Educational Psychology

Second Edition

Educational Psychology
Applications in Canadian Classrooms

Alan Edmunds and Gail Edmunds

Oxford University Press is a department of the University of Oxford.
It furthers the University's objective of excellence in research, scholarship,
and education by publishing worldwide. Oxford is a registered trade mark of
Oxford University Press in the UK and in certain other countries.

Published in Canada by
Oxford University Press
8 Sampson Mews, Suite 204,
Don Mills, Ontario M3C 0H5 Canada

www.oupcanada.com

Copyright © Oxford University Press Canada 2015

The moral rights of the authors have been asserted

Database right Oxford University Press (maker)

First Edition published in 2010

All rights reserved. No part of this publication may be reproduced, stored in a retrieval system, or transmitted, in any form or by any means, without the prior permission in writing of Oxford University Press, or as expressly permitted by law, by licence, or under terms agreed with the appropriate reprographics rights organization. Enquiries concerning reproduction outside the scope of the above should be sent to the Permissions Department at the address above or through the following url: www.oupcanada.com/permission/permission_request.php

Every effort has been made to determine and contact copyright holders.
In the case of any omissions, the publisher will be pleased to make
suitable acknowledgement in future editions.

Library and Archives Canada Cataloguing in Publication

Edmunds, Alan Louis, 1956–, author
Educational psychology : applications in Canadian
classrooms / Alan Edmunds, Gail Edmunds. — Second edition.

Includes bibliographical references and index.
ISBN 978-0-19-901100-1 (pbk.)

1. Educational psychology—Textbooks. 2. Teaching—Textbooks.
I. Edmunds, Gail, 1956–, author II. Title.

LB1051.E35 2015   370.15   C2015-900374-1

Cover image: Image Source/Getty Images

Chapter-opening photo credits: Page 2: Olga Tremblay/Getty Images;
page 34 Dennis McColeman/Photographer's Choice/Getty Images;
page 72: iStock/© MachineHeadz; page 112: iStock/© Izabela Habur;
page 146: iStock/© STEEX; page 190: Stefan Cioata/Moment Select/Getty Images;
page 283: Michael Krinke/E+/Getty Images;
page 266: iStock/© MachineHeadz.

Oxford University Press is committed to our environment.
Wherever possible, our books are printed on paper which comes from responsible sources.

Printed and bound in the United States of America

1 2 3 4 — 18 17 16 15

Brief Contents

Tables, Figures, and Guiding Principles   xiii
Preface   xv
Special Features   xix
Topic Concordance   xxii
Acknowledgments   xxiii
Timeline   xxiv

1 EARLY AUGUST
Planning for the Upcoming School Year   2

2 LATE AUGUST
Considering Child and Adolescent Development   34

3 FIRST WEEK OF SCHOOL
Establishing a Positive Learning Environment   72

4 MID-SEPTEMBER
Making Instructional Decisions   112

5 LATE SEPTEMBER
Assessing Student Progress   146

6 EARLY DECEMBER
Individual Differences—Intellectual Abilities and Challenges   190

7 EARLY FEBRUARY
Socio-cultural Considerations   238

8 END OF SCHOOL YEAR
Standardized Achievement Tests   266

Glossary   292
References   294
Index   300

Tables, Figures, and Guiding Principles   xiii
Preface   xv
Special Features   xix
Topic Concordance   xxii
Acknowledgments   xxiii
Timeline   xxiv

EARLY AUGUST
Planning for the Upcoming School Year

From the Authors' Notebook   3

Primary Learning Objectives   3

The Little Red Schoolhouse   4
Teaching Considerations   4
Educational Psychology   8

Commonplaces of Education   8
Applying Psychological Theories to Education   10
Foundational Topics of Educational Psychology   10
Research in Educational Psychology   12

The Students of *The Little Red Schoolhouse*   17
Teacher Planning   19

Curricular Planning   20
Instructional Planning   23

Assignment—My Approach to Teaching   23
Annette's Journal   28
Annette's Exploration of the Research   29
Annette's Resource List   31
From the Authors' Notebook   32

Reflecting on Practice   32
Chapter Summary   32

New Terms   33
Review Questions   33

Contents   vii

2 LATE AUGUST
Considering Child and Adolescent Development

From the Authors' Notebook   35
- *Primary Learning Objectives*   35

Teaching Students of Different Ages   36

Developmental Influences   37
- *Principles of Development*   38
- *Physical/Biological Development*   43
- *Cognitive/Learning Development*   45
- *The Psychological Structures of Learning*   48
- *From Disequilibrium to Equilibrium*   51
- *Domain-Specific Learning*   54
- *Challenge the Brain: Enhancing Learning*   55
- *Language Development*   56
- *Personal and Social Development*   58
- *Moral Development*   62

Societal Influences   64
- *Ecological Theory*   65

Annette's Journal   67

Annette's Exploration of the Research   68

Annette's Resource List   69

From the Authors' Notebook   70
- *Reflecting on Practice*   70
- *Chapter Summary*   70

New Terms   71

Review Questions   71

3 FIRST WEEK OF SCHOOL
Establishing a Positive Learning Environment

From the Authors' Notebook   73
- *Primary Learning Objectives*   73

viii   Contents

Deciding on an Approach to Classroom Management   74
Dynamic Classroom Management (DCM)   76
Motivational Underpinnings—Behaviour   76
The First Day of School   83
Several Days Later   101
ADHD—Addressing Zach's Classroom Behaviour   102
Annette's Journal   106
Annette's Exploration of the Research   107
Annette's Resource List   108
From the Authors' Notebook   110

Reflecting on Practice   110
Chapter Summary   110

New Terms   111
Review Questions   111

MID-SEPTEMBER
Making Instructional Decisions

From the Authors' Notebook   113

Primary Learning Objectives   113

Determining the Starting Point for Instruction—Diagnostic Assessment   114
Determining Exactly What to Teach   117
Learning Objectives and Lesson Plans   117

Backward Design   118
Bloom's Taxonomy   122

Choosing Effective Instructional Mechanisms   126
My Instructional Practices   126

My Preferred Instructional Mechanisms   126
My Three Guiding Principles   127
Theoretical Basis for My Instruction   128
Motivational Underpinnings   130
Direct Instruction   132
Student Problem-Solving   133
Summary   136

Putting Teacher Knowledge into Practice   136
Annette's Journal   139

Annette's Exploration of the Research   140
Annette's Resource List   142
From the Authors' Notebook   143
    Reflecting on Practice   *143*
    Chapter Summary   *143*
New Terms   144
Review Questions   144

5 LATE SEPTEMBER
Assessing Student Progress

From the Authors' Notebook   147
    Primary Learning Objectives   *147*
Deciding on an Approach to Assessment   148
Talking to Students about Assessment   149
Assessment of Student Learning   158
    The Purposes of Assessment   *159*
    The Assessment Design Process   *161*
    Testing Issues   *164*
Assignment—My Use of Assessment Tools   173
    Authentic Assessment   *173*
    Portfolios   *174*
    Evaluating Effectiveness of Assessment Tools   *178*
The Student Teacher's Role in the Classroom   180
Annette's Journal   183
Annette's Exploration of the Research   184
Annette's Resource List   186
From the Authors' Notebook   187
    Reflecting on Practice   *187*
    Chapter Summary   *187*
New Terms   188
Review Questions   188

6 EARLY DECEMBER
Individual Differences—Intellectual Abilities and Challenges

From the Authors' Notebook 191

Primary Learning Objectives 191

Parent Concern—Our Son Doesn't Seem as Smart as the Other Students 192

Intelligence 193

Is Intelligence a Structure or a Process? 194
The Source of Intelligence 198
Why Is It Important for Teachers to Understand Intelligence? 199
An Example of an Intelligence Test 199

Special Education 201

Who Are the Students Who Receive Special Education? 202
Controversies Surrounding Special Education 202
Individualized Education Programs 204
The Cognitive Abilities of Students with Exceptionalities 206
Students with ADHD 208
Students with Autism Spectrum Disorder 212
Students Who Are Gifted and Talented 215
Students with Mild Intellectual Disability 218
Students with Specific Learning Disorders 220

Cognitive Styles, Learning Styles, and Temperament 226
Annette's Journal 230
Annette's Exploration of the Research 231
Annette's Resource List 234
From the Authors' Notebook 236

Reflecting on Practice 236
Chapter Summary 236

New Terms 237
Review Questions 237

Contents xi

EARLY FEBRUARY
Socio-cultural Considerations

From the Authors' Notebook   239

  Primary Learning Objectives   239

Cultural Differences in *The Little Red Schoolhouse*   240
Socio-cultural Perspectives   248

  Differences within Identified Groups   249
  Positioning Cultural Identity within the Individual   250
  Stereotype Threat and Socio-economic Status   252
  Multicultural Education   256
  Aboriginal Education   258
  Conclusion   259

Annette's Journal   261
Annette's Exploration of the Research   262
Annette's Resource List   263
From the Authors' Notebook   264

  Reflecting on Practice   264
  Chapter Summary   264

New Terms   265
Review Questions   265

END OF SCHOOL YEAR
Standardized Achievement Tests

From the Authors' Notebook   267

  Primary Learning Objectives   267

Determining Student Achievement   268
Testing Issues   270

  What Is a Standardized Test?   271
  Achievement versus Aptitude Tests   271
  Stakeholders' Views of Standardized Testing   272
  Misconceptions   274
  Constructing Better Standardized Tests   276
  Connections between Classroom Curricula and Standardized Tests   278
  Preparing Students for Test-Writing   279

Contents

Interpreting Test Results 279
Summary 280
Canadian Standards for Student Achievement Testing 280

Canadian Debate over Standardized Testing 282
Annette's Journal 286
Annette's Exploration of the Research 287
Annette's Resource List 289
From the Authors' Notebook 290

Reflecting on Practice 290
Chapter Summary 290

New Terms 291
Review Questions 291

Glossary 292
References 294
Index 300

Tables, Figures, and Guiding Principles

Tables

Table 2.1 Development—First Grader   42
Table 2.2 Development—Late Adolescence   43
Table 2.3 Piaget's Four Stages of Cognitive Development   52
Table 2.4 Erikson's Eight Stages of Psychosocial Development   60
Table 2.5 Kohlberg's Stages of Moral Reasoning   64
Table 2.6 Bronfenbrenner's Ecological Theory   65
Table 3.1 On-Task Self-Monitoring Checklist   105
Table 4.1 Bloom's Taxonomy   123
Table 4.2 Verbs Used in Learning Objectives   124
Table 4.3 Stiggins's Taxonomy of Achievement Targets   125
Table 4.4 Cognitive Credit Card—Math Operations   138
Table 5.1 Table of Specifications—Educational Statistics   164
Table 5.2 Assessment Questions according to Bloom's Taxonomy   167
Table 6.1 The Theory of Multiple Intelligences   195
Table 6.2 Cognitive Indexes of the WISC–IV   200
Table 6.3 Levels of Severity in Autism Spectrum Disorder   213
Table 6.4 Common Learning and Behavioural Characteristics of Students with Learning Disabilities   223

Figures

Figure 1.1 Steps in the Research Process   15
Figure 1.2 Curriculum Planning Template   20
Figure 2.1 Anderson's Four Executive Functions   44
Figure 2.2 Assimilation and Accommodation of Incoming Information   50
Figure 2.3 Stress—Performance Connection   56
Figure 4.1 Learning Objective—Relationship to Assessment, Lesson Planning, and Instruction   119
Figure 4.2 Lesson Plan Template   120
Figure 4.3 The Common Thread of Learning Objectives   122

Figure 4.4	Diagram of the SOI Model of Meaningful Learning	129
Figure 4.5	Diagram of the HPL Framework	132
Figure 5.1	Interplay between Teaching, Learning, and Assessment	158
Figure 5.2	Social Studies Writing Portfolio—Evaluative Criteria	177
Figure 6.1	Carroll's Hierarchical Model of Intelligence	193
Figure 6.2	Sternberg's Triarchic Theory of Intelligence	197
Figure 6.3	The Six Phases of the Assessment and IEP Process	205
Figure 6.4	Twelve Fundamental Questions for IEP Formulation	206
Figure 6.5	Example of a One-Page IEP	207
Figure 6.6	Diagnosing ADHD	210
Figure 6.7	Diagnosing Autism Spectrum Disorder	213
Figure 7.1	Banks's Dimensions of Multicultural Education	258

Guiding Principles

Reflective Practice   7

Curriculum Planning   22

Good Teaching: Ten Best Practices and Twelve Generic Guidelines   26

Early Learning—Significant Factors   46

The Resilient Student   75

Strategies to Nurture Three Fundamental Student Needs   88

Teacher Behaviours That Diminish Student Behavioural Problems   90

Successful Students   95

Classroom Management   100

Elements of Backward Design   119

Stiggins's Achievement Targets   125

How People Learn (HPL) Framework   131

Homework   152

Formative Assessment   160

Authentic Activities, Problems, and Questions   175

Building an Inclusive Practice   203

The Aptitude x Treatment Interaction (ATI) Approach   229

Diverse Learners   245

The Critical Consciousness of Teachers   250

The Purpose, Outcomes, and Future of Standardized Testing   275

Preface

The second edition of *Educational Psychology: Applications in Canadian Classrooms*, like the first edition, is unique among textbooks in this domain. Throughout the entire volume, we present one teacher's story to demonstrate how educators can properly apply the principles of educational psychology to their teaching, where *teaching* means anything and everything a teacher does or deals with when carrying out his or her duties.

To begin, we would like to make readers aware of:

1. the importance of understanding educational psychology within the context of real classroom situations;
2. how this book is unique; and
3. how the components of this book were carefully designed to make teaching and learning educational psychology interesting and engaging.

Real Classroom Contexts

Given the importance of integrating the concepts of educational psychology into all aspects of all learning environments, we feel that it is essential that educators clearly understand how this type of assimilation can occur on a daily basis in their classrooms. Too often, students who aspire to be teachers learn about the discipline of educational psychology through a review of theories and research findings. We contend that this is a direct reflection of the matter-of-fact and decontextualized manner in which the majority of textbooks present the material. As a result, students find it difficult to fully comprehend how they might apply this academic-type information when they begin their teaching careers. They typically end up with hypothetical, generic understandings that are far removed from reality-based applications. By contrast, their practicum experiences are usually filled with moment-by-moment, real-life teaching challenges that require mindful and on-the-spot decisions. They rightly wonder how they could possibly find the time to consider theories and research findings that relate to these immediate situations. Even if they were to accurately consider the relevant concepts, how could they conceivably apply them appropriately under such pressing conditions? After these practicum experiences, students often comment that some of their university course material is not related to what really happens in classrooms. It is not surprising, therefore, that experienced teachers also express the same sentiments when they reflect on their education training. We feel that this disconnect between research and practice must be addressed so that education students have the greatest chance for success in their future teaching positions. Our intent, then, was to write a book grounded in the activities of an actual classroom, albeit a fairly unusual classroom, and in doing so present concepts of educational psychology as they directly apply to the educators and students involved. In other words, we have attempted to portray how and when the principles of educational psychology can be applied by teachers.

In older educational psychology textbooks, relevant research information about various aspects of educational psychology was simply presented as facts and details, and it was up to the instructor or the students to make sense of how this information applied to education. As James (1899/1983) stated in his description of the field, "Psychology is a science, and teaching is an art; and sciences never generate arts directly out of themselves. An intermediary inventive mind must make the application, by using its originality" (p. 8). While many older texts are nothing more than watered-down introductory psychology books, modern educational psychology texts tend to contain educational examples and case studies that enable instructors and students to better understand the relationships between conceptual theories, research findings, and educational practices. In fact, entire texts are now devoted solely to case studies in educational psychology. In this text, we take the case study concept a step further by using the entire book to fully explore a comprehensive case, a case that depicts all of the interpretations and applications of educational psychology that take place in one teacher's school year. We chose this approach because it has been apparent for some time that educational psychology texts have not kept pace with the context-rich research that is starting to dominate the field (Berliner, 2012; Calfee, 2012). Commenting on the absence of textbooks adequate for these changing times, Calfee stated, "Today's methods texts encompass a broader array of techniques than a decade or so ago, often promising an integrated approach. The reality seems closer to parallel play" (p. 8). In other words, research and practice are like the two rails of a train track: they are both definitely going in the same direction and toward the same destination, and each assists and complements the other, but they never intersect.

Another reason we wrote this text from the standpoint of classroom practice was to avoid adding to the conceptual confusion that Bredo (2006) so clearly identified as existing within the discipline of educational psychology. Conceptual confusion occurs when a field or discipline chops its overall conceptual framework into fragments and expects the various and sometimes only distantly related fragments to individually define the whole. In the case of educational psychology, some basic fragments are vital to our understandings (e.g., motivation and self-concept), but they cannot be directly linked to teaching or education without a great deal of intermediary intervention. In an attempt to bring about a modicum of conceptual clarity, we have chosen to highlight and define educational psychology by how the broader and more relevant aspects of the domain directly affect everyday occurrences in classrooms. This meant omitting considerable detail on some long-standing issues (such as brain physiology and behavioural views of learning) in favour of more illustrative information about the interactive nature of relevant topics (such as behaviour in classrooms, student motivation, and the emerging emphasis in the field on self-regulated learning). For example, we do not arbitrarily divide teaching and learning into the typical dichotomy of behavioural versus cognitive perspectives. Rather, given the very dynamic and inclusive nature of the teaching and learning process, we present and advocate for an integrated perspective that constantly and purposefully utilizes the dual benefits of teacher-centred and student-centred learning. We also elected to integrate the pertinent aspects of motivation into each chapter as they apply to different classroom situations instead of presenting all aspects of motivation in a separate chapter.

Commenting on the growing acknowledgment of the need for an integrated theory of learning and motivation, Perry, Turner, and Meyer (2006) stated, "Contextual understandings are more integral to research on motivation today, reflecting the general shift in educational research toward situated and social perspectives on learning" (p. 328). In adopting this approach, we want to redirect teachers' thinking away from easily identifiable but sometimes overly simplistic conceptions of educational psychology and toward a more comprehensive set of concepts that are embedded within interactive classroom activities. With this framework as a starting point, we feel that teachers can then use the tenets of educational psychology to better understand how students interpret and respond to their experiences in classrooms. There is no one "best practice" for teaching, but some practices are better than others in some contexts. Educators should conceptualize teaching as a variety of practices that have to be tailored to fit different types of students, with the full acknowledgment that students' actions and reactions are dependent on both the teacher and the environment.

The Little Red Schoolhouse

The one-classroom school we depict in this text is not based on any particular classroom; rather, it is based on all the classrooms we have had the privilege of working in over many years. Many of these classrooms were the multi-grade and split-grade configurations found in schools in northern Canada, while others were the more typical configurations found in schools elsewhere in Canada. Regardless of the size of the classes or the types of students, the good teaching and learning we witnessed was always due to the teachers' excellent understandings of the teaching and learning process. Our version of *The Little Red Schoolhouse* seemed the perfect vehicle for addressing the fundamental tenets of educational psychology, because it allows us to clearly delineate developmental differences across students of all ages (Grades 1–12). This unique perspective should encourage instructors and students to readily draw comparisons, see contrasts, and make connections.

A Unique Approach

Compared to typical educational psychology textbooks, this book is unique in two significant ways. First, we present pertinent educational psychology topics and principles as they become relevant throughout the school year. For example, in Chapter 1 readers are introduced to the classroom teacher, Annette Elkins, as she spends part of August planning for the months ahead. Subsequent chapters outline her experiences in a sequential manner, from September to June. This framework presents educational psychology not only as it applies to the classroom but also as it applies to the day-to-day, week-to-week, and term-to-term experiences that students and teachers encounter over the course of the school year.

Second, unlike most texts that are literally peppered with references and citations, we deliberately limited the number of citations. Many of the numerous citations in other texts merely define singular terms and/or explain the results of studies that may be very important from the perspective of furthering research understandings but do not dramatically influence what teachers or students do. For all the major topics, therefore, we elected to cite the overarching theories and research findings (some older, some very current) that most influence classroom practice and can be functionally translated into teacher actions. In this way, we provide an instructive rather than exhaustive portrayal of educational psychology principles.

Throughout the text, we consciously avoided jargon and technical language. Instead, we used plain and clear language to illustrate complex concepts and transform them into efficient understandings. We felt that this mode of presentation was in keeping with the flow and readability of the overall educational story we are offering. We wanted to keep the emphasis of the book on the applications of concepts rather than on definitions, names of researchers, and dates.

Ultimately, the overall purpose of the book is to develop *teacher self-efficacy*: teachers' belief in their own ability to be effective despite the numerous challenges they will encounter. Not only will this make for better teachers, but the research clearly indicates that teacher self-efficacy leads to better student achievement.

Special Features

In addition to the one-classroom scenario and the minimal use of citations, we have employed a number of special features designed to present information in an interesting and insightful manner. As mentioned, the text follows a year in the life of one teacher—Annette Elkins. Each chapter opens with **From the Authors' Notebook**, a brief overview of the chapter, as well as a list of **Primary Learning Objectives** that inform the reader of intended learning outcomes. Within each chapter, the reader learns about educational issues from Annette's point of view. Her thoughts as well as her preparations for teaching and her actions in the classroom are described in detail. She also has ongoing **e-mail correspondence** with Dr. Andrew Cameron, a university professor who taught a summer course she recently completed. These e-mails provide the reader with explanations of educational psychology concepts, particularly in regard to the questions teacher candidates and practising teachers may have about the relevance of these concepts to classroom activities. The correspondence also emphasizes the importance of mentorship for teachers, a growing facet of educational practice. Annette, while already an experienced teacher, expands her knowledge and teaching skills by continuing to learn from an expert. Reciprocally, Dr. Cameron's exchanges with Annette help him to update and hone his ability to explain concepts and classroom applications to teacher candidates. The reader also learns more about educational psychology through **Annette's Readings**. These readings are either recommended by Dr. Cameron or are papers written by Annette herself when she was a student.

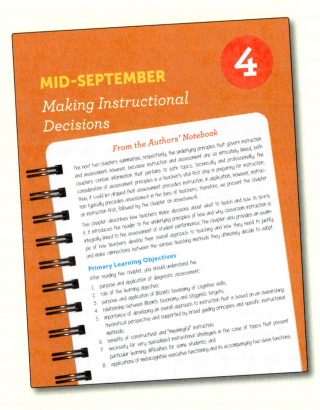

Special Features

Other special features within each chapter include Guiding Principles, Think Boxes, Annette's Journal, Annette's Exploration of the Research, and Annette's Resource List. The **Guiding Principles** feature briefly outlines the underlying educational psychology concepts that form the basis for Annette's thinking and actions (and/or others' thinking and actions). These foundational concepts are presented in textboxes within the pertinent passages of Annette's story. In this way, the foundational concepts are literally and figuratively embedded within the narrative. The **Think Boxes** encourage readers to reflect on the material presented in the text. Entries in **Annette's Journal** informally summarize Annette's teaching experiences during the school year. **Annette's Exploration of the Research** exposes readers to current educational psychology research so that they can learn how the findings are directly related to classroom learning. **Annette's Resource List** includes print and on-line resources that readers can access should they wish to explore the chapter topics further.

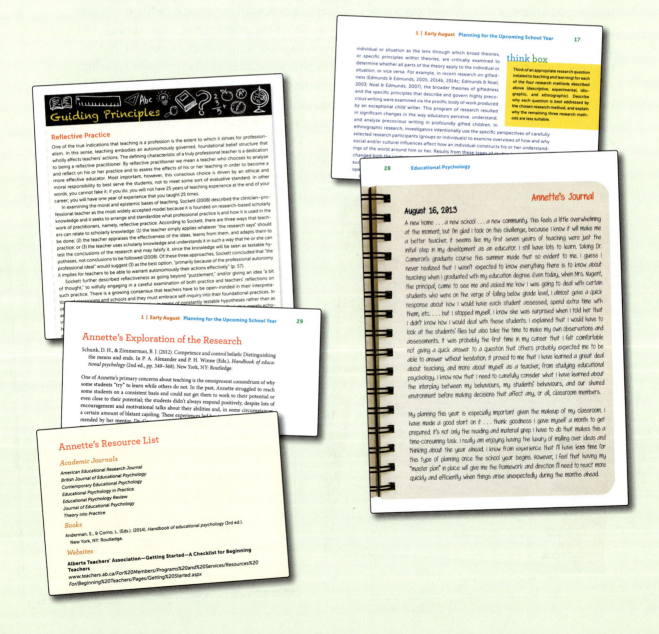

Each chapter ends with another **From the Authors' Notebook** entry that provides closing comments; a **Reflecting on Practice** exercise, which gives readers an opportunity to reflect on chapter contents and knowledge acquired and to identify further knowledge that may be gained through additional resources; a **Chapter Summary**; a list of **New Terms**; and **Review Questions**.

We hope readers will find that this text presents educational psychology in a manner most interesting and relevant to educators and to those who aspire to be educators. We aim to facilitate meaningful learning through meaningful stories. In that spirit, we hope you will enjoy reading about Annette's experiences in *The Little Red Schoolhouse!*

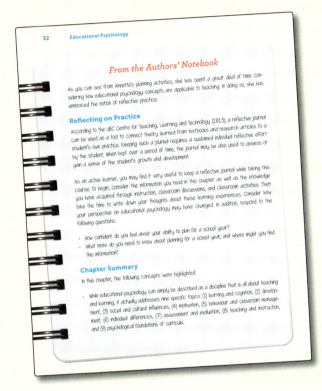

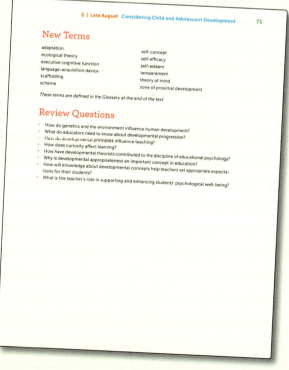

Topic Concordance

	Student Behaviour	Teacher Planning	Instruction	Motivation	Assessment	Child Development	Learning	Special Education	Diversity	Standardized Testing
Ch. 1		✓	✓	✓	✓					
Ch. 2	✓		✓	✓		✓	✓		✓	
Ch. 3	✓			✓				✓		
Ch. 4		✓	✓	✓	✓		✓			
Ch. 5		✓	✓		✓		✓			
Ch. 6			✓	✓			✓	✓		
Ch. 7			✓	✓					✓	
Ch. 8			✓		✓		✓			✓

Acknowledgments

The idea for this text came from students. In our experience, education/psychology students want to know what happens in actual classrooms and how that applies to what they are learning. So first and foremost, we thank students for helping us to bring educational psychology concepts to life. Second, we both would like to express our gratitude to the mentors who have helped us throughout our academic and professional careers. Their support and guidance have enabled us to reach the point where we are today, just as Annette's mentor helped to guide her through her first year at *The Little Red Schoolhouse*.

In keeping with the narrative style of this text, we incorporated original photography to help us tell our story. Many of the photos were taken purposely to depict events in *The Little Red Schoolhouse*. We are indebted to our models (Lindsey Edmunds, Ryan Amos, Rachel Vanderheyden, Amberly Holman, and Matteo Salazar-Ciruz) for patiently posing as we searched for just the right image. Thanks as well to Esso Family Math for sharing their photos.

We would also like to thank the following individuals who reviewed our manuscript and provided excellent feedback during the proposal and development stages of both editions, and we express our gratitude to those who chose to remain anonymous but whose comments were also critical in shaping the text:

Tara Flanagan, Concordia University
Deani Van Pelt, Redeemer University College
Ken Pudlas, Trinity Western University
Stefan Sikora, Mount Royal College
M. Drysdale, St Jerome's/University of Waterloo
Linda Chmiliar, Athabasca University
Eva Gabriele van der Giessen, Laurentian University
Audrey Kinzel, University of Saskatchewan
Ibrahim Sumrain, MacEwan University

Last, but certainly not least, we would like to express our sincere thanks to the Oxford University Press family who assisted us throughout this exciting process. In particular, thanks to Jodi Lewchuk for keeping things flowing as smoothly as possible and Dorothy Turnbull for her acute attention to detail and her great ideas.

Alan Edmunds
Gail Edmunds

Timeline

This timeline identifies the starting point for many of the activities that Annette undertook during the school year. She continued to carry out several of these activities throughout the year.

Late August
- Reviews developmental principles to better understand students and to inform teaching and learning

Mid-September
- Uses diagnostic assessment to situate teaching
- Uses backward design to construct lesson plans
- Uses theoretical principles to construct an overarching approach to teaching

Early Summer
- Engages in professional development (graduate course in educational psychology)

 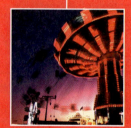  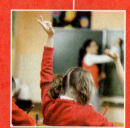

Early August
- Reviews student files
- Starts curricular and instructional planning
- Develops diagnostic assessment tools

First Week of School
- Meets new students
- Uses behavioural principles to establish a psychologically secure learning environment

Early December

- Uses learning ability principles to inform teaching
- Addresses parental concerns about student learning
- Learns more about students with exceptionalities
- Builds an inclusive practice

End of School Year

- Reviews the principles and purposes of standardized assessment
- Considers the role that standardized assessment plays in student assessment and evaluation
- Reads about how classroom curricular objectives can be used to build better standardized tests

Late September

- Uses assessment principles and backward design to build the questions, assignments, and tests that form an overarching approach to assessment

Early February

- Uses socio-cultural considerations to inform teaching and learning
- Takes advantage of a student's cultural differences to enhance performance
- Uses diversity principles to eliminate disparities in students' educational opportunities
- Develops a critical consciousness to build a culturally responsive practice

EARLY AUGUST
Planning for the Upcoming School Year

1

From the Authors' Notebook

This chapter introduces the reader to Annette Elkins, a teacher preparing for the upcoming school year. In an effort to improve her teaching, Annette applies her knowledge of educational psychology to her planning activities. By determining an outline of her curricular and instructional planning, she establishes an overall educational compass that will guide her throughout the coming months.

Primary Learning Objectives

After reading this chapter, you should understand the importance of

1. reflective practice;
2. understanding the central topics that constitute educational psychology;
3. the steps involved in the research process;
4. the different methods used in educational psychology research;
5. curricular planning;
6. constructing a coherent approach to teaching; and
7. using research to explain educational phenomena.

The Little Red Schoolhouse

Annette Elkins looks around the empty classroom and wonders about the 15 faces that will be staring back at her a month from now. She is just as excited to start the new school year as she was when she was a child. This is her first year at George Lake School, better known as *The Little Red Schoolhouse* by the local residents. The red-brick building, located in a remote but readily accessible area of Canada, was built as a one-room school many years ago. Over the years, renovations were made to accommodate a growing population. However, given the downturn in the area's economy, the number of school-aged students has decreased significantly.

Annette has taught a number of different grades during her seven-year teaching career, including both elementary and secondary grade levels. This was excellent preparation for her current placement, because *The Little Red Schoolhouse* now has only one active classroom; this classroom includes students from Grades 1 to 12, with preschool and kindergarten classes held in an adjoining building. The school staff includes a principal (Mrs. Nugent), a preschool teacher (Ms. Martino), a resource-room teacher (Mr. Parker), two educational assistants (Mr. Hayes and Mrs. McCarthy), and Annette, the regular classroom teacher. The school is well equipped, with a resource room, a small gym, a lunchroom, and all of the latest technology that can be found in schools in larger Canadian centres.

Teaching Considerations

As Annette contemplates teaching in this unique situation, she re-reads some recent e-mail correspondence she has had with a professor who teaches educational psychology.

Ed Psych Course

Annette Elkins <annette_elkins@schoolmail.com>

Date: Saturday, August 3, 2013 10:22 AM

To: Andrew Cameron <acameron@university.ca>

Hello Dr. Cameron,

I would like to thank you for such a great course this summer. As an experienced teacher taking coursework during my summer break, I appreciated learning more about how educational psychology applies to the regular classroom. It is relatively easy to study the key concepts, but it is much more effective if this material is presented in the context of everyday life in the classroom. In many ways, I feel like a new teacher since taking your course. I have a much better understanding of how students learn in classroom settings, and therefore I feel better prepared to provide rich and challenging educational experiences for all of my future students.

I am excited about my new teaching position for the coming year. I have just moved to George Lake, which you may not have even heard of . . . it is a remote town with one small school that has all the modern conveniences found in urban schools. My class will include students from Grades 1 to 12 (thankfully, there are two educational assistants to help, plus a resource-room teacher). From what I have been told by the principal, the students are a great group of kids. She also mentioned that the school receives lots of support from the community. I grew up in a similar small town, so I should fit in just fine. As for the teaching aspect of the job, knowing how to apply the educational psychology concepts we discussed has definitely helped me feel more confident about this new teaching challenge. In fact, I am already thinking about how I will do things differently this year. I will keep in touch to let you know how things are going.

Annette Elkins

Re: Ed Psych Course

Andrew Cameron <acameron@university.ca>

Date: Monday, August 5, 2013 3:10 PM

To: Annette Elkins <annette_elkins@schoolmail.com>

Hello Annette,

Thanks for updating me on your plans for the coming school year. I'm glad you enjoyed the summer course. It's nice to know that students appreciate learning educational psychology through the discussion of classroom applications. Your new teaching assignment sounds very unusual but very exciting, and I'm sure you'll have many opportunities to implement the concepts we talked about in the course.

Obviously, teaching a variety of ages and grades—all at the same time—will be very demanding, so I've taken the liberty of providing what I think are five of the basic planning concepts that could help you as you work your way into your new school. While my suggestions are mostly designed for efficiency because of your unique teaching situation, they are fundamentally sound concepts that all teachers should employ.

1) Classroom and behaviour management is always an important issue, but it will be an even bigger issue for you because of your students' inherent age and social interaction differences. Immediately establish the calm, assertive atmosphere we discussed in the course. Take the time to engage the students in discussions about classroom rules. Allow them to negotiate rewards and consequences with you. As was mentioned several times, nothing is more conducive to excellent learning than psychological security. Conversely, nothing undermines learning more than a chaotic classroom.

2) Rather than presume what students have learned up to this point, construct some short but targeted pre-instructional assessments to determine the proper curricular starting points for each student/group. If available, modify and shorten the previous teacher's end-of-year tests. By constructing your own assessment indicators, you'll avoid misinterpreting someone else's grades.

3) Analyze your various curriculum guides (by grade and subject) for common themes among educational outcomes, and use these commonalities to prepare sets of teaching lessons and units. For example, while teaching new fractions concepts to Grades 4/5, use the same notes to review fractions concepts for Grade 9/10 algebra. Similarly, all students can do project presentations (usually an English learning objective) on the same day and to the whole student body, even though they are presenting on different topics and at different levels of complexity and ability.

4) Be sure to construct your **formative assessment** and summative assessment instruments when you are constructing your daily lesson and unit plans. Not only will this process save you from later having to build all your assessment tools at the same time, but it will ensure that all your tests, quizzes, and assignments evaluate students based on exactly the same educational outcomes that you used to plan your lessons.

5) Finally, and this is a tip to help you start on track and stay on track, after one or two lessons, make sure that everything you are teaching is doing two basic things: (1) building on what students already know and (2) presenting tasks that are both challenging and attainable. Continuing this type of personal exercise will ensure that you are engaging in reflective practice.

Hope this advice helps. Let me know how things unfold. I'd be happy to help you any way I can during your school year.

Andrew

Dr. A. Cameron
Associate Professor
Faculty of Education

Reflective Practice

One of the true indications that teaching is a profession is the extent to which it strives for professionalism. In this sense, teaching embodies an autonomously governed, foundational belief structure that wholly affects teachers' actions. The defining characteristic of a truly professional teacher is a dedication to being a reflective practitioner. By reflective practitioner we mean a teacher who chooses to analyze and reflect on his or her practice and to assess the effects of his or her teaching in order to become a more effective educator. Most important, however, this conscious choice is driven by an ethical and moral responsibility to best serve the students, not to meet some sort of evaluative standard. In other words, you cannot fake it; if you do, you will not have 25 years of teaching experience at the end of your career; you will have one year of experience that you taught 25 times.

In examining the moral and epistemic bases of teaching, Sockett (2008) described the clinician–professional teacher as the most widely accepted model because it is founded on research-based scholarly knowledge and it seeks to arrange and standardize what professional practice is and how it is used in the work of practitioners, namely, reflective practice. According to Sockett, there are three ways that teachers can relate to scholarly knowledge: (1) the teacher simply applies whatever "the research says" should be done; (2) the teacher appraises the effectiveness of the ideas, learns from them, and adapts them to practice; or (3) the teacher uses scholarly knowledge and understands it in such a way that he or she can test the conclusions of the research and may falsify it, since the knowledge will be seen as testable hypotheses, not conclusions to be followed (2008). Of these three approaches, Sockett concluded that "the professional ideal" would suggest (3) as the best option, "primarily because of the professional autonomy it implies for teachers to be able to warrant autonomously their actions effectively" (p. 57).

Sockett further described reflectiveness as going beyond "puzzlement," and/or giving an idea "a bit of thought," to wilfully engaging in a careful examination of both practice and teachers' reflections on such practice. There is a growing consensus that teachers have to be open-minded in their interpretations of classrooms and schools and they must embrace self-inquiry into their foundational practices. In other words, teachers must see their practice in terms of constantly testable hypotheses rather than as an established or permanent way of being. This position on teaching is not new. Sockett is merely echoing Dewey's (1934) long-held position that the professional educator's imaginative insights cannot allow his or her accomplishments to be a final and/or complete standard of excellence. Like an artist, the true educator has the interminable problem of creating something new from something old, and while it has to be similar, it cannot be an exact duplicate.

After reading Dr. Cameron's e-mail, Annette cannot help but think back to what she learned during the very first days of her latest summer course. She finally came to understand what educational psychology really is, how critically important empirical research of all types is to defining the discipline, and how the two are, and always will be, inextricably linked. The course reinforced the dual purposes of educational psychology: (1) to expand the fundamental theoretical research framework of the discipline and (2) to improve educational practice for teachers by providing them with sound and relevant research results upon which to base their instruction. Annette's thoughts turn to a paper that Dr. Cameron authored and distributed during the summer course. She decides this is precisely the time to go over that paper again as she prepares for the new school year. She pulls out one of her binders, finds the paper she is looking for, and begins to read.

Educational Psychology

Educational psychology is not simply psychology applied to education. While psychology is the understanding of the principles that govern human behaviour, education is the understanding of the principles that govern teaching and learning. Therefore, educational psychology is best described as the understanding of the psychological principles that govern the interactive human behaviours involved in the teaching and learning process. This fundamental tenet is what has defined educational psychology as its own distinct discipline for more than 30 years.

Commonplaces of Education

Schwab's (1973) prophetic and oft-cited words stress that while educational psychology adheres to the research concepts and methods of psychology, it uses them to explore and make sense of the four commonplaces of education: someone (the teacher) teaches something (the curriculum) to someone else (the student) in some setting (the classroom). These unique, complex, and dynamic characteristics fully identify education and would be sorely missed if one were to simply apply psychological principles and theories to education. Psychological theories without tangible educational applications are merely exercises in academic exploration. Similarly, teaching practices without valid support from educational psychology research are simply a waste of valuable instructional time. It is only at the intersection of meaningful research based on *teacher x student x topic x setting* that truly beneficial educational outcomes can be realized. Further, more fruitful education outcomes require that Schwab's four commonplaces be given equal rank and importance in the eyes of teachers and researchers.

If beginning teachers are not careful, they can easily fall into adopting one of two very common but naïve perspectives on education. The first naïve perspective focuses on teaching subjects (*teacher x topic*) with little emphasis on the students and the classroom environment. This is not an unnatural focus (especially for secondary teachers), because every teacher wants to be recognized as competent in his or her subject area. The major problem with this perspective is that it concentrates on teacher needs and fails to take student needs into account. This often leads to a teaching approach that involves presenting the curriculum in an exact but non-engaging fashion. The second naïve perspective focuses on teaching students (*teacher x student*), with less regard for the topics and the environment. This is also not an unnatural focus (especially for elementary teachers), because every teacher wants to be known as a person who is thoughtful and considerate of his or her students. The major problem with this perspective is that it typically concentrates on students' emotional needs at the expense of curricular standards. This often leads to a teaching approach that involves presenting the curriculum in

an enjoyable but non-purposeful fashion. Both perspectives, unfortunately, pay little attention to the environment. This is primarily because classrooms, gymnasiums, and labs have typically only been considered from a physical perspective, not from the perspective of the atmosphere and attitudes that they foster. In the past 10 to 15 years, however, research on how the tone of the classroom can either negatively or positively affect student learning is dramatically changing teachers' perspectives on how teaching should be constructed and implemented. While it is obvious from Schwab's interactive formula that all four education commonplaces need to be addressed, only recently are considerations of the environment gaining prominence.

The complexities of Schwab's four-part research equation become exponential when one considers how each of the four commonplaces can represent wide-ranging and unique sets of possible attributes. For example, what would it be like for a newly certified teacher to have to teach math to a class of 37 uninterested Grade 9 students in a school that has a poor history of graduation rates? What if we simply changed the student commonplace by replacing "uninterested" with "eager," or by changing "37" to "17," or by changing the setting commonplace from "poor" to "great"? By understanding the underlying principles of "why we need to do or not do certain things" when teaching, teachers are better able to design and implement effective instructional strategies that engage students and foster their personal growth and academic development. This overarching conceptualization of education gives teachers an unparalleled ability to better predict what will happen in learning situations and correctly interpret and understand what has just happened in their classrooms.

think box

Using Schwab's four commonplaces, describe and compare two classrooms you have experienced as a university student. How did the uniqueness of these two settings affect your learning?

Applying Psychological Theories to Education

There is no doubt that the psychological theories and principles derived from long-established research findings constitute the essential underpinnings of educational psychology, but there is also no doubt that these findings are only meaningful to teachers when they are applied to actual school situations. In other words, to understand the principles of the discipline is to know the fundamental reasons "why" certain things happen in everyday classrooms. Not only does educational psychology carefully consider how core psychological principles and concepts affect educational practice, but in a reciprocal manner and in a way much different from that in psychology, educational psychology also carefully considers how educational practice frames psychological research and perspectives. According to Sternberg (2008), there are five inter-related reasons why psychological theories about learning and instruction need to be applied to education:

> First, doing so enables one to have a scientific basis for education in how people think, feel, and/or motivate themselves rather than only to guess what intuitively might make sense. Second, good theories are specific enough to specify what the educational interventions should look like. Third, if the theory is sufficiently specific, it will also specify what the assessments of instruction should look like. Fourth, good theories are disconfirmable, so they provide the basis for discovering whether the intervention actually does or does not work. Finally, one of the best ways to test theories and advance is through practical implementations (pp. 150–151).

It is apparent, then, that educational psychology research has a very significant impact on what happens in classrooms. Most of this research is conducted because teachers and researchers encounter classroom situations that are not necessarily well explained by existing theories and principles. As Berliner stated in regard to the discipline of educational psychology, "our essential concern is a set of related fundamental topics about human teaching and learning, with particular emphasis on the empirical study of those phenomena" (2012, p. 5). In sum, it is definitely within the purview of educators to pose thoughtful questions about teaching and learning; it is equally obligatory, therefore, to diligently implement the research principles of educational psychology to solve them.

Foundational Topics of Educational Psychology

As previously mentioned, at the core of educational psychology is the understanding of teaching and learning. It is a broad and deep domain, because everything that happens between teachers, students, and curricula within classrooms has its essence here. While many of the other disciplines within the social sciences influence education, such as philosophy, sociology, and psychology, it is educational psychology that explains it:

> . . . from the emergence of *Homo sapiens*, whoever reflected on teaching probably had thoughts that we would now label as mainstream educational psychology. It could not

have been otherwise. Our roots are seen to be deep within the corpus of work that makes up Western intellectual history (Berliner, 2012, pp. 4–5).

As Berliner further stated, nine foundational topics are examined within educational psychology. They are listed below. Alongside each topic are some of the questions most germane to educators.

1. **Learning and Cognition**—How do students think and learn best? What are potential barriers to efficient learning? How can teaching be constructed to suit learning needs?
2. **Development**—At what ages/grades can students be taught/not taught particular curricular concepts? How do changes in students' cognitive, social, emotional, moral, and physical development influence the teaching and learning process?
3. **Social and Cultural Influences**—How do classrooms and/or culturally unique neighbourhoods affect teaching as well as student learning and development?
4. **Motivation**—Why do students engage or not engage in certain activities/tasks? How can teachers use student interest to facilitate learning? How can students self-regulate their learning and behaviour?
5. **Behaviour and Classroom Management**—How can teachers construct classroom environments that are academically effective, psychologically and socially comfortable, and properly managed?
6. **Individual Differences**—How can teaching be constructed to take advantage of the inherent differences between students' cognitive and behavioural abilities? Why do some students need more instructional help than others?
7. **Assessment and Evaluation**—How can teachers best determine whether or not students have learned what has been taught? How is assessment linked to instruction? How is instruction guided by assessment?
8. **Teaching and Instruction**—What types of teaching methods are best, and under what circumstances should they be applied? What are the student, topic, and environmental factors that determine the use/non-use of particular instructional methods?
9. **Psychological Foundations of Curricula**—How does curriculum design affect teaching and learning? What are the preferred methods for teaching particular skills such as reading and for teaching broader subjects such as Grade 12 social studies?

It is no surprise that each of the above nine foundational topics, and the accompanying questions, is directed toward helping teachers do a better job of facilitating student learning. Many years of educational practice by thousands of teachers (novices and experts), combined with many research studies, have produced fairly cogent answers to nearly all of these questions, but as with all disciplines, few things in teaching and learning are always exactly the same. Therefore, it is critical that educators realize that subtly different questions about similar topics must be carefully considered and investigated.

> **think box**
>
> To test the pervasive application of educational psychology to all things educational, think about all that you have learned about teaching thus far, and see if you can come up with a topic or issue that does not fit within at least one of the nine major topics above.

Research in Educational Psychology

Educational psychologists, often collaborating with teachers, conduct different types of research to provide educators with appropriate answers to their questions. These answers, or findings as they are sometimes called, provide vital understandings so that educators can decide how to teach, how to teach differently to help different students, how to structure their curricula, and how to effectively carry out these duties within the confines of their classrooms, labs, gymnasiums, theatres, and playgrounds.

History of Educational Psychology

The research methods that prevail in educational psychology come from a long line of efforts by many individuals who dominated the emergence of the field more than a century ago, nearly all of whom were psychologists. A brief history of the global influences on how and why particular approaches to research evolved is presented below so that current research methods can be properly situated, appreciated, and understood.

The early beginnings of educational psychology research can be traced to the work of Johann Friedrich Herbart and his disciples who, in the mid- to late 1800s, were the first to make pedagogy, or teaching, the focus of systematic research. Despite their own research shortcomings, Herbartians convinced teachers and educational administrators that education was a field to be taken seriously and studied scientifically. G. Stanley Hall, the organizer and first president of the American Psychological Association and co-founder of the child-study movement, delivered a series of public lectures on education under the auspices of Harvard University in the 1880s. A decade later, William James, the individual most instrumental in establishing educational psychology as its own discipline, gave a similar series of lectures on educational topics that were later detailed in his book *Talks to Teachers on Psychology* (1899/1983). The work of Hall and James, and especially their unique-for-the-time lecture series, reveals an early desire among both psychologists and educators to develop better psychological understandings of teaching. In the early 1900s, Edward Lee Thorndike, widely considered the progenitor of educational psychology, further entrenched the discipline by purposefully and systematically focusing psychological research on educational matters. Thorndike's divergence from mainstream psychology admirably sought to separate education from psychology based solely on underlying psychological functions. However, because of his "science-will-cure-all" mindset and society's overwhelming reverence for scientific thought at the time, Thorndike was able to convince educational psychologists to retain an exclusive affinity for rigorous and controlled laboratory research, with a heavy reliance on statistical methods. This steadfast adherence to strict quantitative and experimental research was a product of Thorndike's stubbornness and his outright dismissal of the use of qualitative forms of scholarship, including both clinical and naturalistic observations, to examine and explain educational phenomena. This position still resonates somewhat today.

Despite this focus on educational matters, the entire discipline of psychology at the time fell out of love with schooling, and Thorndike, in particular, developed a considerable disdain for actual school practices. In fact, he abhorred the context of the classroom and the social dynamic of teachers interacting with students so much that he was noted for his absence from schools. The emphasis on rigorously quantifiable elements of human behaviour, espoused by individuals in the field of psychology during this period, meant that anything that could not be observably measured, such as one's thoughts or the subtleties of social interaction, was marginalized because it could not be proven or replicated. Thus, Thorndike and many of his contemporaries found classrooms too messy and too complicated when they tried to "control for" all the variables that could affect or explain an experimental outcome. Unfortunately, this narrow perspective on research, which was devoid of contextual influences, governed educational psychology for the better part of 80 years.

In the late 1970s and early 1980s, two monumental occurrences irreversibly changed the research landscape. First, the prolific growth of findings about complex cognitive processes (instead of simple stimulus–response mechanisms) moved educational psychology away from **behaviourism** and "psychology applied to education" toward a discipline that conducted fundamental research about its own essential processes—instruction and learning. Simultaneously, the trivialization of the notion of self-regulation by behaviourists led to the demise of behaviourism (replete with quantitative studies solely about reductionist conceptions of human activity). For behaviourists, the idea that we have a conscience and can choose to do or not do certain things flew directly in the face of the simplistic, but measurable, explanations of behaviour provided by stimulus–response (SR) theory.

In light of these advances, the narrow spectrum of research that previously ignored the inherent contexts of human interaction had to give way to a much broader gamut of context-rich studies. So it was during this period that educational psychologists rediscovered the psychology proposed by several of its founding fathers, including William James and, especially, John Dewey. While Dewey made several notable contributions to educational psychology, his consummate passion and vision was that the classroom was the perfect research laboratory for educational exploration. Nonetheless, just like the efforts of James, who argued against measuring individual mental faculties, and of Hall, who proposed the child-study movement, Dewey's broader conceptions of contextual educational psychology were drowned out by the wave of Thorndikian science that swept the times. Dewey was a functionalist psychologist who held deep holistic views about educational processes and believed, idyllically, in a personal and idiosyncratic plan of learning for each and every student. It is not hard to imagine how Dewey's desire to see how things functioned within classrooms clashed resoundingly with Thorndike's contention that his experimental laboratory at Teachers College was the "only" place to study education.

Cognition and learning are still the predominant topics within educational psychology, but views on what they are and how they operate have changed considerably over the past 30 years or so. In concert with better understandings of self-regulation, socio-cultural influences on thinking and learning are gaining ground, and the entire discipline is building much more reverence for the context-rich perspectives of James, Dewey, Piaget, and Vygotsky. Not only has there been a considerable shift from behavioural to cognitive psychology, but there has also been a shift away from studying the individual to studying the individual within his or her contexts of influence. This emphasis has led to far more encompassing conceptions and models of situated learning theory, a real turnabout from the narrow mental faculty conceptions that prevailed in days gone by. These broadened perspectives have not necessarily changed the methods of inquiry used in educational psychology, although idiographic study has recently been added, but modern conceptions of underlying psychological processes have certainly changed how particular research methods are considered and applied.

Research Methods

In everyday terms, research implies legitimacy and credibility. Credible researchers in educational psychology adroitly adhere to the following maxim: Good research is not as much about *what* is studied—it is more about *how* it is studied. Another fundamental tenet of good research, then, is the importance of asking good questions. Taking time to think carefully about the topic under scrutiny and to examine all of its related issues always results in better questions and frequently results in a question better than and/or slightly different from the original. At its core, the process of answering the well-crafted research question involves a systematic approach and thoroughness in order for the answer (and the researcher) to be considered credible. In educational psychology, such an answer usually includes a demonstration of how the research findings have been (or can be) applied within various educational contexts.

Credible research is the judicious application of appropriate investigative procedures in an effort to best answer the questions being asked. The way in which research is conducted is referred to as the method. This term speaks to three important features that separate proven and reliable research from the logical assumptions, intuitive hunches, and common-sense applications that are often erroneously used to describe or explain educational phenomena. The first feature of good research is that it is systematic; systematization makes research reliable because it demonstrates that the researcher has methodically considered all of the possible factors related to the question. By carefully documenting all the steps and procedures involved, the researcher ensures that the study can be replicated by others. The second feature of good research is that the researcher tries to remain as objective as possible; this consideration tends to eliminate researcher bias as much as possible, and it prevents the findings from being influenced by assumptions, hunches, and common sense. The third feature of good research is that it is testable; this usually means that the variables examined by the research question can actually be applied and observed in educational settings. This is the predominant feature that distinguishes educational psychology from psychology, because many of the experimental findings in psychology are not applicable in classrooms. Moreover, it is this testability that gives research its **validity** and **reliability**. When all three of the above features are properly applied, the findings of a study are said to be valid (they answer the question asked) and reliable (the same answer is highly likely if the research is repeated).

This does not mean, however, that assumptions, hunches, and common-sense explanations do not play an important role in educational research. Very often, highly perceptive teachers identify perplexing situations that defy logical or accepted explanations, and this leads to the most intriguing research questions. Or a teacher or researcher encounters a perplexing situation for which there may be several different theoretical explanations. (A theoretical explanation, or **theory**, is a description, based on scientific findings, of why things happen in classrooms or what might happen if a teacher were to do or not do certain things. Theories are usually made up of collections of guiding principles that explain the relationships between a series of related topics or events.) Regardless of whether an educational scenario defies accepted explanations or appears to be explained by conflicting theories, the next crucial step for an educator is to avoid a quick and easy "common-sense" explanation and, instead, critically examine the situation using the tried and accepted research features described above.

The process of conducting research (see Figure 1.1) produces a series of defined outcomes that occur at different points along a hierarchical structure:

Step 1   Research is typically initiated by a teacher's or researcher's intuition or hunch that an observed educational phenomenon does not fit within current or acceptable explanations.

Step 2   Research questions are generated by carefully considering the observed phenomenon and contrasting it with current explanations of identical or similar occurrences.

Step 3   The critical features of proven research methods are employed to determine relationships between phenomena.

Step 4   Several similar research outcomes regarding the same topic become guiding principles.

Step 5   Collections of established and replicable principles about sets of related phenomena are merged into overarching theories that tend to govern our understandings and guide further research—that is, of course, until a teacher or researcher runs into a perplexing educational situation that is not satisfactorily explained, and then the whole process starts again.

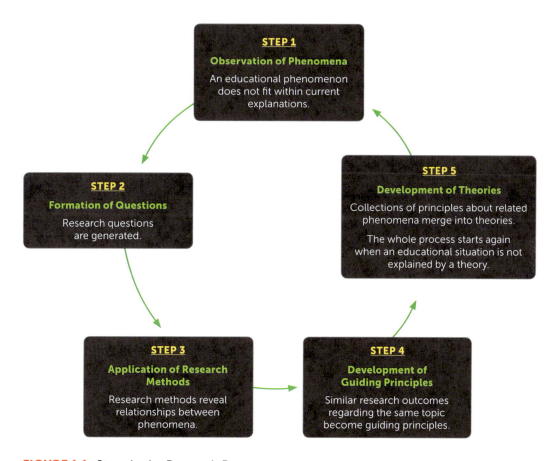

FIGURE 1.1   Steps in the Research Process

Approaches to Research

There are two fundamental approaches to research in educational psychology, and each approach is conducted using two basic methods. Therefore, four methods predominate research in the discipline. Each involves far more detail than can be described here, but the brief explanations below should facilitate an understanding of how all four contribute to the development of the principles and theories that govern educational psychology. Depending on the thrust and purpose of the research question(s) being asked, researchers will employ one of these four methods to obtain a suitable answer, or they will combine two methods because one by itself cannot sufficiently answer the question.

Quantitative research

Descriptive research and **experimental research** are the two dominant methods within the **quantitative** approach. Descriptive studies do exactly what the phrase implies—they seek to describe how or what a situation is as it actually exists. In descriptive studies, researchers gather numerical and non-numerical data about what appear to be related variables. They perform statistical analyses to determine whether or not relationships exist and then describe the strength of these relationships. Because these are relational findings, researchers and educators can use one variable to make predictions about the other. For example, numerous studies have repeatedly shown that there is a positive relationship between high school grades and university performance (Cyrenne & Chan, 2012; Geiser, 2003; Geiser & Santelices, 2007; Hoffman & Lowitzki, 2005). This relationship is the primary reason that high school grades are used to make decisions about university admission; these grades have consistently predicted a reasonable expectation for university success.

Conversely, rather than merely describing a situation as it exists or outlining the strengths of relationships between variables, experimental studies manipulate one of the variables (independent variable) within the situation to see if the manipulation causes a change in the target variable (dependent variable). As much as possible, researchers try to control all other potential influences on the dependent variable so that they can say, with some authority, that the independent variable produced the observed effect. For example, to test whether a new way of teaching spelling is more effective than the one currently in use, a teacher could simply change his or her way of teaching halfway through the spelling curriculum. Student scores on spelling tests for the first and second half of the curriculum could then be compared to see whether or not the new teaching approach (the cause) changed students' spelling performances (the effect). A more rigorous way to carry out this experiment would be to match teachers and students according to grade and spelling curriculum and then have one teacher use the new instructional method while the other teacher uses the old one. The test scores of students who received the new method (the treatment group) would then be compared to those of students who received the old method (the control group).

Qualitative research

The **qualitative research** approach is dominated by two methods: **idiographic research** and **ethnographic research**. In idiographic research, the investigator uses a unique individual or situation as the lens through which broad theories, or specific principles within theories, are critically examined to determine whether all parts of the theory apply to the individual or situation, or vice versa. For example, in recent research on giftedness (Edmunds & Edmunds, 2005, 2014b, 2014c; Edmunds & Noel, 2003; Noel & Edmunds, 2007), the broader theories of giftedness and the specific principles that describe and govern highly precocious writing were examined via the prolific body of work produced by an exceptional child writer. This program of research resulted in significant changes in the way educators perceive, understand, and analyze precocious writing in profoundly gifted children. In ethnographic research, investigators intentionally use the specific perspectives of carefully selected research participants (groups or individuals) to examine overviews of how and why social and/or cultural influences affect how an individual constructs his or her understandings of the world around him or her. Results from these types of studies have dramatically changed both the content contained in school texts and the ways in which teachers deliver such content. Careful and precise consideration is given to the diverse worlds that students operate in and from.

Overall, the key to effective and useful research, whether it is quantitative or qualitative in nature, is asking good research questions. Excellent questions arise when teachers and researchers are observant and thus become inquisitive about perplexing situations that occur in classrooms.

> **think box**
>
> Think of an appropriate research question (related to teaching and learning) for each of the four research methods described above (descriptive, experimental, idiographic, and ethnographic). Describe why each question is best addressed by the chosen research method, and explain why the remaining three research methods are less suitable.

After re-reading Dr. Cameron's paper, Annette feels even more excited about facing the challenges of her new placement. She knows that she does not have to find all of the answers herself—there is a wealth of information at her disposal as a result of research conducted within the discipline of educational psychology. She feels that she can now use this vast array of information more effectively and more confidently because she has a better understanding of how it was carefully determined to be both valid and applicable to classrooms.

The Students of *The Little Red Schoolhouse*

Moving on to more pressing issues, Annette looks at the 15 school files sitting on her desk. She settles back into her chair and begins to read about the individuals who will learn and grow under her guidance during the coming year. As she goes through the files, she summarizes each student's apparent strengths and challenges and records them in the new files she has set up for herself. While she will certainly remain open to learning more about her new students as the year unfolds, reading what others have written about these students will help with her initial planning activities.

Name: Jacob White
Age: 6
Grade Level: 1
Strengths: excellent gross motor skills; gets along well with peers
Challenges: difficulty with fine motor skills and pre-literacy skills

Name: Lily Carter
Age: 6
Grade Level: 1
Strengths: good pre-literacy skills; motivated learner
Challenges: shy

Name: Troy Lee
Age: 7
Grade Level: 2
Strengths: working well at grade level across all subject areas
Challenges: English is second language

Name: Amanda Pritchard
Age: 8
Grade Level: 3
Strengths: excellent organizational skills; focuses well in class
Challenges: difficulty getting along with peers

Name: Zach MacMillan
Age: 9
Grade Level: 3
Strengths: artistic; good verbal skills
Challenges: impulsive and inattentive (diagnosed with ADHD)

Name: Jacqueline Dion
Age: 10
Grade Level: 4
Strengths: creative; performs well in activities that involve music, art, or drama
Challenges: lacks interest in academics

Name: Liam Carter
Age: 10
Grade Level: 4
Strengths: excellent reading skills; independent learner
Challenges: needs extra help with mathematics

Name: Caleb Johnston
Age: 12
Grade Level: 5
Strengths: athletic; interested in nature; strong ties to his First Nations culture
Challenges: working below grade level; disruptive classroom behaviours

Name: Tara MacMillan
Age: 13
Grade Level: 7
Strengths: performs above grade level in reading and writing
Challenges: perfectionist

Name: Jackson Roberts
Age: 15
Grade Level: 8
Strengths: average intelligence (has the ability to be successful in school)
Challenges: lack of effort in class; rarely completes homework; little communication between home and school

Name: Sophie Dion
Age: 16
Grade Level: 10
Strengths: average academic achievement across all grade levels; likes to help others
Challenges: works evenings and weekends to help with family finances

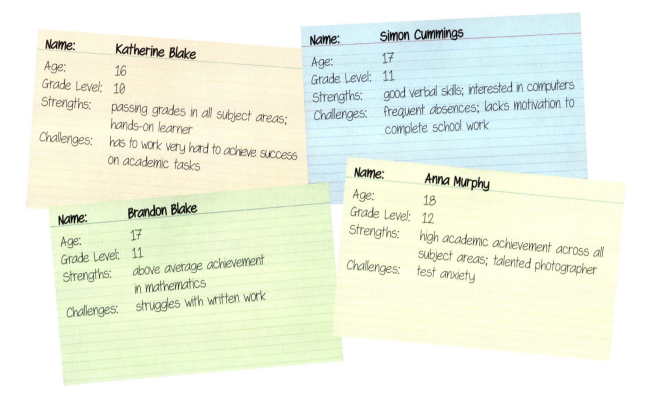

Teacher Planning

Now that Annette has reviewed the files and has a better feel for each student's strengths and weaknesses, she turns her focus to planning the instruction that will meet their educational needs. Thinking back to when she was a beginning teacher, Annette remembers feeling that the actual act of teaching was the most important thing she had to accomplish. She now knows through her years of experience, however, that next to reflective practice, the most important element of her profession is planning. As Dr. Cameron emphasized in class, good planning results in excellent teaching, enhanced student learning, and exemplary environments within which effective teaching and learning can take place. He also emphasized that the opposite of good planning is not poor planning; it is not planning at all. Poor planning may result in occasional mistakes and setbacks, but not doing any planning will certainly result in instruction that is vague and directionless, students who do not learn despite their best efforts, and classrooms that lack predictability, structure, and routine. Annette has learned that good planning involves a careful and simultaneous consideration of (a) what she will teach, (b) the order in which it will be taught, (c) what teaching methods and materials she will use, (d) the type of environment she will teach in, and (e) how and when her students will be assessed.

think box

Imagine that you are Annette and her 15 students are the students you will have in your classroom this year. What are your first impressions? Are there any student strengths or challenges that will test your current knowledge or teaching skills? What types of additional information might you seek out before school begins?

Curricular Planning

Annette has already decided that she will plan what she will teach by following a top-down approach. This approach (see Figure 1.2) includes (a) determining the curricula for the year and for each term, (b) breaking the curricula down into units that extend over several weeks, and (c) determining what will be taught on a daily basis.

Year- or Term-Long Curriculum
Outline the global curricular objectives for the entire course/subject.

Topical/Thematic Units
Design plans that extend over several weeks.

Daily Lesson Plans

FIGURE 1.2 Curriculum Planning Template

To get things started, Annette sets about conceptualizing her entire year. This process is not difficult, because she has access to the various curriculum guides produced by the Ministry of Education in her province. Curriculum guides are year-long, or term-long, outlines of school subjects, differentiated by grade. These comprehensive guides specifically outline what students are to be taught and the knowledge and skills that they are

expected to acquire for each subject at each grade level. Sometimes the guides also outline provincial/territorial expectations for student achievement.

Annette spreads all the guides out on a large table so that she can organize them into groupings. She carefully divides the year and the terms of the year into large units of instruction centred around topically related themes and/or clusters of educational outcomes or learning objectives. Her units of instruction cover no less than one week of teaching. Some units extend over several weeks because she wants to incorporate more and/or broader issues related to the topic being taught. She also likes to leave a little room in her units for unexpected circumstances that might arise, such as breaking news on the topic at hand or the sudden availability of a guest speaker whose particular expertise would contribute toward an expansion of the information provided in the unit. The main objective of her planning process at this point in August is to establish and visualize "the big picture" for all of her teaching and to determine the basic sequencing of all topics. Annette uses some of the sequences and thematic units suggested in the curriculum guides, modifies several others to suit her teaching preferences, and designs completely new and different units based on her inherent need to teach common topics across various grades, as well as on her growing knowledge about her students and the community and region where they live. She constructs just a few daily lesson plans now (enough to get her started in September) and will develop the rest as the year unfolds. Nonetheless, while she is in the moment, she labels them all with probable but tentative headings for the time being. She knows that nothing is more frustrating than failing to recall her great ideas because she did not take the time to jot them down during her previous planning processes. When she does start to design her lesson plans in earnest, she will follow two well-proven rules: (1) the purpose of each lesson will be clear, and (2) the theme or essence of each lesson will be flexible enough to accommodate interruptions (systemic or behavioural) and teachable moments.

Because she has only a general idea of what her students were taught last year, Annette decides to follow Dr. Cameron's advice and start the school year by assessing their current levels of knowledge and skills. This is known as diagnostic assessment—the determination of students' existing knowledge and skills for the purpose of guiding future instruction. Since it is impractical to expect to assess her students' knowledge and skills in all curricular domains, Annette decides to assess the language arts and math skills of the Grade 1–6 students and the English and math abilities of the Grade 7–12 students. Not only will these choices give her a global overview of student abilities in the essential elements of schooling—reading, writing, and calculation—but they will also provide an indication of the relative strengths and needs of all her students in these critical areas. This knowledge will enable her to better differentiate her math and language arts/English instruction by grade. It will also allow her to take advantage of where the curricula overlap across grades. Another potential benefit will be that students in Grade 6 or higher who are particularly skilled at writing can be identified as possible mentors for younger students who are just learning to write or are struggling with writing. The same is true for math. Annette concludes that in addition to directing her instruction, the information she will glean from the diagnostic tests will offer endless benefits. It will be her first opportunity to see whether the information in each student's file is confirmed by the observations she makes during the assessment sessions.

As recommended by Dr. Cameron, Annette assembles her pre-instructional assessment indicators by modifying the final tests or other evaluation methods that were administered at the end of the previous school year. While this process initially seemed an onerous task, it actually turns out to be relatively easy once she gets started. Annette reads a copy of each test or evaluation method for each grade, and using information from respective curriculum guides, she reduces each one to between 10 and 20 questions (10–14 questions for the younger students and 15–20 for the older ones). On each assessment tool, more than half the questions assess global or general curricular objectives, while the remaining questions assess specific knowledge or skills. Annette knows that after the summer holidays, students will remember general concepts better than specific topical details. Allowing time for differing student abilities, she estimates that each pre-instructional assessment will take between 45 and 60 minutes. Recognizing the limited attention span of the younger students, Annette will have them complete each test in two shorter time periods.

Curriculum Planning

To lay people, "curriculum" is simply what is taught in schools. They are unaware of the knowledge, planning, and analysis of curricula that form the basis for expert teacher practice. Without a firm understanding of curriculum design and planning, good teaching would be impossible, even for experienced educators. Darling-Hammond et al. (2005) define curriculum planning as the learning experiences and goals that teachers develop for their classes in light of students' characteristics and the teaching context. They (p. 200) outline the following three interrelated elements of the curricular planning process:

1) **Educational purpose** is a conception of what is important for students to study based on social needs and expectations, learning standards, and research and the translation of these broad goals into more discrete objectives that can guide particular lessons and units of study.
2) **Learning experiences**, systematically selected and organized into what is often called a *scope and sequence*, refer to the kinds of information, demonstrations, models, inquiry opportunities, discussion, and practice students need in order to acquire the requisite knowledge and skills.
3) **Evaluation** is the collection and analysis of student academic performance data to provide feedback about the effectiveness of teaching and learning relative to the desired curricular objectives.

Based on the topics covered in the diagnostic assessment, Annette also prepares the lesson plans she needs for the start of school. These lesson plans address both language arts/English and math for each group of students. She knows that unless her pre-instructional assessment tools are way off the mark, these lessons will only require minor modifications in order to be suitable instructional starting points. In the past, these lessons, which she typically prepared in August, have saved her time. More important, they have allowed her to start the year with confidence, knowing that her lesson plans match where her students are in their learning.

Annette lets out a sigh as she reflects on her progress. The time has flown by, and she notices it is already dark outside. However, she is content that her general planning activities are almost complete and she has accomplished all she wanted to do, at least for today. She realizes that one of her primary concerns has now been addressed. She was worried that she lacked the knowledge and expertise required to teach the younger students (Grades 1–3). Her worst fear was that she would teach or do something that was inappropriate for their ages. However, in reading over the curricular documents for those grades and organizing them into coherent units, she sees that that the guides were designed and structured with developmental appropriateness in mind. As she read more and more of each guide, what could be and should be taught became clearer, and she intuitively recognized where and how she could extend student learning and where she would probably need to go more slowly.

Annette wearily packs up her knapsack, turns off the classroom lights, and makes her way through the empty hallway, satisfied with the curricular planning she has accomplished.

Instructional Planning

The next component in Annette's planning process, laying out her approach to teaching, is waiting for her the next morning. She remembers that this was not an easy task when she first started her career. Her initial approach was a combination of a variety of methods that, for a considerable period, she had difficulty articulating as a coherent whole. Her thoughts on what accurately described her overall approach to teaching were finally consolidated by an assignment in Dr. Cameron's course. The assignment required her to outline her entire methodology and to rationalize why each element was included. She pulls this assignment out of her binder to see whether her established approach is still a good fit for her current situation.

Assignment—My Approach to Teaching

My preferred way of teaching combines elements of the teacher-centred approach and the student-centred approach, since they offer contrasting but complementary elements of good teaching. I definitely have an affinity for the highly structured nature of teacher-centred instruction. I believe that teachers are primarily responsible for the overall direction that instruction takes, for the way the classroom is managed and governed, and for the establishment of the academic and social tone that students operate in. Within this model, I appreciate the highly formalized elements of direct instruction whereby the teacher directs the curriculum, plays a predominant role in selecting learning activities, has high performance expectations for students, and devotes most of her students' class time to academic tasks. But I know that direct instruction is not always suitable for all teaching situations. For example, I use more direct instruction when teaching students in the elementary grades because they have to learn specific skills, and I use it less in the higher grades because students' problem-solving and critical-thinking skills are more mature. I should note, however, that I do not subscribe to the element of teacher-centred instruction that suggests that teachers should minimize non-academic conversations between and among students and teachers. This may work for some teachers, but it does not really match my personality or my way of doing things.

While I generally like student-centred approaches to education, I do not feel that the focus of education should be predominantly student-driven. I think that some of the suggestions used in this approach can cause teachers to mistake student-pleasing activities for meaningful learning activities whereby the simple performance of classroom activities can mistakenly take the place of the meaningful learning that is supposed to occur. Nevertheless, I am a firm believer in the contribution that **constructivism** has made to teaching. I like how it stipulates that rather than simply absorbing information, students develop their own cognitive structures and actively construct their knowledge and skills. This tells me that as an educator I must first consider the knowledge that my students bring to school and then design and deliver curricula to expand and develop their knowledge by connecting it to new learning.

As a result of my constructivist understandings, my approach to teaching contains the following three student-centred elements that take full advantage of the constructivist perspective: (1) each of my lessons contains specific learning outcomes that fall under the umbrella of overarching themes, allowing my students to see where and how new and specific information is related to larger frames of knowledge; (2) students get to construct their own meaning and knowledge under my watchful guidance; thus, I can prevent them from constructing knowledge only on their own and/or constructing knowledge that is obviously incorrect; and (3) students in my classes engage in problem-based learning (emphasizing problem-solving processes) and project-based learning (emphasizing a product or artifact as an outcome) because while these types of activities are mostly student-directed, they are still teacher-facilitated and they are ideal for collaborative efforts by groups of students. In my classroom, these combined instructional strategies require students to utilize a wide-ranging set of academic abilities to solve authentic, real-life problems and/or academic problems while producing related academic products. My students have considerable input into the selection and design of "vague" problems that act as the catalysts for these activities, and they also have a say in how these activities are evaluated.

Finally, I have always felt that an important result of my overall approach to teaching is that it should directly influence student self-regulated learning (SRL), another valuable contribution from the constructivist perspective. My interest in SRL began with an exploration of what self-regulation really means, especially as it applies to young children. The best description I have found is one provided by Stuart Shanker (2010), who described self-regulation as:

> . . . the ability to stay calmly focused and alert, which often involves—but cannot be reduced to—self-control. The better a child can stay calmly focused and alert, the better he integrates the diverse information coming in from his different senses,

assimilates it, and sequences his thoughts and actions . . . self-regulation nurtures the ability to cope with greater and greater challenges because it involves arousal states, emotions, behaviour, and—as the child grows older—thinking skills.

This explanation allowed me to better understand the importance of facilitating self-regulation in students at the early grade levels so that they will eventually experience more success when required to engage in SRL in later grades. According to Paris and Winograd (2003), SRL emphasizes the autonomy and responsibility of students to take charge of their own learning by

- being aware of what effective thinking entails and comparatively analyzing their own thinking habits (metacognition);
- being strategic in their approaches to learning and problem-solving (including knowing what the strategy is, how the strategy operates, and when and why the strategy is applied); and
- making motivational decisions about the goal of an activity, the perceived difficulty and value of the task, the self-perceptions of the learner's ability to accomplish the task, and the potential benefit of success or liability of failure.

I feel that my approach to teaching contributes to self-regulated learning because it involves processes that assist students in the development of all of the above skills. It helps them develop the basic skills of self-regulation, and, when developmentally appropriate, it presents them with comprehensive, complex, and meaningful tasks; it involves them in self-determined processes and products; it encourages them to engage in collaborative and cooperative efforts; and it gives them input into the self-design, self-monitoring, and self-evaluation of their academic activities.

"Not a bad description of how I feel about teaching," Annette confirms as she puts away her old assignment. She decides to take the rest of the day to think about what she wrote. As she attends to some of the more mindless classroom tasks, such as photocopying handouts and gathering together general classroom supplies, she reflects on how well her stated approach to teaching will fit with her new classroom situation. She finally concludes that the approach is a good one and it already accounts for the challenges she will face when teaching both younger and older students.

As Annette tidies up her desk, she gives herself some good advice: "It's important for me to feel confident, not only in my teaching knowledge but also in my choice of teaching approaches. By taking the time to plan and think things through, I'm providing myself with the best opportunity to be an effective teacher."

Good Teaching: Ten Best Practices and Twelve Generic Guidelines

In her paper on teaching, Annette refers to the two predominant approaches to instruction employed by most teachers. In the teacher-centred approach, the teacher determines the content and the direction of lessons. This traditional view establishes teachers as those who have knowledge to impart and students as those who will learn that knowledge. By contrast, in the student-centred approach, teachers consciously consider more of their students' perspectives when preparing and teaching lessons. The primary shift from being teacher-centred to being student-centred typically involves teachers adopting a constructivist perspective on education, often called constructivism, which emerged from cognitive and social psychology. In adopting this perspective, teachers recognize that students do not merely absorb what is taught; they are acutely aware that students actively and constantly construct their own understandings and knowledge. Therefore, teachers must consciously prepare and teach lessons to suit students. While it is certainly more demanding to design and teach lessons in this manner than simply to deliver a lecture, there is considerable evidence that teaching from the constructivist perspective makes student learning more meaningful and much more effective.

Regardless of what an approach to teaching is called or labelled, there appears to be some common ground in the methods used by good teachers. Brophy's (2012) analysis and synthesis of the considerable research done on "good teaching" resulted in two useful lists: (1) *Ten Best Practices* and (2) *Twelve Generic Guidelines*. It is best to think of the 10 best practices as specific teaching methods that teachers can use in classrooms and to think of the 12 generic guidelines as broader rules that teachers should always be considering as they construct and deliver their teaching.

Ten Best Practices

The following practices were derived from a distillation of instructional commonalities that have consistently proven effective across all subject areas.

1. **Teach for understanding, appreciation, and life application:** teaching for the understanding of networks of connected knowledge that are structured around big ideas and retained in forms that make them available for life applications.
2. **Address multiple goals simultaneously:** attending to multiple mixtures of knowledge, skill, attitude, value, dispositional goals, and content and process goals in particular, in a balanced way.
3. **Employ inquiry models:** using models that engage students in problem-solving and decision-making after sufficient orientation, structuring, and scaffolding.
4. **Engage students in discourse management:** teaching students to use related discourse, typically involving the co-construction of understandings through discussion and collaborative problem-solving.
5. **Design authentic activities:** including activities that engage students in doing what disciplinary practitioners do and activities that allow students to apply what they are learning to their lives outside of school.
6. **Include debriefing:** teaching students to use post-activity discussions to assess and reflect on what was learned.

7. **Work with artifacts:** in association with authentic activities, having students work with the artifacts of a field of study.
8. **Foster metacognition and self-regulated learning:** teaching in ways that help students become metacognitively aware of goals and strategies and better able to self-regulate their learning (also connected to inquiry models and discourse management).
9. **Be aware of trajectories, misconceptions, and representations:** being familiar with typical trajectories in the development of understanding or skill; scaffolding students' progress through trajectories; and avoiding false starts, dead ends, and misconceptions by using well-chosen sets of representations to ensure that students do not construct overly specific or otherwise distorted understandings.
10. **Recognize the social aspects of learning:** learning is most likely to be meaningful and accessible for use when it is socially negotiated through classroom discourse culminating in whole-class debriefings (pp. 774–775).

Twelve Generic Guidelines

The following guidelines have consistently shown to be applicable under typical classroom conditions and are associated with fostering progress towards desired student outcomes. Moreover, these guidelines are considered to be mutually supportive components within a coherent model of teaching that can be applied across school subjects.

1. **Create a supportive classroom climate:** students learn best within cohesive and caring learning communities.
2. **Provide opportunities to learn:** students learn more when most of the available time is allocated to curriculum-related activities and the classroom-management system emphasizes maintaining students' engagement in those activities.
3. **Ensure curricular alignment:** all components of the curriculum are aligned to create a cohesive program for accomplishing instructional purposes and goals.
4. **Establish learning orientations:** teachers can prepare students for learning by providing initial structuring to clarify intended outcomes and cue desired learning strategies.
5. **Provide coherent content:** to facilitate meaningful learning and retention, content is clearly explained and developed, with emphasis on its structure and connections.
6. **Facilitate thoughtful discourse:** questions are planned to engage students in sustained discourse structured around powerful ideas.
7. **Include practice and application activities:** students need sufficient opportunities to practise and apply what they are learning and to receive improvement-oriented feedback.
8. **Scaffold students' task engagement:** the teacher provides whatever assistance students need to enable them to engage in learning activities productively.
9. **Teach effective strategies:** the teacher models and instructs students in learning and self-regulation strategies.
10. **Include cooperative learning:** students often benefit from working in pairs or small groups to construct understandings or to help one another master skills.
11. **Utilize goal-oriented assessment:** the teacher uses a variety of formal and informal assessment methods to monitor progress towards learning goals.
12. **Establish achievement expectations:** the teacher establishes and follows through on appropriate expectations for learning outcomes (pp. 775–776).

Annette's Journal

August 16, 2013

A new home . . . a new school . . . a new community. This feels a little overwhelming at the moment, but I'm glad I took on this challenge, because I know it will make me a better teacher. It seems like my first seven years of teaching were just the initial step in my development as an educator. I still have lots to learn. Taking Dr. Cameron's graduate course this summer made that so evident to me. I guess I never realized that I wasn't expected to know everything there is to know about teaching when I graduated with my education degree. Even today, when Mrs. Nugent, the principal, came to see me and asked me how I was going to deal with certain students who were on the verge of falling below grade level, I almost gave a quick response about how I would have each student assessed, spend extra time with them, etc. . . . but I stopped myself. I know she was surprised when I told her that I didn't know how I would deal with these students. I explained that I would have to look at the students' files but also take the time to make my own observations and assessments. It was probably the first time in my career that I felt comfortable not giving a quick answer to a question that others probably expected me to be able to answer without hesitation. It proved to me that I have learned a great deal about teaching, and more about myself as a teacher, from studying educational psychology. I know now that I need to carefully consider what I have learned about the interplay between my behaviours, my students' behaviours, and our shared environment before making decisions that affect any, or all, classroom members.

My planning this year is especially important given the makeup of my classroom. I have made a good start on it . . . thank goodness I gave myself a month to get prepared. It's not only the reading and material prep I have to do that makes this a time-consuming task. I really am enjoying having the luxury of mulling over ideas and thinking about the year ahead. I know from experience that I'll have less time for this type of planning once the school year begins. However, I feel that having my "master plan" in place will give me the framework and direction I'll need to react more quickly and efficiently when things arise unexpectedly during the months ahead.

Annette's Exploration of the Research

Schunk, D. H., & Zimmerman, B. J. (2012). Competence and control beliefs: Distinguishing the means and ends. In P. A. Alexander and P. H. Winne (Eds.), *Handbook of educational psychology* (2nd ed., pp. 349–368). New York, NY: Routledge.

One of Annette's primary concerns about teaching is the omnipresent conundrum of why some students "try" to learn while others do not. In the past, Annette struggled to reach some students on a consistent basis and could not get them to work to their potential or even close to their potential; the students didn't always respond positively, despite lots of encouragement and motivational talks about their abilities and, in some circumstances, a certain amount of blatant cajoling. These experiences led her to review research recommended by her mentor, Dr. Cameron, about the basic motivational processes that cause seemingly capable students to stop trying. Her search for an answer was rewarded when she read Schunk and Zimmerman's (2012) extensive review of how both competence beliefs and control beliefs affect student learning behaviours in classrooms. She condensed the salient points of Schunk and Zimmerman's analysis into a few manageable concepts and wrote down the implications it had for her as a teacher.

Salient Points

According to Schunk and Zimmerman, competence beliefs are students' evaluative perceptions about their means, processes, and capabilities to accomplish certain tasks; control beliefs are students' perceptions about the likelihood of accomplishing tasks under certain conditions. In the past, before they separated these two functions, researchers and educators considered and treated competence and control in the same way. As a result, teachers attempted to motivate competent students by telling them to try harder or to try again, and when that approach did not work, they used shame or bribery as last-resort motivators. But for many non-motivated students, no amount or type of reasonable or unreasonable persuasion worked.

Implications for My Teaching

There are two explanations for this phenomenon; one is obvious, while the other is less readily apparent. First, students who feel competent about learning generally expect success for their efforts, but they do not have the same success expectations if they feel that they have little or no control over contextual influences that can determine the outcome of the task. In other words, students need to be effective self-regulators of learning rather than teacher-controlled learners. Students have to truly believe that they can, within reason, exert some semblance of control over the classroom factors that govern their learning. Therefore, my approach to teaching this year will include the development and use of methods that require various facets of the self-regulation function (meaningful tasks, self-determined processes and products, cooperative learning, self-design, self-monitoring, and self-evaluation of academic activities).

The second explanation for the unmotivated-student phenomenon is that students who do not feel competent about learning do not typically experience a lot of academic success. This is exactly the type of student I have in mind and want to reach. As the research indicates, rather than continuing to try to learn and failing despite good effort, these students find it psychologically safer to "fail-by-not-trying." While they always seem to have a never-ending litany of excuses about why they did not or could not learn, they have essentially given up. This is a psychologically protective tactic that preserves their overall well-being. Moreover, it is a stronger psychological function in these individuals than the threat of failure or embarrassment due to failure or even the embarrassment of being caught lying about why they did not try to learn (e.g., I left my homework on the bus). In fact, "failing-by-not-trying" is even more powerful than the many enticements or threats adults can offer. In many cases, teachers and parents often provide students with more self-determinant and self-regulatory control than usual to get them back on track. What is not realized is that no amount of control over external influences will calm students' inner fears of the psychological risks presented by the challenges inherent in new learning tasks. As a result, the learning task still does not get done, and teachers and parents feel frustrated by the fact that the allowance of more control was ignored or abused.

The implication for my teaching, then, is that students with low-perceived competence in an academic domain must be taught the skills they require, whereas students with low-perceived control must be led through low-risk, high-success tasks that demonstrate to them that their skills can accomplish the desired outcomes. Once some low-risk, high-success learning activities have been completed, these students will feel more in control because they will see that their competence can produce desired results. Instead of initiating the remedial instructional process with student motivators, I need to initiate it with student successes.

Annette's Resource List

Academic Journals

American Educational Research Journal
British Journal of Educational Psychology
Contemporary Educational Psychology
Educational Psychology in Practice
Educational Psychology Review
Journal of Educational Psychology
Theory into Practice

Books

Anderman, E., & Corno, L. (Eds.). (2014). *Handbook of educational psychology* (3rd ed.). New York, NY: Routledge.

Websites

Alberta Teachers' Association—Getting Started—A Checklist for Beginning Teachers
www.teachers.ab.ca/For%20Members/Programs%20and%20Services/Resources%20For/Beginning%20Teachers/Pages/Getting%20Started.aspx

American Psychological Association—Educational Psychology
www.apa.org/about/division/div15.html

Canadian Association of Educational Psychology
www.csse.ca/CAEP/html/newsletter.html

Education World—Planning for Your First Day at School
www.educationworld.com/a_curr/curr360.shtml

ERIC—Education Resource Information Center
www.eric.ed.gov/ERICWebPortal/Home.portal

Teacher Tools
www.thecanadianteacher.com/tools

From the Authors' Notebook

As you can see from Annette's planning activities, she has spent a great deal of time considering how educational psychology concepts are applicable to teaching. In doing so, she has embraced the notion of reflective practice.

Reflecting on Practice

According to the UBC Centre for Teaching, Learning and Technology (2013), a reflective journal can be used as a tool to connect theory learned from textbooks and research articles to a student's own practice. Keeping such a journal requires a sustained individual reflective effort by the student. When kept over a period of time, the journal may be also used to assess or gain a sense of the student's growth and development.

As an active learner, you may find it very useful to keep a reflective journal while taking this course. To begin, consider the information you read in this chapter as well as the knowledge you have acquired through instruction, classroom discussions, and classroom activities. Then take the time to write down your thoughts about these learning experiences. Consider how your perspective on educational psychology may have changed. In addition, respond to the following questions:

- How confident do you feel about your ability to plan for a school year?
- What more do you need to know about planning for a school year, and where might you find this information?

Chapter Summary

In this chapter, the following concepts were highlighted:

- While educational psychology can simply be described as a discipline that is all about teaching and learning, it actually addresses nine specific topics: (1) learning and cognition, (2) development, (3) social and cultural influences, (4) motivation, (5) behaviour and classroom management, (6) individual differences, (7) assessment and evaluation, (8) teaching and instruction, and (9) psychological foundations of curricula.

- There are two fundamental approaches to educational psychology research—quantitative and qualitative; quantitative research can be either descriptive or experimental, while qualitative research can be either idiographic or ethnographic.
- Curricular and instructional planning is much more than preparing units and lessons; this process establishes the fundamental scope and direction of teaching.
- A coherent approach to teaching involves (a) knowing your students and (b) carefully selecting instructional methods that complement each other while providing ample variety and diversity.
- Teachers can and should use research to explain educational phenomena. This investigative process improves teachers' foundational knowledge and avoids misconceptions.

New Terms

behaviourism
constructivism
descriptive research
ethnographic research
experimental research
formative assessment

idiographic research
qualitative research
quantitative research
reliability
theory
validity

These terms are defined in the Glossary at the end of the text.

Review Questions

- How can teachers benefit from being reflective practitioners? How, by extension, might their students also benefit?
- What are the foundational topics of educational psychology, and how do they relate to the classroom?
- What are the steps of the research process?
- How does qualitative research differ from quantitative research?
- What planning activities should a teacher complete before the school year begins?
- Why is it important for teachers to consider and recognize their own approach to teaching?
- How can teachers use current educational psychology research findings to improve their practice?

LATE AUGUST
Considering Child and Adolescent Development

2

From the Authors' Notebook

This chapter presents the aspects of child and adolescent development that are important to educators. It also describes how Annette applies developmental concepts to her teaching. For the most part, developmental issues, when applied to educational psychology, focus on children's attainment of physical, cognitive, social, and emotional skills. Attention is paid to (a) the skills children have mastered, (b) the skills they are in the process of acquiring, and (c) the skills they need to acquire in order to maximize their developmental potential. This information is critical to teachers, because they must constantly adjust their teaching to suit each child's growing needs.

Primary Learning Objectives

After reading this chapter, you should understand that

1. development is influenced by genetics and the environment;
2. development is orderly in progression but does not follow a constant rate of advancement;
3. there are both intra- and inter-individual rates of developmental progression;
4. developmental principles significantly impact teaching;
5. learning is a natural cognitive function that is driven by our innate curiosity to understand the world around us;
6. developmental theorists have made valuable contributions to the discipline of educational psychology;
7. developmental appropriateness is important to all things educational;
8. developmental concepts must be applied in both elementary and secondary classrooms; and
9. teachers play an important role in supporting and enhancing students' psychological well-being as well as their intellectual and academic growth.

Teaching Students of Different Ages

With two weeks of preparation behind her, Annette sets out early Monday morning on her walk to school. The air is cool, but the sun is shining down from a cloudless blue sky. The only sound she can hear is the water rushing down the Cartier River. Annette feels energized once again by her surroundings. She cannot keep from thinking about what she wants to accomplish in the next few days. Since arriving in George Lake, she has been realizing more and more that teaching students of different ages requires some very careful thought. Her goal for today, then, is to review and hone her understanding of developmental differences. In the past, she was able to focus on the developmental abilities of one age group according to the grade level she was teaching. Most of her past teaching experiences took place in the upper grades of a K–8 school. However, she also taught secondary math and English in Grades 9–12, and early in her teaching career, she held two nine-month-term replacement positions in the early elementary grades (one in Grade 1 and the other in Grade 3). Annette laughs and shakes her head at the position she finds herself in now. She chides herself as she approaches the school grounds: "As if teaching isn't challenging enough, now I'm facing all grade levels at once. Annette, you really have pushed yourself to the limit this time. You'd better use these last few prep days to your best advantage!"

Instead of stopping to chat with other staff members upon entering *The Little Red Schoolhouse*, Annette grabs a cup of coffee, waves to her colleagues, and heads straight to her classroom. There, she pulls out the reading material she has on development and decides to start at the very beginning.

Developmental Influences

Development is a proficient evolutionary process that occurs across the lifespan. Throughout childhood and into adulthood, this process results in a progressively more complex and sophisticated individual. In educational psychology, development is specifically defined as a series of physical, cognitive, and social changes that occur within children. These changes allow children's learning to become more organized and more efficient and their resultant behaviours to be more adaptive to the environment in which they live.

Why is an understanding of development so important for those who work in the field of education? The first and most obvious reason to consider developmental differences is that the grade-by-grade structure of schools is designed and differentiated according to children's ages. At different ages, children acquire certain physical, cognitive, and social abilities. In a variety of children across various grades, any given physical, cognitive, or social trait or ability may be non-existent, just emerging, or fully formulated; it may even have transformed into a much more advanced ability. Therefore, educators must carefully choose instructional methods and curricular topics that are age- and grade-appropriate for their students. For example, reading is taught in the primary grades because this is the earliest time in cognitive development that most students' brains are ready and capable of learning to read in an efficient manner. Information gleaned from research on reading and observations of classroom practice over the past several decades has revealed which aspects of reading are taught in which grades (and even in which parts of the school year), but this has not changed the developmental fact that the best time for most students to learn to read efficiently is between Grades 1 and 3. Similarly, algebra is taught after elementary school because students' brains cannot efficiently understand and manipulate abstract algebraic concepts until the middle or high school developmental time frame.

There are three other foundational and highly influential reasons why knowing about developmental principles is important for teachers. They are:

1. Developmental principles apply to all students in all grades; they do not only apply to younger children in the elementary grades. The changes that occur in adolescence (ages 12–20 for girls and ages 14–20 for boys) are as important for teachers to understand as those that happen in the elementary grades (ages 5–12). Often, educators associate development with the earlier grades because of the frequent, dramatic, and easily noticed developmental changes that occur during that time. The subtler changes of adolescence are not as easily recognizable but are just as significant.

2. Developmental differences exist not only among children in the same grade but also within some children. For example, not all students in the same grade will learn and understand particular math skills at the same time, and for some students, their math proficiency for their age or grade will be more advanced than their English skills.
3. Developmental principles provide teachers with foundational understandings of the learning process. Nothing has changed the teaching profession more than the discovery of how learning takes place and how students' learning processes differ from those of adults.

In essence, development explains who students are, how they differ from one another, and how and why they learn. However, the status of being a child is not static. Children naturally grow and change from initially helpless and dependent individuals into capable and self-sufficient adults. They accomplish this transformation via a series of simultaneous and often interactive changes in physical growth, cognitive abilities, and personal and social understandings. These changes may be minor or major and are all governed by a series of universal or guiding principles.

Principles of Development

Much has been written about what constitutes development and what influences various developmental processes, but there are five guiding principles about which there is little argument. These principles have evolved over time through the research efforts of many theorists and practitioners, who often did not necessarily agree with each other. Nonetheless, their differing opinions, carefully tested and examined by accepted fundamental research processes, have consistently found support. The following five developmental principles are highly relevant to educators:

1. Development follows an orderly and logical progression. Individuals walk before they can run, talk before they can read, and master sentences before they can write essays. In this sense, prerequisite milestones or indicators are not skipped or eliminated, although they can sometimes overlap somewhat with milestones that immediately follow them.
2. Development is a gradually progressive process, but it does not necessarily occur at a constant rate. While development is typically devoid of quantum or overnight changes, it is certainly marked by periods of relatively rapid or slow growth. Time is the critical factor, and while some developmental milestones/indicators can be compressed or accelerated (but not skipped), most require close-to-normal time frames to be fully consolidated.
3. Development involves quantitative and qualitative changes. This means that in addition to knowing more about something (e.g., there are three territories and 10 provinces in Canada), individuals learn to think differently about these very same things (e.g., Canada is a country with a federal government and regional governments defined by the three territories and 10 provinces). Similarly, not only do children learn to walk 10 more steps than the 20 they could walk before, but a commensurate increase in their fluidity and grace when walking 30 or more steps signifies a qualitative change in their behaviour/ability.

4. Individuals develop at different rates. While all children undergo simultaneous changes in their individual physical, cognitive, and social development, not all children achieve the same developmental milestones at the same time, despite being the same age. This principle has serious implications for classrooms of same-age students (e.g., some students will learn more rapidly than others, and some students will be physically smaller than their peers). It also has implications for students who are the same age but, because of different school-entry cut-offs, are placed in different grades.

5. Development results from the combinatorial influences of genetics (nature) and the environment (nurture), with genetics setting the limits of developmental potential and the environment determining how much of that potential is realized. At a basic level, genetic inheritance and the effects of environmental surroundings combine to determine the abilities an individual develops and the behaviours and outcomes that result from these abilities. On a more relational level, it has been suggested that development is also a function of how individual factors, such as personality and temperament, interact with environmental factors, such as methods of teaching and classroom management, to produce particular behaviours. In this way, not only are individuals affected by genetics and their environment, but they also learn to effect changes within their environment (that is, to manipulate it) to suit what they want or feel that they need.

These five guiding principles point to the following key teaching considerations:

1. Teachers must teach each topic in its respective learning progression.
2. Teachers must allow time, and preferably practice, in order for academic concepts to be fully understood.
3. Teachers must strive to improve *how* students know, not just *how much* they know.
4. Teachers must consider that within their classrooms it is normal and expected that some children will learn faster or slower than others.
5. And, perhaps most important, teachers must recognize their ability to either positively or negatively affect how much of each child's academic and social potential is realized.

Annette pauses for a moment. The list she has just read seems straightforward and logical, but she knows it has much more meaning embedded in it. She puts the reading material aside and sits back in her chair. She ponders the effect she has had on her past students' academic and social growth. "Did I pay enough attention to the guiding principles of development? Did I ask too much of some students and too little of others? Oh, how easy it is to get caught up in the day-to-day work of a teacher and forget these good ideas . . . I really need to be able to keep these ed psych concepts in mind when I'm making teaching decisions. I wonder if Dr. Cameron has any suggestions about how to accomplish this . . ."

> **Development Issues**
> **Annette Elkins <annette_elkins@schoolmail.com>**
> **Date:** Monday, August 19, 2013 9:22 AM
> **To:** Andrew Cameron <acameron@university.ca>
>
> Hello Andrew,
>
> Today I'm reading about development. All the material you gave us this past summer has taken on a greater importance now that I'm faced with teaching students of all ages. I can't help but think this is good for me, because when I taught classes where all the students were the same age, I didn't really think too much about development. Basically, I knew what kids of a certain age were supposedly capable of, and I taught them the curricula I was given. I'm sure I did some students a disservice at times by not consciously considering developmental principles and issues. I want that to improve this year . . . I really have no choice—developmental differences will be staring me in the face!
>
> I was wondering if you might help me with the practical side of this. I have just re-read the section about the five guiding principles of development and how they are relevant to educators. Their relevance is indisputable, yet in the past I don't think I consciously took them into consideration when I was faced with teaching decisions. Do you have any ideas on how I can bring these concepts to the forefront of my everyday life in the classroom? I want to be sure that all of my new students reach their academic and social potential this year.
>
> I hope your preparation for your new grad course is going well!
>
> Many thanks,
>
> Annette

Annette sends off her e-mail and decides to take a break from reading. She sets about organizing the computer lab at the far end of the classroom. An hour later, she checks her e-mail and finds a response from Dr. Cameron.

> **Re: Development Issues**
> **Andrew Cameron <acameron@university.ca>**
> **Date:** Monday, August 19, 2013 10:32 AM
> **To:** Annette Elkins <annette_elkins@schoolmail.com>
>
> Hello Annette,
>
> First of all, I want to impress upon you that your teaching skills are always developing and you shouldn't be too hard on yourself about how you handled certain situations in the past. I'm sure you did the best you could with what you knew at the time. The important thing is to keep building on your skills and your knowledge, and I see you are doing just that!

Now, let's consider what you can do to keep on top of the developmental differences in your classroom. From my experience and the experiences of the teachers I know, completing the following steps can be quite helpful:

Step 1: Become familiar with what is known about developmental differences in school-age children. You can accomplish this by reviewing the course material I gave you earlier this summer (which you are already doing) and by finding other relevant information on-line. You should be able to locate tables or lists that outline the skills you can expect to observe in different-age children . . . this will most likely be presented by grade level rather than by age.

Step 2: Determine how these developmental differences will likely relate to your students. I suggest that you consider each of your students individually, starting with the youngest. Using the information you have collected in Step 1, make a few notes about what you can expect from each of your students. (If you have created files for each student, this is a great place to record your notes.) When you move from youngest to oldest, the developmental differences within your classroom will become even clearer. Your notes will then provide you with a quick resource when you need it. Remember, though, as you get to know the students better, you may need to modify these notes. Not all children will fall into the developmental level that corresponds with their age and/or grade level.

Step 3: When a student is having difficulty with a task, review your notes and consider any developmental issues that may be contributing to the problem. As well, ask yourself these questions: Has the student acquired the prerequisite skills that are needed to complete this task? Does this student typically learn more slowly than others? Have I given him or her ample time and practice opportunities to learn the new skill? Have I presented the material in a number of meaningful ways, all of which are appropriate for the student's developmental understanding?

By following these steps, you'll automatically begin to think more about developmental differences in your everyday school life. You'll also find that you'll retain more of the information you have read about this topic by regularly applying it to classroom situations. Hopefully, your knowledge of ed psych will continue to grow, and you'll see first-hand how it can facilitate more effective teaching. I'm eager to see how your year unfolds! Keep me posted . . .

Andrew

Annette likes Dr. Cameron's ideas. She pulls out her students' files and decides to attach some key developmental information to each one. This information will help to remind her of the abilities expected of students at each grade level. She starts with the youngest students just as Dr. Cameron suggested. Jacob's and Lily's files are first. Using her resource books and credible websites, Annette summarizes the key "expected abilities" for a child who is in Grade 1 (see Table 2.1) and attaches a copy to both students' files.

Annette continues attaching key developmental information to the remaining students' files, and in less than an hour, she finishes with her oldest student, Anna (see Table 2.2). Just as Dr. Cameron indicated, she has found it useful to do this exercise in ascending age order. In a very short time, Annette has a clearer picture of the expected abilities of her students and how they differ across the full range of school grades. It is quite clear that in the case of *The Little Red Schoolhouse*, developmental differences must be closely considered in terms of all classroom activities.

Annette smiles as she thinks of Dr. Cameron. His enthusiasm for all things related to teaching is very contagious. She hopes that someday she will be as effective a teacher and mentor as he is. Annette looks out the window and gets lost in her thoughts for a few moments. The noise of a motorcycle passing by brings her back to the present. "Okay, time to get back to my reading . . . gotta follow Dr. Cameron's advice . . . I need to review this stuff before I can expect to use it in my teaching."

TABLE 2.1 Development—First Grader

Physical Development	Social and Emotional Development
Developing fine motor skills Learning to distinguish left from right Has a good sense of balance	May exhibit some problematic behaviours (e.g., tantrums, teasing, tattling) Interested in rules and rituals Likes to spend time with friends, especially same-sex friends Learning to work with peers as a unit

Intellectual Development

Loves to ask questions
Learns best through discovery and concrete evidence
Developing an understanding of the past when tied closely to the present
Developing classification skills
Uses comparisons ("bigger than a car")
Starting to understand time and days of the week

By the end of first grade:

Listening
  Remembers information
  Responds to instructions
  Follows two- to three-step directions in a sequence

Speaking
  Speech is easily understood
  Provides more complex answers to "yes/no" questions
  Tells and retells stories and events in a logical order
  Expresses ideas with a variety of complete sentences
  Uses most parts of speech (grammar) correctly
  Asks and responds to "wh" questions (who, what, where, when, why)
  Stays on topic and takes turns in conversation

Reading
  Identifies sounds in short words
  Blends separate sounds to form words
  Matches spoken words with print
  Knows how a book works (e.g., reads from left to right and top to bottom)
  Identifies letters, words, and sentences
  Sounds out words when reading
  Has a sight vocabulary of 100 common words
  Reads grade-level material fluently
  Understands what is read

Writing
  Expresses ideas through written productions
  Prints clearly
  Spells frequently used words correctly
  Begins each sentence with capital letters and uses ending punctuation
  Writes a variety of stories, journal entries, or letters/notes

TABLE 2.2 Development—Late Adolescence	
Intellectual Development	**Social and Emotional Development**
Able to think abstractly Able to solve complex problems Able to appreciate subtleties Can project into the future Able to make independent decisions Can sense what others are thinking Increased thoughts regarding global concepts May develop idealistic views	Able to delay gratification Able to compromise Greater concern for others Spends more time with friends than family Emotional issues may influence decision-making May still act without thinking May push the limits May be focused on career and life plans

Physical/Biological Development

Physical development, or maturational change, is not typically influenced by anything that educators do or have control over. Humans follow a genetically predetermined path of physical/biological development, and except for nutritional or medical impairments, this development proceeds unabated. However, it is important for teachers to understand how certain physical changes interact with co-occurring cognitive and social changes, especially during the early school years and during puberty and early adolescence.

As early elementary children get older, their brains grow, and so does their capacity to learn. This growth allows teachers to present more complex material and place more demands on students' learning abilities. As suggested previously, this is why concerted efforts to teach students to read only occur from Grade 1 onwards—it makes sense developmentally. Similarly, knowing that puberty is a time of several significant and important developmental changes affects educators' practices in the later grades. In adolescence, biological maturation activates hormones, which change how individuals think and, as a result, how individuals behave. This change in behaviour is not necessarily a direct result of hormonal changes. Rather, it occurs because adolescents' behaviours are mediated through psychological processes, such as thinking and judging, and by contextual influences, such as home and school environments. As these biological changes are occurring, adolescents also face significant changes in the structure of their schooling—the middle-school rotary system involving multiple teachers is substantially different from the single-teacher/single-classroom experience of elementary school. Many school districts, therefore, have responded to these dual challenges by either dropping the beginning of middle school to Grade 6 (from Grade 7) or establishing K–8 structures. Both approaches prevent students from having to make two significant and potentially troublesome adjustments at the same time—adapting to changes in their school structure and adapting to uncontrollable changes in their biological structure (Wigfield & Eccles, 2002; Wigfield, Eccles, & Pintrich, 1996).

A further example of how research into physical/biological development influences teaching and learning has emerged from recent studies on how and when the brain reaches its full development. Prior to adolescence, it is accepted and expected that children will exhibit certain levels and amounts of impulsivity and therefore will need to be guided in their thinking processes. When children reach adolescence and move toward adulthood, society expects them to reduce or eliminate their impulsive behaviours gradually in favour of more controlled actions. However, it is now known that it takes about 20 years for the prefrontal cortex to become fully functional (Spear, 2000; Weinberger, 2001). This is the part of the brain that is responsible for higher-order executive functioning skills such as (a) decision-making and goal-setting, (b) controlling attention/impulsivity, (c) cognitive flexibility, (d) information processing, and (e) managing risk-taking (Anderson, 2002; Weinberger, 2001). The developmental trajectories for Anderson's four executive functions are found in Figure 2.1.

The implication of this research finding is that teachers and parents cannot merely assume or expect adolescents to automatically and easily engage in setting rules, boundaries, and limitations for their behaviour. Even if adolescents do accomplish these tasks, it is likely that they will experience difficulty carrying through on the rules and parameters they have set. This is a classic case of a developmental conundrum. While adolescent students will "know" what they are being asked to do and be able to do it if they work at it, their brains are not fully prepared to do it instinctively or naturally. Not being aware of this subtle but important difference, adults will often make the mistake of assuming that because adolescents "know it" then they should be able to "do it." Instead of faulting adolescents for seemingly irresponsible behaviour, teachers and parents should help adolescent children establish and live within their own learning and behavioural conventions. This is best accomplished by consistently engaging them, from middle school onwards, in the dynamic process of first determining and then adhering to mutually agreeable rules and limitations. This process will enhance and expand their decision-making processes and help to control their impulsive or non-boundaried and/or non-governed behaviours.

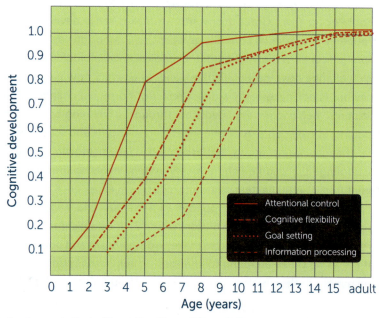

FIGURE 2.1 Anderson's Four Executive Functions

Source: Anderson, P. (2002). Assessment and development of executive function (EF) during childhood. *Child Neuropsychology, 8*(2), 71–82. Reprinted by permission of the publisher (Taylor & Francis Ltd, http://www.tandfonline.com).

Annette pauses and puts a large asterisk next to the note about "mutually agreeable rules and limitations." She knows this will be an important concept to remember and consider when she deals with classroom management. There will be a number of adolescents in her new classroom, and she wants to make sure she does not unrealistically expect them to act like adults just because they are older and bigger than their younger classmates. From what she has read so far, it appears that she will have to pay as much or more attention to their behavioural needs as she does to the behavioural needs of the younger students. She turns her focus back to the material on development.

Cognitive/Learning Development

Perhaps the most important facets of development for educators to understand are how and why learning occurs or does not occur and how learning processes evolve and change over time. If teachers do not understand these fundamental elements of learning, they will not recognize why students can or cannot understand or manipulate certain types of information. As a consequence, their teaching will likely be ineffective, and their students will be denied opportunities to learn in the most advantageous and efficient manner.

Developmental research has taught us, for example, that the cognitive skills and concepts learned in the early school years are critical for all other later achievement expectations. In fact, we know that the best predictor of continued academic success into adolescence and adulthood is the early mastery of essential numeracy and literacy skills (Duncan et al. 2007). Consequently, the attainment of these skills has now become the focus of programming that occurs outside of schools. For example, in Ontario there are numerous community family math programs that are designed to help parents learn how to facilitate their young children's mathematical development.

Early Learning—Significant Factors

Paris, Morrison, and Miller (2012) conducted an extensive review of the research on early schooling. They noted that efforts to understand and improve the academic skills of children continue to be the central focus of educational psychology. Their research revealed the following important influences on children's pathways into school (p. 63):

1. Meaningful individual differences in language, literacy, and foundational skills for learning emerge before children begin formal schooling.
2. The early variability in language, literacy, and foundational skills for learning is the result of many factors (e.g., the child, family, preschool, and larger socio-cultural context).
3. The early schooling experiences of children are highly variable, in some cases exacerbating the differences established prior to school entry.
4. The cumulative impact of these factors means that children begin formal education with vastly different preparation for academic learning and their pathways for early academic success have already begun to diverge.

Despite the variability in children's preschool preparation for learning, early formal schooling has consistently demonstrated that the explicit teaching and motivation of young children has resulted in academic progress for the vast majority of students. "The best predictor of a successful pathway is early mastery of essential skills involved in literacy and numeracy, because so much of elementary education depends on the fluent application of these skills" (p. 79).

Executive Cognitive Functioning

Recent developmental research has also demonstrated that the major change in adolescents' thinking is not so much the development of abstract thinking, as was previously theorized, but the capacity to engage in **executive cognitive functioning** whereby individuals organize, co-ordinate, and reflect on their thinking to achieve more efficient processing outcomes (Steinberg, 2005). For example, younger students quickly learn that they can acquire a simple math fact by saying it over and over, either out loud or silently, using a rote learning process called rehearsal. If they do not already have it, students usually acquire this learning tool from elementary teachers who frequently use choral or group rehearsal as a strategy to facilitate learning and understanding. As students get older and become more cognitively capable, they realize, usually through trial and error, that simple rehearsal is ineffective when learning a complex math process, such as the order of operations. Despite the child's best efforts, the volume and complexity of information required to "know" the order of operations is simply too much for their simple rehearsal strategy to handle. Their non-success with rehearsal forces them to use an executive learning strategy, such as an acronym, which attaches more meaning to what is being learned. Acronyms are words formed from the first letters of words in a process or string of related information. They make complex and/or detailed information easier to remember. For example, BEDMAS is a short and catchy term used to remember the precise and consistent order of executing math operations when solving detailed and/or multi-step problems:

- B—Brackets
- E—Exponents
- D—Division
- M—Multiplication
- A—Addition
- S—Subtraction

Students are usually assisted in switching or progressing from simple strategies (e.g., rehearsal) to more complex learning processes (e.g., acronym) by teachers who use or demonstrate the required executive strategies when teaching. Parents can also influence their children in the same way. Students then simply follow their teacher's or parent's example. Later on, as students' abilities develop further along the learning process continuum, they are eventually able to identify their own preferred executive strategies. For example, some students prefer to read something over two or three times to better or fully understand it, while others prefer to take notes on the first read-through and then rely on studying their notes for full comprehension. Because, as in this example, the executive function element of cognition enhances vital learning and problem-solving skills, understanding how cognition operates and changes is important to educational psychology and to teachers. The question is, how, exactly, does learning take place?

> **think box**
>
> Which executive strategies do you use when learning something new? For example, how are you processing the material presented in this book, and how would you prepare for a quiz on this material? Consider how your use of particular executive strategies may affect the way you teach.

Innate Curiosity

A critical but often overlooked feature of the learning process is that human beings are born with an innately powerful curiosity about the world around them. This instinctive psychological function is characterized by a deep and constant desire to understand the environment so as to adapt one's behaviours in order to exist and survive within it. It explains how and why newborns, after a very short time in the world, "learn" to cry when they are hungry. They have learned about themselves (I am hungry), made sense of their surroundings (food is available), and adapted their behaviour to suit their needs (if I cry, I can get food). Naturally, because the world consists of individuals as well as objects, children instinctively use the very same curiosity mechanism to learn about people. Thus, in addition to learning and adapting innately, young children also learn by observing others (they mimic people) and through the direct guidance/instruction provided by others (teaching). By understanding more about people as well as objects, newborns who have "learned" to cry when they were hungry soon learn to adapt their crying to different situations: they cry to be picked up and comforted, and later they use crying (and/or other behaviours) to avoid having to do something, just as older children and adults do. It cannot be overstated that understanding and adapting to the social realm is an important innate function, because it enables children, adolescents, and adults to "fit in" with the many other individuals who affect their world.

Curiosity, our deep psychological desire "to know," sets all humans on a pervasive and life-long exploration to seek understanding. In theory, curiosity is a mental or cognitive switch that is always "on," and this constant search for understanding provokes and promotes learning. Knowing that students possess this instinctive catalyst for all learning processes, modern teachers present curricular material in interesting ways so as to arouse students' attention and pique their curiosity. Once the brain perceives something that it does not fully understand, it instinctively tries to figure it out. In fact, this process is so automatic that a person would have to consciously turn off their curiosity (ignore it) if they did not want to learn about something. This function partly explains why individuals seem to learn about some things even though they were not paying direct attention to them.

Learning How to Learn

As well as learning about things and people, children also have innate psychological mechanisms that allow them to learn how to learn. The brain uses different learning mechanisms depending on what is encountered in the environment. In fact, the ability to adapt one's learning is the cognitive quality considered by many to be the *sine qua non* of intelligent individuals. In young children, the process of learning and adapting is largely an unconscious and natural mental procedure, but there is no doubt that it becomes a more consciously manipulated mechanism as children get older.

It may be helpful to think of a child's psychological curiosity as a car motor that is always running, even when the car is parked; all the child needs is for a teacher or parent to slip their mind into gear by asking them a question or presenting them with something that is interesting or odd. Like the engaged car, the child's learning then moves ahead.

The Psychological Structures of Learning

The learning process, then, revolves around our innate curiosity; humans are always observing, testing, or manipulating the objects and people in their environment to see what happens. Jean Piaget, a Swiss philosopher, natural scientist, and developmental theorist, provided the best explanation of the psychological structures that are active during this process (Piaget, 1970). According to Piaget, humans have two basic learning instincts that originate from our natural curiosity.

Innate Drive to Organize

The first is an innate desire to organize our behaviours and thoughts into coherent systems. As children gather information through observation and manipulation, the brain naturally and instinctively looks for patterns in the information and organizes it into groups or clusters of knowledge according to similar traits, actions, or thoughts. The brain is constantly combining, arranging, recombining, and rearranging what it knows. This process results in what Piaget termed mental "schemes" and "**schemas**." A scheme is a particular way in which children repeatedly act or think about particular items or happenings. For example, a child develops a "shake-and-rattle" scheme because this action tells her something important about her world or it is amusing and entertaining for her to hear and feel the rattle. She will instinctively, therefore, shake and rattle everything that comes into reach because she is trying to use her learned and understood action to find out more about new objects or to be more amused. On the other hand, a schema is a simple mental representation of an item or happening. For example, a bird schema might be animals that have wings (trait), or animals that fly (action), or animals that look nice (thought/idea). As children get older, their schemas become more complex and encompass more features. Thus, the bird schema might expand to include all animals that have wings, fly, make whistling noises, etc. (It should be noted that although scheme and schema are slightly different terms, the term "scheme" is often used to imply thoughts and actions as well as representations.)

Innate Drive to Adjust

Our second basic learning instinct is what Piaget called **adaptation**: this is an innate drive to adjust to one's surrounding environment. When the brain encounters new information, its patterning and organizing abilities instinctively and immediately classify the new information into something that is either similar or dissimilar to an existing scheme. Piaget said that when the new information (traits, actions, or thoughts) is comfortably and easily explained or understood by existing schemes, the brain is in a state of balance, or equilibrium—think of a playground teeter-totter that is perfectly balanced in the horizontal position. However, when the new traits, actions, or thoughts cannot be easily explained or understood by existing schemes, the clash of unexplainable new information with comfortable old information creates a mental discomfort referred to as disequilibrium—one end of the teeter-totter moves up while the other moves down, and it is out of balance. If the new information is only slightly different from existing schemes—if the ends of the teeter-totter only move up or down a little—the brain experiences a little discomfort, but it quickly and often immediately assimilates the new information into an existing scheme, and it readily returns to a state of equilibrium—the teeter-totter returns to horizontal balance. However, if the new information cannot be easily assimilated into existing schemes, the brain experiences considerably more discomfort—think of one end of the teeter-totter almost touching the ground while the other is high in the air. The brain now has to accommodate what is new by either modifying an existing scheme or creating an entirely new scheme. This usually takes more time and mental effort, but eventually equilibrium is accomplished, and the brain (or teeter-totter) returns to balance. In this process, assimilation and accommodation are said to work hand in hand as the brain is continually confronted with new incoming information (see Figure 2.2).

It is the brain's preference for mental balance over mental discomfort that causes it to automatically react to new information by trying to understand it. The brain always seeks to understand what it encounters. The process of moving from disequilibrium back to equilibrium, or bringing the teeter-totter back to balance, is referred to as learning.

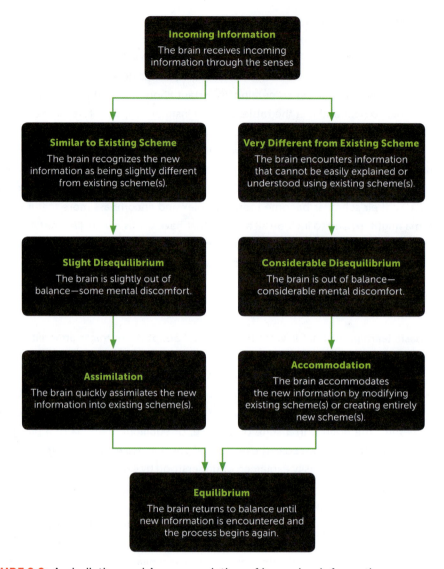

FIGURE 2.2 Assimilation and Accommodation of Incoming Information

Annette pauses as she imagines hearing Dr. Cameron's voice asking his familiar question: "So, what is the motivation here . . . why do we want to learn?" One of the key features of Dr. Cameron's course that Annette particularly appreciated was the way he always linked motivation to the different topics of educational psychology. He posted his views in the classroom and often brought them to the attention of his students:

All that happens in classrooms is motivated in some way.

Student's perspective—the essence of school is <u>learning</u>.
Students are trying to understand and adapt to all elements of their environment.

Teacher's perspective—the essence of student learning is <u>motivation</u>.
Students have the internal drive to understand so they can adapt.

Educational psychology perspective—understanding motivation is key to understanding why things happen in classrooms.
Knowing why is infinitely better than simply knowing what or how.

Rather than devote a single class to motivation issues, Dr. Cameron made them an ongoing theme of the course, including them in discussions on learning, classroom management, instruction, and assessment. Annette appreciated this approach, because it made the principles of motivation much more meaningful and therefore easier for her to understand and eventually apply. Throughout the course, Annette labelled her notes on motivational issues "Motivational Underpinnings" because of the way they permeate and support all parts of teaching.

Annette turns her attention back to Piaget and his explanation of how children learn. She contemplates what motivates learning (mental balance–mental discomfort) as she reads on.

From Disequilibrium to Equilibrium

An 18-month-old girl learns that the family's four-legged animal who has brown fur, a tail, and two ears is a cat (scheme) called Socks. One day, the child's parents take her to visit one of their neighbours, and she encounters another four-legged animal with brown fur, a tail, and two ears and automatically says, "Oooh, Socks!" Her parents correct her by pointing out that although the animal is a cat and virtually identical to Socks, its name is Fluffy. Because the animal is similar to Socks in every regard except for its name, Fluffy is easily assimilated into the child's cat scheme. The same child later goes to her cousin's house and encounters another animal with four legs, brown fur, a tail, and two ears. Because her previous learning mechanism worked, the child again says, "Oooh, Socks." Her parents respond, "No, honey, that's not Socks. That's a dog and his name is Fido." The parents also point out that Fido makes sounds much different from those made by Fluffy and Socks. Because the dog's features are quite different from the identifying features of her cat scheme, the child's brain attempts to, but cannot, assimilate the differences. The child's brain then automatically shifts gears and accommodates this new information by modifying her cat scheme to include dogs or by creating an entirely new scheme. This automatic learning process occurs in all children. Later on, as children age and their thinking becomes more sophisticated, their schemes become more organized and structured. This enables them to incorporate more and different types of information. They are then able to combine schemes into broader conceptions and classifications based on more widely related traits, actions, or thoughts. Consequently, the child's cat scheme may eventually evolve into all things feline (from miniature Persians to lions), the dog scheme may evolve into all things canine (from dachshunds to Irish wolf hounds), or both schemes may evolve into an even broader scheme that encompasses all animals, and so on.

Piaget felt that the brain's constant desire for equilibrium is the mark of intelligence. He reasoned that moving from disequilibrium to equilibrium leads to more and better organized thinking and this organized thinking produces more intelligent behaviours. He also suggested that this process enables children to learn about how they learn. In fact, the different ways that individuals think and mentally manipulate information to reason and problem-solve forms the basis of Piaget's four-stage theory of cognitive development (see Table 2.3). The stages in this

TABLE 2.3 Piaget's Four Stages of Cognitive Development

Level	Cognitive	Description of Thinking
Sensorimotor	0–2	Object permanence by 18–24 months Can reverse actions such as emptying/filling container Beginnings of symbolic representation of items
Preoperational	2–6/7	Rapid language acquisition Symbolic/semiotic thought (e.g., pretend play) consolidated but only with one-way logic Animism: thinking that inanimate objects can do or say things Egocentrism: the inability to differentiate between someone else's perspective and their own Centration: focusing exclusively on one trait at the expense of others Lack of conservation/reversibility: illogically thinking that if objects change shape, they also change in amount Emerging logical problem-solving ability limited to intuition One-dimensional classification skills Inability to seriate; ordering objects by quantifiable dimension
Concrete Operations	6/7–11/12	Can logically solve problems related to real (concrete) objects Two- or multi-dimensional classification skills Can simultaneously consider multiple aspects of an object or event Awareness of other people's perspectives on the world Conservation/reversibility: amount of object does not change with appearance/can mentally undo an activity Can arrange objects in serial order by dimension
Formal Operations	11/12–adulthood	Can think in logical, idealistic, and abstract ways Can develop hypotheses about problems and devise systematic ways to solve them, inductively and deductively Egocentrically believe everyone else finds them as unique and as interesting as they do Hypothetical reasoning: can logically formulate and solve untrue problems Developing concerns for identity and social issues

model focus on four qualitatively different types of thinking that are universally applied by all individuals across a variety of contexts.

While the finiteness of Piaget's stages has been questioned, the model is still considered the most comprehensive and influential in the discipline. Piaget was most concerned about the actual types of different thinking that individuals were able to demonstrate. In fact, each of the four stages is characterized by particular kinds of thought that individuals use and/or construct to enable their reasoning. According to Piaget, individuals create their cognitive functioning abilities to achieve mental equilibrium. In other words, the brain's constant drive for cognitive balance forces it to design thinking and problem-solving strategies to achieve the required equilibrium.

It is obvious from this explanation of the learning process that the minds of children are constantly and actively building and developing understandings, and in doing so, they construct their own knowledge. They observe the world around them, and they constantly test it and manipulate it to find out more. Their brains automatically interpret the findings and adjust their own cognitive structures. This is a departure from previous contentions that children merely learn what they are

think box

Imagine that you teach physical education to both elementary and secondary students. According to Piaget's stages of cognitive development, how might your instructional methods change when teaching sportsmanship skills to a group of 7-year-olds versus a group of 14-year-olds? What kinds of discussions might you have with each group in order to facilitate their understanding of sports etiquette?

taught in a receptive and passive manner. The critical implication for teachers here is that the brain is a naturally efficient and effective learning machine all on its own. Its built-in curiosity mechanism automatically asks questions, and its preference for equilibrium automatically forces it to learn from the answers to these questions. Teachers, therefore, can enhance this natural learning ability in children by stimulating their minds with various forms of new information.

Annette takes a break from reading to further consider Piaget's stages of development. She thinks about her new students. She is fairly certain they will all fall into one of two stages—either concrete operations or formal operations—because of their ages. Some will be just entering these stages, and new cognitive abilities will be just emerging, while others will have already acquired many of the abilities encompassed by their current stage of development. Annette makes a note to be very aware of students whose ages would indicate that they are about to enter a new stage of cognitive development (Jacob—age 6, Lily—age 6, Troy—age 7, and Caleb—age 12). She wants to be sure that she does not assume that they have developed abilities that they are not yet capable of.

Since it is time for lunch, Annette puts the reading material aside and heads to the staff room. She has already arranged to meet the two educational assistants who will be working in her classroom. Since they have both worked at the school for a number of years, she wants to hear their views on how her new students have been progressing academically and behaviourally. Annette knows that her new colleagues will have some useful information to share, and she wants to be sure that they feel valued and respected. In previous schools in which she worked, the role of educational assistants was not always clear. Sometimes they were given too much responsibility (e.g., developing lessons for students), and other times they were not given enough (e.g., spending much of their time gathering materials for

the teacher rather than working with students). Annette will be clear with the educational assistants in this school that she is responsible for instruction in her classroom but, under her guidance, they will play a major role in assisting particular students with learning.

Two hours later, after a long but productive lunch meeting, Annette heads back to her classroom. She wants to finish perusing the material on development before the end of the day. She settles into her chair and continues to read with a determined focus.

Domain-Specific Learning

Like many other theories in educational psychology, Piaget's ground-breaking explanations of cognitive development and the learning process have been tested and criticized, and as a result, new theories and explanations have emerged. This was due, in large part, to the 1970s movement away from behaviourism toward cognitive science. Neo-Piagetian researchers retained and expanded Piaget's conceptions of thinking and knowledge construction by infusing them with newly found concepts from information processing theory, such as how strategic thinking, memory, and attention affect children's learning structures. One of the most prominent neo-Piagetian developmentalists was a Canadian, Robbie Case. Case's theory of central conceptual structures (1992; 1998) is an expanded and more interactive version of Piaget's scheme concept. According to Case, "central conceptual structures" are groups of interrelated and incorporated concepts and cognitive processes that establish conceptual frameworks for thinking and learning in content-specific domains. Some of these specific domains are motor development, spatial concepts, social skills, reasoning about physical objects, and numerical concepts. Case reasoned that as children's thinking becomes more complex and sophisticated, their cognitive automaticity when using certain structures allows them to merge and combine two or more structures into more efficient ways of thinking and processing (identical in process to Piaget's assimilation and accommodation functions). As children increase their quantity and quality of conceptual structures, they develop mental efficiency, which frees up mental processing capacity. For example, as a child's conceptual structures for both printing and language become more automatic and integrated, he does not have to use as much mental energy as he did before to either "print" or "think" and, instead, can simply write (a combination of physical and language skills). Similarly, later on as his writing structure incorporates other writing-related concepts and becomes a more holistic structure, his writing efficiency progresses to the point where he can write different types of paragraphs and, ultimately, essays that are quite complex. The same is true for the cognitive structures that children use for reading as they transition from decoding words to understanding whole sentences to being able to read for overall comprehension.

Nonetheless, children's abilities and expertise in different domains do not all emerge or develop evenly or at the same time. This temporary difference in children's ability levels across various cognitive domains was what Piaget called "horizontal decalage." Not only are some thinking processes and abilities more advanced than others, but all abilities seem to progress with some amount of slippage, and the child's thinking has to momentarily pause or even back up a little before the ability or process becomes fully consolidated. This is why reviewing and/or redoing some of the mental processes associated with school tasks is important. It affords children the opportunity to settle their thinking before they move on to more demanding tasks.

Challenge the Brain: Enhance Learning

Lev Vygotsky, a prominent Russian psychologist, proposed a slightly different view of how learning takes place. Although he agreed with Piaget's basic view that children construct their own knowledge, Vygotsky felt that Piaget's theory only described cognitive processes that children had mastered; therefore, children were mostly learning from earlier cognitive successes. Piaget's theory primarily presents learners as independent entities who are making sense of their environment with the abilities they have. Because of Piaget's keen interest in an individual's ability to adapt, he intentionally did not teach or provide instruction to any of his research subjects. In comparison, Vygotsky was far more concerned about emerging learning abilities and skills. He contended that children learn more, and with greater efficiency, when they receive some assistance from more competent individuals to complete tasks that are just beyond their independent abilities (Vygotsky, 1962; 1978). According to Vygotsky, the range of tasks that a child cannot perform independently but can perform with the help of others is his or her "**zone of proximal development**." This zone includes all tasks requiring cognitive abilities, and it changes in complexity as the child ages. Vygotsky also claimed that the social environment of the child does more than merely influence cognitive development, as intimated by Piaget. Because people make up the bulk of one's environment, Vygotsky's theory proposes that social interactions and shared social activities actually create an individual's cognitive structures and cause individuals to think in certain ways.

Vygotsky's notion that more efficient learning is due to the influences of more competent others speaks to the obvious importance of teachers and teaching. It is not surprising, then, that Vygotsky's theory underpins much of how modern instructional practice is conducted. His concept of **scaffolding** is a dynamic teaching process that focuses on active instructional support while considering, relating to, and interacting with students' responses to instruction. The key for teachers, then, is to tailor their instructional support so that students are given opportunities to "respond" to the task on their own and then receive support relative to their understandings. For students who catch on quickly, teachers provide less assistance but do not remove assistance completely. Conversely, for students who struggle to understand, teachers provide more assistance but not so much that the student has no responsible or active role in the learning process.

If educators hold true to Vygotsky's concept that there is an optimal zone or range of task difficulty that improves learning and stretches and improves learning abilities, the best stimulation for effective and efficient learning is to present students with challenging-but-attainable tasks. In other words, the tasks must include questions, problems, or types of information that cause enough cognitive disequilibrium to engage the brain's natural learning process but not enough to cause so much disequilibrium that the brain finds the task too difficult and decides to ignore it.

The psychological basis for making learning tasks challenging-but-attainable is derived from the Yerkes–Dodson law, which describes the relationship between motivation and performance. Motivational theory requires that a certain amount of basic cognitive

think box

Imagine that Piaget and Vygotsky are both Grade 2 teachers in an elementary school. What do you think a math lesson might be like in each teacher's classroom? What similarities and differences would you predict?

Now imagine that Piaget and Vygotsky are both science teachers in a high school. What do you think a biology lesson might be like in each teacher's classroom? What similarities and differences would you predict?

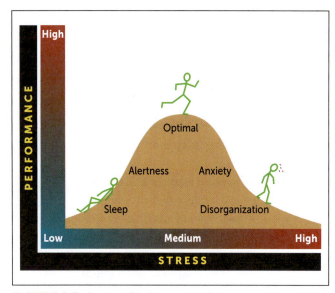

FIGURE 2.3 Stress–Performance Connection

arousal must exist (motivation) in order for any amount of learning to occur (performance). An individual's basic learning motivations come from their inherent cognitive curiosity about the environment—a motivation to resolve anything perceived as cognitively confusing. In school, learning motivations can be broadened or increased by the presentation of academic tasks that increase cognitive challenge. By resolving these challenges, students' learning performance is enhanced. However, the relationship between challenge intensity and resulting performance is not linear; it is an inverted U-shaped function (see Figure 2.3).

The Yerkes–Dodson law dictates that while learning performance increases with task challenge (psychological stress), tasks that are either too easy or too challenging actually decrease learning. This is because an individual's internal mental motivations are instinctively switched off by tasks they perceive as too easy (very boring) or unattainable (highly stressful). Therefore, for maximum learning performance, students need to be presented with moderately motivating tasks, tasks that are challenging-but-attainable.

Knowing that with help and guidance students can take on more challenging tasks than they could if learning on their own, teachers can slowly but consistently move students through an entire year of advancing curricular topics. Achieving this challenging-but-attainable balance, however, is a delicate function for educators, and it is often one of the more difficult aspects of teaching. Novice teachers find this function especially difficult because they enter the profession armed with an abundance of teachable information but they have limited understandings of what constitutes a suitable entry point and an appropriate pace of delivery. Typically, newer teachers prepare too much material for many of their daily lessons and find themselves re-teaching the same material later because their lesson demanded more than their students could manage.

think box

How can Annette ensure that all of her students are presented with learning tasks that are challenging-but-attainable? Consider how she might determine the starting point for each student (current level of competency in a particular subject) and the rate at which the student can manage new information. Once Annette has collected some of this basic information about her students, how might she construct her lesson plans to best support this challenging-but-attainable approach?

Language Development

It is not really possible to talk about learning and learning processes without examining the role of language. Children's language develops at the same time as their other cognitive skills. In much the same way as cognition develops, young children learn language by being curious about, and striving to make sense of, the verbal world that typically bombards them. The language centres of the brain automatically look for patterns in the words and sentences that children hear. Rules are established to knit together a coherent way of processing and using language. As time goes on, the brain organizes and tests its rules for language processing and proper usage and, based on feedback from more proficient language users, reorganizes and restructures its rules as needed. Amazingly, the brain does all this without formal instruction.

Piaget and Vygotsky had considerably different views on the role of language, especially relative to the influences of inner language, or self-talk. From Piaget's perspective, children's cognitive thinking structures develop first, and then language emerges as a function of developed cognitive structures/thoughts. He stated that as children's language capacity develops and they have more interactions and disagreements with peers, they learn to listen more and exchange ideas, and thus, they develop more socialized and global applications of speech. Piaget categorized children's self-talk as a function of their egocentrism because they talk to themselves without regard for others. From Vygotsky's perspective, children's inner language drives their reasoning abilities and builds cognitive structures because they use inner language to carry out important executive mental functions such as planning, forming concepts, problem-solving, and directing their attention to or away from objects of interest. Vygotsky felt that this was a better explanation of how children move toward self-regulation in their thinking.

Language-Acquisition Device

So how does a child actually learn language? Early conceptions of language and language development purported that children learn language simply by mimicking adults. Noam Chomsky (1957; 1965), who was a linguist and not a psychologist, provided evidence that humans have a biological basis for language that hard-wires us to learn language at a certain time and in a certain way. His theory posited that humans have a **language-acquisition device** (LAD), an innate capacity (or, perhaps, need) to learn, understand, and acquire language. Chomsky rejected the notion of children simply mimicking or repeating the sounds and words of others to acquire language, because he felt that this theory did not fully explain how children can instinctively and easily produce never-before-heard sentences/phrases and ask their very own insightful questions. In fact, children from all nations and cultures of the world acquire the same language milestones at about the same time and in approximately the same order, regardless of the language environment they are born into. Amazingly, very young children master words, the meaning of words, the proper sequence of words, how asking questions differs from stating facts, and when it is appropriate to say something in a two-way conversation. According to Chomsky, the LAD fosters this complex learning of language and all its various parameters without instruction because it provides humans with a built-in ability to (a) analyze and synthesize spoken language and (b) work out what the rules of engagement are in language/communication. Just as innate curiosity leads us to seek an understanding of the world around us, Chomsky proposed that the LAD leads us to actively attempt to make sense of what we hear by analyzing sounds and spoken words for patterns and then we use these patterns to interact verbally with others.

There are three especially important components of language development that teachers need to understand:

> **think box**
>
> Think back to your early school years. How did you learn about the structure of language? For example, did your teachers use direct instruction (e.g., specific drills and worksheets) to teach you correct grammar, or were you taught using a whole language approach (e.g., more focus on the meaning of language and less emphasis on skill instruction)? How might your early language learning experiences affect the way you assist students with their language development?

1. **Function** refers to the use of language to think, problem-solve, and communicate ideas to others.
2. **Structure** refers to all the rules that govern language use, such as syntax (grammar), semantics (meaning), and pragmatics (the appropriateness of language in context).
3. **Infinite generativity** refers to the ability to creatively and functionally generate an infinite series of meaningful phrases, sentences, and questions based on a finite set of words and language rules.

Students of different ages will obviously exhibit varying levels of competency within these three components of language development. Teachers can certainly facilitate further language development by recognizing students' current levels of functioning and providing appropriate language experiences and language instruction. As well, teachers who are well versed in the area of language development can help to identify students who may need special services in order to achieve the level of language development required for learning at their grade level.

Personal and Social Development

Despite the fact that educators emphasize academic progress and accomplishment, our most powerful memories of school typically revolve around our social and emotional experiences. This is why an individual's psychological well-being is considered by many educational psychologists to be one of humankind's highest priorities. Our psychological well-being comes from feelings of comfort and ease about ourselves within our social environments. Humans face a constant inner battle that pits our deep desire to stand apart from the world as a unique individual against our deep desire to be a part of the world and fit in with other people. In regard to schooling, psychological well-being is a basic human need that has to be met, or at least mostly satisfied, before teachers can expect students to concentrate on learning. There is clear evidence that nothing makes the learning process less efficient than emotional worries. In cases of persistent emotional duress, no learning takes place at all. Therefore, the proactive promotion of psychological well-being within each student and among all students has to be a very high priority for teachers, if not the highest priority. After all, what good is a great lesson with excellent learning activities if students are worrying about their next meal or threats from a bully?

Fundamental Psychological Needs

Our psychological well-being is made up of three fundamental and interrelated needs. Self-worth is a person's sense that he or she is a competent individual who is capable of overcoming challenges and living adequately within his or her environment. It is also vital that individuals sense that they can autonomously, and within reason, control their day-to-day actions and the overall direction of their lives (self-determination). But none of this is accomplished in a social vacuum, because all individuals, young and old, have a fundamental need to be socially connected and socially interactive (relatedness). In fact, how we are viewed by others, either positively or negatively, is one of the most powerful motivators for many of our actions.

Fulfilling these three fundamental psychological needs is the underlying driving force behind all our motivations to do or say certain things and/or not to do or say other things. In theory, these needs are never fully realized or satisfied. Rather, they are constantly changing and evolving. When some of these existing needs are not met, however, we typically have enough psychological resilience to be partially comfortable and at ease but not completely so. This partial psychological satisfaction is often referred to as "putting it on the back burner," and it indicates that despite our mental need or urge to immediately resolve concerns and issues as they happen, we are willing to be temporarily dissatisfied until we can get back to them. It is this constant striving-to-satisfy psychological process that keeps our emotional state active and moving along, thus preventing stagnation. By accomplishing or satisfying our current needs within reasonable levels, we eliminate enough of our concerns and worries to be mostly at ease. Because not all of our concerns and/or worries are ever totally taken care of, we constantly have a much-needed mental "to-do" list, which keeps our minds active and stimulated.

Making Choices

Achieving or satisfying these three internal needs innately performs another important psychological function. It is the motivational structure that forces us to purposefully set goals and take actions to attain them, and by doing so, we make choices. This process helps to establish who we are as individuals. Some theorists contend that our emotional need to establish the "self" gives rise to our cognitive speculations about what our possible selves could look like and it is our sense of the possibilities of "who I may be" that motivates all that we do. By doing things and seeing what kinds of personal and/or social reactions we get, we constantly test our environment and adjust our behaviours. In this manner, the function of making conscious choices connects our cognition and learning to our actions and behaviours. For example, the biggest motivational difference between younger and older students becomes apparent in adolescence. Adolescents have many more options and choices than their younger counterparts. What adolescents choose and how they make their choices is affected by their beliefs, values, and goals. Their choices ultimately affect how they act and behave. Therefore, how individuals exercise and control their competence-related beliefs (**self-efficacy**) is important for teachers to understand. By age 10, for example, students demonstrate self-efficacy for different scholastic domains and start to govern their learning energies according to their interests/non-interests and their perceptions of potential academic success/non-success. The transition from elementary to middle and then to secondary school is well managed by most students, but for a considerable proportion of students (15–50%, depending on ethnic group and socio-economic status), this period marks a downward spiral in motivation for school-based choices. This often leads to dramatic decreases in academic achievement and for some, dropping out altogether.

Emotionality

Just as our day-to-day actions to meet our psychological needs are not conducted in a social vacuum, our actions to meet our personal needs are not experienced in an emotional vacuum. "Affect" is the term that describes the broad category of emotions that people bring to bear on what they are doing, or about to do, and their emotional responses to events that occur, either to themselves or to others. There is considerable evidence that how we emotionally react or respond to any given situation is at least partially due to a behavioural predisposition that comes from our genetic code. A person's **temperament** is made up of various behavioural tendencies that account for the type, quality, and intensity of emotional actions and reactions that are displayed. While temperament tends to be universally established in childhood and is fairly stable through adolescence and adulthood, there is evidence that an individual's behavioural tendencies can be affected by other individuals and by various social environments (Berk, 1996; Thomas & Chess, 1977).

Self

The foremost explanation of personal development within the social sphere is Erikson's psychosocial theory (1963; 1968; 1980), which emphasizes a lifelong process of establishing who we are (self) and how we relate to others (see Table 2.4). Erikson's eight-stage framework explains the various and universal needs of all individuals at different stages in their life and how these needs can be satisfied by society.

Erikson felt that each of the eight stage-specific needs is represented by an emotional crisis that is fraught with both vulnerability and potential. The emergence and establishment of the self happens as individuals face each type and level of crisis and experience either positive or negative outcomes. Combined and accumulated, these experiences have a long-lasting effect on a person's self-image and his or her view of the world. When an individual has increasingly more successful resolutions of these various identity crises, he or she experiences an enhanced psychological well-being, which in turn results in more effective social interactions. This occurs because, when faced with a crisis, individuals are forced to develop coping strategies. Since

TABLE 2.4 Erikson's Eight Stages of Psychosocial Development

Stages	Ages	Identity Crisis	For Successful Resolution
1. Trust vs. Mistrust	0–1	World is safe/predictable **or** world is risky/chaotic	Bonding through nurturing caregiving
2. Autonomy vs. Shame and Doubt	1–3	Established independence **or** an inability to cope	Provide opportunities to exercise independence
3. Initiative vs. Guilt	3–6	Engage, be assertive, and take initiative **or** be anxious and irresponsible	Allow decisions and choices and respective consequences
4. Industry vs. Inferiority	6–12	Mastery and productivity **or** incapability and non-success	Realistic self-evaluation of abilities on challenging-but-attainable tasks
5. Identity vs. Role Confusion	Adolescence	Unified sense of self and life direction **or** confused sense of self and unsure future	Opportunities to realistically explore different roles and life paths
6. Intimacy vs. Isolation	Early adulthood	Close positive relationships **or** disconnected from others	Provide examples of successful, meaningful relationships
7. Generativity vs. Stagnation	Mid-adulthood	Positive contribution to future generations **or** no contribution	Help younger generations develop and lead useful lives
8. Integrity vs. Despair	Late adulthood	Meaningful, fruitful life **or** missed opportunities	Evaluate from broader, holistic perspective

these developed strategies involve social interaction and/or negotiation, socialization skills are enhanced. Erikson did not contend that each crisis had to be absolutely resolved. His model allows for individuals to be in moratorium, a period when an individual is exploring options or experimenting with different outcomes while on the road to making some sort of decision.

The self is a conscious reflection of who we are and what we represent; it is our identity. It has often been suggested that identity formation is both the biggest transition and the foremost challenge for adolescents, because it is during this period that individuals develop an overall psychological sense of who they are and how they fit into the world around them. As adolescents experience all that happens in their lives—such as school, friends, career possibilities, and community and family activities—they have to integrate these experiences into a coherent sense of self—one's identity.

As Vercillo (2012) noted, students now experience much diversity within their classrooms (e.g., different races, different sexual orientations, different religious beliefs), and this must be recognized in any discussion of self and identity formation. Students, like individuals of all ages, want to fit in. When they feel different from their peers, their sense of self and their identity can be negatively affected, resulting in self-destructive behaviours. Therefore, teachers must take steps to ensure that all students feel accepted and valued within the classroom. A psychologically secure classroom is one where different cultures and different ways of life are acknowledged and celebrated. For example, in Canada it is recognized that culturally responsive educational practices are critical when teaching students of First Nations heritage. As stated by Alberta Education (2014):

> First Nations, Métis and Inuit students experience greater success when learning is relevant to their personal values and life experiences. Having warm, caring teachers and welcoming classroom environments; integrating First Nations, Métis and Inuit cultures and content into current educational practice; having high expectations of students and recognizing and celebrating student academic progress and success also supports students. Understanding a community's unique relationship with the land also helps teachers become more effective in developing culturally responsive educational practices.

This type of approach is clearly recommended for all classrooms where diversity is an issue.

Self-Concept and Self-Esteem

While **self-concept** is our cognitive understanding of who we are, **self-esteem** is our emotional judgment of ourselves. Combined, these constructs contribute to our self-worth, or how we value ourselves. It is a common misconception that enhancing an individual's self-concept or self-esteem is about making him or her happy; nothing could be further from the truth. Rather, it is about helping individuals make reasoned and good choices that result in positive outcomes. These positive outcomes automatically lead to feelings of happiness and pride and increase one's feelings of self-worth.

It is imperative, then, that educators do as much as they can to enhance their students' self-concepts and self-esteem by requiring them to (a) engage in the process of making well-thought-out decisions, (b) take action to accomplish their goals, and (c) reflect on what they have done and on what others tell them about what they have done. It is not simply a matter of requiring children to make choices and then letting them live with the consequences. Children, being children, will often make naïve or poorly informed choices. Because of inexperience, they will fail to anticipate all the potential outcomes and consequences of their actions. Educators, therefore, must take the time to help students "talk through" the choice-making process, always being cognizant of the fact that there are some choices that students should not be allowed to make because they will obviously result in negative outcomes. If children are constantly allowed to make such poor choices and then act on them, they will never appreciate the value of reflective choice-making. As well, they will not appreciate the guidance offered by educators and other adults. Rather, they will continually allow themselves to put impulsive decisions into action. It should be noted, however, that it is important not to overprotect children so that they can never make a poor choice. They must acquire the ability to learn from their mistakes.

Children's reflections about who they are and how they feel about themselves as students (student identity) should be based on comparisons with their own expectations and others' expectations of them. Research indicates that individuals have either positive or negative student identities or a mixture of both. Those with positive student identities usually have positive experiences with regard to school and peers, positive emotions regarding school and themselves as students, and a commitment to learning. Conversely, those with negative student identities usually have negative experiences with regard to school and peers, negative emotions regarding school and themselves as students, and a dwindling or non-existent commitment to learning. The implications for teachers are obvious.

Moral Development

In the early stages of children's development, the adults in their lives, such as parents and teachers, design all the rules and work hard to have children follow these rules. As children get older, adults expect them to autonomously distinguish between right and wrong and to decide, within reason, what the rules might be and what the outcomes may be if the rules are enacted. Over time, a child's sense of morality develops; he or she learns to differentiate between right and wrong, and eventually he or she will use that differentiation to evaluate the actions of others as well as his or her own. The rules we are talking about are the basic rules of life, rules that dictate how to get along in society.

In order to understand and live by the collective rules of our society, we have to appreciate that there are other people in our world and that they, too, have thoughts, beliefs, feelings, wants, and perceptions about all that is in the world. This understanding is called **theory of mind**. Without this understanding, we are not able to appreciate the emotions or feelings of others or the fact that others may see things differently from the way we see things. In this case, we would not adjust our actions to accommodate anyone but ourselves. For example, lacking a theory of mind is one of the principal identifying features of individuals with autism; they are unable to understand and properly react to the emotions and behaviours of others. This, unfortunately, makes them appear aloof, uncaring, and insensitive, even toward those who care deeply for them. Being able to understand and take the perspective of others is crucial to moral development because, over time, our sense of morality grows as we learn to resolve social conflicts and to cooperate with others in establishing and living by the rules of our society.

Heteronomous and Autonomous Morality

Piaget, in addition to his explanation of cognitive development and how learning takes place, proposed one of the first theoretical models of moral development. Not surprisingly, he made direct connections between his stages of cognitive development and moral reasoning ability. Piaget's (1964) theory postulated that children's cognitive abilities and structures develop first, and it is these mental structures that enable children to reason about moral and social events. As with his predictable stages of cognitive development, Piaget claimed that up to about 10 to 12 years of age, moral development is made up of a very egocentric and naïve form of moral reasoning. Once children are beyond this age range and capable of formal operations, their morality changes into a more refined and adult-like sense of social justice based on a universal cooperative effort. Piaget called the first type/level of moral development "heteronomous morality," morality that is subject to the rules of others and is evaluated based on its eventual outcomes, not on the intentions of the individual. For example, if a Grade 3 boy leans over to pick up the pencil his seatmate dropped but accidently steps on her sandwich, the young girl will probably "not like" her good Samaritan friend because her sandwich was ruined. At the older type/level of morality, which Piaget called "autonomous morality," children will more likely base their evaluations of someone's actions on their intent, not necessarily on the outcome of their actions. As much as Piaget argued that children need the prerequisite matching cognitive structures to progress from heteronomous to autonomous morality, he also believed strongly that morality was enhanced by children resolving social conflicts with equal-status peers and coming to consensus about the rules that govern their shared environments.

Kohlberg's Six-Stage Theory

Piaget's early work on moral reasoning was later elaborated on and refined by Kohlberg (1969). While Piaget's theory evolved from talking to children about the rules involved in their games of marbles and how these rules were or were not applied, Kohlberg is famous for having devised his theory of moral reasoning by analyzing people's responses to a variety of moral dilemmas. Like Piaget, he evaluated his subjects' reasoning, not necessarily their final decisions or actions.

Based on what children and adults perceived as more correct or higher moral actions under certain circumstances, Kohlberg determined that there are six stages of moral reasoning across three distinct levels (see Table 2.5). Similar to other development-stage theories, Kohlberg's perspective was that each stage of moral reasoning is more sophisticated and complex than the previous stage and that most individuals progress through the stages in much the same order. It is implied that lower-stage reasoning is subsumed under higher-stage reasoning.

From an educational perspective, teachers can help children develop their moral reasoning by introducing and discussing issues dealing with morality and justice. While it does appear that there are some cultural influences on moral reasoning, Kohlberg's stages seem to occur in the same order and at relatively the same ages around the world. Similarly, while males tend to focus their moral reasoning on a

> **think box**
>
> Students are often faced with the moral dilemma of whether or not to cheat on tests or exams. While many students would never cheat under any circumstances, some students will cheat if they know they can get away with it. Other students cheat with no fear of punishment. What do you think are the critical elements that Annette should include in her discussion with her students about cheating? How can she discuss this topic without making any of them feel that she mistrusts them or suspects them of cheating? How might her discussion differ with students of varying ages?

TABLE 2.5 Kohlberg's Stages of Moral Reasoning

Level I Preconventional	Level II Conventional	Level III Postconventional
Rules are set down by others.	Individual adopts rules and will sometimes subordinate own needs to those of the group. Expectations of family, group, or nation seen as valuable in own right, regardless of immediate and obvious consequences.	People define own values in terms of ethical principles they have chosen to follow.
Stage 1: **Punishment and Obedience Orientation** Physical consequences of action determine its goodness or badness.	Stage 3: **"Good Boy–Good Girl" Orientation** Good behaviour is whatever pleases or helps others and is approved of by them. One earns approval by being nice.	Stage 5: **Social Contract Orientation** What is right is defined in terms of general individual rights and in terms of standards that have been agreed on by the whole society. In contrast to Stage 4, laws are not frozen—they can be changed for the good of society.
Stage 2: **Instrumental Relativist Orientation** What is right is whatever satisfies one's own needs and occasionally the needs of others. Elements of fairness and reciprocity are present, but they are mostly interpreted in a "you scratch my back, I'll scratch yours" fashion.	Stage 4: **"Law and Order" Orientation** Right is doing one's duty, showing respect for authority, and maintaining the given social order for its own sake.	Stage 6: **Universal Ethical Principle Orientation** What is right is defined by decision of conscience according to self-chosen ethical principles. These principles are abstract and ethical (e.g., Golden Rule), not specific moral prescriptions (e.g., Ten Commandments).

Source: Kohlberg, L. (1969). Stage and sequence: The cognitive-developmental approach to socialization. In D. A. Goslin (Ed.), *Handbook of socialization theory and research* (pp. 347–380). Chicago, IL: Rand McNally.

strong sense of justice and females tend to focus their concerns on caring and responsibility for others, there is no research that indicates that these trends result in differences in moral maturity. The most common criticism of Kohlberg's stages and theory, or perhaps it is a comment about our society as a whole, is that the theory depicts what people's reasoning is when facing moral dilemmas, not necessarily what their actions are. It is not hard to imagine that it is relatively easy to say the morally right thing in such situations; it is much harder to actually carry out the action.

Societal Influences

We are inherently born into a society of people, and we spend the rest of our lives learning about people, and learning from people, so that we can effectively interact with people. It is the combined influences of emotion, motivation, and cognition that determine social skills. Within the school setting, these skills, according to Masten and Coatsworth (1998), are geared toward accomplishing three primary goals:

1. adjusting to the social demands of school;
2. getting along with others;
3. conducting ourselves according to the routines and conventions of school.

As Erikson articulated, the development and attainment of effective social skills determines the quality of our interactions with others, and because of our inherent need for relatedness, social interactions affect our feelings of self-worth. Therefore, while students bring a particular set of emotional tendencies and ways of reacting to school, they can expand their emotional repertoires by adapting the way they interact with others and by adjusting to the demands of school. It is not as if who they are when they arrive on the first day of school remains the same throughout their school years.

Ecological Theory

Bronfenbrenner's **ecological theory** (1979; Bronfenbrenner & Morris, 1998) is the most prominent description of the influences that environmental contexts have on the social development of individuals. It focuses on the existing and changing relationships between individuals and their environments and consists of five environmental systems, ranging from the immediate and most powerful influences of family to the broader and often less impactful influences of culture and history (see Table 2.6). These five systems represent complex layers of interactive influences that are driven by an individual's need to evolve within his or her society and to be somewhat guided by the societal pressures he or she encounters. A ripple effect occurs whenever one of the layers changes. Therefore, both the immediate and the broader environment should be examined when teachers are attempting to fully understand what may be influencing a child's social skills or his or her actions within the social sphere called school.

One of the most important aspects of the ecological model is the relationship and influence of individuals within a child's immediate sphere of influence. For students, these are parents and teachers. While Bronfenbrenner acknowledged that teachers do not provide the complexity of interaction that comes from a child's parents, teachers are certainly in a position to provide an environment that welcomes, influences, and nurtures children's social abilities. According to ecological theory, if relationships and positive influences within immediate spheres (e.g., family and school) break down, children will not have the skills to appropriately explore and grow in other less immediate environments, such as society at large. For example, students who do not get the influential affirmations typically found in child–parent or student–teacher relationships will look for them in other, often inappropriate, social milieus (e.g., on-line chat rooms or gangs). Obviously, these inappropriate milieus do not facilitate the development of the social skills needed to interact in broader social organizations.

Another important aspect of ecological theory is that each system is characterized by its own expected behaviours and relationships. When individuals are with family members at home, they act differently from the way they do with their peers and teachers when they are at

TABLE 2.6 Bronfenbrenner's Ecological Theory

Environmental System	Influences
Microsystem	Includes influences from an individual's family, peers, school, and neighbourhood and the way an individual exerts influence over these individuals and settings
Mesosystem	Links the influences between different microsystems—either complementarily or in opposition
Exosystem	Includes influences from distant social settings within which the individual does not have an active role
Macrosystem	Involves cultural influences including respective values and beliefs
Chronosystem	Involves influences from environmental patterns and transitions that arise from socio-historical circumstances

school. Bronfenbrenner felt that development progresses more smoothly when the relations and interactions within different microsystems are compatible; children will perform better when role expectations do not differ substantially between settings (e.g., home and school).

In summary, how we feel emotionally depends largely on whether or not our needs are being met and whether or not our goals are being accomplished. The more we make and carry out purposeful plans and reflect on the outcomes of our decisions and actions, the better we feel and the more likely we are to be motivated to do more of the same. When we are successful at something, especially if we had a hand in determining what the task or objective was, we significantly enhance our self-worth. This connects our emotions and feelings to how we think (cognition), how we make choices (motivation), and how we act.

After Annette finishes reading, she contemplates the importance of fostering feelings of self-worth and competency in her students. Clearly, it is vital to establish a classroom environment that supports and enhances the psychological well-being of all students. This is the type of environment she wants to teach in, and she knows it is the type of environment that students want to learn in.

From her lunch meeting with Mr. Hayes and Mrs. McCarthy, Annette realizes that she has more work to do, especially in regard to the psychological well-being of a few students in particular. Before packing up for the day, she adds some further comments to the notes she made at lunchtime and updates the following students' files:

Name: Simon Cummings

Staff Input: keeps to himself; does not put much effort into school work; family with lower SES; at risk to drop out of school

- I need to determine his interests, including possible career interests.
- I need to incorporate his interests into required school tasks.
- I must give him responsibilities that make him feel valued.

Name: Amanda Pritchard

Staff Input: good self-worth and self-determination; does not always relate well with others; bossy behaviour; intense temperament

- I need to help her understand how her behaviour is perceived by others.

Name: Jackson Roberts

Staff Input: unstable home environment; little guidance and support from parents; loves to get attention from teacher and other adults

- I need to provide him with much guidance and support.
- I must ensure that school is a safe environment for him.
- I need to increase communication between home and school.

Name: Caleb Johnston

Staff Input: does not persist with academic tasks; tries to be class clown; has developed negative school identity over past year

- I need to determine what difficulties he has with academic tasks.
- I must design tasks that guarantee he will have some academic successes.
- I must ensure that learning is relevant to his personal values and life experiences.

Name: Zach MacMillan

Staff Input: does not think before acts; fidgety and talkative; peers find him annoying; tries too hard to be accepted by others

- I need to help him understand what ADHD is and how it affects him and those around him.
- I need to provide him with a learning environment that has few distractions.
- I need to help him develop better social skills.

Annette knows that helping these students with their psychological well-being will take some time. However, she also knows that she has no choice but to focus on this aspect of their development. It is clear from the literature that school success is as much about personal and social development as it is about cognitive development. "Hmmm, things always seem to be much more complicated than they first appear," Annette realizes. "I was pretty naïve years ago when I entered my teacher education program. If only it was as easy as teaching a concept, testing the students, and moving on to the next curriculum unit!"

Annette's Journal

August 20, 2013

I'm well on my way to being prepared to teach in *The Little Red Schoolhouse*, and it sure is a good feeling. While the work I'm doing is time-consuming and some days I'd rather be out hiking on the trails around George Lake, I feel a real calmness about the upcoming school year. In past years, especially when I was teaching the same grade as the previous year, I'd try to get my prep done a couple of days before school started. The essential things would get done, but I'd be running around like a madwoman and starting the first day of school exhausted . . . and wondering what I'd forgotten. There was certainly no time for pondering ideas and considering different ways of doing things. With only some minor tweaking, I really just repeated the same way of teaching year after year. This new teaching assignment has forced me into becoming a better prepared and more thoughtful teacher. I have learned that good prep is the key to starting the year with a feeling of optimism and confidence. Surely the students will be able to sense my positive attitude. It's better than having them arrive on the first day to see a teacher who is tired and anxious . . . that's not the first impression I'm aiming for!

I have completed my reading on developmental differences. I really appreciate the info that Dr. Cameron gave us during the summer course, because it's presented in terms of how it relates to teaching. I have taken several university courses that addressed the same developmental concepts . . . I think I have read about Piaget, Vygotsky, and Erikson more times than I can count! But oh how different it is when the information is presented with applicability in mind. Suddenly, I find myself lingering over every concept as I think about what it means for my classroom.

I also took Dr. Cameron's advice on how to incorporate what I learned about developmental differences into my everyday school life. I made notes about the likely developmental levels of each of my students, and I'll confirm and refine my notes as the year

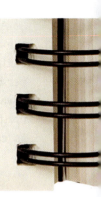

unfolds. As well, I wrote down the questions that Dr. Cameron suggested I consider when a student is having difficulty. These questions are perfect because they will encourage me to stop and think about developmental issues before making any definite decisions regarding how to help a student. I'll also be sure to consider motivational issues and a student's psychological well-being, since they are obviously key to successful learning experiences.

Annette's Exploration of the Research

Piaget, J. (1970). Piaget's theory. In P. H. Mussen (Ed.), *Carmichael's manual of psychology*. New York, NY: Wiley.

Vygotsky, L. S. (1978). *Mind in society*. Cambridge, MA: Harvard University Press.

Annette has certainly increased her understandings of developmental issues, but she feels she needs to consolidate them into some sort of working model that will benefit her teaching. Of all the theories she has read, the conceptions of cognition and learning presented some years ago by Piaget and Vygotsky seem to resonate with her the most. She realizes, however, that at least on a theoretical level, Piaget's and Vygotsky's ideas will not necessarily direct her teaching in the same manner. For example, Piaget viewed language as a by-product of thinking, whereas Vygotsky viewed language as the most important mechanism for thinking. On the other hand, both theorists advocated for social experiences and learning environments that facilitate student-constructed knowledge; she definitely wants to use that approach. She resolves that both theories are too important to discard and opts for a compromise; she utilizes what she feels are the very best facets of each position to assist and expand her teaching methods.

Annette decides to use Piaget's notion of learning via cognitive disequilibrium as the basis for using questioning and problem-presenting as an instructional strategy. These methods promote curiosity and can be widely applied in in-depth school projects that cover a broad spectrum of abilities and skills. She feels that students will benefit from discovering information and deriving answers for themselves, especially if their interest is aroused and maintained by a variety of topic choices and project completion options (e.g., essays, models, and artifacts).

At the same time, Annette decides that she definitely wants to use Vygotsky's concepts of prompted learning facilitated by more capable others to both challenge and support her students. These approaches use instructional conversations to propel students slightly beyond their cognitive scope while providing teacher support as necessary. These ideas also sit very well with Annette's preference for collaborative and cooperative learning tasks.

In the end, Annette feels that this methodological blend holds true to the main tenets of both theories. The combination suits her personality and teaching style and will allow her to offer the best learning opportunities for her students.

Annette's Resource List

Academic Journals

Child Development
Cognitive Development
Cognitive Psychology
Developmental Psychology
Learning and Individual Differences

Books

Bergin, C., and Bergin, D. (2011). *Child and adolescent development in your classroom.* Belmont, CA: Wadsworth.

Elkind, D. (1976). *Child development and education: A Piagetian perspective.* New York, NY: Oxford University Press.

Mareschal, D. (2007). *Neuroconstructivism.* New York, NY: Oxford University Press.

Websites

Child Development—The Physical, Intellectual, Social, and Emotional Development of Elementary-Age Children
http://childparenting.about.com/od/childdevelopment

Child Development: 13- to 16-Year-Olds
www.greatschools.org/parenting/health-nutrition/middle-adolescence.gs?content=870

Education and Child Development—Parent's Guide to Children's Developmental Characteristics in Each School Grade
www.education.com/grade/first

Temperament in the Classroom—Helping Each Child Find a Good Fit
www.greatschools.org/special-education/support/942-temperament-in-the-classroom-helping-each-child-find-a-good-fit.gs

From the Authors' Notebook

This chapter emphasized why and how all teachers must consider a variety of developmental issues if they want their teaching to best match where their students are in terms of cognitive, physical, social, and moral growth. Not only is this consideration beneficial for teaching and learning, but it will also help children continue and expand their growth in these important psychological domains.

Reflecting on Practice

Consider the information you have read in this chapter as well as the knowledge you have acquired through instruction, classroom discussions, and classroom activities. Then take the time to write down your thoughts about these learning experiences. Consider how your perspective on educational psychology may have changed. In addition, respond to the following questions:

- How confident do you feel about applying developmental concepts to your teaching?
- What more do you need to know about the relationship between developmental concepts and instruction, and where might you find this information?

Chapter Summary

In this chapter, the following concepts were highlighted:

- Development is driven by both our genes and our surroundings, and it follows an orderly progression. Because schools match children's ages with particular grades, curricula and instruction must be developmentally appropriate.
- Learning is a naturally occurring human phenomenon that is driven by our natural curiosity about our surroundings. By satisfying our curiosities, we develop a variety of cognitive skills as well as a vast store of knowledge.

The six most influential developmental theorists and their major contributions to educational psychology are:

- Piaget, who explained how cognitive development and learning take place;
- Vygotsky, who emphasized why it is important to allow students to construct their own knowledge;
- Chomsky, who described how and why language develops;
- Erikson, who focused on how an individual's sense of self develops;
- Kohlberg, who clarified how our sense of right and wrong (morality) develops;
- Bronfenbrenner, who outlined how different spheres of influence affect an individual's social development.

New Terms

adaptation
ecological theory
executive cognitive function
language-acquisition device
scaffolding
schema

self-concept
self-efficacy
self-esteem
temperament
theory of mind
zone of proximal development

These terms are defined in the Glossary at the end of the text.

Review Questions

- How do genetics and the environment influence human development?
- What do educators need to know about developmental progression?
- How do developmental principles influence teaching?
- How does curiosity affect learning?
- How have developmental theorists contributed to the discipline of educational psychology?
- Why is developmental appropriateness an important concept in education?
- How will knowledge about developmental concepts help teachers set appropriate expectations for their students?
- What is the teacher's role in supporting and enhancing students' psychological well-being?

FIRST WEEK OF SCHOOL
Establishing a Positive Learning Environment

3

From the Authors' Notebook

This chapter introduces the reader to the underlying psychological principles of behaviour and the motivating forces that cause students to act as they do. It also describes how teachers can implement <u>Dynamic Classroom Management</u>, an effective model of behaviour and classroom management.

Primary Learning Objectives

After reading this chapter, you should understand that effective classroom management

1. requires a well-planned and comprehensive approach (preferably school-wide);
2. engages students in discourses about appropriate classroom and school rules;
3. includes student-negotiated rewards and consequences (for adhering or not adhering to established rules); and
4. is ever-changing as teachers and students deem necessary.

You should also understand that

5. the absence of good student behaviour is a performance deficit rather than a skill deficit;
6. the way teachers achieve classroom order is critical to long-term effectiveness;
7. teachers cannot be the only individuals responsible for classroom order;
8. classroom order must be explicitly defined, reasonably flexible, and firmly implemented;
9. the psychological and behavioural needs of students can be met and transformed into a positive student mindset when exemplary environments are created; and
10. students with behavioural disorders such as ADHD can be properly managed if they are provided with specific behavioural strategies.

Based on all of the above, teachers can design and implement a comprehensive approach to behaviour and classroom management that results in more positive student behaviours, enhanced student psychological security, and better teaching and learning.

Deciding on an Approach to Classroom Management

It is Saturday morning, and Annette wakes early with thoughts of what still needs to be accomplished before her new students walk through the door of her classroom. Because the first day of school is less than a week away, she turns her focus to a remark Dr. Cameron made in an earlier e-mail. He reminded her that **classroom management** must be an essential element of her teaching repertoire if her multi-grade classroom is to function effectively. So how should she set up and manage her classroom so that her students feel completely comfortable as they go about their daily activities? While Annette is aware that some stress and anxiety is necessary for optimal learning (Yerkes–Dodson law), she does not want her students to experience the psychological insecurity that occurs when a classroom is poorly managed. Annette pours herself a cup of coffee, opens the window to let in some fresh morning air, and peers through the screen as the sun appears just above the treetops.

She recalls her approach from previous years. She always took time to make the classroom look inviting, she emphasized the importance of respect among classroom members, and she made sure she implemented appropriate consequences for misbehaviour (e.g., time outs, trips to the principal's office, and phone calls to parents). For the most part, her approach worked. However, there were a couple of years when student misbehaviour got out of hand and she had difficulty finding consequences that were effective. In those instances, she felt frustrated because she was forced into being reactive rather

than proactive. It just seemed that once things got out of control, she struggled to regain the positive environment she had created before the misbehaviour occurred. She remembers feeling more like a classroom "police officer" than a teacher, constantly dealing with infractions and minor uprisings. Even with the older students she taught, it sometimes seemed as though she was the only one in the room concerned with maintaining order. In these situations, the stress of having to settle persistently occurring behavioural conflicts left her feeling exhausted at the end of the day. At times, she seriously questioned whether she really enjoyed teaching. She also recollects that her frustrations were exacerbated by the realization that the valuable energy she was expending on behavioural issues could be better spent on activities related to teaching and learning. Now as she looks back on these experiences, it is clear to Annette that a well-run classroom is not simply a matter of knowing about the importance of having a well-managed and psychologically secure classroom; it is a matter of establishing and retaining this type of environment.

Annette thinks back to the readings presented in Dr. Cameron's course. There is ample evidence from **process-outcome research** on classroom management that students learn better and more efficiently in environments that are orderly and psychologically secure. However, as Dr. Cameron emphasized, this does not mean that classrooms are always devoid of minor and/or distracting behaviour problems, but it does mean that at no time should a classroom feel out of control or chaotic or be home to recurring and persistent problematic behaviours.

According to Dr. Cameron, one approach to classroom management that presents a logical method of implementation for teachers is Dynamic Classroom Management (DCM), a school-wide approach designed by Alan Edmunds at the University of Western Ontario (Edmunds & Edmunds, 2014a; Edmunds & Edmunds, 2014b; Johnson & Edmunds, 2006). Annette pours a second cup of coffee and reaches for her binder of course material. It is time to re-read the material on this approach. She remembers being impressed by it, so she is eager to see how it might be implemented in *The Little Red Schoolhouse*.

> **think box**
>
> From our own school years, we can all recall classroom environments that we enjoyed more than others. Think back to a classroom environment that you found particularly positive. What do you remember about that classroom (e.g., general atmosphere, teaching style, class rules, types of discipline, frequency of disruptive behaviour)? Is there a classroom that you found much more stressful? If so, what do you remember about that classroom?

The Resilient Student

Schools have changed. No longer can educators focus on academic skills while ignoring the emotional well-being of students. This change in perspective should not, however, be considered a mere moral obligation for teachers, something that they may choose to implement or ignore. There is compelling evidence that a student's sense of belonging and security supports the educational bases for motivation, learning, and self-discipline. Additionally, there is equally strong evidence that nothing undermines academic learning as much as poorly managed classrooms and problematic behaviours that result from students feeling disconnected.

In their comprehensive analyses of behaviour and classroom management, Goldstein and Brooks (2007a) stressed the importance of *resiliency* in students, stating that

> . . . schools must now provide social, emotional intervention hand-in-hand with academic education . . . instilling what we have called a resilient mindset in students. The basic feature of resilient children is that their self-esteem and sense of competence are intact . . . [they] possess feelings of hope and optimism, of ownership and personal control . . . nurtured by charismatic educators capable of providing experiences to reinforce their strengths and their feelings of self-worth. When students are actively involved in the learning process, when they feel connected and make contributions, discipline, as E.B. White once wrote, "will take care of itself" (p. 4).

Dynamic Classroom Management (DCM)

DCM (Edmunds & Edmunds, 2014a) is an approach to classroom management that incorporates the most current research principles available in the discipline. All of these principles can be found in the *Handbook of Classroom Management: Research, Practice, and Contemporary Issues* (Evertson & Weinstein, 2006a), which is viewed as the gold standard for issues related to classroom management. According to Evertson and Weinstein (2006b), the impetus for the handbook came from the following consistently reported observations by numerous researchers and educators:

> Classroom management is a topic of enduring concern for teachers, administrators, and the public. Beginning teachers consistently perceive discipline as their most serious challenge; management problems continue to be a major cause of teacher burnout and job dissatisfaction; and the public repeatedly ranks discipline as the first or second most serious problem facing the schools (p. 3).

Along the same lines, Charles (2002) made a very bold but accurate statement when identifying the most serious educational problem facing teachers:

> That problem is student misbehaviour. If you are now teaching, you have had ample experience with it. If you are preparing to teach, be forewarned: It is the major obstacle to your success and has the potential to destroy your career (p. 1).

Annette stops reading to consider this strong statement once again. She remembers how this very issue generated a great deal of discussion in her summer course. The comments of her fellow students made it quite clear that misbehaviour is a very significant problem in some classrooms. Dr. Cameron was quick to ask his familiar question, "So, what is the motivation here . . . why do students misbehave?" Annette flips the page she was reading and finds the notes she made in response to Dr. Cameron's question.

Motivational Underpinnings—Behaviour

Behaviours do not happen randomly or for no reason. All behaviours are an effort to get something or an effort to avoid something, and all behaviours are maintained, changed, or shaped by consequences. Behaviour is both an intrapersonal (within-person) and an interpersonal (between-person) phenomenon.

In schools, good student behaviour is rarely an issue; bad student behaviour is always an issue. The most widely accepted explanation about why individual students behave badly comes from Dreikurs and Cassel (1992). Their theory holds that while humans

have an innate and prevailing need to be well received and appreciated, some feel they can obtain this desired acceptance by engaging in negative behaviours to

- gain attention (negative attention is better than being ignored or considered non-important—nobody pays attention to me when I am good);
- gain power/control (I only feel good about myself when I have control—I won't try because I don't like taking risks);
- exact retribution for personal slights (I protect/enhance my personal well-being by attacking others); and/or
- conceal inadequacy (I cannot do it—if I demonstrate I cannot do it, I cannot be held responsible).

Behaviours also emanate from human interaction; this makes behaviour a relational phenomenon. Bandura's (1977; 1986) concept of <u>reciprocal determinism</u> explains that the constant social interactions between students and teachers reciprocally determine how each of them will interact with each other in the future.

Annette nods her head in agreement with the notes she wrote. They only confirm the importance of addressing classroom behavioural issues. If a classroom environment is set up to recognize and foster positive behaviour among students, the motivation for engaging in negative behaviour should decrease, especially if the negative behaviour is exhibited as a way to gain acceptance. Annette flips the page and continues reading.

So what exactly is classroom management? It is generally defined as the actions teachers undertake to create environments that support and enhance academic learning and appropriate social-skill development. This does not mean that classroom management is a "bag of tricks" that is suddenly whipped out by teachers whenever students act improperly, nor is it a method of "controlling" students so that they obediently respond to teacher demands. Rather, classroom management is a coherent set of principles and skills that are applied and integrated into the everyday activities of teachers and students who are interacting and working together. From this perspective, the teacher is not the only person responsible for order in the classroom.

Most educational psychology textbooks present various models of what classroom management is made up of, and the authors encourage teachers to adopt one of them based on their personal predilections and/or the characteristics of the classroom or school they are working in. The teacher is still left with the task, however, of interpreting the various and often multi-faceted components of the chosen model and incorporating them into a usable plan. DCM appears to be one of the first approaches to transform research findings into a comprehensive and systematic plan for teachers. The approach brings together many of the effective components found in several models and presents them in an applicable format that can be easily adapted by all teachers.

DCM strictly adheres to the five global principles of effective classroom management as summarized by Evertson and Weinstein (2006b):

- Develop caring, supportive relationships with and among students.
- Organize and implement instruction in ways that optimize students' access to learning.
- Use group management methods that encourage students' engagement in academic tasks.
- Promote the development of students' social skills and self-regulation.
- Use appropriate interventions to assist students with behaviour problems (p. 5).

Emerging from these five principles are the following three fundamental understandings and implications that guide and direct all teacher actions when implementing DCM:

1. Relative to student behaviour, there is no evidence whatsoever that the absence of good classroom behaviour is a skill-deficit problem; rather, it is widely viewed as a performance-deficit problem (Gresham, 2002; Lane, Falk, & Wehby, 2006; Maag, 2004). This means that all students have the skills to behave appropriately: they are just not using them or being encouraged to use them properly. Keeping this in mind, teachers must provide an atmosphere and a structure that models, encourages, and supports the optimum use of desired behaviours. DCM is therefore based on the theoretical and behavioural constructs that form the foundations of **positive behaviour support**. Positive behaviour support was first conceptualized by Sugai and Lewis and their colleagues (Lewis and Sugai, 1999; Sugai et al., 2000) in response to the US Surgeon General's call for systems of behaviour that address the contextual factors within schools that contribute to problematic behaviour. It was clearly mandated that such systems should proactively emphasize universal, primary prevention methods and at the same time include a continuum of intervention supports for students with chronic behavioural concerns.

2. While it has been well known for some time that orderly environments promote student learning and enhance student social growth, current research now emphasizes that how a teacher constructs and maintains order in the classroom is as important as whether or not order is achieved (Nucci, 2006; Fallona & Richardson, 2006). To adhere to this principle, DCM applies two primary instructional tenets of **classroom discourse research**: (1) an emphasis is placed on proactive and explanatory teacher–student discourses that collaboratively establish classroom rules and routines; and (2) it includes overtly explicit, rather than implicit, rules and routines as well as the development and use of reminder

mechanisms so that explicit rules and routines do not become invisible after extended or regular use (Morine-Dershimer, 2006).

3. The modern classroom contains far too many interactions and complexities of human behaviour for the teacher to be the lone manager; students of all ages have the capacity and the ability not only to help manage the classroom but also to regulate their own behaviour within it. That said, DCM intentionally uses the powerful motivational dynamics evident in self-regulated behaviour management (McCaslin et al., 2006). The process of creating student self-regulated behaviour has moved beyond simply providing students with choices that allow the transfer of behaviour "control" from the teacher to the student. Current conceptions of effective student-regulated behaviour advocate strongly for teachers to provide students with, and engage students in, explicit cognitive strategies for (a) making choices, (b) reflecting on the personal meaningfulness of these choices, (c) seeing their choices through to completion, and (d) reflecting on the outcomes of their actions. To maximally enhance the overall behavioural tone of a classroom, these strategies are best implemented collectively. The student discourses that take place while working through all the strategies will draw disparate behavioural perceptions and attitudes into the conversation. Through discussion and compromise, the process promotes more universally accepted student responsibility for behaviour. In this light, classrooms are better conceived as being co-regulated environments. By proactively engaging all students in the design of explicit rules and routines, teachers promote classroom-wide student self-control and commitment to the rules and impede student impulsivity. This enables students to award (or suffer) self-determined consequences for behaviours that they have a vested interest in promoting (or diminishing). The same self-regulation strategies can be used with individual students whose behavioural or social-skill levels are not commensurate with those of their peers.

By combining all these factors, DCM includes various effective classroom and behaviour management strategies that have a history of strong empirical support (see Gettinger & Kohler, 2006). Most important, perhaps, DCM is explicitly prescriptive about the types of discourses teachers need to use to convey their intentions for how exemplary management processes can regulate student behaviour and produce excellent learning. They include:

- an emphasis on the explicit clarification of what students are expected to do—this diminishes student passivity and/or compliance-only attitudes;
- a collaborative and collective emphasis by teachers and students on before-the-fact problem prevention while only using after-the-fact disciplinary measures as needed—this diminishes punishment-based management and the perception that the only owner and enforcer of the rules is the teacher; and
- an emphasis on classroom management as an integral part of instruction rather than as a separate and disconnected part of teacher practice—this increases the coherence and continuity of all that takes place in the classroom.

As Annette considers the material on DCM, she realizes that she has some questions for Dr. Cameron. She contacts him again by e-mail.

DCM
Annette Elkins <annette_elkins@schoolmail.com>
Date: Saturday, August 31, 2013 9:56 AM
To: Andrew Cameron <acameron@university.ca>

Hello Andrew,

Sorry to bother you on a Saturday, but I know you like to catch up on e-mail on the weekends. I have just a few questions about the DCM approach to classroom management. I have re-read the material you presented in class, but I still need a few specifics on how to implement the approach in my classroom. It would be most helpful if you could remind me of the key implementation elements. What do I need to do before school starts? What do I need to cover during the first day of classes? What practices are necessary to maintain a positive classroom environment throughout the school year?

School starts on Tuesday, and I really want to be sure that I start the year on the right note. I understand the importance of being very clear about my learning and behavioural expectations for the students during our first meeting. It is not something I have consciously done in the past, but I can see how it would be beneficial. I am excited about this approach to classroom management. It just seems to make so much sense. It will be interesting to see what classroom rules the students come up with. I'll let you know how it goes.

Thanks again for your time,

Annette

Annette receives a reply from Dr. Cameron within the hour. She is eager to read his response, since he always seems to provide exactly the information she needs. "I'm so lucky to have a mentor like Dr. Cameron," she muses as she begins to read the e-mail.

Re: DCM
Andrew Cameron <acameron@university.ca>
Date: Saturday, August 31, 2013 10:40 AM
To: Annette Elkins <annette_elkins@schoolmail.com>

Hi Annette,

I was just about to leave the office when I received your e-mail. I came in early today to do some planning for the first semester. I'm teaching a new grad course on research methods, so I have more prep than usual this year. It's a lot of work, but I enjoy the challenge!

It sounds like your preparation is going well. I'm glad to hear that you are giving some serious thought to classroom management issues. It will certainly pay off in the long run. Dynamic Classroom Management is a great approach—just be sure you tailor it to suit both the younger and the older students in your classroom. As you may recall, one of the reasons why I like this approach so much is that it allows the teacher and the students to create such a great rapport with one another. Implementing negative consequences for misbehaviour is simply a matter of doing what has been mutually agreed upon prior to the occurrence of the misbehaviour. It's not about a teacher being especially hard on a student or not liking that student. One of my students wrote to me about an incident that occurred during her recent practicum. With her permission, I have included her e-mail here:

During my first practicum, in the Grade 9 music class, there was a boy, Richard, who had a history of causing a lot of problems. He rarely played his instrument and was often very disruptive, so his teacher had arranged for him to go to the adjoining practice room to rehearse on his own when he was getting out of hand. In the last week of my practicum, when I was in charge of teaching the music classes, Richard began to act out again, so I sent him to the practice room. The next day he called out in the middle of the class, "You don't like me!" I responded, "I do like you, Richard . . . I just don't always like what you do." He seemed surprised by this comment. Later on in the class, I had to ask him to leave because of more disruptive behaviour. After only a couple of minutes in the practice room, he returned to class, picked up his instrument, and actually played without any disruptions for the rest of the period! I suspected that my supervising teacher had sent him back to the classroom, but when I talked to him later, he said he hadn't. As it turned out, Richard decided that he was ready to behave and returned on his own!

I like sharing this student's story because although she didn't have control over setting the class rules during her short practicum, she let her student know that his punishment was about his behaviour and not about what she thought of him as a person. Her actions brought about very positive results.

Now, back to those questions you need answered. Here's a flowchart of the primary steps of DCM and a list of the key DCM implementation points.

DCM—PRIMARY STEPS

↓

Concept presented to all students at school assembly

↓

Teacher and students develop classroom rules as well as
rewards and negative consequences

↓

"Wall of Rules" posted in classroom

↓

Administrators visit each class for presentation of rules by students
A copy of the classroom rules/rewards/consequences kept in office

↓

Rules/rewards/consequences for non-teaching spaces are determined

↓

Parents are informed about the new approach

↓

DCM is discussed at every staff meeting

KEY IMPLEMENTATION POINTS

Before school starts,
- decide on the non-negotiable rules that you will put in place for the year (you can collaborate with the principal and other colleagues on these rules, but your students will have no input);
- discuss your classroom management plan with the principal and other school personnel (e.g., educational assistants, resource-room teacher), and decide how these staff members can support your approach; and
- think about how you will go about setting a positive, engaging, and determined tone on the first day of school.

On the first day of school,
- welcome the students, and let them know that your goal is for everyone to have a successful school year;
- be explicit about how the class will be managed, and let students know that your goal is to be fair and firm;
- introduce the non-negotiable rules;
- allow students to develop additional classroom rules;
- allow students to participate in the design of meaningful rewards for adhering to the rules and meaningful consequences for breaking the rules;
- post a completed rules list on the classroom wall (you will likely have two sets of rules—one for the younger students and another for the older students);
- have the students present the class rules to the principal; and
- set a time frame to review the rules.

To maintain a positive classroom environment,
- immediately and consistently enforce the agreed-upon rules (enforcement is the teacher's responsibility);
- ensure that all stated rewards and consequences are implemented;
- plan how you will deal with a student who is displaying problematic behaviour (suggested dialogue: What is the problem we are having? Which of our rules is being broken? What did we agree the consequence would be if this rule was broken? Let's do what we decided upon. Let's check in later and see how we are doing);
- plan how you will deal with a student who is returning to class after being sent to see the principal (suggested dialogue: Welcome the student back to the class. Have a private conversation with the student about what has transpired, emphasizing his or her behaviour, not the punishment. Indicate to the student that you have confidence in his or her ability to be better behaved from now on. Tell the student you will be monitoring his or her behaviour and in one to two days you will review with him or her how things are going); and
- review the rules with the class periodically, and make adjustments where necessary.

According to Edmunds and Edmunds (2014a), educators who use this approach report that they see:

- ✓ demonstrable improvements in student behaviours
- ✓ demonstrable reductions in office referrals
- ✓ heightened student awareness of the negative impact of misbehaviour
- ✓ overall enhancements of the tone of classrooms and schools

Educators also report that because of DCM students are:

✓ more respectful
✓ less disruptive in class
✓ better at resolving conflicts
✓ better at following rules
✓ less argumentative
✓ better at helping others
✓ better at paying attention

I hope this helps. Remember to adjust the approach to what best suits your situation. If you stick to the key concepts, I'm sure you'll create a great environment for you and your students to work in. Good luck!

Andrew

Annette gets busy making notes on how she will greet the students on Tuesday, what non-negotiable rules she wants to implement, and what activities she will include in order to establish the classroom rules.

The First Day of School

The bell rings, and all 15 students file into the large classroom. Some appear nervous, especially the younger children, while others are comfortably chatting among themselves. Eventually, they each take a seat at one of the available desks. "Hello everyone," Annette says. "My name is Ms. Elkins, and I'm very happy to be here as your new teacher. I've just arrived in George Lake, and I live on Pine Street, down by the river. I've seen a few of you around town since I got here in August but I don't know anything about you except what I've read in your school files. I know most of you know each other fairly well, but I'm sure some things have changed since you finished school in June. Many of you have probably been away on a family holiday or maybe you even had a job during the summer, so you must have some interesting things to tell us." As Annette passes out a sheet of paper to each student, she says, "Let's do this activity together so I can get to know you better and everyone can catch up on the classroom news." Annette instructs the students to form pairs (she makes herself available so that there are eight pairs) and then interview each other regarding their favourite memories of the summer holidays. She then indicates that the students must depict what they have learned about their partner's summer experiences either in writing or in a drawing and present it to the whole class.

Once the activity is over, and the students have shared their completed work, Annette prepares to discuss the classroom rules. She splits the students into three groups: Group 1 consists of the three youngest students (Grades 1–2), Group 2 includes the students in Grades 3–6, and Group 3 is made up of the students in Grades 7–12. Annette makes these divisions because she wants to be sure that what she says to the students about classroom behaviour suits their level of language and comprehension skills. She also knows from experience that the three groups will have different preferences for both the rewards for adhering to the rules and the consequences for not following the rules. She has Mrs. McCarthy, one of the educational assistants, take the two younger groups into the lunchroom for some reading time. Annette will talk to these students about the class rules when she finishes with the older students. As the younger ones cheerfully exit the room, she turns her attention to Group 3.

"Now, let's talk a little bit about how we are going to do things in our classroom this year. First, I want you to know that I sincerely want all of you to be very successful in your school work. Yes, it's important that you all get good grades and pass your courses, but did you know that being successful in school is also very important because it satisfies your brain's natural desire to understand what is happening around you? Learning new things is exciting, and that's what I'd like our year together to be—exciting and stimulating. I also want you to learn about things that interest you, not just what you need to know in order to complete your assignments and pass your exams. Let's see if we can find a way to make this year a successful and enjoyable journey. I'll do everything I can to make school fun and keep you motivated, so please don't be shy about asking me for help at any time. If you ask about something that I don't know much about, we'll work together to find the right information." Annette pauses.

"So, tell me what you think about school." She wants to get a sense of what their concerns are before she starts their discussion about classroom rules.

Tara, a 13-year-old who is working at the Grade 7 level, puts up her hand. "Miss, I'm not sure about the others, especially Jackson who hates school, but I think school is fun, and I get all my work done. Are we going to do anything different this year?"

"I only hate it because it's always too noisy for me to concentrate and everybody makes fun of me because I get bad marks," says an exasperated Jackson, a Grade 8 student. He appears somewhat embarrassed that he has been singled out, but Annette can tell from the looks on the other students' faces that there is some truth to his remarks.

"Well," Annette says, as she slowly looks into each set of eyes, "that's the second thing I want to talk about. You see, in order for everyone to enjoy school and have a good chance of doing their best, we are all going to have to be very careful about how we behave toward each other. I'm sure that no one here wants to be teased or made fun of, so we will have to do something to eliminate that as much as possible. And I also know that no one in this room will do well academically if they feel threatened or scared in any way. So let's take some time to decide together what our rules and routines will be. I'm sure we all want this classroom to be a safe and pleasant place."

Tara immediately pipes up, "Miss, before . . . uh, Mr. Dawe just told us all the rules, and we had to obey them . . . when we did something wrong, he would yell at us or make us write lines . . . and some of his rules weren't even fair." Her voice softens, "Are you going to do that, too?"

"What wasn't fair?" Annette asks. She can sense from their rapt attention that several other students feel the same way as Tara.

"Well . . . ," Tara looks to her classmates for support, "some of us didn't like having to put up our hand every time we wanted to get out of our seat, and if we forgot to put up our hand, we had to stay in during recess. Mr. Dawe didn't trust us. He thought we would make too much noise if we got up and walked around. He just never gave us a chance . . . it was so not fair."

"Yeah," Katherine, a 10th-grader, chimes in, "I always got in trouble for that, and I had to spend recess with the little ones. They had a blast and I was so-o-o bored. I was supposed to do school work as my punishment, but I never got anything done because of all the racket . . ."

"See!" says Jackson, happy that someone else finally understands how noise can be bothersome.

". . . then I'd have to take it home to do as homework," Katherine continues, "on top of all my other homework . . . all for getting out of my seat without permission." Her impression of a male teacher's "very serious" voice draws giggles of approval.

Based on the discussion so far, Annette is even happier that she split the students into groups. From her understanding of moral development, this issue of the fairness and appropriateness of rules would be completely lost on the younger students. "Well, I'm not going to say that we won't have punishments for misbehaviour," she says, "but I think we can make the rules fair for everyone and only use punishments that are suitable and ones that you agree to. I also want to emphasize that I'd prefer to give you rewards for good behaviour rather than for you to be good just to avoid being punished." She notices how this gets their attention.

Very sceptical, Katherine asks slowly, "What do you mean punishments that we agree to? I don't want to be punished for anything."

"I don't mean that you will always agree to being punished, but if it's necessary, it will be a punishment that you have agreed to beforehand, one that's appropriate. As a class, we can decide together what is acceptable and unacceptable behaviour in our school and decide, also in advance, what rewards people can get for doing things right and what negative consequences people will have to accept for doing things wrong."

Not yet convinced, Katherine says, "Like, what kind of rewards? What do I have to do to get them—sit still and not say or do anything except school work for the whole day? That's just boring."

The quiet stillness of the other six students lets Annette know that she is on a roll. "No . . . nothing quite that drastic. Actually, it's quite easy. Let's just say, for example, that we agree that one of our rules is that no one is allowed to talk while someone is speaking to the class, like me or another adult who works in our school. If no one breaks the rule during all of the morning classes, every student can have 15 minutes of free time just before lunch. How would you feel about that?"

"Can we use the computers during free time?" Simon asks, "I'd rather do that than anything."

Katherine asks, "What if we break the rule about not interrupting? Then what happens?" Her tone clearly indicates a here-it-comes negative expectation. Annette wonders if Katherine's scepticism is due to unpleasant punishments she has experienced in the past.

think box

If you were implementing DCM in your classroom, what mandatory rules would you require your students to follow? In other words, what rules do you consider so important that they are not up for discussion in terms of their inclusion on the list of classroom rules?

"Well," Annette explains, "when we decide on a rule and its reward, we will also decide on what the consequence will be if someone breaks the rule."

"What's a consequence, Miss?" asks Tara.

"In this case, consequence is another word for punishment," explains Annette. "Let's say that the consequence, or punishment, for breaking the interrupting rule is that there will be no free time or computer time before lunch. But the consequence can be anything we want it to be, like a detention or a visit to the principal's office. We just have to agree on what it will be . . . then, when the rule is broken, everyone knows what will happen, and there will be no arguments."

"So if one person breaks the rule, we all get punished? That doesn't sound fair," exclaims Katherine, who is clearly becoming more agitated. "What if only one person breaks the rule and spoils it for everyone? That just sounds like the rules we had before. What's the point of being good if someone else can ruin it for the whole class?"

"Well, then maybe we shouldn't have a rule where the punishment applies to everyone. As a group, we can decide ahead of time if the punishment will apply only to the individual who breaks the rule or to the whole class." Annette can see that her new students like the idea of having "fair" rules. "If we decide it only applies to the individual and someone breaks the rule, that person loses their free-time privilege while everyone else gets free time.

"You see, rules can be fair," Annette continues while looking Katherine directly in the eye, "but what really makes rules, rewards, and punishments fair is when everyone in the class has a chance to understand them, talk about them, and then agree to them by a majority vote. Except for a few mandatory rules that Mrs. Nugent and I have decided

are best for everyone in our school and our classroom, everybody here today will help me decide what our other rules will be. We will also decide what happens when the rules are either followed or broken."

Silence descends on the classroom. Annette can sense that the students are thinking hard about what she has just said. Undoubtedly they are struggling to grasp these new concepts because they haven't experienced them before. "Rather than talk about rules that don't exist, why don't we work together to figure out what our actual rules will be? That will make things a lot clearer," she promises. "Before we begin, I'd like to tell you the five mandatory rules that we will use as our starting point. I call them *The Big Five*. As I said before, these are the rules that Mrs. Nugent and I have decided are in the best interests of everyone in the school. As you will see, they are fair and necessary, but they are not negotiable. Once everyone understands these five basic rules, we can set up whatever other rules we want as long as the new ones do not go against *The Big Five*." She turns and starts writing on the large chalkboard at the front of the room. "Okay, our first rule is . . ."

> Rule #1: All our rules will be fair and reasonable, and they will be democratically decided upon. They will be posted on the wall for everyone to see, and they will be enforced.

"I think this is a pretty straightforward rule, but is there anyone who doesn't understand what it means?" She gets no response, but she is not surprised at this because the rule doesn't really state anything that the students have not heard from her already. Eventually, a hand goes up. "Yes, Anna?"

Anna is a quiet but bright girl, the oldest in the class. "This all seems pretty obvious to me," she says quite matter-of-factly. "Why do we even have to have such a rule?"

"Thank you, Anna. That's a very good question. There are several good reasons for this rule, but the main reason is that in many classrooms the teacher seems to be the only one who knows all the rules and students have to guess what they can and cannot do. This especially happens in the higher grades, because many teachers simply assume that older students will know how to act properly. The teacher mistakenly thinks that all the students in the room have implicitly learned over time what is good and bad classroom behaviour when, in fact, every student needs to be explicitly told exactly what the rules will be. I don't want you to have to guess what my rules are. I want you to know precisely what the boundaries are for your behaviours. By talking about the rules and deciding on them in a democratic fashion, we can all be on the same page. That way, nobody can later claim that they didn't know a certain rule existed or get into trouble because they broke an 'invisible' rule."

Strategies to Nurture Three Fundamental Student Needs

Deci's research on motivational factors (Deci & Chandler, 1986; Deci & Flaste, 1995; Deci, Hodges, Pierson, & Tomassone, 1992) indicated that students are more motivated to engage in all types of school activities and to be resilient in the face of adversity if teachers construct school environments that satisfy the three following fundamental student needs:

1. to belong and feel connected and to sense that teachers believe in them and will treat them with respect—satisfying this need reduces the likelihood of disruptive, angry student behaviours;
2. to feel autonomous and possess a sense of self-determination and to feel they are expected and permitted to have ownership, responsibility, and accountability for their actions—satisfying this need increases positive behaviours; and
3. to feel competent, successful, and accomplished—satisfying this need appeases our basic motivation to enhance our self-esteem, the primary motivating force for all human activity.

Brooks and Goldstein (2007) extended these research findings by outlining the following six strategies that teachers can use to nurture these fundamental student needs:

1. Provide an orientation period at the very beginning of the school year/term to plant the seeds for a positive student mindset of behavioural responsibility and an overall attitude that will promote a successful classroom climate.
2. Develop realistic expectations and goals for behaviour and learning, and make accommodations when necessary.
3. Reinforce responsibility by providing opportunities to contribute to the welfare of others.
4. Provide opportunities to make choices and decisions and solve problems, thus reinforcing a sense of ownership.
5. Establish self-discipline by learning to discipline effectively.
6. Assist students to deal more effectively with mistakes and failures.

The purpose here is to help students develop a mindset of being behaviourally effective participants in their school environments.

"Yeah, that's what happened to me last year," Jackson states with authority. "I got the stapler out of the teacher's desk and ended up in b-i-i-i-g trouble." Lots of laughter erupts. "How was I supposed to know we weren't allowed in his desk? He never said anything."

"My point exactly!" Annette appreciates the example and makes a mental note that Jackson seems to experience a lot of misunderstandings. "Don't forget that an important part of Rule #1 is that all the rules will be posted on the wall of the classroom where everyone can see them, every day. The other reason we need Rule #1 is that it refers to the democratic process, which is so important. We all want our rules to be fair and reasonable. Our group discussions will allow everyone to get a better understanding of the intent of each rule. That way, everyone will develop ownership of them. It isn't just Mrs. Nugent and I who are responsible for them. Clearly stating that the rules will be enforced also reminds everyone of what they are supposed to do or not do, and it reminds me, as your teacher, that I am ultimately responsible for everything that goes on in this room. I don't like having to punish people, because I like all of my students and I want them to be successful, but I will hand out punishments if I have to because that's what will make our classroom function best. There's no sense setting up rules if they will not be enforced."

"Uh, Miss . . .," the ever-sceptical Katherine raises her hand. "So it will be your job to give us rewards too?"

"Katherine, you took the words right out of my mouth," Annette says cheerfully. "In fact, I would love to give out lots of rewards for good behaviour every day, because that would mean that we are all getting along and having the best opportunity to learn and enjoy school."

"Can time in the gym be a reward?" asks Brandon. "Free time would be better if we didn't have to stay in the classroom with the younger kids."

"Yes, because we have so many different ages in the same classroom, we can agree on different rewards for different age groups if you like." Annette can tell that they are coming to grips with the basic idea, so she goes back to writing on the chalkboard. "Let's have a look at our next rule in *The Big Five* . . ."

> Rule #2: We will not tolerate any disrespectful behaviour.

As she reads it out loud, she can tell that she has all the students' undivided attention. She continues, "This rule applies to anything that is disrespectful, like rude or improper gestures or saying mean things, and it also includes saying mean things in a teasing manner, because what is said is still hurtful. I'm not including this rule because I'm worried that you will be disrespectful to me. I don't think you will be. Mrs. Nugent and I like this rule because the vast majority of disrespectful acts in classrooms are directed at other students. Nothing makes a person feel more psychologically insecure than being called names or being teased, threatened, bullied, or put down. Furthermore, I cannot think of anything positive that can come from allowing or tolerating disrespectful behaviour. Can any of you?" Annette pauses again so the students can think this over and then continues, "All disrespectful behaviour ever does is make people feel bad. It also makes people feel angry with each other." Annette sees that Jackson has raised his hand.

"Does that mean they can't tease me because I suck at school?" he asks pleadingly. This is obviously troubling him.

"Yes, that's right, Jackson. No one will be allowed to tease you about your grades," says Annette. "However, I don't think that will even happen because no one has come up with a good reason why we should allow disrespectful behaviour in our classroom. I think you can safely assume that you won't be treated that way anymore. However, that's not to say that it will never, ever happen again. So, what do you think the consequence should be if someone does tease you about your grades or if anyone does anything else we consider disrespectful?" The recess bell rings before anyone can give Ms. Elkins an answer. "Perfect timing!" Annette says to herself. "Why don't you all think about it during recess, and we'll talk about it when you come back."

Once the room has cleared, Annette sits at her desk and takes a moment to think about what has transpired to this point. It is very clear to her that her students know exactly what constitutes disrespectful behaviour, and it is equally obvious that they do not like it and do not want it as part of their school life. It also appears that there haven't been many intentional instances of disrespectful behaviour in the past with this group, but what has happened—usually taunting, teasing, and name-calling—has been hurtful. Annette knows that her approach will do a good job of preventing this very problem in the future. She feels positive about what has been accomplished so far and sits back to relax a little before recess ends.

Teacher Behaviours that Diminish Student Behavioural Problems

Teachers are the linchpins that hold all models of classroom management together. According to Goldstein and Brooks (2007a), persistently disruptive and problematic student behaviours, and especially aggressive and non-compliant behaviours, are consistently diminished, if not eliminated, when teachers consciously engage in the following actions:

- provide positive feedback to students;
- offer sustained feedback to students;
- respond supportively to students in general;
- respond even more supportively to low-ability students;
- respond supportively to students with behaviour problems;
- ask questions that students are able to answer correctly;
- present learning tasks for which students have a high probability of success;
- use time efficiently;
- intervene in misbehaviour at a low rate;
- maintain a low ratio of punitive to positive interventions;
- are punitive at a low rate;
- use criticism at a low rate;
- keep the need for disciplinary interventions low through positive classroom interventions;
- waste little student time on transitions; and
- keep off-task time to a minimum (p. 18).

Once the students return from their break, there is considerable conversation. The class decides that there will be a list of escalating consequences for disrespectful behaviour and that Ms. Elkins will mete out these consequences according to what she thinks is appropriate based on the offence. As a bare minimum, the offending student will have to publicly acknowledge that they have been disrespectful and sincerely apologize to the victim. Tara thoughtfully interjects, "You know, if everybody knows the rules and the punishments for breaking them, then everybody will know when someone has crossed the line and what will happen next! I think that will definitely make us stop and think before we do something. Besides, who wants to be embarrassed by having to stand up in class and make an apology? Not me!"

The group also agrees that if the disrespectful behaviour requires a stronger punishment, the following additional consequences are to be levied:

- no computer privileges (variable duration);
- no free time (variable duration);
- after-school detention (variable duration);
- a note to parents; or
- a visit to the principal's office.

Amid all the animated conversation about negative consequences, it suddenly dawns on Katherine that they have not yet determined how students will be rewarded for being respectful of each other. She reminds Ms. Elkins of this part of the process.

"Well, what do you think you should be rewarded for?" asks Annette, only somewhat rhetorically. "Don't you think it's fair and reasonable to expect people to treat each other with respect without being rewarded for it?"

"Uh, yes," says Katherine, feeling a little embarrassed for asking to be rewarded for this behaviour. "Oh, . . . I don't know, it's just that you said that you wanted us to be good and there would be rewards . . ." Her voice trails off.

"I know what you mean," says Annette with a smile. "So what I propose is rather than rewarding people for being overtly respectful, because that can quickly become fake and meaningless, we decide on a reward for being basically polite and not being disrespectful. That way we will see more good behaviour from everyone. You have to remember, we are also talking about your judgments about what are respectful and disrespectful behaviours, not only mine or Mrs. Nugent's."

After more discussion, they agree that their reward for not being disrespectful for a whole day will be 10 minutes of free time the following day. Those who break the rule will lose the free-time privilege as well as suffer any of the previously agreed-upon tougher consequences. But aside from the reward, Annette feels that it is much more important for the students to see themselves as having the potential to exceed the behavioural expectations implied in the rule. She gets them to agree that after a two-week trial period, they will need two days of good behaviour in order to get the same free-time reward. She also gets them to agree to re-evaluate the whole idea two weeks after that. Annette does not want her students to get the sense that the rules, rewards, and consequences are rigid or fixed. She wants them to understand that, within reason, things can be changed or modified to better suit the conditions of their classroom.

think box

Consider classrooms that you have visited or been assigned to for a student-teacher practicum. What rules did the students have to follow? Were these rules made explicit in any way (e.g., posted on a classroom wall)? How well were these rules understood by the students? How could you tell? Were there rewards for good behaviour and negative consequences for bad behaviour? How consistently were these rewards and negative consequences applied?

Annette allows a few moments for the students to talk among themselves while she prepares to present the next rule in *The Big Five*. She can tell that the process of discussing and collectively deciding on the rules is actually making the students much more aware of the intent of each rule. "This understanding and level of ownership never would have happened if we did not discuss the rules in this way," she realizes. Because they will all know that everyone knows the rules and has agreed to them, she expects, as Tara so obviously stated, that they will be much more vigilant about adhering to them. "More important," she concludes, "they now have good behaviour to consciously and meaningfully work on instead of simply obeying the rules to avoid punishment. This level of student awareness and responsibility is something I never really considered before, but it makes a lot of sense."

Annette picks up where she left off. "Okay, I need your attention please. Our next mandatory rule is just as important as the previous one. In fact, you might think of this one as merely dealing with another form of disrespectful behaviour. Here it is." She points to what she has written on the chalkboard and reads it out loud.

> **Rule #3: Students are not to touch other students or their things without permission.**

Unknowingly, and almost imperceptibly, all the students' heads are nodding in approval. This tells Annette that the rule has struck a universally appreciative chord, so she forges ahead. "The reason for this rule is that the unwanted touching of people or their things only causes bad things to happen. It hurts people's feelings and can cause arguments and fights to occur. Rarely does anything positive come of it. This is because we are all very protective of ourselves and our personal things, as I'm sure you can all appreciate. Like the disrespect rule, this rule is necessary because almost all unwanted touching happens to students, not to teachers or other adults in schools. Can you think of any time when this rule might not apply?"

"What about when we are helping other students and passing out things that belong to others, like books and scribblers and papers?" asks Sophie. "That isn't the same thing, right?" She obviously likes being the teacher's helper.

"You're correct, Sophie. That's not what this rule is for. Everyone here will still be able to do all those sorts of things. The intent of the rule is to keep people from touching or hitting others, because even if it's done in a friendly or teasing manner, it can be very irritating and it often leads to bigger behaviour problems. If you think about it, touching someone or their things when they don't want you to is a very disrespectful act. This rule is also in place to keep people from going into someone else's packsack, desk, or lunch box. These types of behaviours create nothing but problems and hard feelings. So, to start with, we will all assume that no one here has given anyone else in this classroom permission to touch them or their things. That way, everyone is on the same page. Now, let's discuss some possible rewards for following this rule and some consequences that will be applied if the rule is broken."

The students' concerted efforts at working through the elements of the disrespect rule pay off, and they come to a consensus about the no-touching rule in less than half the time. They decide that since "no touching" is a logical extension of disrespectful behaviour, the rewards and punishments will be the same. But Katherine has been paying close attention and is obviously worried that the reward element is too good to be true.

"Um, Miss, so, does that mean that we can get 20 minutes of free time each day if we obey both rules? That would be a lot of free time in one week. Shouldn't we be spending that time on school work?" There are audible groans from the other students who had figured this out but did not want to spoil their good fortune.

"You have a very good point, Katherine," Annette acknowledges, "but I'm not worried, because the free-time reward is earned when many positive behaviours occur in the classroom. You know as well as I do that when disruptive behaviours happen, teachers have to interrupt their teaching to correct the student or use up even more class time to stop everything and deal with the student directly. Without explicit rules, these types of extended interruptions happen over and over again and waste a lot of valuable time. Often, these interruptions also involve heated arguments, and both the teacher and the student experience high emotions. Not only does this make everyone in the room feel uncomfortable, but everybody also lives with a constant worry about when the next eruption will occur. If that's the alternative, I'm more than happy to let you have 20 minutes of free time because you were behaving yourselves. You may conclude that teaching time is lost either way, but you also have to conclude that free time puts that time to much better use and sets a much nicer tone for our classroom." She wants to close this part of the discussion on that important point, so she goes back to the chalkboard. "Now, the next rule in *The Big Five* is a little bit longer than the others, but it's one that I think you will definitely like."

> Rule #4: Students will be allowed to talk. Other than when Ms. Elkins is teaching, speaking to someone, or giving directions, students can talk among themselves quietly.

As she turns back to the group, she spots several ear-to-ear smiles and a few looks of incredulity. She smiles right back, not only because of the positive impact of the rule itself but because she knows that this will go a long way toward maintaining harmony in the room. "I know that you want to talk to each other, and I think it's a good thing for you to do. I don't have any problem with you talking to each other as long as it doesn't interfere with what I have to do and as long as the noise in the room doesn't get too loud. Now, I don't expect you to automatically understand what an agreeable noise level is, so let's do a little activity to set a reasonable volume for talking. I'd like you all, at the same time, to say your full name and repeat it over and over until I tell you to stop. While you're talking, I'll raise or lower my hand to indicate that you should either raise or lower your voices. When my hand is level with my waist," she demonstrates this position, "that will be the acceptable volume for talking."

After the acceptable volume is established, Annette moves on. "Another time that students like to talk is after they've completed their seatwork, but sometimes talking at that time can be distracting to those who are still working." Annette quickly looks at Jackson to let him know that this is specifically for his benefit. "What I'd like us to agree on is that no one will talk until everyone has finished their work. Once everyone is finished, and if there is time, you can all talk about whatever you like until we move on to the next part of the lesson. My only condition is that you must stop talking and give me your full attention when I ask for it. If everyone is okay with that, then let's add that part to the rule."

As Annette is writing this amendment to the rule on the chalkboard, Tara asks, "Ms. Elkins, do we have to just sit here while other students are finishing their work?" Annette remembers Tara was one of the students who had gotten into trouble for getting out of her seat without permission so she has obvious reason for concern.

"No, that would be a waste of your time," Annette replies, "and I have a better solution. What I'd like each of you to do is write out a list of the five things you would like to do whenever you're finished your seatwork, such as reading a book or magazine, working on an assignment, drawing, or just sitting quietly. This can also include moving around the room or using the computer as long you're very quiet. Let's call these things *After Seatwork Options*."

"Can we listen to music on our iPods?" asks Brandon.

"Yes, but you can only have an earphone in one ear. It will be very difficult for me to get your attention when you have both earphones in and the music on," Annette explains. "Besides, you're already allowed to listen to your music before school, during recess and lunchtime, and after school while waiting for the bus, so I think this is a good compromise when in the classroom." Brandon is obviously pleased.

"In addition to your list, I'll also make a list of the five things I would like each of you to do once your work is done, such as working on a project, revising a draft, reading for the next lesson, getting extra help from me, or helping me get ready for another class activity. I'll meet with each of you individually, and we'll review both lists to make sure we aren't duplicating anything. You can put both lists in your desk or your planner, and I'll have copies of everyone's lists in my planner. Then, when you're finished your seatwork, you can choose something from *your* list on Mondays, Wednesdays, and Fridays, and something from *my* list on Tuesdays and Thursdays. We can change what's on the two lists every month or so, especially if you finish something and it needs to be removed. That way, you'll always have something to do while waiting for the others to finish. How does that sound?"

"Aw, that sounds like everyone will be bugging me to hurry up because I'm always last and they will want to talk and I'll never get to talk because I'm so slow," says Jackson, not happy at all at that prospect.

"No, Jackson, the others won't pester you to hurry up, because that would be disrespectful," says Annette quite pointedly. She can tell that this seemingly innocuous behaviour was not something that they had previously thought of as disrespectful, but their nods clearly indicate that they agree with her logic. Nonetheless, Annette knows she has to address Jackson's worries. "So, I'll tell you what, on days when there are at least five minutes left of class time after everyone else is finished their seatwork, you can stop working too and take the rest of your work home as part of your homework. That way, nobody will bother you and you will get to talk like everyone else, or you can do something from your *After Seatwork Options*. It will be your choice, but you will have to be responsible for doing the work at home or I cannot let you have that privilege. How do you feel about that?"

"That's okay, I guess, but it means I'll always have more homework than everybody else." Jackson is obviously not fully convinced that the deal is worth it.

"Yes, that's one way to think of it, but here's a better way," says Annette. "The seatwork I give you is very important, because it's a chance for you to practise what you've learned and to get help if you need it. You just have to decide whether you want to do it here or finish it at home. It's completely up to you."

"But . . . if I don't do it at home . . . I won't be allowed to take it home anymore, and then I can't have free time and talk like all the other kids." Jackson's statement is almost a question.

Guiding Principles

Successful Students

Students emulate their teacher's behaviours, and they will adjust their own behaviours to suit the positive, energizing environments that teachers create. The predominant mindset of successful students is that they believe that they are active participants in their learning environments. This belief is driven, in part, by a strong desire to be involved in the processes that govern their environments. Goldstein and Brooks's (2007b) synthesis of the characteristics of successful students highlights the following commonalities:

1. They believe that whether they learn or not is based in great part on their own motivation, perseverance, and effort. If students view themselves as passive recipients of what is being taught, their interest and enthusiasm for learning will greatly diminish.
2. They recognize that making mistakes and not immediately understanding certain concepts or material are part of the learning process. They appreciate that learning takes time and effort.
3. They perceive the teacher as a supportive adult. When confronted with difficulty with academic or non-academic issues (such as behavioural concerns), successful students feel comfortable in taking the initiative to ask their teachers for assistance.
4. They understand their learning style, learning strengths, and learning vulnerabilities. The more that students gain an understanding of their learning profile, the more they can develop strategies for learning actively and successfully.
5. They treat classmates with respect and avoid teasing or bullying, recognizing that such behaviours work against a positive school climate and adversely affect the learning of all students (p. 29)

Rather than let him dwell on all the possible ways that this could go wrong or end badly, Annette intervenes, "I understand. For now, let's put our special plan in place for the first couple of weeks and see how it goes, then we can decide if we want to continue." Jackson shrugs his shoulders and grins; he seems willing to at least give it a try.

Jackson's issues aside, the essence of the talking rule seems understood and appreciated by the rest of the students. However, Annette knows that the bane of many teachers' existence is getting students to stop talking and pay attention as needed. She decides to turn their tacit agreement into an explicit understanding. She informs the class that along with the privilege to talk comes a responsibility to stop talking and pay full attention to her when she asks them to. Annette also knows that yelling "Can I have your attention, please?" or "Please stop talking!" does not work, because in the past she used these attention-getters without attaching student responsibility for a proper response. In fact, the more she raised her voice, the less effect it seemed to have and the louder the talking became. Annette informs her new students that when she wants their attention, she will briefly turn the lights off, then back on, and when this happens, all students are to stop whatever they are doing, stop talking, and face her. She attaches student responsibility by having them decide on a consequence for not following this rule and a reward for appropriate behaviour. After some concerted discussion, the students agree that a failure to adhere to this aspect of the talking rule constitutes a breach of the overall rule and, thus, the same consequences should follow. However, and this takes a lot of explaining on Annette's part, they eventually agree that being quiet and paying attention to the teacher is a respectful, necessary, and vital component of the teaching and learning process. They also agree, ruefully, that it does not warrant a reward.

"I've been around students long enough to know that your conversations with one another do not always fit nicely into the segmented times that talking will be allowed in the classroom. I also know how hard it will be for you to suddenly have to stop talking when you're in the middle of a really important conversation. So keep this in mind . . . in the vast majority of instances when I ask for your attention, it will only be to give you a brief direction or a small, but important, piece of information. The sooner you stop talking, the sooner I'll be able to say what I need to say, and then you can go back to what you were talking about. On the other hand, the longer it takes me to get your undivided attention, the less time you will have left to talk to each other. Does everyone see the benefit of giving me your full attention right when I need it?" The students respond affirmatively by nodding in agreement.

Annette proceeds to write the final rule on the chalkboard. "Here is the last rule in *The Big Five*."

> **Rule #5: The principal will be aware of all our class rules and will support us for our good behaviour as well as deal with our bad behaviour.**

From their startled looks, Annette can tell that this concept is new. "There are several reasons why this rule is necessary. First, while I am ultimately responsible for what goes on in our classroom, Mrs. Nugent is responsible for what goes on in the entire school. It makes sense, therefore, that she knows exactly what our rules and routines are and the rewards and punishments that go along with them. She also needs to know about the democratic process we went through to develop our rules. If I have to send someone to see Mrs. Nugent, she can then deal with that person according to our rules and whatever other rules she has designed for the school." Annette knows that because all the students will be aware that the principal is cognizant of the rules and the process used to come up with them, students will not be able to plead ignorance if they break one of them. According to what she has read about classroom management, simply "knowing that the principal knows" will be an effective behavioural deterrent for many students, because it eliminates their ability to pit the teacher against the principal (or their parents) and it increases their accountability for their conduct beyond the comfortable confines of the classroom.

To complete the rule-setting process of DCM, Annette tapes two large pieces of chart paper on the wall and then divides the students into two groups. She directs each group to pull up their chairs next to one of the charts. "I want each group to come up with three to five rules that they want to implement in our classroom. Remember to only choose rules that are not contrary to *The Big Five*. Once you have listed your rules on the chart paper, I want you to come up with reasonable rewards and punishments for each one. Write them down next to the rules." The students get busy with the activity. After they complete the task, Annette says, "Okay, switch chairs now. I want you to read and discuss the rules developed by the other group. When you're finished, we'll discuss all the rules as a class, and everyone can provide feedback or change what's been written."

When the groups are finished, Annette asks two of the older students, Sophie and Simon, to take down the chart paper and record all of the possible rules, rewards, and punishments on the chalkboard at the front of the room. Annette then allows both groups to offer suggestions and feedback. This results in several animated discussions followed by a vote on each rule and its matching rewards and punishments. A majority vote is required before a rule can be added to *The Big Five*. Annette is prepared to veto a rule if it is approved by the majority but would negatively affect a student or group. She purposefully asks Sophie to be part of the recording and voting process because she seems particularly attuned to the concept of fairness. Annette's instincts prove right as Sophie and Simon consistently require the groups, especially during the voting process, to explain why a rule, reward, or punishment is both fair and reasonable. She is also impressed by how fair-minded all the students are despite their youth.

In the end, three rules (along with rewards and punishments) are added to *The Big Five*:

> **Rule #6:** No cellphones allowed in the classroom. Students who do not bring their cellphones into the classroom may use them during the lunch break. If a student brings a cellphone into the classroom, the teacher will keep the cellphone until class is dismissed for the day.
>
> **Rule #7:** Students must be on time for class. Each month, if there are fewer than eight instances of students being late, the class earns the privilege of watching a movie during class time. A student who is late must apologize to the class and stay in the classroom during the morning recess.
>
> **Rule #8:** Students must be prepared for class. Only those students who complete all of their homework during the week will have no homework assigned for the weekend. A student who is not prepared for class must write a list of what they need for the next school day and have it signed by the teacher and a parent.

Before the rule-making process started, Annette had formulated a series of other rules that she thought would be helpful based on her past teaching experiences. She keeps careful track of her students' deliberations to make sure that nothing important is overlooked. In the end, Annette is extremely pleased with their overall rules.

"Congratulations, you've been a great help in establishing our rules. We have one final step in our rules procedure, but I need a few minutes to set it up. In the meantime, I'd like all of you to prepare your list of five activities for your *After Seatwork Options*, and obviously, you can talk while you're doing it. This will be our very first test of working and talking at the same time, which I'm sure you can handle with no problem."

Annette waits until they get started and slips out of her busy but composed room to see whether Mrs. Nugent can spare a few minutes for them at the end of the day. Annette is sure that the students' attention to the activity and their "permission" to talk to each other will keep them on-task for the two minutes she needs. Her heart leaps as she returns to a chatty but busy classroom, and she is encouraged at her first success. Not only is the noise level quite acceptable, but the students are nearly finished their lists, and they appear happy. She walks around the room and watches as they all complete the assigned task, stopping to ask about some individuals' lists and helping others come up with interesting ideas. She eventually steps over to the wall nearest the door and briefly turns the lights off, then back on. Annette is not exactly sure whether the immediate silence and inactivity in the room is due to the unexpected darkness or because the students remember her attention-getting rule, but she gives them the benefit of the doubt.

> **think box**
>
> Now that you know how Annette established the classroom rules with the older students, consider how she might alter her approach with the younger students. What should she do differently?

"Well," she says with a genuine smile, "Thank you for stopping what you were doing and paying attention. And thank you for working on your lists and for talking in such a reasonable fashion while I stepped out of the room."

"She was gone?" Katherine quietly asks her brother Brandon.

Annette walks over from the doorway and leans against the front edge of her desk. "Yes, Katherine, I was gone for about two minutes, but it didn't seem to matter because all of you carried on as if I was still here. I am very impressed, and you should be too."

"Why?" asks Tara. "I mean, all we did was talk and do our lists. It was kind of normal. We didn't break any rules."

"Tara, that's exactly my point. This is the way we want our classroom to be at all times . . . the whole class adhering to all our rules. Doing your lists and talking quietly and paying attention when I flicked the lights are the obvious things, but a lot more happened, or didn't happen, during that time. There was no disrespectful behaviour, nobody touched anyone else or their things, and nobody was acting out or using their cellphones or iPods when I came back. Now, while this was just our first little experiment with the rules, I think it went exceptionally well. I don't see any reason why we can't conduct ourselves like this all the time."

Annette continues, "After lunch, I'll be doing exactly the same thing with the younger students to see what rules they want. At the end of the day, we'll all come together to talk about all of the rules. We'll also discuss how the different rules will be enforced. It's almost time for lunch now, so you can head to the lunchroom. By the way, job well done!"

At the end of the day, after Annette has established the rules with all of her students, Mrs. Nugent arrives at the classroom door. Annette invites her in. "Students, as you will remember, one of our rules states that Mrs. Nugent will be aware of all our rules and the rewards and punishments that go with them. Let's start with Group 1. Lily would like to share the rules they came up with. Then I'd like Sophie and Simon, our discussion leaders for the older students, and Jacqueline and Liam, our discussion leaders for Group 2, to tell Mrs. Nugent about the rules they established. When everyone is finished and all of Mrs. Nugent's questions have been answered, I'll make a final copy of all the rules to put up on the wall. I'll also pass along copies to Mrs. Nugent, Ms. Martino, Mr. Parker, Mr. Hayes, and Mrs. McCarthy."

Guiding Principles

Classroom Management

The key to effective classroom management is for teachers to design and implement a management system that always requires students to think about how they will behave in their environment rather than simply reacting to their environment without thinking. The more invested children are in helping design the classroom management system, the more they will think about their behaviours, especially if they are to be rewarded and acknowledged for good behaviour.

The group's discussion with Mrs. Nugent finishes about 15 minutes before the end of class. Annette has no difficulty convincing the students to use one of their *After Seatwork Options* as they wait for the dismissal bell. When the bell finally rings, Annette congratulates the students again for a very successful first day. As the students head home, Annette gets busy making copies of the rules. She is tired but happy to have achieved so much, even though it took nearly the whole school day to do so. She is hopeful that the tone for the school year has been set and the focus can now turn to learning.

Several Days Later

Annette is quite happy with the atmosphere and tone of her classroom. For the most part, her implementation of DCM is going well, even though there were a few minor missteps by some students as they adjusted to the overall routine. She is reminded of Dr. Cameron's prophetic words about children's behaviour—"We never actually change children's behaviour, we change their thinking and they change their behaviour."

While Annette was somewhat sceptical of using rewards to entice good behaviours, the students have latched on to the idea, and consequently, the classroom has been calm and conducive to learning. Within a few days, however, Annette notices that Zach seems to be getting on the nerves of several of the other students. While he is basically a pleasant boy and very friendly, he has two distinctively noticeable problems that overshadow his amiable personality and his underlying academic abilities. In the first instance, he is very distractible, and he has considerable difficulty staying on-task. Once off-task, which sometimes does not take very long at all, he annoys his peers by chatting and trying to get them to pay attention to him rather than to their work. He also does not seem to pick up on his classmates' subtle cues to mind his own business, and when someone pointedly rebukes him for bothering them, he takes it personally. This usually sets off extended periods of pouting and sulking and other time-wasting behaviours such as aimlessly moving around the room, pretending to clean out his desk, or asking to leave the room for one reason or another. While none of these behaviours on their own is particularly bothersome, Zach's repertoire of constant annoyances is an aggravating collection of behaviours that persistently puts a damper on the overall positive climate that Annette is trying to create. He also seems to know exactly where the danger point of breaking one of their class rules lies and is usually very careful not to cross that line. Therefore, while his behaviours are annoying and aggravating to almost everyone in the room, Zach usually only suffers mild verbal rebukes and no significant or meaningful consequences for his actions. Annette found it very interesting, however, that when she taught a lesson on the solar system, which included a lot of classroom discussion, Zach was very attentive and his overall behaviour was better than most other days. But despite his high level of interest in space-related issues, Zach's distractibility still caused him, and others, some difficulties.

Annette notes that Zach is also impulsive, which is evident by his apparent lack of control over his actions (e.g., blurting out answers, interrupting when others are talking, fidgeting during the singing of *O Canada*, and disruptively going to the window on the other side of the room to check out passing airplanes when Annette is teaching). Like most impulsive individuals, he certainly does not think of the potential outcomes or consequences of his behaviours beforehand, but he is almost always remorseful and understanding once the reality of the situation is pointed out to him. Zach's apologies are genuine, but because his impulsive behaviours recur, his regrets eventually wear thin, and people are no longer convinced of his intended apologies. Again, neither of his isolated impulsive behaviours warrants a dramatic or constant response on Annette's part, but it is evident that Zach's litany of distracted behaviours represents a persistent irritation to her and the rest of the class.

Annette is troubled by Zach's behaviours for a variety of reasons: (a) they keep him from completing his work, which affects his academic performance; (b) except for recess and lunch time, the other students avoid him during class activities (this is a problem during group work); and (c) he does not seem to have any strategies to get himself back on track, even when directed by Annette to do so. He may be obediently sitting quietly and not bothering anyone, but he is not doing any work either.

In her review of the students' files in August, Annette noted that Zach was diagnosed as having attention deficit hyperactivity disorder (ADHD), a behavioural disorder of inattentiveness, hyperactivity, and/or impulsiveness. Because Annette had never taught a student with ADHD, she consulted Mr. Parker, the resource-room teacher, at that time. He gave her information about ADHD and offered to work with Zach when needed. She goes to him now and explains what is happening in class. He quickly agrees to work with her and Zach on an intervention that will address his distractibility issues. Annette is pleased that Mr. Parker has opted to deal with Zach's distractibility before focusing on his impulsivity, because his impulsivity seems to get worse when he is distracted and has nothing to focus on. A few days later, Annette receives a plan from Mr. Parker. She sits down and begins to read.

ADHD—Addressing Zach's Classroom Behaviours

While everyone in society occasionally engages in all of the 18 identifying behaviours of ADHD from time to time, the official diagnosis is only rendered when an individual (a) exhibits these behaviours much more frequently, (b) displays very intense emotions associated with the behaviours, (c) exhibits the behaviours and the accompanying emotional intensity for longer than normal durations, (d) mostly engages in these behaviours in completely inappropriate situations, and (e) persistently exhibits all these symptoms before age 12. Individuals with ADHD are usually aware of their behaviours and the problems their actions create, but they typically cannot control their behaviour without specific interventions.

The difficulty teachers face is knowing how to distinguish between purposeful problematic behaviours (student is wilfully acting out) and ADHD-caused behaviours (student has little or no control over his or her actions). The following scenarios from *Special Education in Canada* (Edmunds & Edmunds, 2014b, pp. 70–71) highlight the behavioural differences.

Scenario 1:
A child gets up in the middle of the class to sharpen his pencil, and he stubs his toe on the leg of a chair. Despite an instinctive attempt to be quiet and suffer in silence, he yells out, gets angry, utters a few choice words under his breath, and maybe takes a swipe at the chair. All the while, he is trying to do so quietly. After a short time, he gets himself under control and hobbles back to his desk, trying to be quiet and hoping he has not disturbed anyone.

This example portrays a fairly common and acceptable way of dealing with an uncomfortable situation, despite the fact that many of the behaviours the student exhibited could be construed as problematic.

Scenario 2:
Now let's look at what typically happens to an individual with a behaviour disorder (or little self-control) who also stubs his toe. He yells out, but with little or no inhibition, and yells and curses loudly and frequently. He gets almost uncontrollably angry, topples the chair, and feels so angry for so long that he cannot get back to attending to his seatwork. He intentionally disturbs everyone and has little or no consideration for their need for quiet. The remaining 40 minutes of class time are a disaster, and at the end of the class he is still going to great lengths to tell everyone of his mishap.

This example points out the degrees of behaviours and reactions that differentiate students with behavioural problems from those who may engage in the same behaviours but are not considered to have a behavioural problem.

Teachers, therefore, face two problems in their classrooms:

1. How should a student be treated differently because of his ADHD issues but also be treated fairly, relative to the rest of the students in the room? ADHD should never be an excuse for bad behaviour, because the diagnosis does not diminish the effect of annoying behaviours. At the same time, a student should not be punished for behaviours he or she cannot control.

    Consider another example—two students are engaging in the identical disruptive and annoying behaviour of calling out answers when they are supposed to raise their hand or wait their turn. The teacher will obviously react very differently to the student he knows is impulsive and cannot control blurting out her answers than he will to the student who has no such control problems and is merely trying to get attention. The way the teacher perceives and deals with each student will be different, but only because he has an understanding of the causes of the observed behaviour. Without this understanding, most teachers would suspect that both students were simply trying to be annoying and would deal with them in the same manner. To treat both students fairly, the teacher has to make sure that both students are operating with the same understandings and both can act on these understandings. In this case, the teacher must help the student with ADHD to devise a strategy that helps her resist blurting out answers. For example, it is obvious that the student is highly motivated to answer questions, but it is also likely that she feels the need to get her answers out quickly so that she is not overlooked by the teacher. A possible solution is to have the teacher guarantee that the student can answer every fourth question. While waiting for her next turn, the student must count 1 . . . 2 . . . 3 . . . as the intervening questions are asked and answered. This counting requirement gives the student something to focus on, and it replaces the impulse to blurt out the answers. Once the student with ADHD has learned this control strategy, she can be expected to properly raise her hand or wait her turn just as the other students are required to do. She can also suffer the same consequences for not doing so.

2. How can a teacher help a student with his distractibility? Like most individuals with ADHD, Zach is fairly aware of the impact his annoying actions have on others around him. The problem is that he only realizes this after he does something wrong and/or gets reprimanded. Often, this mistakenly focuses the teacher's attention and scrutiny on his annoying behaviours but not on his distractibility. Also, making Zach's annoying behaviours the focal point sets up an unsolvable dilemma for his teacher, because distractible students have such a

broad range of annoying behaviours that it is difficult for anyone, especially the student, to pinpoint what he needs to stop doing. In this case, there are three things for the teacher to consider and act on. The first step in helping someone like Zach is to engage him in a conversation that makes him aware of the fact that it is only when he gets off-task that bad things seem to happen. This will let him know that there is something that happens before his "annoying behaviours" kick in that he has to watch out for. According to teacher reports in his school file, Zach's off-task behaviour occurs most often when the teacher is teaching or during seatwork. The teacher can solve both of these problems with a student-regulated monitoring system that is teacher-facilitated. This approach places the primary regulatory responsibility in the hands of the student while the teacher provides support and supervises the overall process. The second step in helping a student like Zach is to get him to monitor his own on-task behaviours—by checking whether he is on-task, he will immediately know when he is off-task. Self-monitoring will relieve the "picked on" feeling that can arise when a student's behaviours are monitored by the teacher. To accomplish self-monitoring, Zach will be provided with a watch or timer that emits a quiet beep (and/or flashes) at regular intervals (one or two minutes, depending on the severity of the problem), and every time he hears the beep, Zach will verify whether or not he is doing what he is supposed to be doing. If he is on-task, he will put a check mark in the On-Task column of the On-Task Self-Monitoring Checklist opposite the appropriate interval (see Table 3.1). This self-documentation process will give Zach clear indications of his successful on-task behaviours—something he needs to appreciate and something the teacher can acknowledge. If Zach is not on-task, he will check the Not On-Task column. This mark will be a tangible signal to immediately inform the teacher, who will help him get back on-task. Furthermore, the check mark and immediate report to the teacher will replace Zach's predominant habit of chatting with other students or otherwise trying to get them to pay attention to him. (Note: It would be very useful to make it clear to Zach that this is precisely the behaviour that the teacher wants him to avoid rather than telling him "not to bother the others," because such a generic, non-explicit statement will not have much impact.) The third step in helping a student like Zach is to consider that most students with ADHD lack the metacognitive ability to effectively review where they were in the learning process before they were distracted. Without help, they cannot restart their thinking; they will be just as cognitively lost as they were when they were distracted. To effectively get Zach back on-task, the teacher must talk him through what he was doing or thinking before he became distracted so that he can restart his thinking processes and move on in the task. If the distraction occurs during instruction, the teacher should do a quick review of the material and ask Zach to verbally describe the general gist of the information to accomplish the cognitive restart, and the lesson will move on from there. This can also be done privately while the other students are working, but short reviews of this nature are always beneficial to all students, so the teacher should not worry about wasting other students' time unless this occurs frequently. Once Zach is back on-task, he will signify his successful return to the activity with a check mark in the Back On-Task column. This concrete documentation will give Zach clear evidence that he can successfully return to whatever task he was supposed to be doing, which in turn will eliminate his prevalent sense that once he gets off-task, everything goes badly and he always ends up in trouble. It also will prevent teachers and parents from perceiving that the student is hopelessly adrift once distracted.

TABLE 3.1 On-Task Self-Monitoring Checklist			
Intervals	On-Task	Not On-Task	Back On-Task
2 minutes			
4 minutes			
6 minutes			
8 minutes			
10 minutes			
Etc.			

After a period of moderate success (good monitoring coupled with a majority of on-task and back on-task check marks), the intervals can be extended, but this entire concept and the reasons for the changes need to be explained and discussed in detail with the student. Zach's active involvement and complete understanding of the purpose of the process are vital to its success. His parents can have him use the very same beeper/timer and checklist when doing school work or projects at home. This will help him consolidate his monitoring abilities and provide even more evidence to everyone that he can stay on-task or get back on-task and do what is required. Both the teacher and the parent will probably have to closely supervise the initial process until Zach learns how to do it properly.

In summary, by providing Zach with a strategy to monitor and control his own behaviours (with some help), the teacher can hold Zach more accountable for his actions, and his behaviours will be less annoying to his classmates; both effects will immensely please the other students, some of whom feel he already gets away with too much. Finally, his own constant self-regulation for distractibility should also diminish his impulsive behaviours. Teaching Zach a self-regulated but teacher-facilitated strategy is designed to

- change his behaviours for the better;
- provide him with a self-regulation strategy;
- relieve the teacher of having to constantly police his behaviours;
- allow the teacher to hold him accountable because he now knows what to do when he is distracted;
- improve his status with the other children; and
- improve his academic performance.

Annette is optimistic about Mr. Parker's plan. She is thankful that she has a colleague with his expertise, since she is not as knowledgeable about special education as she would like to be. It is comforting to know that she will have his support as she deals with problems like Zach's. It also makes her feel more confident about her classroom management plan, knowing that she can effectively address specific behavioural problems exhibited by students with special needs.

think box

From your own school years, can you recall a student who frequently exhibited problematic behaviours? How did this student's behaviour affect the overall classroom environment? How did you and your classmates respond to this student? What do you remember about how this student was disciplined? Can you think of ways that this student's behaviour could have been addressed more effectively?

Annette's Journal

September 8, 2013

I've survived the first week of school! And the time I spent on preparation in August sure made a difference. Things just flowed so smoothly during what is usually a bit of a hectic time. I thought that having students from many grade levels in one classroom would make things so hard to manage, but so far it has been the opposite. Our classroom feels like a little community—everyone seems to play a different but important role. It really seems like everyone is enjoying being together. I know that I'll have to be diligent about keeping the older students content within this multi-age-level environment, but at least we are off to a good start.

I think the key to this positive beginning to the school year has been my new approach to classroom management. I was really taken aback at the students' positive response to helping make the classroom rules. Even the younger students were able to come up with some very relevant rules. In fact, while their rules were more simply stated, they were not that different from the ones established by the older students. The whole process of talking about possible rules and discussing why they were or were not important was an excellent exercise. I learned a lot about the individual students, and I think the students were better able to understand the perspectives of their fellow classmates. They also had fun coming up with consequences for breaking and adhering to the rules. It won't be hard for me to monitor classroom behaviour, because the students have already been quite vocal about who is breaking, or verging on breaking, any of the established rules. But I'm going to have to watch a few of them who are a little overzealous about reporting their peers' behaviours to me. I also want to make sure that students who adhere to the rules are given as much attention as those who misbehave. In addition, I think Mr. Parker and I have made some good progress in planning an approach that will address Zach's behavioural difficulties. This is new to all of us, so I'm sure things will get even better over the coming weeks.

Annette's Exploration of the Research

Wentzel, K. R. (2006). A social motivation perspective for classroom management. In C. M. Evertson & C. S. Weinstein (Eds.), *Handbook of classroom management: Research, practice, and contemporary issues* (pp. 619–644). Mahwah, NJ: Lawrence Erlbaum.

Prior to Annette's decision to implement Dynamic Classroom Management, she seriously considered why and how this approach to managing the classroom might be effective. Its reliance on positive and collective teacher–student and student–student interactions certainly seemed to make a lot of intuitive sense, but Annette had to satisfy her own curiosities and concerns before she could trust it in her own classroom. In other words, she had to fully understand the concepts behind DCM before she could believe in and implement it.

In her search for answers, Annette came across Wentzel's (2006) comprehensive summary of how and why social motivation plays such a vital role in classroom management. Although she found many other articles and books on classroom management, Wentzel asked two very important and simple questions that caught Annette's eye: "If teachers are able to implement specific practices and conditions that result in socially competent students, what is it about these practices that motivates students to participate willingly in classroom activities and even contribute in positive ways to the overall climate of the classroom? Are there ways in which students enable each other to adapt to the demands of the classroom?" (p. 635).

Wentzel's responses to these questions included information similar to the descriptions Goldstein and Brooks (2007a) provided about successful students. Wentzel stated that socially and behaviourally competent students are those who have positive beliefs about themselves, have an effective repertoire of behavioural skills, can solve social interaction problems, and have positive interpersonal relationships. Social competence is fostered when all of these personal abilities are exercised within the broader contexts and boundaries of various social environments. In turn, these experiences influence the further development and refinement of one's personal social skills and resulting behaviours. Like all other abilities, social competence is a goal-directed behaviour, and individuals will naturally strive to strike a balance between achieving their own goals and helping to achieve the goals of their different social groups. According to Wentzel, "social competence is achieved to the extent that students accomplish social goals that have personal as well as social value in a manner that supports continued psychological and emotional well-being" (2006, p. 620).

Wentzel also pointed out that the motivational influences of teachers and peers are significant when they create contexts and goals that make individual students feel as though they are an integral and valued part of the process. Teachers typically promote pro-social and responsible behaviours, and peers typically communicate expectations and values for social behaviours, although they do not necessarily promote the same behaviours as teachers. These implicit or explicit social understandings of what is expected behaviourally have a considerable effect on student self-regulatory behaviour. Given that teachers and peers are the most influential people that students encounter in school, it follows that their overall influence on the behaviour of others increases if they agree on a common set of behavioural goals and expectations. This influence is increased further if the collective goals and expectations are made explicit, discussed, and mutually agreed to. This enhances students' sense of self-determination and why it is important to behave in certain ways and not in others.

All students like to achieve successes (individual or group goals) as measured by their own standards and by the positive social reactions they receive from teachers and peers for those successes. From Wentzel's perspective, social competence "is achieved not just by one person's efforts but often as the result of compromise or conflict resolution among two or more individuals" (2006, p. 621).

Wentzel's explanation went a long way toward satisfying Annette's query about whether or not DCM is a sound approach to managing classroom behaviour. She could now see that if she made her behavioural expectations and goals very clear to the students, and if she allowed them to establish their own personal and collective goals that complemented her expectations, this would provide them with a very personal motivation to "buy into" the process. And because all of them would want to protect their own vested interests (rewards) and maintain their own psychological well-being, they would readily, and with just cause, exert positive pressure on students who misbehave.

Annette's Resource List

Academic Journals

Education and Treatment of Children
Exceptional Children
Journal of Applied Behavior Analysis
Journal of Emotional and Behavioral Disorders
School Psychology Review
Teaching Exceptional Children

Books

Dreikurs, R., Cassel, P., & Ferguson, E. (2006). *Discipline without tears: How to reduce conflict and establish cooperation in the classroom.* Mississauga, ON: Wiley.

Evertson, C. M., & Weinstein, C. S. (2006). *Handbook of classroom management: Research, practice, and contemporary issues.* Mahwah, NJ: Lawrence Erlbaum.

Websites

Classroom Management Strategies for Novice Teachers
www.ernweb.com/public/1004.cfm

Dr. Mac's Amazing Behaviour Management Advice Site
www.behavioradvisor.com

Dynamic Classroom Management
www.edu.uwo.ca/dynamic-classroom-management/dcminfo.asp

Education World—Classroom Management
www.educationworld.com/a_curr/archives/classmanagement.shtml

National Education Association—Classroom Management
www.nea.org/tools/ClassroomManagement.html

ProTeacher—Classroom Management
www.proteacher.com/030001.shtml

From the Authors' Notebook

This chapter emphasized how all teachers can construct exemplary learning environments that are well managed and devoid of constant and persistent student misbehaviours. It also demonstrated how teachers, via purposeful and meaningful student investment in managing the classroom, can encourage students to engage in more positive behaviours, more often.

Reflecting on Practice

Consider the information you have read in this chapter as well as the knowledge you have acquired through instruction, classroom discussions, and classroom activities. Then take the time to write down your thoughts about these learning experiences. Consider how your perspective on educational psychology may have changed. In addition, respond to the following questions:

- How confident do you feel about your ability to establish a psychologically secure environment for your future students?
- What more do you need to know about student behaviour and classroom management, and where might you find this information?

Chapter Summary

In this chapter, the following concepts were highlighted:

- The absence of good behaviour is a performance-deficit problem, not a skill-deficit problem.
- To elicit students' good behaviour skills, effective classroom management requires a comprehensive approach with explicit rules and appropriate consequences for adhering to or breaking those rules.
- How teachers achieve classroom order is as important as establishing order; teachers cannot be the only ones responsible for classroom order.
- Basic student psychological and behavioural needs can be satisfied and transformed by exemplary teacher behaviours.
- Students with behavioural disorders can be properly managed with specific behavioural strategies.
- DCM results in more positive student behaviours, enhanced student psychological security, and better teaching and learning.

New Terms

classroom discourse research
classroom management
positive behaviour support

process-outcome research
reciprocal determinism
resiliency

These terms are defined in the Glossary at the end of the text.

Review Questions

- Why do students engage in negative behaviour?
- What is classroom management?
- What are the global principles of effective classroom management?
- What are the primary steps in the Dynamic Classroom Management approach?
- How should a teacher introduce a classroom management approach like DCM to students?
- How should teachers handle students with behaviour disorders?

MID-SEPTEMBER

Making Instructional Decisions

4

From the Authors' Notebook

The next two chapters summarize, respectively, the underlying principles that govern instruction and assessment. However, because instruction and assessment are so intricately linked, both chapters contain information that pertains to both topics. Technically and professionally, the consideration of assessment principles is a teacher's vital first step in preparing for instruction; thus, it could be argued that assessment precedes instruction. In application, however, instruction typically precedes assessment in the lives of teachers; therefore, we present the chapter on instruction first, followed by the chapter on assessment.

This chapter describes how teachers make decisions about what to teach and how to teach it. It introduces the reader to the underlying principles of how and why classroom instruction is integrally linked to the assessment of student performance. The chapter also provides an example of how teachers develop their overall approach to teaching and how they need to justify and make connections between the various teaching methods they ultimately decide to adopt.

Primary Learning Objectives

After reading this chapter, you should understand the

1. purpose and application of diagnostic assessment;
2. role of the learning objective;
3. purpose and application of Bloom's taxonomy of cognitive skills;
4. relationship between Bloom's taxonomy and Stiggins's targets;
5. importance of developing an overall approach to instruction that is based on an overarching theoretical perspective and supported by broad guiding principles and specific instructional methods;
6. benefits of constructivist and "meaningful" instruction;
7. necessity for very specialized instructional strategies in the case of topics that present particular learning difficulties for some students; and
8. applications of metacognitive executive functioning and its accompanying two slave functions.

Determining the Starting Point for Instruction—Diagnostic Assessment

It is Friday, and Annette does some last-minute preparation before the first bell of the day. Through the open window she can hear the students greeting each other as they enter the school grounds. She thinks about her plans for the morning. With the tone and atmosphere of her classroom fairly well established, her next educational hurdle is to determine exactly what she will teach her students. To accomplish this, she will start by having the students complete the two tests she developed as part of her **diagnostic assessment**. Annette knows that determining "what to teach" is not as straightforward as it seems. Among other things, teaching certainly does not involve simply opening a book or curriculum guide and teaching whatever is found there. She also knows that she cannot merely start at the very beginning of any particular curriculum without first establishing her students' current level of knowledge and skills.

Annette purposely took time in August to review the necessary curriculum guides from her province's Ministry of Education. Knowing the overall framework of what needs to be covered for each grade level, and having considered how she will chunk the curricula into smaller parts, has helped her feel very confident about the start of the school year. However, while Annette knows that she can easily design unit plans and daily lessons, she first needs a more precise indicator of where to start each course and where each student fits in. The last thing she wants to do is teach material that is too advanced or bore students by re-teaching something they have already mastered. She also does not want to cloud her academic judgment of any student by basing it solely on their grades from last year.

The bell rings, and the students pile into the classroom, still chatting about what happened on their favourite reality television show last night. After the usual early morning rituals of taking attendance, singing *O Canada*, and making sure everyone has their forms signed for the field trip, Annette asks Jacob, Lily, and Troy to join Mr. Parker in the resource room. Mr. Parker has agreed to conduct some early literacy and early numeracy assessment measures with these students while the older students complete the diagnostic tests designed by Annette. As soon as they have left the room, Annette flicks the classroom lights off and on to gain the full attention of the remaining students. They settle down quickly, and Annette explains the purpose of the two short tests. After a few questions from the students, mostly in reference to the concern that they may have forgotten a lot of what they did last year, and some reassurances from

Annette that these are not pass/fail tests but rather tests designed to determine what they need to work on this year, everyone gets down to work. Mr. Hayes and Mrs. McCarthy, the two educational assistants, supervise the testing session and provide help to students when needed. This allows Annette the opportunity to unobtrusively observe all her students while they work and to make notes about their work habits, their motivation to achieve/complete the tests, and any problems they have with the demands of the tests.

Once the tests are completed, Annette sends the students outside for recess and begins marking. Since Mrs. Nugent has organized a field trip to the public library for the rest of the morning and a local theatre group is giving a workshop for the students in the afternoon, she has ample time to determine the test results, contemplate what they mean, and make relevant notations in each student's file. Three hours later, just before the lunch break is over, Annette surveys her initial findings.

Name: Amanda Pritchard
Language Arts: 81%
Math: 76%
Focused on task. Did not require any help. Completed tests on time.

Name: Zach MacMillan
Language Arts: 55%
Math: 68%
Had to be reminded several times to stay on-task. Did not complete either test but did fairly well on those questions he did complete.

Name: Jacqueline Dion
Language Arts: 67%
Math: 64%
Complained about having to do tests. Completed all questions but did not seem to expend a great deal of effort. Spent more time doodling in the margins.

Name: Liam Carter
Language Arts: 82%
Math: 60%
Completed the language arts test quickly. Asked many questions when completing the math test and appeared to be anxious.

Name: Tara MacMillan
Language Arts: 86%
Math: 88%
Worked quickly and meticulously. Extremely neat. Excellent handwriting. Continued checking work until asked to pass in completed test.

Name: Caleb Johnston
Language Arts: 60%
Math: 46%
Put in a good effort at the beginning but soon showed signs of frustration. Seemed to give up midway through first test and failed to put in much effort after that. Did not ask for help. Stared out the window for much of the testing session.

Annette takes a few bites of her sandwich as she thinks about the students' performance. She concludes that the test results reveal few surprises; they simply validate the information she previously collected from school files and from school personnel. With few exceptions, the students are performing at grade level. She is a little concerned about the math performance of the younger students, but she will address the weaknesses she has identified in the next few weeks and see if that resolves the problem.

Annette is convinced that some of the students, whose test scores fell in the 50s and 60s, have the potential to perform much better. She notes that (a) she needs to ensure that Zach continues to receive help with his behavioural disorder (ADHD) so that he can be more focused in class; (b) she must address motivational issues in regard to Jacqueline and Simon; (c) she needs to determine why Liam, Caleb, Jackson, and Katherine appear to have difficulty with academics, particularly with math; and (d) she must experiment a little to see if Brandon might benefit from using a keyboard and/or

think box

What did you learn about the students in *The Little Red Schoolhouse* from Annette's observations during the testing sessions? How do the students' test results and their behaviours during the testing sessions compare to the information Annette collected from the students' files in August?

being tested orally because of his apparent physical problem with writing. In the meantime, Annette plans to begin teaching using the lesson plans she prepared in August. She had already built some review time into her overall plan, so she feels confident that the lesson plans will provide a good starting point for instruction.

As she walks down the hallway to join her students for the theatre workshop, she considers whether or not the effort she spent on designing and conducting the diagnostic assessments was worthwhile. She quickly concludes that while the process of constructing the assessments for all her students was somewhat time-consuming, it has certainly paid off. She now feels confident that she will initiate her instruction at exactly the right curricular junctures. This will set the stage for orderly and systematic progress for the rest of the term and the year. She opens the door to the gym and is happy to see her students immersed in theatre activities. Annette cannot wait to join in the fun . . . a perfect end to the week!

Determining Exactly What to Teach

The next afternoon, Annette decides to continue reading. It is a rainy Saturday, so she curls up on the couch and pulls out more material that Dr. Cameron provided during the summer course. She is most interested in reading his paper on the development of lesson plans, since this is where most of her attention will be focused in the coming weeks. It is information that she is familiar with, but it seems there is always something worth reconsidering when relating the material to a new class of students. She begins to read.

Learning Objectives and Lesson Plans

At its core, education is about two predominant teacher functions: teaching and then assessing whether or not students have learned. The symbiotic interrelationships between teaching, learning, and assessment cannot be overstated, but this critical interplay only occurs when assessment and instruction are planned and designed together, not separately or sequentially. Often, teachers are very good at teaching but less skilled at designing good assessment tools. This disconnect typically occurs because most teaching is designed and delivered without *a priori* consideration of the principles of assessment. In fact, many teachers do one of two things when it comes to assessment, neither of which results in a very reliable or effective assessment process. They either wait until after they have finished teaching a unit or a series of lessons to construct their assessment tools (tests or exams), or they simply use the same tests or exams they used the last time they taught that very unit or topic. While both methods appear to save time and effort, they are actually inefficient, and both have the potential for glaring problems. Making up tests or exams after teaching a unit (especially a long unit delivered over several weeks) usually results in

think box

Consider some assessments of your work that you have received recently (e.g., marks on tests, feedback on presentations, feedback on essays and papers). Do you feel that these assessments of your work were fair and accurate? Why or why not? How well did the in-class instruction you received prepare you for the assessment tasks you were required to complete? How could the instruction have been more effective in preparing you for these tasks?

completely forgetting to assess something that was taught or assessing it incorrectly relative to how it was taught. In a similar vein, using the same tests over and over usually results in assessing something that was not taught. Assessing material that was not covered during instruction is the most unpopular aspect of assessment for students, especially for older students who are more aware of what has or has not been included in classroom instruction. In both of the above instances, teachers lose credibility and respect in the eyes of students (and parents) and find this type of assessment practice very difficult to justify to principals and administrators.

Backward Design

Fortunately, there are proven systematized methods of constructing assessment tools that consistently and accurately reflect what has been taught. As strange as it may sound, this can only be done when instruction accurately reflects what is to be assessed. In order for the underlying principles of teaching and assessment to be properly considered and implemented, teachers must consciously put assessment considerations ahead of instructional considerations when planning their teaching. They do this by asking and answering two key assessment questions and then doing the same for two key instructional questions:

1. What do I want my students to learn?
   What I want students to learn is called an instructional goal/learning objective.
2. How will I determine whether or not they have learned?
   The educational device that determines whether or not the learning objective has been learned is called an assessment question.
3. What will I teach?
   I will teach topics/units/lessons that directly address the intended instructional goal/learning objectives.
4. How will I teach?
   I will choose the best way to teach the topics/units/lessons so that objectives are fully achieved/realized.

This critical approach to planning for teaching is known as *backward design*: the development of curricular units and lessons that are derived from the identical instructional goals/learning objectives that are used in creating assessment tools. In this process, the key element for teachers is first knowing where they want to take their students and then charting a map that allows them to both take them there and confirm that they have arrived in good order. Figure 4.1 further illustrates how knowing the precise learning objective, and how it will be assessed, predicates what will be taught and how teaching will take place.

For example, let's say the specific learning objective is *to be able to successfully calculate two-column addition without carrying*. To properly determine whether students have learned this skill, the teacher will assess their abilities using the following questions (and/or other variations):

$$\begin{array}{ccc} 23 & 11 & 71 \\ +\ 15 & +\ 55 & +\ 18 \\ \hline \end{array}$$

Now that the teacher knows precisely what students are supposed to learn and how their understanding and/or application of this knowledge/skill will be assessed, he or she can properly

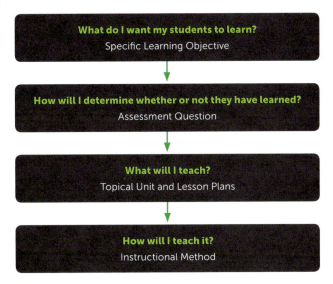

FIGURE 4.1 Learning Objective—Relationship to Assessment, Lesson Planning, and Instruction

and confidently design his or her teaching to make sure this happens. Accordingly, the lesson plan will contain the following learning objective: *As a result of this lesson, my students will be able to calculate two-column addition without carrying.* The reason the learning objective is so clearly stated within the lesson plan is that it acts as the precise focal point for all other lesson

Elements of Backward Design

The theoretical and practical basis for backward design emanates from the work of Wiggins and McTighe (1998). They recommend that when designing instruction, teachers should "map backward" from the desired results of student assessment. In other words, instead of simply listing which topics need to be covered, teachers should let desired educational outcomes dictate what their instructional plan looks like. A variation on this "backward" approach is often used by teachers when they start lessons with a question. Just as this type of question is designed to lead students' thinking and to force them to address the key topical elements of a lesson, backward design requires teachers to first consider assessment questions and then proceed to design instruction that facilitates student learning.

The core elements of backward design are:

- instructional activities that connect to and build understanding;
- assessment that deliberately measures student progress toward curricular goals;
- the development of a variety of ongoing formal and informal assessment tools; and
- the articulation of why certain assessments are appropriate and for what purpose.

plan components, such as the material required and how the material will be taught (see Figure 4.2). The teacher then decides on the best way to teach the material (usually by explanation and demonstration) and proceeds to teach the lesson. Once the teacher is satisfied that the students have learned, he or she uses the previously constructed test questions to assess their understandings/skills. In other words, what is expected to be learned, what is taught, how it is taught, and the questions used to assess student learning are all derived from the same learning objective. This approach provides the entire process with instructional continuity and integrity. Furthermore, by devising assessment questions when planning each daily lesson, teachers have a comprehensive and ready-made test once they have finished teaching the lesson. They do not have to try to remember what they did or did not teach. It is these direct and explicit connections between teaching and assessment generated via adherence to the underlying learning objectives that make assessment authentic.

Daily Lesson Plan

Subject _____ Date/Time/Period _____

Topic of Lesson _____

Administration
- ❑ Reminders/due dates for homework, projects, etc.
- ❑ Field trip permission

1. Learning objective statement (be very precise):
   - ❑ As a result of this lesson, my students will be able to . . .

2. Assessment questions:
   - ❑ Build test items immediately

3. Teaching method:
   - ❑ Select best teaching approach "for the objective"
   - ❑ Review previous day—make explicit connections
   - ❑ Teach, demonstrate, discuss, etc.
   - ❑ Review lesson?

4. Materials required:
   - ❑ Handouts/overheads/videos/music/tools
   - ❑ All parts for demonstrations

5. Anything special about this lesson or this day?

FIGURE 4.2 Lesson Plan Template

Another important function of having a specific learning objective as the critical element within each lesson plan is that teachers can use this objective to direct student expectations. For example, the teacher can say (or indicate on an overhead, a PowerPoint slide, or the board), "Today we are going to learn about fractions. At the end of this lesson, I expect you to be able to add and subtract fractions with different denominators." The teacher's statement acts as a cognitive readiness cue, or prompt, and allows students to get into the right frame of mind. Teachers can support and reinforce the purpose of the learning objective by asking some students to repeat it and explain their understanding of it. When students are explicitly aware of what they are expected to learn, they can better direct their learning energies, and they can better monitor and evaluate their understandings. This sets up an active, rather than a passive, learning process and creates a dynamic relationship between teachers and learners.

The learning objective also has a greater influence that extends far beyond the classroom. At any moment in any day, teachers should be able to relate what is happening in their classroom to the broader objectives of the curriculum and to the overall philosophy of education espoused by their school board (and/or province or territory). Figure 4.3 demonstrates how specific learning objectives permeate throughout the entire foundation of education. In this process, society decides on the overall purpose of education (philosophical objectives), and the government is charged with designing curriculum guides that outline the various topics to be taught/learned in order to properly educate a member of society (global curricular objectives). Teachers break down curricula into large manageable units of instruction (broad learning objectives) and then into daily lesson plans (specific learning objectives) and assessment questions. The complexity and broader application of a specific learning objective builds from the

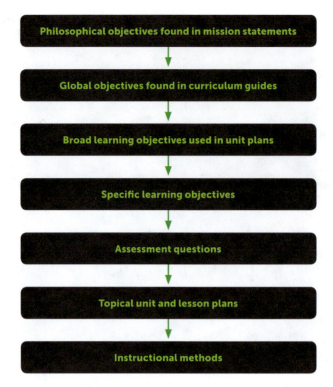

FIGURE 4.3 The Common Thread of Learning Objectives

bottom up. The skills, knowledge, and attitudes contained in each level are embedded within successive higher levels. In this way, every one of a teacher's daily lessons is directly connected to a coherent thread of continuity.

It should be noted that the general or broad educational goals and objectives found in most curriculum guides are fundamentally meaningless as guidelines for everyday teaching. However, in the past five to eight years, many regions of Canada have begun providing more and more specific learning objectives within curriculum guides. These details help standardize instruction and assessment.

Bloom's Taxonomy

Obviously, then, learning objectives play an important role in teaching, learning, and the assessment of learning. But not all learning objectives are created equal; some address fairly simple concepts and only require basic cognitive skills to understand and apply, while others are much more complex and require far more sophisticated thinking skills. This means, therefore, that teachers have to use different types and levels of assessment questions to properly address the various concepts covered in their lessons. Educational psychologist Benjamin Bloom (Bloom, Englehart, Furst, Hill, & Krathwohl, 1956) established a hierarchical classification of cognitive learning objectives that is commonly referred to as **Bloom's taxonomy** (see Table 4.1).

This taxonomy explains and clarifies the complex, hierarchical series of intellectual abilities involved in the acquisition and use of knowledge. Educational objectives, and the types of

TABLE 4.1 Bloom's Taxonomy

Level	Cognitive Objective	Description of Thinking
1	Knowledge	Remembering or recognizing something factual
2	Comprehension	Interpreting/understanding information
3	Application	Being able to use information to solve a problem
4	Analysis	Breaking concepts into parts; indicating relationships
5	Synthesis	Bringing ideas together; generating/creating new ideas from other related ideas
6	Evaluation	Judging the respective worth/value of something

thinking required to learn and apply them, are sorted into six distinct levels, from simple recall to the ability to judge and evaluate learned material: (1) Knowledge, (2) Comprehension, (3) Application, (4) Analysis, (5) Synthesis, and (6) Evaluation. Bloom's six categories are "progressively inclusive," meaning that in order for students to successfully process the information demanded in higher-order categories, they must first understand the information contained in lower-order categories. For example, students cannot be expected to answer their teacher's questions about how the respiratory system works (Level 3: Application) unless they first understand the basic parts that make up the system (Levels 1 and 2: Knowledge and Comprehension). Similarly, in order to be able to properly evaluate a position or theory (Level 6: Evaluation), students must first be able to use the fundamental knowledge and thinking skills required to analyze and synthesize the material (Levels 4 and 5: Analysis and Synthesis). It is especially important to note, therefore, that the same principle must be applied when assessing student learning. Students cannot be expected to answer a question requiring knowledge or skills that they have not yet acquired.

The advantage of utilizing Bloom's taxonomy is that it clearly separates different types and goals of thinking. This allows teachers to easily generate a variety of different but related learning objectives for a course or unit of study. By paying close attention to the cognitive verbs used in their learning objective statements, teachers can be sure that each learning objective is well conceptualized and taught at its intended level of understanding. Cognitive verbs are used to specifically delineate the way that teachers want students to think as a result of participating in any given lesson. Consider the learning objective that was used earlier to calculate *two-column addition without carrying*. This objective, like each and every learning objective in each and every lesson plan, has three required parts:

Part 1
Basic Form   *As a result of this lesson, my students will be able to . . .*

Part 2
Cognitive Verb   *calculate . . .*

Part 3
Topical Description   *two-column addition without carrying*

Furthermore, to be sure that the intended thinking required for a particular learning objective is properly assessed, the same cognitive verb is used in building the assessment questions. In the example below, the test directions tell the student what to do (using the same cognitive verb), and the test includes the test questions the teacher formulated when initially planning the lesson.

Calculate the following:

$$23 + 15 \qquad 11 + 55 \qquad 71 + 18$$

To make sure that the intended thinking of the learning objective is properly realized, teachers use the cognitive verbs that are associated with the six cognitive levels of Bloom's taxonomy (see Table 4.2).

TABLE 4.2 Verbs Used in Learning Objectives

Cognitive Objective	Cognitive Verbs That Activate Learning Objectives
Knowledge	list, name, identify, show, define, recognize, recall, state
Comprehension	summarize, explain, interpret, describe, compare, paraphrase, differentiate, convert, demonstrate, visualize, restate
Application	solve, illustrate, calculate, use, interpret, relate, manipulate, apply, classify, modify, put into practice, compute, determine
Analysis	analyze, organize, deduce, choose, contrast, compare, distinguish, differentiate
Synthesis	design, hypothesize, support, schematize, write, report, discuss, plan, devise, compare, create, construct, formulate
Evaluation	compare, critique, evaluate, choose, estimate, judge, defend, criticize, justify

From Bloom's list, we can see that all forms of thinking can be classified into six basic cognitive processes: remembering, understanding, applying, analyzing, creating, and evaluating. These six processes can be brought to bear on four different types of knowledge: factual, conceptual, procedural, and metacognitive. Therefore, another easy way for teachers to determine the proper cognitive verb for learning objectives is to analyze the cognitive processes involved in the learning tasks and focus on the process that is most relevant. For example, the various mental processes involved in solving a math word problem are (a) reading for understanding, (b) determining the math calculation form (addition, multiplication, etc.), (c) recalling and properly using memorized math facts, and (d) solving the problem. By the time word problems are introduced in the math curriculum, math facts (knowledge) and calculation abilities (application) are mostly consolidated. Therefore, the learning objectives for lessons on word problems will likely focus on verbs that address the cognitive skills involved in reading, analyzing, and deciphering word problems (e.g., analyze, organize, deduce). This example also illustrates how simple cognitive tasks (remembering and calculating) are often embedded in more complex tasks (analyzing). It stands to reason, therefore, that students who cannot remember math facts, or the processes required to perform calculations, will not be able to complete word problems, even if they have good deciphering skills.

It is important to note that the approaches described above are simply the building blocks for designing and delivering effective lessons. Once these fundamental elements are understood and in place, teachers are free to be as creative and inventive as they wish to make their lessons suit their personality, their teaching approach, and their students.

Stiggins's Achievement Targets

Stiggins (1997; 2001) is said to have furthered Bloom's taxonomy by creating a hierarchical structure for "achievement targets": a set of specifications for what students should learn or do (see Table 4.3). Two of the primary differences between Bloom's and Stiggins's taxonomies are that Stiggins purposefully targets the development of (1) the combined use of knowledge with specific thinking processes to create products and (2) the preferred attitudes and dispositions that students should bring to bear on their academic endeavours. Stiggins's "attitudes and dispositions" target is consistent with mainstream conceptions of educational psychology, which advocate that students need to be encouraged to be mindful of their learning and to be explicitly purposeful in applying their thinking and learning processes.

TABLE 4.3 Stiggins's Taxonomy of Achievement Targets

Targets	Description
Knowledge	Declarative knowledge: facts, terms, concepts, and generalizations Procedural knowledge: procedures or problem-solving methods
Reasoning	Process of answering questions through analytical problem-solving
Skills	Abilities required to put procedural knowledge to use in a fluent fashion and in the appropriate context
Products	Student creations that reflect current skill and ability levels
Attitudes and Dispositions	Interests in certain topics; the desire to learn more about a topic

Annette loves the paper's concluding reference to creativity. While she definitely agrees with the careful construction of learning objectives and lesson plans, she has always enjoyed finding new ways to make learning fun for her students. As she knows from past experience, engaging students in stimulating and challenging learning experiences makes everyone in the classroom, including the teacher, feel excited about school. On that note, Annette puts away the reading material for the day. The rain has stopped, so she decides it is a perfect time for a visit to the local library to find out more about the history of George Lake. "You never know where I might find a lesson plan idea," she muses as she pulls on her jacket and heads out toward Main Street.

Choosing Effective Instructional Mechanisms

Annette wakes on Sunday morning and, as is her routine, pours a cup of coffee and sits at her desk to check her e-mail. She smiles when she sees a message from Dr. Cameron.

Instructional Practices

Andrew Cameron <acameron@university.ca>

Date: Sunday, September 15, 2013 7:10 AM

To: Annette Elkins <annette_elkins@schoolmail.com>

Hello Annette,

I hope things are going well with the start of school. Did you use the DCM approach? How did the students react to the rule-making process?

I was wondering if I might ask a favour of you. Some of my students are having difficulty selecting instructional practices as they prepare for their upcoming practicum. Since you have developed a very good understanding of what works for you, I wonder if you might share your thoughts. I know you are busy, so perhaps you could simply expand a little on the paper you completed for me ("My Instructional Practices"). Let me know if this is a reasonable request!

Andrew

Annette is not surprised that Dr. Cameron would want to share her ideas with his current students. She remembers how frequently he used other teachers' ideas to explain or consolidate a concept he wanted the class to understand. She quickly locates the paper he is referring to. "No better time than now to get this done for Dr. Cameron," she tells herself. "It will only help me further consolidate my own teaching methodologies before I develop my lesson plans for the term."

Annette gets settled at her computer desk and begins to write. The task is not that difficult, because she has several papers and assignments from which to cut and paste her ideas. Several hours pass before she even pauses for a coffee refill. She has enjoyed putting her thoughts together; she feels like a student again. As she sips the steaming liquid, she edits her work and makes changes where needed. Just before sending it to Dr. Cameron, she does a final read-through.

My Instructional Practices

My Preferred Instructional Mechanisms

There are a variety of instructional mechanisms that teachers can choose to implement, but it is rare that any one mechanism or teaching method will do everything a teacher requires. In much the same way, it is also rare that a teacher will use a particular teaching method exactly as it is described or make complete use of the entire method. For the most part, teachers choose and modify different parts of various instructional mechanisms to develop their own approach. I will first describe the theoretical basis that governs my overall approach to teaching, and I will then describe how and why I use certain elements from a variety of established methods. Together, all these parts form a cohesive and congruent instructional whole that is consistent with (a) my views of teaching; (b) my approach to classroom management; and (c) the ways that I think about, and conduct, student assessment.

My Three Guiding Principles

There are three foundational principles that guide my teaching. The first is the principle of **universal instructional design** (UID). The roots of UID originate in the architectural concept of "universal design," which advocates for physical spaces and objects that consider the needs of all users and especially those of individuals with disabilities. It is a concept of equitable accessibility and utility. By extension, universal instructional design conceptualizes teaching as an instructional system that, when designed and delivered with the needs of the least independently able students in mind, is more accessible and effective for all students (Rose & Meyer, 2006). With inclusiveness and equity as its core elements, UID creates classroom environments that respect and value diversity. I have incorporated the fundamental principles of universal instructional design into my integrated approach to teaching; this includes my instructional approach as well as my approach to classroom management. The UID principles I adhere to are as follows:

1. Create a welcoming classroom environment that emphasizes academic and behavioural success.
2. Determine the essential academic components to be taught/learned and the preferred behavioural outcomes.
3. Provide students with both clear expectations for learning and feedback about their learning progress and social conduct.
4. Implement a variety of topically suitable instructional methods.
5. Provide a variety of ways for students to demonstrate what they have learned (assessment).
6. Make appropriate use of technology to enhance learning.
7. Encourage and initiate teacher–student and student–student discourses about learning topics/tasks and behavioural expectations.

The second principle that guides my teaching comes from my realization that the vast bulk of teaching is accomplished by either explaining or demonstrating, or both. I use examples, pictures, questions, models, manipulatives, student discourse, student-read passages, and various forms of teacher and student re-explaining to reinforce the concepts I am teaching. Therefore, my overall approach is constructivist in nature, even though it includes several teacher-centred applications. I want to allow students to formulate and construct their own knowledge and their own knowledge-producing structures with my guidance. My teaching methods include carefully selected elements of student-centred approaches to instruction, yet at the same time

I make specialized use of certain facets of teacher-centred approaches, such as direct instruction, to satisfy my responsibility as the instructional leader. All of these elements, in conjunction with the meaningful tasks inherent in problem-, project-, and inquiry-based learning, are used collectively to have a direct, positive influence on student achievement and student self-regulated learning. My primary instructional purpose, therefore, is to guide and assist students toward constructing their own understandings and acquiring the skills necessary to responsibly regulate their own learning.

Finally, the third principle that guides my teaching is based on the realization that learning is a highly complex function that involves academic skill acquisition, the development of cognitive understanding, and the formation and enhancement of a variety of cognitive processes used for further learning. All of these student abilities are dependent upon learners' constructing knowledge, and making skill adaptations and adjustments, based on their social environment and the level and type of cognitive stimulation they encounter. If learning is a function of student thinking, then student thinking must be a function of teacher instruction. For me, good teaching is certainly about the various teaching elements I choose to use during the instructional process, but more important, it is about using these elements to cause students to think. Therefore, my overall approach to teaching is primarily geared toward generating student thinking; without thinking, neither knowledge construction nor the regulation of learning can happen.

Theoretical Basis for My Instruction

Thinking is the processing of information. In my opinion, the best explanation of the thinking processes that facilitate learning was provided by Michael Pressley and his colleagues (Pressley, Borkowski, & Schneider, 1987) through their "good information processing" model of effective thinking. I was impressed to discover that the fundamental conceptual principles of this model are contained in all other contemporary models of information processing.

Cognitive Strategies

According to Pressley, Borkowski, and Schneider, to be a "good thinker" an individual must effectively use cognitive strategies; his or her thinking must be strategic and systematic. A **cognitive strategy** is a purposeful and controllable thinking process that actively promotes the understanding and retention of knowledge; essentially, it is knowing how to do things cognitively. Effective thinking also involves the use of working memory, a short-term store of relevant information, and long-term memory, which is replete with procedural and declarative knowledge. And finally, effective thinking is also a product of metacognition. Sometimes referred to as thinking about one's own thinking, **metacognition** actually refers to the executive thinking processes, such as planning, gauging comprehension, and evaluating, that actively control the cognitive processes that become engaged when the brain is required to think or learn. I find it useful to think of cognitive strategies as the processes that achieve specific academic goals, such as writing a paragraph, and I think of metacognition as the overall supervisory procedure that governs an entire process, which in the case of writing would include (a) making an outline for the paragraph (planning), (b) choosing a specific strategy to complete the paragraph (strategy selection), (c) making sure the writing strategy is working properly (monitoring), and (d) checking to make sure that the completed paragraph is what was initially intended and planned for (evaluation).

Select–Organize–Integrate

In order to encourage active thinking in my students, as opposed to simple rote memorization, my teaching must make what is to be learned meaningful. The theoretical foundations for my teaching, therefore, come from the select–organize–integrate (SOI) information-processing model of meaningful learning (Mayer, 2001; 2003). According to this model, meaningful learning occurs when students engage in three cognitive processes: (1) selecting relevant information; (2) organizing the selected information; and (3) integrating the organized information with prior knowledge. Based on these principles, meaningfulness does not happen only because students are interested in particular information (i.e., they like it); it also happens primarily because of the manner in which students are required to manipulate the information (i.e., use it). There are two reasons that I like this model: (1) it prevents teachers from feeling pressured to design lessons that are solely about "interesting stuff," such as music videos and sports, and (2) teachers can use the SOI model to make all material cognitively stimulating, even if it is not about music videos or sports. Figure 4.4 provides a schematic diagram of the SOI process.

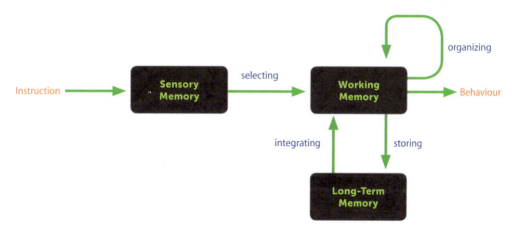

FIGURE 4.4 Diagram of the SOI Model of Meaningful Learning

Source: Mayer, R. E., & Wittrock, M. C. (2006). Problem solving. In P. A. Alexander & P. H. Winne (Eds.), *Handbook of educational psychology* (2nd ed., pp. 287–303). Mahwah, NJ: Lawrence Erlbaum.

According to this figure, when information is presented to a learner, the sound and symbol representations of the information are stored in sensory memory. The representations the individual perceives to be important are selected and transferred to working memory, where they can be organized as a group and/or integrated into prior knowledge retrieved from long-term memory. This produces two related results. First, the thinking process makes the information meaningful and coherent (it is learned). Second, the entire thinking process that gave the information meaning and caused it to be learned is stored as a coherent cognitive structure. Thus, not only does teaching for meaningfulness result in students acquiring more knowledge, it also results in students developing and acquiring more effective cognitive learning processes that are retained for future use. Together, the availability of a larger knowledge base and numerous learning processes make an individual's thinking far more efficient. In other words, the more often information and learning processes are used, the more automatic thinking and learning become. From a teacher's perspective, this means that instruction that fosters selecting, organizing, and integrating will lead to more meaningful learning than instruction that does not cause students to engage in these mental processes. This type of inefficiency happens, for example, when students simply have to copy a teacher's notes from an overhead slide or from the blackboard—they hardly have to process the information; therefore, little learning occurs and no new thinking/learning processes are developed. A further implication of the SOI model is that in order for meaningful learning to occur, "the learner must select relevant information from the presented material, the learner must mentally organize the material into a coherent structure, and the learner must mentally integrate the organized knowledge with existing knowledge retrieved from long-term memory" (Mayer & Wittrock, 2012, p. 291). From my perspective, this clearly indicates that teaching for meaningful learning via the selecting, organizing, and integrating processes fosters self-regulated learning.

Motivational Underpinnings

So, how do I motivate my students to learn? While educational psychology has long maintained the need for an integrated theory of learning and motivation, most research to date has either focused on isolated features of teaching and learning or has had little to do with actual classroom contexts. Descriptions of students who are motivated to learn (or not) can no longer focus solely on an individual's behaviour, cognition, and affect; these descriptions must include the contexts within which student motivation and engagement take place. This perspective does not eliminate the fact that some students will purposefully choose to disengage from learning; rather, it simply states that explanations of learning motivation must also include understandings and portrayals of the instructional elements that can enhance or detract from motivations to learn. "Contextual understandings are more integral to research on motivation today, reflecting the general shift in educational research toward a situated and social perspective on learning" (Perry, Turner, & Meyer, 2012, p. 328). In their comprehensive review of factors that affect student motivation within classrooms, Perry, Turner, and Meyer identified classroom tasks, instructional practices, and classroom relationships as being the critical contextual factors that significantly influence student engagement.

Tasks

Teachers can actively engage students' motivations to learn with challenging and meaningful tasks that are dynamic in purpose and open to a wide range of student-selected topical variations. This results in tasks that appeal to a broad range of student engagement and interests.

Instructional Practices

Teachers who teach students learning and problem-solving strategies, and how to use them effectively, foster student motivations to learn. Providing and adjusting instructional support to suit students' individual needs is also motivating, but these supports are more powerful when accompanied by motivational messages about the importance of verifying student understandings. By challenging students to demonstrate their understandings and abilities, teachers appeal to students' needs for personal relatedness, external and personal approval, and intellectual respect.

Classroom Relationships

Students report more positive motivational outcomes when they sense that their teacher cares about them as well as their academic well-being. Similarly, teacher interest in students' personal lives and teacher support for student autonomy during learning promotes student willingness to engage (be motivated) in classroom learning activities. These types of teachers (a) encourage student engagement, (b) encourage student discussions, (c) elicit student perspectives on nearly all instructional topics, and (d) withhold judgment about student perspectives during the interim. While it is still the teacher's responsibility to eventually correct student misconceptions, students must feel at ease in voicing their thoughts and exchanging ideas with the teacher as well as with their peers.

One of my primary goals for my students is that they become intrinsically motivated learners. These are learners who have a tendency to look for and follow through on academic challenges that test their personal interests. These types of learners do not need the threat of tests, exams, or grades to study and learn; they do it for the sake of learning. It has been said that **intrinsic motivation** is what makes people do things when they do not have to do anything. On the other hand, extrinsically motivated learners are not actually interested in academic tasks; they simply complete them to get passing grades, to avoid punishment by their parents, or to receive other types of rewards. It has been said that **extrinsic motivation** is what makes people do what they do not really want to do.

How People Learn (HPL) Framework

To organize what is known about teaching and learning, the National Academy of Sciences Committee (National Research Council, 2000) developed the *How People Learn* (HPL) framework. The four components of this framework incorporate the various "mini theories" that educators tend to have about teaching (modified from Bransford, Derry, Berliner, & Hammerness, 2005, p. 41):

Knowledge-Centredness: What should be taught, why is it important, and how should this knowledge be organized?
Learner-Centredness: Who learns, how, and why?
Community-Centredness: What kinds of classroom, school, and school-community environments enhance learning?
Assessment-Centredness: What kinds of evidence can students, teachers, parents, and others use to see if effective learning is really occurring?

Continued

Figure 4.5 provides a schematic diagram of the HPL framework.

FIGURE 4.5 Diagram of the HPL Framework
Source: Bransford, J., Darling-Hammond, L., & LePage, P. (2005). Introduction. In L. Darling-Hammond & J. Bransford (Eds.), *Preparing teachers for a changing world: What teachers should learn and be able to do* (pp. 1–39). San Francisco, CA: Jossey-Bass. Reprinted with permission from John Wiley and Sons.

Effective teachers balance and integrate all four components of the HPL framework in the following ways (modified from Bransford et al., 2005):

Knowledge-Centredness: Teachers consult their respective national, provincial, and district standards in deciding what to teach and why.

Learner-Centredness: As well as intensive curricular and instructional planning decisions, teachers need to make moment-by-moment teaching decisions based on their ongoing assessments of their learners' current levels of understanding.

Community-Centredness: Teachers need to create climates of shared learning and respect for learning, the sense of community among fellow teachers and other adults in the school, and build on the goodwill and intellectual resources of the community.

Assessment-Centredness: Teachers focus on ways that different teaching and learning goals affect the assessment of academic progress.

In conclusion, Bransford et al. (2005) illustrated how the HPL framework influences student motivation:

If students know they are learning content and skills that will be important in life, this is motivating. If courses connect with their interests and strengths, and provide interesting challenges to their preconceptions, this is motivating. If students receive frequent feedback that allows them to see their progress in learning and gives them chances to do even better, this is motivating. And if students feel as if they are a valued part of vibrant, "high-standards" learning communities—at the classroom level, school level, and overall community level—this is motivating as well (p. 75).

Direct Instruction

Direct instruction (DI), or explicit teaching as it is sometimes called, is a systematic instructional method that is often portrayed as teaching small amounts of information and providing lots of practice so that students can master basic facts and skills. I feel that this is an overly narrow view of its application that loses sight of the larger functional benefits that can be garnered by teachers. I find the following aspects of direct instruction appealing:

1. DI emphasizes well-developed and carefully planned lessons with clear learning objectives that are purposefully presented to students. Not only do such lessons provide structure and predictability for both my students and me, but I feel that the rich structure and clear instruction based on well-planned lessons eliminates misinterpretations that inhibit student learning. While I am a constructivist at heart, I know of far too many instances of student-centred teaching and learning that led students off-track and fostered misconceptions of lesson content.

2. DI requires teaching via some form of explanation (either lecture or demonstration, or both) and guiding students through complex concepts/problems (either as a group or one-on-one). In my mind, I must lead my students' learning, since no one else knows the intended learning objective of each of my lessons better.
3. As part of every lesson, DI requires students to complete problems or exercises related to the material and/or to explain their understandings of the concepts to the class. Once I have explained the key parts of the content, I always use two linkage questions: "Can anyone tell me how this is related to what we already know?" and "Why is this information important?" By assigning in-class problems and tasks and by having the students respond to my linkage questions, I activate my students' own constructions of knowledge. I also like the way that teaching in this manner provides all of us with constant interaction. It is much better than teaching that is primarily me talking and them listening.

Therefore, when I teach, I strictly adhere to the following aspects of direct instruction for the structure it provides:

1. I review previous related material to activate students' prior knowledge and/or to immediately clear up any lingering misunderstandings.
2. I explicitly describe how new material is related to previous lessons.
3. I allow for both guided and independent practice/homework through the use of in-class problems/tasks and questioning for student understanding.
4. I provide feedback about guided and independent practice.
5. I provide a "common thread" review at the end of related lessons or units of study whereby the common thread links all the concepts. I also do this between all units of instruction to connect everything back to the broader curricular objectives.

I am confident that my constructivist alterations and additions to these elements, such as problem- and project-based learning (outlined in the next section), keep my lessons from feeling stiff or rigid. Most important, I have found that this modified approach helps my students both prepare for learning and organize how they will approach learning tasks.

Student Problem-Solving

One of the main objectives of teaching is to facilitate students' acquisition of knowledge, skills, attitudes, and thinking strategies. In keeping with the current emphasis on teaching thinking skills, educators want to help students develop "routine thinking expertise" whereby students become more efficient at solving recurring forms of academic problems, problems that, as children progress though each grade, become more sophisticated and complex. Problem-solving, then, from the teacher's perspective, is turning non-routine or new problems into routine problems by teaching students how to develop and apply new thinking strategies and procedures.

The more strategies students have, the better their learning. Children are able to use more strategies as they get older; some they develop on their own as they work through academic tasks, while others need to be taught explicitly. If I have learned one thing about students' thinking abilities over the years, it is that I should never assume that students of a particular age or grade have developed the use of a particular thinking or learning strategy or that they can use it in the most efficient fashion. Invariably, when I have helped students who did not utilize an effective strategy, I have found that all students in the class benefited from direct instruction in strategy knowledge and application. On many occasions, several of my very competent students have stated that they learned something new when I re-explained a strategy or demonstrated its use again by utilizing a different example.

Although my constructivist propensities make me more inclined to allow students to "discover" thinking strategies for themselves, I know that the research in this area indicates that students do not do this very well on their own, and even if they do, they do not consistently use their newly developed strategies in the most efficient ways. Student self-development of thinking strategies is not a substitute for teacher-taught strategies. Students cannot replicate a teacher's ability to think of all the variations of strategy use that are possible, nor can they anticipate the probable errors or misuses of particular strategies. Also, teachers know what the efficient use of a strategy looks like; students do not. Pressley and Harris (2012) summed up this perspective in their analysis of cognitive strategy development and use by students of all ages across curricular domains:

> we have encountered little evidence in any task domain that children certainly discover and consistently use the most effective strategies that can be used to accomplish tasks. . . . there is one approach that works better than any other for ensuring that learners actually learn strategies: strategies instruction (p. 270).

Moreover, students' abilities to consistently and efficiently use domain-specific learning strategies improves significantly under two specific teacher-lead instructional conditions: (1) when instruction is metacognitively rich (the teacher explains and demonstrates his or her own use of executive processes) and (2) when instruction relies on student self-regulated use of strategies (students are encouraged to select from and/or improve their own repertoire of proven strategies).

Verbal Protocol Analysis

Ultimately, there are only two ways that teachers know when students have made efficient use of a thinking or learning strategy: (1) students attempt a task or problem, and teachers infer their strategy ability from the demonstrated outcome, or (2) students describe their thinking and/or talk out loud as they complete a task. Because I am highly interested in determining my students' learning and problem-solving abilities, most of my teaching processes require students to explain their thinking. Interestingly, I discovered that having students do this is one of the few instances in education when a preferred and effective instructional practice is also preferred as a research methodology. According to Pressley and Harris (2012), verbal protocol analysis—documenting conscious cognitive processing—has proved to be one of the most illuminating approaches to studying efficient strategy use by students. There is also clear evidence that requiring students to explain their problem-solving strategies (procedural knowledge) improves their understandings of facts (declarative knowledge), enables them to refine their strategies, and improves their ability to transfer their strategies to other types of problems. This happens because when students are asked to explain their thinking about either acquired knowledge or a new problem they have encountered, they consciously activate their working and short-term memory. These efficient cognitive functions allow students to think about and manipulate information and processes stored in long-term memory and then apply them to their knowledge and/or to the problem to be solved. In other words, student explanations of their own understandings and/or problem-solving strategies act as a self-feedback mechanism that allows for reflection and/or refinement because attention is paid to the logic behind their thinking. I especially like to use these underlying features of strategic thinking as the basis for problem-, project-, and inquiry-based learning.

Problem-, Project-, and Inquiry-Based Learning

Problem-, project-, and inquiry-based learning are slightly different teaching methods, but each conforms to the fundamental teaching and learning principles found in all information-processing approaches to instruction. While each method can be used on its own, I prefer to use them together. Therefore, I think of problem-, project-, and inquiry-based learning (PPIL) as a student-centred constructivist instructional approach in which students (a) help teachers design comprehensive curricular tasks (inquiry base), (b) complete tasks with peers collaboratively (problem base), (c) create specific educational products (project base), and (d) reflect on their learning experiences. I like PPIL because while it maintains my role as instructional leader, I am predominantly a learning process facilitator and guide rather than simply a provider of curricular knowledge. I also like the way that the combined PPIL elements are used as an interactional entity that closely mirrors real life outside of school; individuals are involved in figuring out which problems to solve, they collaborate to solve them and design an end product, and they collectively reflect on what they have learned and how efficient the learning process was. As a result of this reflection, students are in a much better position to solve complex problems more efficiently. Learning these types of cognitive courses of action is as important as the information acquired and/or the final product presented.

In my use of PPIL, learning is predominantly driven by challenging, open-ended problems that are teacher- and student-designed and mediated. With teacher guidance, students work in small collaborative groups and take primary responsibility for their group's activities in organizing and directing their learning. During the process, learners discuss problems, define what they know, generate hypotheses, set out learning goals, organize their work to achieve these goals, and reflect on their learning. To round out the entire process, I also require each group to present the results of the activity to the rest of the class. This allows students to develop and demonstrate their presentation skills (a commonly required learning objective), and it provides me with an added educational element that can be assessed.

It should be noted that teachers have to model the entire PPIL process with well-constructed examples before students can be expected to take on such comprehensive learning activities. Just as students cannot be expected to develop efficient thinking and learning strategies on their own, they cannot be expected to process and organize all the new information included in problems that have such wide-ranging applications. It is critical, therefore, that teachers provide lots of support to facilitate the original processes and then reduce their support as student autonomy increases and their thinking and problem-solving abilities become more routine (i.e., scaffolding).

think box

Consider what you have read in this chapter as well as in the previous chapter. What are the commonalities between Annette's approach to classroom management and her approach to instruction? Imagine that you are a student in Annette's class. How do you think you would react to her approaches to classroom management and instruction?

I also like the way that the information-processing emphasis of PPIL simultaneously taps into a broad range of cognitive and social skills. Students have to analyze the overall problem and pick out the important aspects, activate their prior related knowledge, individually and collectively process and construct new understandings, form hypotheses, problem-solve, and present their findings/solutions, and throughout the entire process, they have to carefully monitor and evaluate their progress. I feel that the most important aspect of this learning strategy is that it makes both the curricular content and the learning process highly contextual and meaningful and it requires considerable social interaction for implementation. I have also found that these wide-ranging and comprehensive forms of academic assignments improve students' content knowledge and foster the development of communication, problem-solving, and self-directed/self-regulated learning skills. Many of these skills would not develop as well if student assignments had an overly narrow focus or were predominantly completed individually.

Summary

In summary, I think the most interesting thing about my overall teaching methodology is that it is very different now from what it was when I began my career. I was always encouraged to have an open mind, and while in the early days I still had to "survive" in my classroom, I found that trying new ideas every now and then freshened and expanded my approach. Not all my ideas worked well; some failed miserably, while others took me some time to get comfortable with, but I cannot imagine still teaching the way I did when I started. Knowing what I know now, I am very careful to try only well-researched and substantiated teaching methods that I can modify to suit myself and my classrooms—those, by far, have proved to be the most helpful and worthwhile.

Annette is quite pleased with her paper and sends it off to Dr. Cameron right away. Again, she is somewhat surprised about how much she benefits from examining and re-examining her ideas.

Putting Teacher Knowledge into Practice

Early Monday morning, Annette meets with the educational assistants before the students arrive at school. She has an idea that has grown out of all the reading and thinking she has been doing over the past few days. On Friday, the math diagnostic assessment revealed that almost all of Annette's younger students need additional instruction in solving word problems. Annette observed that most of the students encountered difficulties in deciphering which math operation was required. She wonders if one or more of her students may even have a learning disability, because while they seemed to be able to "do the math," they could not identify or understand the one key word that unlocked the calculation mystery embedded within each problem. Annette explains this dilemma to Mr. Hayes and Mrs. McCarthy. "Over the past two decades, math has evolved from a series of straightforward calculations to an emphasis on math as problem-solving, communication, connections, and reasoning. This change has made math more challenging for some students, particularly those with learning disabilities (LD). Just look at these two comparable problems:

1. How many marbles would you have if you combined Bill's with Stephanie's?
2. How many marbles do Bill and Stephanie have together?

It is implied in both problems that the marbles will be added, but this is exactly the type of inference that students with LD do not usually grasp. Their cognitive confusion is further complicated by the fact that many other different words and phrases can also imply that the marbles are to be added together."

Before Annette continues with her explanation, she pulls out an academic journal that describes research on learning strategies. In one of the articles, she has found a specific learning strategy that was designed to improve the math achievement of students with LD. While she is not sure that any of her students have a learning disability, the strategy is also described as being relevant for any student who is having difficulty solving word problems. According to the authors, the vast majority of students with LD have short-term memory processing difficulties that prohibit the self-generation of cognitive strategies and metacognitive executive functions that are used to solve problems and enhance learning. These processing problems include difficulty with (a) determining what the problem is asking, (b) choosing a strategy to solve it, (c) getting started, (d) using the strategy, (e) staying on-task, and (f) monitoring to see if their eventual solution is reasonable given the initial problem. Learning strategy interventions that effectively overcome such deficits typically provide students with cognitive and/or metacognitive cues or prompts that elicit or trigger a learning process or the cognitive execution of a particular thinking skill. Once the proper cognitive stimulus is provided, these students are often able to execute the academic task at hand. The researchers, Edmunds and Blair (1999), used the cognitive credit card (CCC) model (Edmunds, 1999) to help students design their own math prompts to solve word problems.

Annette shows the article to Mr. Hayes and Mrs. McCarthy. "I'd like to use the CCC method in my math class, because it will help all the students who are learning to solve word problems and it will be particularly helpful to those who have difficulty with math. Because both of you will be helping these students, let's walk through the method together." Annette presents the following steps:

Step 1: Explain to students what a key word in a math problem is, and together read through word problems in our teaching units and identify all such words.
Step 2: Help students identify, discuss, and understand the various terms that can be used to indicate one of the four primary math operations. Record all of these terms, and group them accordingly.

Step 3: Have a student volunteer type the identified terms into a word processing program, and then print out copies (using poster board) of the entire set for all students in the class. The printed copies should be the size of a credit card (see Table 4.4), and ideally they should be laminated to make them more durable.

Step 4: Show students how to use their cognitive credit cards when doing math problems.

Step 5: Monitor each student's use of the card, and make corrections if needed.

"The element of the CCC strategy that I'm most happy about," says Annette, "is that it helps students independently execute the same kind of thinking that naturally occurs for their peers who easily solve such problems. Most students don't mind getting a little help, but when teachers have to provide a long, drawn-out explanation, students tend to feel self-conscious, and they stop asking for help as often as they should. With the CCC, if a student gets stumped, all we have to do is to get him or her to connect the words in the problems with the words on their card, and they can move on."

Mr. Hayes nods his head. "I think this will work, because it really involves the students in the process. We won't just be giving them a list that we put together. They'll identify and choose the terms that go on the card themselves, and therefore they will better understand them. I like that they'll have their own concrete system for solving math problems right there in front of them. It means they'll be able to try the problems without having to ask for help, and that will prevent some students from simply doing nothing because they are so confused."

Mrs. McCarthy adds, "Yes, and the fact that they'll be involved at every stage of the CCC process, from development to usage, will provide them with much needed repetition. That means they'll probably make better connections between all the math operation terms."

"Yes, this type of relational thinking is excellent for enhancing and transferring overall processing skills," explains Annette. "And the strategy design and development process is mostly student-mediated, so it encourages self-regulation. I think it's a win-win situation. It also offers an excellent opportunity to get the students to talk about their thinking and hear how other students use their cards. Sometimes, the students who struggle with certain concepts think that everyone else is smarter than they are and never have problems with school work."

TABLE 4.4 Cognitive Credit Card—Math Operations

"+" Add	"−" Subtract	"x" Multiply	"/" Divide
together	less	times	share
combine	difference	combine	equal
how many	least	product	split into
total	from	price per	separated
and	remaining		how many in
unite	fewer		
sum	take away		

Source: Edmunds, A. L., and Blair, K. (1999). Nova Scotia teachers' use of the cognitive credit card. *ATEC Journal*, 5(1), 7–13.

4 | Mid-September Making Instructional Decisions

Annette wraps up the meeting with her colleagues and prepares for the morning ahead. She makes a mental note to closely monitor the implementation of the math-related CCC to see if it may be worthwhile to develop other CCCs to assist learning in other subject areas. Her prediction is that the students will enjoy having special "credit cards" that help them complete their work successfully and independently. The use of this type of learning strategy is another complement to her overall approach to effective instruction.

> **think box**
>
> How does the cognitive credit card strategy fit with Annette's use of universal instructional design? How might the use of the CCC facilitate the creation of a classroom environment that respects and values diversity?

Annette's Journal

September 20, 2013

Well, now that I have everything else out of the way, it's time to start teaching, and that means I need to start developing more lesson plans. I love this part of my job. It challenges me to be creative while developing instruction that meets the needs of my students. A big challenge this year will be designing global lesson plans that can be used for the whole class. I would like to use one global plan a week. It's important that we do things together despite the age differences in the class. While some of the older students may lack enthusiasm at first, that will quickly change. I just need to come up with the right kinds of activities—ones that give all students important, but appropriate, roles. It really won't be much different from when I had to design class lessons that recognized the strengths and abilities of students with special needs. I'll just have to be sure that everyone is included and that they have the opportunity to learn while feeling like a valued member of the class.

There's no doubt that I'll depend more and more on my support staff now that the real teaching is about to begin. Mr. Hayes and Mrs. McCarthy will be instrumental in helping me keep the classroom activities running smoothly. I have to admit, though, I was a little concerned about their interpretation of their job responsibilities based on their past experience. It seems that they've been accustomed to taking on actual teaching duties, even designing some lesson plans, but they responded rather well when I made it clear that their roles would be changing a little this year. While I've encouraged them to provide some input into my instructional decisions, I

have also made it clear that it is my job to be the "teacher" and it is their job to "assist" me. Because of the age range in the classroom, there will certainly be times when they'll find themselves implementing a lesson plan with one or more students. However, it will always be my responsibility to develop the lessons and to ensure that learning objectives are met. I think I need to set aside some time every Monday and Friday to meet with both of them and perhaps Mr. Parker as well. On Mondays we can discuss the week ahead, and on Fridays we can just talk about how the past week went. I want to give everyone a chance to voice their opinions and concerns. I really couldn't do this job without their help, and I'll certainly let them know that.

It's also time for me to begin regular communication with the parents of my students. I think I'll schedule an informal "Meet the Teacher" get-together for next week. It will give me a chance to introduce myself, and it will give parents an opportunity to ask questions they may have about my plans for the year. Together, we can also decide on the best way for me to communicate with them on an ongoing basis. I'm going to need their input and support if this school year is to go smoothly.

Annette's Exploration of the Research

Ackerman, P. L., and Lohman, D. F. (2012). Individual differences in cognitive function. In P. A. Alexander and P. H. Winne (Eds), *Handbook of educational psychology* (2nd ed., pp. 139–162). New York, NY: Routledge.

After several years of teaching, Annette, like a lot of teachers, began to ask herself, "Why do some students fail to learn despite good cognitive functioning and good instruction?" She remembers her mentor, Dr. Cameron, saying that this query is one of the long-time perplexing questions in education. He mentioned a possible answer to this dilemma that is now gaining prominence in educational psychology. It appears that a number of typical academic tasks are difficult for students because these tasks exceed students' capacity to store and manipulate information in working memory. This commonly happens when teachers ask students to complete higher-order thinking tasks before basic facts and lower-order thinking processes are consolidated or when there is simply too much new information to be effectively understood at one time.

To illustrate, Dr. Cameron first explained that working memory is made up of a central executive function and two slave functions. The central executive function is responsible for supervising the integration of information by directing attention to relevant information, by discounting irrelevant information and inappropriate cognitive processes, and by co-ordinating an individual's thinking, including the slave functions, when multiple tasks are done simultaneously. One of the slave functions is called the phonological loop. This cognitive process stores the sounds of language and retains that information by continuously refreshing it in a rehearsal loop. This is the function at play when individuals silently repeat a phone number, a short grocery list, or the steps required to complete a task. In a similar fashion, the other slave function, the visuo-spatial sketch pad, is responsible for setting up and manipulating visual and spatial information. This is what individuals do when they visualize different views of three-dimensional objects or create mental maps. When working memory is activated, the central executive function constantly reminds the brain to be aware of the information it wants to use, and the slave functions cooperate by providing constant updates of the specific details required to complete the task. This enables us to monitor and execute very precise thinking, even over long periods of time or numerous repetitions of similar or different tasks.

Dr. Cameron then recommended that his students read Ackerman and Lohman's (2012) report on what they found when conducting an extensive review of individual differences in cognitive functioning. Annette located the article and found that the researchers supported the idea presented by Dr. Cameron—learning in classrooms is often compromised because too many academic tasks exceed students' working memory capacity. Ackerman and Lohman outlined that when teachers attempt to make academic tasks easier to learn, they mistakenly off-load problem-solving and reasoning skills because these processes often require more cognitive attention and work than merely learning facts. While this type of cognitive off-loading might allow students to learn factual content, it diminishes the development of the higher-order thinking skills crucial for further manipulating the content. The students' learning, therefore, remains highly dependent on someone else to do their thinking and reasoning. To address both issues properly, Ackerman and Lohman recommended that it is better to reduce students' cognitive load by:

- automatizing the elemental component skills required for more complex tasks (i.e., writing words is consolidated before students are required to write paragraphs);
- redesigning large tasks into smaller tasks but making sure that the smaller tasks still require thinking (i.e., writing sentences and paragraphs is consolidated before students are required to write essays);
- off-loading non-critical attention-demanding executive processes, such as monitoring, until students have acquired enough practice (e.g., allowing students to write inventively/creatively before they are required to adhere to the conventions that govern writing paragraphs or books).

Annette's decision to base her instruction on the guiding principles of development is reaffirmed by the findings reported in Ackerman and Lohman's study. Their research makes an even greater case for the importance of being sure that academic concepts are fully understood and mastered before moving on to new and more complex tasks.

Annette's Resource List

Academic Journals

Academic Exchange Quarterly
Elementary School Journal
Harvard Education Letter
Harvard Educational Review
Teaching and Teacher Education

Books

Darling-Hammond, L., and Bransford, J. (Eds.) (2007). *Preparing teachers for a changing world: What teachers should learn and be able to do.* San Francisco, CA: Jossey-Bass.

Websites

CBC Digital Archives—For Teachers
www.cbc.ca/archives/teachers

Learning Centre for Teachers—Library and Archives Canada
www.collectionscanada.gc.ca/education/008-1000-e.html

Links for Teachers—Ontario Ministry of Education
www.edu.gov.on.ca/eng/teachers/links.html

Ten Steps to Developing a Quality Lesson Plan
www.lessonplanspage.com/WriteLessonPlan.htm

4 | Mid-September Making Instructional Decisions

From the Authors' Notebook

This chapter emphasized how all teachers can build their own unified approach to teaching and confidently put it into practice knowing that it will produce efficient student learning. A well thought-out approach is a natural complement to the exemplary learning environment depicted in Chapter 3.

Reflecting on Practice

Consider the information you have read in this chapter as well as the knowledge you have acquired through instruction, classroom discussions, and classroom activities. Then take the time to write down your thoughts about these learning experiences. Consider how your perspective on educational psychology may have changed. In addition, respond to the following questions:

- How confident do you feel about your ability to establish effective lesson plans?
- How confident do you feel about selecting the best teaching method for the situation?
- What more do you need to know about lesson plans and teaching methods, and where might you find this information?

Chapter Summary

In this chapter, the following concepts were highlighted:

- Diagnostic assessment should be the starting point for all instruction.
- The learning objective is the foundation of every daily lesson plan; it also has direct connections to student assessment and one's philosophy of teaching.
- The critical element in Bloom's taxonomy of cognitive skills is the verb that accurately indicates what students will learn and/or be able to do as a result of each lesson.
- The critical element in Stiggins's targets is making an outline of what students should be able to do as a result of applying their cognitive skills; it also requires teachers to encourage preferred student attitudes and dispositions.
- Teaching is more than developing a group of lesson plans; it requires adherence to a theoretical framework, guiding instructional principles, and specific instructional methods.
- Meaningful learning stems from effective teaching.
- Discussing and encouraging the use of metacognitive and cognitive strategies enhances student autonomy, student learning, and student motivation.

New Terms

backward design
Bloom's taxonomy
cognitive strategy
diagnostic assessment
direct instruction

extrinsic motivation
intrinsic motivation
metacognition
universal instructional design

These terms are defined in the Glossary at the end of the text.

Review Questions

- What is the purpose of diagnostic assessment?
- Why is it important to establish learning objectives?
- What is Bloom's taxonomy, and how does it relate to Stiggins's targets?
- Why should teachers deliberately develop an overall approach to instruction?
- What are the benefits of constructivist and "meaningful" instruction?
- How can teachers alter instruction to address students' learning difficulties?
- How do metacognitive executive functioning and its accompanying two slave functions relate to student learning?

LATE SEPTEMBER
Assessing Student Progress

5

From the Authors' Notebook

In this chapter, the vital connection between instruction and assessment, already discussed in Chapter 4, is extended with a concentrated focus on classroom assessment. The reader is introduced to the underlying principles of how and why the assessment of student performance must be linked to instruction. The authors also address how teachers can develop an overarching and integrated approach to assessment, and they describe how a well-planned and comprehensive approach provides students with optimal opportunities to demonstrate their learning. This chapter makes it clear that detailed approaches to assessment that are directly connected to instruction allow teachers to professionally justify the assessment choices they make and implement.

Primary Learning Objectives

After reading this chapter, you should understand the importance of

1. considering student assessment before planning and implementing instruction;
2. discussing in-class assessment with students;
3. using formative and summative assessments;
4. establishing assessment validity;
5. applying Bloom's taxonomy of cognitive skills to assessment;
6. knowing how to construct a Table of Specifications;
7. including various types of selected-response and constructed-response questions in assessment;
8. using authentic problems in assessment;
9. analyzing and reviewing the use of assessment tools; and
10. obtaining student feedback on assessment.

Deciding on an Approach to Assessment

After a full week of implementing her newly designed lesson plans, Annette has slipped into a comfortable daily routine. She is amazed at how smoothly things are running in *The Little Red Schoolhouse*. With the help of her colleagues, she has been able to immerse all of her new students in appropriate learning activities. On this Friday morning in late September, she expresses her appreciation to Mr. Hayes, Mrs. McCarthy, and Mr. Parker at the beginning of their early morning meeting. "I want to thank all three of you for the hard work you have put in to get this school year started off on a very positive note. I think we've laid the foundation for a great teaching team. Let's continue to talk openly about our concerns and work collaboratively to resolve any problems that come up. We can definitely learn a lot from each other. I know I've already learned a great deal from each of you. I'm looking forward to having your continuing help and support throughout this school year. The stronger we are as a team, the more our students will benefit."

After listening to her colleagues express their views about how the past few weeks have gone, Annette moves on to her most pressing issue—assessment. "I want to talk a little more about assessment, even though we touched on it last week when I talked about my approach to instruction. I think it would be helpful for you to fully understand how I plan to handle the assessment of student learning. It's really not all that complicated. Just as I was very explicit with the class about the critical elements of good classroom management, I've also decided to be absolutely clear about the critical elements of how their academic progress will be assessed. Again, I believe that student success in the classroom is predicated upon teachers and students understanding and fulfilling their respective roles. I know that if students understand what they have to do to learn effectively and are clear on how their learning will be graded and reported, they are far more likely to positively direct their learning and studying energies. As well as providing them with this important sense of control over their schooling, I want to eliminate any misperceptions they may have about how marks are assigned. My experience has taught me that heightened student awareness about assessment criteria also means heightened student responsibility for assessment outcomes. The clear and simple message I want the students to receive is that they have a responsibility to be active and diligent learners; their grades will reflect how seriously they carry out their role in the process. If they are responsible and do the things they should, they'll do well. If they don't, they won't achieve their potential. Not only will this straightforward message reduce the need for us to pressure them to pay attention during lessons, work hard in class, complete assignments, and study for tests and exams, but it will also virtually eliminate the common excuses that students use to absolve themselves of responsibility for their actions and resulting grades. We've all heard excuses like 'I didn't know it was due today,' 'that test was unfair,' or 'you never gave us enough time.' In cases where assessment methods are appropriate and fair, and clearly understood, these excuses indicate nothing more than poor planning or a lack of effort on the students' part. This isn't to say that students never have legitimate reasons for forgetting to hand in assignments or for failing to plan or study properly. These things happen, so we'll have to judge these situations on their individual merits and provide remedies as we see fit. For example, due date extensions, test rewrites, and alternative assignments are always a possibility. But by being very explicit with the students about everything related to assessment, I hope to significantly reduce excuses like these as reasons for poor scholastic performance." The first bell of the school day interrupts the team's meeting, so Annette quickly summarizes her thoughts on assessment. "My basic message about assessment is that I'll take my usual approach—I'll be explicit with the students about what I expect of them, and I'll also tell them what they can expect from me. Of course, my message to the younger students will be somewhat simplified, but it will still contain the same ideas."

Talking to Students about Assessment

Once the students are settled in their seats and the start-of-the-day activities are over, Annette invites the older students and Mr. Hayes to join her in the lunchroom. Mrs. McCarthy remains in the classroom to help the younger students with a creative arts project. The older students are obviously both pleased to have permission to leave the classroom and curious about what Ms. Elkins has planned.

Annette asks them to have a seat around a large table. She begins by asking for their feedback on how school is going so far. They seem a little surprised by this question, and at first they are hesitant to respond. Once Annette reassures them that they have done nothing wrong and she is simply interested in hearing their views, they begin to talk openly. Their comments are mostly positive, and while they do not like everything about school, they seem to like spending time in the classroom environment that Annette has created. Annette compliments them on their good classroom behaviour to date and turns the conversation to assessment. "Remember when we had our talk a little while ago about establishing the class rules? One of the most important things I said was that 'I want all of you to be very successful in your school work.' So, what does that really mean? Well, in my mind, academic success is all about learning. It's my job to assess how much and how well you have learned so I can determine your progress and assign you appropriate grades. Today, I want to share with you how your work will be assessed and what you have to do to get good grades. I can already tell that you're all very capable students, and I can think of no reason why anyone in this class should not do well. I'm going to do my very best to make our lessons exciting and interesting, and I'll create assignments, tests, and exams that are demanding but fair. That way, your grades will be a true reflection of your learning. I also want you to know that I'm always available for extra help if any of you need it. This can be during class, before or after school, or during recess or lunch. For the most part, I'm going to leave it up to you to ask for help when you need it, but I know that people are sometimes too embarrassed to ask for help, so I'll check with you from time to time to see how things are going."

Annette continues talking as she pulls out a large piece of chart paper and tapes it to the wall. "Here's what you need to do to be successful in my classroom. You don't have to write this down. I'll give each of you a copy in a minute. I just want you to think about these ideas carefully, and then we can talk about them."

How to Be a Successful Learner

<u>Come to school every day</u>—I can only help you learn and achieve if you are here.

<u>Make sure you have everything you need</u> (e.g., pencils, pens, scribblers, calculators, homework, lunch, and indoor shoes)—I cannot help you learn if you are not prepared.

<u>Pay attention during class, take notes, and do the assigned seatwork</u>—I will tell you when seatwork will be marked or not marked.

<u>Complete all assignments</u>—I will not give you very much homework, but what I assign will be important, and you will be marked on all of it.

<u>Study for all tests and exams</u>—I will give you lots of notice about each test and exam, and I will also provide a brief review of the material you will be tested on. It is your responsibility to be well prepared by studying a little bit every day.

<u>Ask questions if you do not understand something</u>—If you have a question, it is very likely someone else in the class is wondering about the same thing. If you do not ask questions, I will not know when you need help.

After the students have read the list and chatted among themselves for a few minutes, Brandon is the first to voice his opinion. "Why are we going to be marked on our homework? Last year we were only marked on the work we did in school, like tests and big assignments. Homework was just work that we didn't finish in class or sheets of questions that gave us extra practice on things we had trouble understanding. We didn't get marks for any of that. Some people never even handed in their homework. And anyway, I don't think we'll do very well if you give us lots of school work to do at night, because some of us have lots of other things to do, like sports and jobs. We won't have time to do tons of homework every night."

"Yeah," says Caleb dejectedly, "I'm on the hockey team, and I have practice almost every day from 4:30 to 6:00. When I get home from school, I have to go to the rink right away, and by the time I get home after practice I'm way too tired to do homework. I usually eat my supper and fall asleep watching TV."

"Well, first of all, let's remember what we already decided about homework when we came up with our class rules," Annette replies calmly. "Rule #8 says that if you complete your homework during the week, I won't assign any homework on the weekends. So that means you will really only have homework on four nights—Monday through Thursday.

Second, I want it to be perfectly clear that when I say homework, I'm only talking about small assignments that should take you less than one hour to complete. Besides, on most days, if you use your class time wisely, most of you will finish the assignment before you even leave school, so your homework should not interfere with your after-school activities. Just as your teacher did last year, I'll use homework to reinforce difficult concepts or to provide you with extra practice. I think it's only fair that if you do the work, you should get credit for it. Your marks for homework won't be worth as much as the marks you get for tests or major assignments, but your overall homework mark could certainly make the difference between a 'C' and a 'B' or a 'B' and an 'A.' I also want to be clear that I'll always make sure that you have plenty of time to complete any homework I give you. I'll never give you homework that's due on the same day as one of your big assignments or on the day of a test, and except for some advanced readings for the older students, which won't be graded, I'll never use homework to introduce new topics. Remember, my overall goal is to give you every opportunity to be successful in this class. I think you'll find that the homework I assign will help you with learning. I have no intention of assigning homework just for the sake of you having to do school work at night."

Annette pauses so that her students can digest what she has just said. She then continues. "I'd like you to keep in mind that homework is a very important learning device that gives you a chance to practise certain skills and demonstrate what you've learned. It also tells me how well things are progressing in each subject area. The other thing you should know is that all of your homework assignments will focus on exactly the same types of things that you'll see on your tests. That means that if you do all your homework, you will be very well prepared. On the other hand, it also means that if you copy someone else's homework instead of doing it yourself, you may get good marks but you certainly won't know the material for your tests."

"And . . . it also means . . . ," says Brandon slowly, as the thought dawns on him, ". . . that if we do all of our homework, we can get good homework marks *and* we won't have to study as much for tests. So it sort of saves us time in a way."

"That's exactly right," replies Annette, "Not only that, you will probably do much better on the tests *because* you did your homework. In fact, you should think of all homework assignments as mini study sessions for your next test. Do all of your homework, and you won't have to study as hard or cram for tests."

She waits while this tidbit registers. "I hope you can see how homework is a vital part of your academic success instead of just an extra part of school that takes up your evenings and for which you get no credit."

"It makes sense to me," states Simon. "Last year we only did our homework if we felt like it. It was never worth anything, except the really big projects. If homework is going to be worth something, and it reduces our studying time, and helps us do well on tests, it's like getting double marks for the same work."

"Hey," says Katherine with a laugh, "wait till I tell my mom that we are going to have less homework than ever before and that it'll be worth a lot more. She thinks that unless I have at least two hours of homework a night, I'm not really learning anything. I like this idea of doing homework for marks. No, actually, I love it!" Katherine grins from ear to ear as the rest of the room smiles along with her.

"Yes, that's certainly one way of looking at it," Annette responds as she begins to pass out copies of her "How to Be a Successful Learner" handout. She muses to herself on how often students are able to boil things down to what truly matters; in this case, it is all about spending less time on homework and getting better grades. She does not really care how they think about it as long as they approach their school work with enthusiasm. She can see that they are all motivated by the fact that they will receive credit for their homework. She knows that by completing homework assignments, they will learn, and that is what is most important. She also knows that her students will figure out soon enough that a little bit of studying intermittently is better than cramming for a test.

"Okay, if there are no further questions, let's break for recess a little early. I'll go over some other details with you when you come back," Annette says as she begins to tidy up her material.

Homework

Much has been written about the benefits as well as the misuses of homework. The following is a synthesis of the benefits that can be realized from assigning homework and the factors that make homework a worthwhile educational endeavour for both teachers and students.

The primary benefits that can be realized from homework include

- additional practice with and/or the reinforcement of concepts and skills learned in the classroom;
- higher educational achievement at the secondary level (Cooper & Valentine, 2001);
- the development and enhancement of study, organizational, and time-management skills (O'Donnell, D'Amico, Schmid, Reeve, & Smith, 2008); and
- the development of elementary students' study strategies and self-regulatory skills even though homework has little, if any, effect on their academic performance (Cooper & Valentine, 2001).

These benefits are minimized or eliminated unless homework is

- linked to high expectations for student academic success (Newmann, 1991);
- governed by an overall homework policy that focuses on how assignments affect learning and how they are related to classroom instruction (O'Donnell et al., 2008);
- made up of smaller, frequent assignments rather than larger, infrequent assignments (Cooper, 1989);
- appropriate, challenging, meaningful, and graded and returned promptly (Berliner & Calfee, 1996); and
- differentiated according to whether the teacher wants students to practise or reinforce concepts, be exposed to new material (usually by reading), or extend their learning beyond the classroom, usually involving student interests and preferences (LaConte, 1981).

As Annette and Mr. Hayes walk back to the classroom, Mr. Hayes says, "Well, Annette, I'm impressed at how the students responded to your description of how homework will be handled this year. They did nothing but gripe about homework all of last year . . . and they usually put little or no effort into completing the assignments. I guess I can't blame them if they felt that their efforts weren't valued."

Annette laughs, "Oh, I'm sure the same types of things will happen this year, but I don't think they'll happen nearly as often. You know, sometimes we just aren't explicit enough with our students. By taking the time to state things clearly, we can at least reduce the chances of students' misinterpreting what we mean or choosing to misinterpret what we mean so they can use it as an excuse for not doing their work. I want to make a point of sending clear and direct messages so that there's no perception that I have any hidden agendas. I want all of my students to be quite clear on what I expect of them. My main goal this morning was for them to be fully aware that they have to work hard to get good grades and they can also get lots of help from us if they need it. By delivering this message, I'm giving them every opportunity to control their learning and their grades. Hopefully, this will have a self-regulatory effect. I don't want them to be apathetic about learning, because I've seen that happen before and it isn't a good situation. Apathetic students often see the teacher as the only person in the room who's responsible for learning and achievement, and as a result, all the effort comes from the teacher rather than the students. Some of my colleagues have fallen into the emotional trap of feeling like they've failed as teachers because despite all the wonderful teaching they did, their students performed poorly. Their guilt then led them to compromise their teaching by spoon-feeding knowledge, making assignments and tests less demanding, and awarding marks for effort and results that were not worthy. That's not what I want to see happen in my classroom. I think we can avoid student apathy by making it clear to them that they have a very important role to fill in the learning process."

"There was definitely a bit of that in this group last year," admits Mr. Hayes. "They had little input into what went on in the classroom, homework often didn't get done, and they were frequently at odds with the teacher over their grades. It got quite uncomfortable at times, especially when some of the parents got involved. The kids seem much more enthusiastic this year. It all started when you laid out your approach to classroom management, and now you've followed that up with a very similar approach to homework and assessment. Just like everybody else, they like to know ahead of time how things are going to unfold. It's really nice to see their upbeat attitudes. Even I feel more excited about coming to school."

Annette is pleased to receive a compliment from Mr. Hayes. She is confident that his openness is a direct result of her efforts to make the educational assistants feel like valued members of the teaching team. She was somewhat apprehensive about having to define their roles more clearly, but her honest and sincere approach seems to have worked.

"Annette," continues Mr. Hayes, almost shyly, "assessment is a topic that has always interested me, but I haven't had the chance to really study it in any detail. I was wondering . . . do you have some material I could read?"

"Of course," Annette replies quickly. "Let me get some stuff together over the weekend, and I'll give it to you Monday. It wouldn't hurt for me to read through it again myself."

"Thanks. I'd really appreciate that," says Mr. Hayes as he leaves to check on Jacob and Troy, who are spending recess inside.

Annette enters her classroom and logs on to her computer to check her e-mail before recess ends. She finds an e-mail from Dr. Cameron.

Practicum Placement

Andrew Cameron <acameron@university.ca>
Date: Thursday, September 26, 2013 11:22 PM
To: Annette Elkins <annette_elkins@schoolmail.com>

Dear Annette,

I hope all is well in your school and that you're enjoying the term so far. We're having a wonderful fall season with warm temperatures and some of the most vivid colours I've seen for a long time. I imagine it's much cooler in George Lake.

I have a very big favour to ask. A Grade 8 teacher from one of our local schools has suddenly taken ill, and she won't be able to supervise the student teacher we assigned to her for the six-week practicum this term. The student, Aaron Jones, is from a small town fairly close to your school, so I was wondering whether you might be willing to be his supervising teacher. You'd only have to fill this role for the initial six weeks, since we'll try to find Aaron other placements for his winter and spring sessions.

Please get back to me ASAP.

Thanks in advance,

Andrew

Annette ponders Dr. Cameron's request. "Hmmmm . . . do I want a student teacher? I guess it would be nice to have an extra pair of hands around here, and you never know what new things he might bring to the table. Maybe this is perfect timing for me with midterm tests for the older students and report cards for the younger students just around the corner. Aaron will certainly get lots of good experience working with students of all ages!"

Annette grabs a granola bar from her lunch bag and munches on it while replying to Dr. Cameron's e-mail. She then tackles the other e-mails that have piled up in her inbox. Before she can finish reading the last one, the bell rings, signalling that recess is over. The students return noisily to the classroom. Apparently, several deer were sighted just across the road from the school, so Annette takes the time to listen to the students' animated descriptions of the deer's activities. Once the excitement has died down, Annette takes the younger students to Mr. Parker's room for a language arts class and then returns to the classroom to resume her discussion of assessment with the older students.

She begins by asking if the students have any questions about what was discussed before recess. "Uh, . . . Ms. Elkins . . . ," Anna says quietly, "we were talking during recess and . . . uh . . . we'd like to know if we are going to have a lot of tests this year. Some of us don't like tests because we never do as well as when we have to write essays or do projects. I know I just get too nervous when I have to write a test." Although Anna is doing all the talking, several other members of the class nod in agreement. They had obviously talked about this issue at length. It was important.

"I do okay on tests," interjects Sophie, "but the fewer essays I have to write, the better, especially if it's on a test. They take so long to do, and I always run out of time. I do way better on essays for homework because I can take as long as I like."

"Yes, we'll have tests," replies Annette, "and we'll also have essays, both for homework and on some tests—it all depends on how I want to test your knowledge."

"Why do we even have to have tests anyways?" asks Simon, feigning indignation. "Can't you just give us a mark based on our homework and how hard we work in class?"

"It's funny you should say that, Simon, since these are exactly the issues I want to talk about this period. I want you to understand how I'm going to mark your work and assign grades. Let's call it our assessment system. This system will consist of the different methods that I'll use to assess your learning. It's going to include tests and essays, but it will also include marks for homework, projects, in-class presentations, and your portfolios. You see, I know that not everybody does equally well on tests, and the same goes for essays or projects and even homework. But by using a variety of assessment methods, I'll give every person a fair chance to show me what they've learned. This system will not only give me a more accurate picture of how well everyone has learned but also let me know how well my teaching is going. Remember, to a certain degree my teaching is guided by your learning. It's my responsibility to be able to make changes to my instruction if your performance indicates that changes are needed. For example, if one of you is having difficulty with an algebra assignment, I need to do something more, or something different, to help you grasp the material. If several of you were to do poorly on an algebra test, then I'd know that we need to spend more time on the concepts covered on the test before moving on to more advanced algebra. In other words, your academic performance is at the centre of everything that happens in this classroom. Without using tests or assignments to find out how well you're doing, we'd have difficulty making any progress at all."

Katherine pipes up immediately. "Are we going to do any of those special tests that we did last year? My cousins in Vancouver did the same ones. Those tests ask you to do stuff that you haven't even done in class before. What's the point of that?"

"Good question, Katherine," Annette responds. "The tests that you're talking about aren't really a part of our classroom assessment system, but you have to do these tests so that the Ministry of Education can capture an overall picture of how well all students in all schools are learning. It's part of the government's system of monitoring everyone's education, but your marks on those tests don't count toward the grades that I'll give you." Annette wanted to keep the conversation on what would happen in their school, not on what happened elsewhere, especially when it did not affect their learning or their grades. "Let's get back to my assessment of your learning. Now, there are also going to be times when I'll ask you to grade your own work so you can see how well you're doing. I'll mark those tests and assignments afterwards to make sure they're graded properly. Each term, I'll also give you the option of dropping your lowest assignment or test mark in each subject."

"I like both of those ideas, but I'm not sure I understand why you're letting us do those things," Anna comments.

Annette is pleased to see Anna talking positively about assessment issues. She obviously has a great interest in how she will be marked, and that falls in line with the fact that she experiences test anxiety. Annette reassures her by saying, "I want these ideas to be a part of our assessment system because I think you'll be more inclined to work and study more effectively if (a) you know exactly how things are graded and (b) you know you can maintain a good average even if you have one bad test or project. After all, none of us is perfect. It's unrealistic to expect that any of you will perform your very best on every single assignment and test that I give you this year. It was the same for me when I was in school. A low mark didn't mean that I was a poor student. It just meant that I scored less than I should have on one of the progress indicators used in my teacher's overall assessment system."

"I get it," says Jackson loudly. "And if I mark my own work, I'll learn how to do better next time." He pauses and then seems less excited after thinking it over. "But how will marking my own work really help? Won't every assignment and test be different?"

Annette smiles at Jackson. "Yes and no. My assignments and tests usually require similar types of thinking and reasoning even though they're about different topics. I'd be extremely happy if you learned how to study better from marking your own work. I want you to feel that your grades are the result of hard work and good studying rather than being lucky in choosing what to study."

"Yeah," agrees Sophie, "I got caught like that last year. I thought we were going to be tested on the systems of government in Canada, but the test was about both Canada and the United States, even though we only spent one day in class talking about the US system. I lost a lot of marks because of that, and I almost failed the test."

"Well, there will be no secrets and no guessing when it comes to my tests," says Annette firmly. "I'll tell you exactly what to study and what to ignore."

"Why?" asks Anna. "Won't that make it easier?"

"Yes, it will make it easier for you to answer test questions that require factual information, but if you don't pay attention in class to the connections we make between different concepts, you won't do very well on the parts of the tests that require you to show me your thinking and reasoning skills."

Annette continues while she has the students' full attention. "I'll use various types of questions to test for factual and conceptual knowledge. That doesn't mean that the tests will be really long. You see, I know that you'll learn more and do better if I give you shorter tests and assignments on a more frequent basis, say a short test every two or three weeks rather than one per month. That way, I'll have more chances to give you accurate and timely feedback about how you're doing and what you can do to improve. The way I see it, the more you know about how well you're doing, and what you can do to improve your grades, the more motivated you will be."

"How will we know exactly what we have to do to improve? What does a mark really tell us?" asks Anna. This question causes a cascade of negative emotions within Annette when she realizes that very little of their previous assessment feedback was in the form of written, constructive comments. "Yes," she muses to herself. "What could they ever learn from a number?" She then takes the time to explain that they will always receive written and oral comments about their work, especially in terms of how they can do better next time. "Any more questions?" she asks as she checks her watch.

Simon has been paying close attention. "Miss? It sounds like we are going to have an awful lot of tests . . . more than we had last year."

"Oh, but I have some good news for you, Simon," says Annette with a wry smile. "Yes, you may have more tests than last year, but my tests will be at least 50% shorter, so you won't have to study as much material. I'll usually have at least two tests per unit, so the studying you do for the first one will also help you on the next one. Even though the second test won't cover the same material as the first, the information will be related. I think that's fairer than expecting you to study and remember everything for one large test that's worth all the marks for the unit. You also have to remember that I'll be marking your homework, so sometimes I'll use those marks for your overall grade instead of a test. As I'm sure you can appreciate, there's no sense having you write a test if it covers exactly the same material you worked on for homework. I'll only do that if I need the test to do something different from what was assessed in your homework."

"So, more frequently actually means less?" Simon laughs. "I like that logic!"

"Yes, in this case, that's exactly what it means," Annette concedes as the period ends. "Okay, time for gym. We can talk about our assessment system again later if you still have some questions."

Later, on the weekend, Annette is tired but content after a morning hike with a friend up Wilson's Peak. The climb to the snow-covered summit took a great deal of effort, but she is happy she persisted with the trek, because the view from the top was spectacular. She took some photos to e-mail to her friends, especially the ones who wondered why she wanted to move to the "middle of nowhere."

> **think box**
>
> Consider the discussion Annette has just had with the older students about assessment. How might she alter her approach when relaying similar information to the younger students? What information on assessment is most important for the younger students to understand?

Now, as she relaxes in her favourite armchair with her tired legs resting on the matching ottoman, she begins sorting through all the material she has on the topic of assessment. She wants to follow up immediately on Mr. Hayes's request for reading material. Before long, she is intently reading through the material herself.

Assessment of Student Learning

Except for the social part of school, most of what happens in education revolves around teaching and then assessing whether or not students have learned. The foremost goal of instruction is to optimize student learning. The best educational interplay between good teaching, excellent learning, and appropriate assessment occurs when assessment principles are used *a priori* to guide instruction (see Figure 5.1). Optimally, teachers first consult curriculum guides to determine what they want students to learn and then decide how to best assess student learning. From there, they establish what to teach to achieve that learning, and finally, they come to a conclusion about how to best teach the material to achieve all of the above.

What educational devices do teachers use when assessing student progress? Classroom assessment refers to the utilization of a variety of teacher-generated assessment tools. The term "assessment tool" can refer either to a single question or assignment that assesses student knowledge and/or skills or to a collection of different types of questions in the form of larger

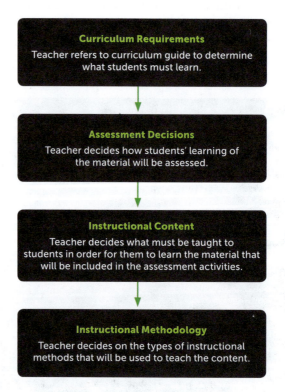

FIGURE 5.1 Interplay between Teaching, Learning, and Assessment

assignments, tests, or exams. Given that teachers teach a variety of concepts and topics while purposefully using a variety of different instructional methods, they must be open to using a variety of different assessment tools so that they can properly ascertain the full scope of student learning. For example, there is no reason why students cannot write paragraphs to explain math concepts (instead of always completing calculation questions), and similarly, there is no reason why students cannot draw and use flow charts to demonstrate their understanding of written material (instead of always writing an essay). Regardless of whether it is one question or several, and regardless of the type of tool used, the primary function of a good assessment tool is to allow students to demonstrate what they have learned; its secondary function is to provide grades to indicate student learning performance.

But where, exactly, do assessment questions come from? Further, how can teachers be confident that their questions, assignments, and tests/exams are appropriate given what is being taught? The following sections present the systematic process of designing appropriate assessment tools, followed by more specific details on the different types of questions available and their appropriate uses. But first, it is important to consider the educational reasons for assessment.

The Purposes of Assessment

As already stated, the overarching purpose of academic assessment is to measure and indicate student achievement. Within an assessment system, there are three subsidiary purposes of assessment, which have significant influence at different stages of the teaching process:

Diagnostic Assessment

This type of assessment is completed before instruction to determine instructional starting points and to refine and adjust teaching methods.

Formative Assessment

There are two types of formative assessment that take place during instruction. Each serves a different but related purpose. In the first type of formative assessment, teachers assess or get a sense of student understandings by constantly asking students curricular questions as lessons are taught and by closely monitoring students' performance and understanding as they complete in-class seatwork and group work. Teachers use this steady form of feedback to refine and modify all aspects of their teaching as it unfolds to ensure that their lessons present information that is suitably challenging-but-attainable. This is one of the main reasons why teacher–student and student–student discourses are important parts of the instructional process. Question-asking and the resulting discourse allow teachers to check for understanding and clear up potential misconceptions. In the second and more common type of formative assessment, teachers use assigned seatwork, homework, class participation, or short quizzes to obtain accumulating grades for student work completed during units of instruction. This data also provides feedback that can be used for monitoring instructional progress, modifying teaching methods, and adapting future assessments. For example, if grades on a short quiz indicate mastery of the material by the vast majority of students, teachers can eliminate further lessons (or parts of lessons) and homework related to that topic. Conversely, if the quiz reveals non-mastery or considerable misunderstandings, teachers should provide a review or assign extra seatwork to make sure that the concepts are consolidated before moving on. This is an important consideration, because many topics and concepts are predicated on student understandings of preceding topics and concepts.

Formative Assessment

There was a time in education and schooling when, for assessment purposes, it was acceptable that teachers would simply construct and administer tests and assignments that matched the learning objectives of the curriculum and then assign grades accordingly. While these elements of assessment are still critically important, research in educational psychology has demonstrated that student assessment is far more effective if teachers also use assessment tools to discover what students do or do not understand. They do this with a view to improving both student learning and teacher instruction. The seven vital elements that underpin this formative type of assessment are as follows (adapted from Shepard, Hammerness, Darling-Hammond, & Rust, 2005, pp. 275–288):

1. Teachers must have a deep understanding of the formative assessment process and understand its close relationship to instructional scaffolding.
2. Students should be afforded multiple ways to demonstrate their proficiency.
3. Student progress should be judged in relation to performance expectations rather than in comparison to other students.
4. Students must have a clear understanding of the criteria by which their work will be assessed.
5. Teacher feedback from assessment must occur strategically throughout the learning process (not only when teaching on that topic is finished).
6. Feedback is most effective when it focuses on particular qualities of a student's work in relation to established criteria, identifies strengths as well as weaknesses, and provides guidance about what to do to improve.
7. Teachers can dramatically improve the effectiveness of feedback by focusing on three questions: What is the key error? What is the probable reason the student made this error? How can I guide the student to avoid the error in the future? (from Elawar & Corno, 1985)

To best discover what students do and do not understand, teachers should use various types of seatwork, assignments, and test questions that examine students' problem-solving and metacognitive abilities, not merely those that examine knowledge and comprehension. In grading these more sophisticated and complex types of questions, teachers have to ensure that they do not simply grade what is easy to count or quantify, but look for the special elements in students' answers that demonstrate the quality of their work.

Summative Assessment

By far the most common of the three stages of assessment, **summative assessment** takes place after instruction, preferably immediately following the completion of an instructional unit. The main purpose of summative assessment is to indicate how well students have learned the material, and when combined with all of the accumulated formative assessment grades mentioned above, it provides an overall grade for a particular reporting period. This data on student performance and progress also forms the basis for teachers' decisions regarding potential reviews of specific curricular material, as well as student promotion and graduation.

> **think box**
>
> Consider your own school experiences. What types of assessment do you remember your teachers using (i.e., diagnostic, formative, summative)? How aware were you of the purposes of these different types of assessment? As a teacher, will you use assessment in a similar way? Why or why not?

The Assessment Design Process

Just as research regarding effective classroom practices for both behaviour management and instruction is founded on systematized and proven design processes, so too is assessment. Effective assessment design produces tools and measures of student achievement (questions or collections of questions) that consistently and accurately test what students know or can do.

Designing Questions

Where do assessment questions come from? As with good lesson planning, the keystone of assessment design is the teacher's adherence to the fundamental principle of backward design. This principle dictates that assessment questions must be derived from exactly the same learning objectives used to create larger units of instruction as well as daily lesson plans (Wiggins & McTighe, 2001). For example, refer again to the lesson plan in Chapter 4 that contains the following specific learning objective—*to be able to successfully calculate two-column addition without carrying*. When developing this lesson plan, the teacher created the following questions to use when assessing whether or not students had attained this particular skill:

$$\begin{array}{ccc} 23 & 11 & 71 \\ +\,15 & +\,55 & +\,18 \\ \hline \end{array}$$

    These questions are conceptually identical to the examples the teacher will use when she teaches the concept, and they are similar in content to the questions her students will tackle during seatwork or for homework. Because the teacher knows precisely what her students are supposed to learn and exactly how she will assess their knowledge/skills, she designs her teaching of the math content to make sure this happens. This process provides her with ready-made assessment questions for that specific learning objective once the lesson or unit is finished. Moreover, because the questions were based on the learning objective, the teacher can be quite confident that the questions are appropriate.

    It is impractical, however, to formatively assess each and every learning objective as it is taught, so teachers often finish a unit of instruction that has taken several days to present and then design a test or assignment that assesses several related learning objectives together. For example, *two-column addition without carrying* would likely be assessed at the same time as *single-column addition without carrying* and *single- and two-column subtraction without borrowing*, or it might be included with *single- and two-column addition with carrying and single- and two-column subtraction with borrowing*. Determining when a learning objective should be assessed, and which other related objectives are assessed at the same time, depends on its placement within the teacher's unit of instruction.

Designing Tests and Exams

Given that the overarching purpose of assessment is to indicate student achievement, then by extension, assessment is also used to hold teachers accountable for student performance. Educators have lived in an era of teacher accountability for several decades, but with the recent growing demand for less reliance on standardized tests and increased reliance on classroom-based assessment, teacher-made tests must be able to withstand considerable scrutiny. The very best criteria by which to judge the suitability of a test, including one made by a teacher, are its reliability and validity. Reliability is the extent to which a test produces consistent results, and validity is the extent to which a test assesses what it is supposed to assess. **Content validity** is the most important criterion in teacher-generated assessments, because it pointedly evaluates whether a test and the questions contained therein properly address the essence of the content that was taught. There is a simple but effective two-step process for making sure a teacher-made test has high validity. The first step establishes the validity of each individual test question, while the second establishes the validity of the entire test:

Assessment validity—Step 1

If the principles of backward design have been followed whereby identical learning objectives were used for lesson plan design and for assessment question generation, then the assessment questions will usually have very high validity. We know this because content validity is typically evaluated and confirmed by comparing test questions to the lessons that were taught to see whether they both address the same curricular content. In other words, when teachers adhere to the principles of backward design, they not only create both precise lessons and suitable test questions, they also ensure that their test questions have high validity. This important first step provides teacher-made tests with curricular credibility. On any given day, it allows teachers to confidently explain, should anyone ask, how their teaching is directly related to indicators of student learning.

Assessment validity—Step 2

With high validity established for all assessment questions, the second step for teachers is to make sure that their entire test is equally well constructed. Building a valid test or exam, however, is not simply a case of using all of the assessment questions contained in all the lesson plans in a unit. First, this would very likely result in too many questions, but more important, it would place too much emphasis on some concepts and not enough on others or too much emphasis on lower-order thinking at the expense of higher-order skills, or vice versa. In other words, even though each of the individual questions has high content validity, the overall test would be inappropriate because it does not accurately reflect the emphasis of what was taught. Such a test would have poor validity.

Table of Specifications

In order to be confident that they are constructing tests that have high validity, educators use a **Table of Specifications** (Chase, 1999; Guskey, 2005). This is a table, or chart, that systematically outlines (a) the topics covered by the test, (b) the number of questions used to assess each topic, and (c) the level of thinking required for each category of questions based on Bloom's taxonomy of cognitive skills (see Table 4.1). For assessment purposes, the six levels of thinking in Bloom's taxonomy are reduced to three levels in a Table of Specifications because (a) the thinking skills within each group are very similar and (b) it is easier to differentiate between the thinking skills across groups. The three levels are (1) Knowledge, (2) Comprehension/Application, and (3) Analysis/Synthesis/Evaluation.

The primary purpose of the Table of Specifications is to ensure that a test contains a fair and representative set of questions that properly reflect the curricular emphasis of the instruction provided. This enhances the validity of the test. Once the purpose and process of creating the Table of Specifications are understood, and if the teacher has used backward design to construct both the lessons and the assessment questions, building a valid test or exam becomes a fairly straightforward fill-in-the-blank exercise. Table 5.1 illustrates a Table of Specifications that a university professor used to construct an end-of-term test in her statistics course.

The professor used a step-by-step process to complete the table. All the steps in the process were predicated on the fact that the university assessment policy required instructors to assign an end-of-term test with a maximum time limit of two hours. In most schools, the time frame for teacher-made tests is usually one instructional period (or less) or, in the case of secondary schools, a set amount of time during an exam period, typically one to two hours (or less).

Step 1 The professor filled in the five Topical Domains (column 1). These are the major units of instruction that she covered in the first half of her course: Measurement, Central Tendency, Norms, Validity, and Reliability.

Step 2 Then, based on the different types of questions contained in her lesson plans, she decided that in two hours students could easily answer a total of 50 questions (bottom right cell) and still have about 15 to 20 minutes left for review. She confirmed this time frame by completing the test herself (in about 25 to 30 minutes) and then allowing three to four times that amount of time for her students.

Step 3 Next, based on her time spent teaching and the emphasis she placed on each unit or topic within a unit, she decided on the emphasis percentage for each topical domain, and as a percentage of 50 total questions, she determined the number of test questions per unit (column 5). For example, her instruction on Norms took 20% of the time and emphasis of the course, so she allotted 10 questions on Norms (20% of 50).

Step 4 Based on the verbs used in her lesson plan objectives, she determined the proportion of Bloom's levels of thinking within each unit and assigned questions to match. For example, her lessons on Measurement emphasized slightly more Knowledge than Comprehension/Application processing but did not require Analytic, Synthetic, or Evaluative thinking; therefore, she allotted three questions, two questions, and zero questions, respectively. It is obvious from this breakdown that her Measurement unit dealt mainly with the knowledge of basic facts and the understanding and use of measurement applications and calculations. Similarly, it is clear that her units on Norms, Validity, and Reliability dealt with more abstract concepts; consequently, she used more higher-order thinking questions. (Note: Details on the types of questions to be used for Bloom's different levels of thinking are contained in the next section.)

Step 5 Finally, she filled in Bloom's Level Totals and cross-checked these numbers with the ones in column 5 to make sure that (a) each level was proportionally reflective of the thinking emphasis in her lessons/units and (b) the total number of questions was consistent at 50.

TABLE 5.1 Table of Specifications—Educational Statistics 521

Topical Domains	Bloom's Levels of Thinking			Topic Emphasis and Question Totals
	Knowledge	Comprehension/ Application	Analysis/Synthesis/ Evaluation	
Measurement	3	2	0	5 (10%)
Central Tendency	1	2	2	5 (10%)
Norms	3	3	4	10 (20%)
Validity	4	6	5	15 (30%)
Reliability	4	7	4	15 (30%)
Bloom's Level Totals	15 (30%)	20 (40%)	15 (30%)	50 (100%)

The primary benefit of using a Table of Specifications is that it recycles many of the instructional tasks that teachers have already completed. Teachers have already divided the entire curriculum/course into smaller instructional units (column 1), and based on the thinking verbs contained in their learning objectives, they have already designed assessment questions for all lessons in each unit (columns 2, 3, and 4). The Table of Specifications simply reuses these instructional elements in a systematized way to ensure that the number of questions per unit, and per type of thinking, accurately reflect the instructional emphasis. When assessment questions and instruction are created using the learning objective principles contained in backward design, and when tests are constructed by following the Table of Specifications process, tests are said to have excellent content validity.

Testing Issues

The two main issues teachers face regarding the testing of student learning are the appropriateness of the test questions and the frequency of assessment. In terms of appropriateness, test questions must be designed as described above—they must match the information that was taught as well as the teaching methodology used. Students should never be surprised or confused by the type and content of the questions on a test.

Annette stops reading for a moment as she remembers something that happened in one of her previous schools, a scenario she later learned was unfortunately common among teachers who were not well versed in designing instruction or assessment. As she was preparing material in her secondary-school classroom, students were filing in and talking about a test they had just finished in their Grade 11 science class. Many of them felt they had failed the test because "who ever heard of the answers to multiple-choice questions being 'A and B but not C or D' or 'A and B and C but not D'? It was totally confusing." One of them stated very firmly, "Well, at least that's better than that stupid 'higher-order thinking test' we did three weeks ago—that was so bad. How could you ever study for that? None of the questions made any sense." Clearly, the students were not happy with what was happening in their science classroom. "Yeah," said another, "that first test he gave us in September was soooo easy . . . it was all about facts and figures, simple stuff that anyone with half a brain would know if they paid attention in class and took a few notes. Maybe that test was a little too easy, but at least I could do it. I practically failed all the tests since then. There's hardly any point in studying anymore because it doesn't make any difference in my marks!" The more they talked, the clearer it became to Annette that the science teacher was caught in a common teaching conundrum. Later, in a staff room conversation, Annette learned what had happened. The science teacher had begun the term by teaching factual knowledge; he did this by simply going through the lists of information found in the curricular guides, teaching the listed facts and having the students write down what he was saying—verbatim. When it came time for a test, the students who studied did very well, and many got perfect or near-perfect grades. Word got around that this teacher's course was easy. To restore his credibility, the teacher tried to make his next test much more demanding by asking mostly higher-order questions. This only compounded the problem, because the types of questions he asked did not match what he taught or how he taught it. It was no surprise that the students did very poorly. Faced with increasing criticism about widespread failing grades and being at a complete loss as to how to test differently, he resorted to using numerous and complicated multiple-choice answers in a naïve attempt to make the simple concepts he was teaching seem a little more demanding. Unfortunately, his poorly constructed answers only made his students feel as though they were being tricked. Eventually, this did nothing except increase the number of failures and exacerbate student, and by now parent, frustrations. Ultimately, the teacher was forced into going back to assessing his students in a way that matched his teaching style. He returned to the easy tests that tested for factual knowledge, and his students' test scores improved markedly.

Annette realizes that this teaching scenario is a good example to share with her teaching team so that they will have a better understanding of her system for dealing with assessment. She jots down a few notes and then reads on.

Frequency of Testing

Rather than assessing students infrequently and using lengthy tests, it is recommended that testing occur more frequently based on natural separations between, or within, units of study. Frequent, shorter tests encourage students to be active rather than passive learners, because they are required to study on a consistent basis. In fact, it has been demonstrated that frequent tests serve as powerful memory enhancers; testing actually enhances the long-term recall of material studied for a test, even if the material does not appear on the test (Chan, McDermott, & Roediger, 2006). As well, given that the cognitive demand of learning new material can interfere with the recall of material that has already been learned, frequent studying and testing can solidify the continuous process of learning new knowledge and skills rather than interrupting it. Ideally, then, testing should occur within one to two days of finishing a unit or a designated section of a unit.

Testing that follows these principles is more effective than testing that is infrequent and typically preceded by curricular reviews by teachers and cramming sessions by students. This is not to say that longer tests that cover more material should be avoided. Shorter, more frequent tests usually emphasize basic knowledge and skills, and they prepare students for the longer tests that occur at the middle or end of a term. These longer, cumulative tests are then designed to have more of an emphasis on integrating knowledge and material.

Types of Assessment Questions

There are a variety of assessment questions that teachers can use, but all questions measure either the retention of knowledge (remembering) or the transfer of knowledge (application) or both. To examine the basic knowledge accumulated by rote learning or memorization, teachers usually ask recognition or recall questions, often called **selected-response questions**—these are questions that require students to select an answer from the options provided. The teaching that occurs before these types of assessment questions are employed indicates to students that "knowing information" is important. To examine the application of knowledge and to assess the transfer skills that are acquired through much more meaningful types of learning experiences, teachers usually ask problem-solving questions, often called **constructed-response questions**—these are questions that require students to think about, construct, and write their answers. The type of teaching that occurs before these types of questions are employed indicates to students that "applying knowledge" is important. It should not be forgotten, however, that there are certain basic knowledge elements within every curriculum that have to be known and established before teachers can examine whether students can extend or transfer their understandings of that knowledge. With the recent educational emphases on higher-order thinking skills, the assessment of basic knowledge and skills using selected-response questions is sometimes dismissed as a less legitimate form of assessment. In reality, assessing only higher-order understandings is just as inappropriate as measuring only basic knowledge and skills. Unless teachers are assured that basic knowledge is consolidated, designing assessment that focuses exclusively on application or transfer questions doubly, and unfairly, penalizes students who have learned the required basic knowledge and skills but are unable to complete the higher-order, problem-solving questions.

An example of how assessment questions address different levels of cognitive complexity across Bloom's taxonomy of abilities is provided in Table 5.2. The assessment questions are ones used to examine students' knowledge about water and/or test their ability to apply and transfer their understandings about the characteristics of this substance. Depending on the age and grade of the students and on the teacher's curricular emphasis, each of the questions could be legitimately included in a test.

TABLE 5.2 Assessment Questions according to Bloom's Taxonomy

Cognitive Objective	Thinking Involved	Sample Questions
Knowledge	Know/Remember	Which of the following is the chemical symbol for water? What are the two elements that make up water?
Comprehension	Understand	Water is two parts X and one part Y. Explain the ratio of hydrogen to oxygen in a water molecule.
Application	Use knowledge "to do something"	Build/draw a water molecule and explain its composition.
Analysis	Deduce	Why does water extinguish fire?
Synthesis	Create/Organize	How is it that we can walk on ice but not on water or steam?
Evaluation	Judge according to criteria	Present a case for/against why water is considered the basis of life.

For several decades, educational psychologists and educators held the view that selected-response or objective questions, such as multiple-choice and matching items, are only suitable for determining students' knowledge and skills, while constructed-response questions are best suited for assessing their problem-solving abilities, even though the marking of constructed answers involves a great deal of subjectivity on the part of the teacher. (As illustrated later in this section, the design of answer rubrics for marking problem-solving questions has removed much of this subjectivity.) In light of the better connections that teachers make between instruction and assessment, this overly negative view of selected-response questions, along with the overly positive view of constructed-response questions, is no longer valid.

More recently, there has been a growing emphasis on the importance of designing assessment that directly supports and complements instruction and learning. Therefore, currently, the primary guiding principle for selecting the best type of assessment question is to choose the question format that provides the most direct measure of the learning objective. A broad rule of thumb for choosing the question type is to simply duplicate the activity or learning mechanism that was used to teach the concept. If a concept in geography is taught using maps, then the best assessment tool for that concept will involve the use of a map. If an English unit focuses on learning how to write a persuasive essay, then requiring students to write a persuasive essay is the best assessment tool. Similarly, if calculation questions are used to teach math concepts, then calculation questions are the best assessment tool. As outlined previously, when teachers generate specific assessment questions based on the learning objectives from their lesson plans, and then use the Table of Specifications to systematically organize questions into suitable tests, these tests will assess their students' use of the same thinking processes that were used to learn the material. However, it should also be noted that while assessment questions are primarily learning objective-dependent, they are also somewhat student-dependent. Students have different learning styles and modes of expressing knowledge, which significantly affect their ability to perform well on different types of test questions. Some students do best on essay-based tests, while others do better on tests made up of selected-response questions. Therefore, if the main objective of assessment is to allow students to demonstrate what they have learned, teachers must use various, yet suitable, types of assessment questions. Adopting this mindset toward assessment provides all students with the very best opportunity to show what knowledge and skills they have acquired.

Selected-Response Questions

The most commonly used selected-response-type items are true/false, matching, and multiple-choice questions. All three types are generated from the specific learning objectives that guide teachers' lesson plans.

True/False questions

These questions require students to indicate whether a given statement is true or false. These questions are best used for examining unambiguous fundamental facts (i.e., Bloom's Knowledge and Comprehension levels) that need to be known in order to complete higher-order cognitive tasks. They place less demand on reading skills than do multiple-choice questions, and a 10- or 15-item true/false test is a quick and accurate way of reviewing material and clearing up misconceptions or misunderstandings. These types of "quick quizzes" are usually used as formative assessment devices within a unit of instruction or as a summative assessment for instruction that involved many small but important details. Once the information and concepts on a true/false test have been learned, reviewed, and clarified, teachers can confidently use higher-order questions about the same material on a future test. True/false questions are good substitutes for multiple-choice items when it is difficult to generate a number of wrong answers.

Matching questions

These questions typically require students to indicate that a concept or term from one list matches or relates to a corresponding concept or term in the second list. Students do this by either drawing a line between the matching concepts or by writing the number or letter of the selected response beside the matching concept. Matching questions usually examine Bloom's levels of Knowledge and Comprehension, because students merely have to recognize or recall information. One way to increase cognitive complexity is to include concepts or terms in the second list that either match more than one item in the first list or do not match any items at all. A matching question can also be transformed into a multiple fill-in-the-blank question to raise the question to Bloom's Application level. In this case, students are required to fill in the blanks opposite the first list with corresponding words or phrases (e.g., naming the capital cities of the listed provinces). Matching questions are best used to assess student understandings of associations and linkages between concepts and can be used in the same formative assessment fashion as true/false questions (i.e., frequent testing to examine whether required knowledge is consolidated before higher-order thinking is addressed). To avoid designing matching questions that are confusing, limit each list to 10 or fewer concepts.

Multiple-choice questions

These questions, by far the most commonly used selected-response format, require students to read a question or statement, or stem, and select one correct answer from preferably four, but sometimes five, options. While multiple-choice questions are mostly used to test factual knowledge, well-thought-out questions can also be used to measure complex reasoning skills and the application of student understandings. Sometimes multiple-choice questions are purposefully designed to have answers with varying degrees of correctness rather than simply one correct answer and several incorrect answers. These types of questions are excellent for examining concepts that have subtle but important distinctions between related pieces of information. However, when designing these types of questions, teachers must be very careful that the most correct answer is not susceptible to interpretation; they must pay very close attention to the learning objectives from which the questions were generated and the content specificity that was highlighted when the material was taught. Excellent multiple-choice tests have clearly stated, unambiguous questions or statements presented in a language that is consistent with the language used to teach and discuss the concept. The use of "all of the above" or "none of the above" as possible answers should only be implemented if, and only if, "all" or "none" of the information forms a critical understanding of the concept that was taught. Otherwise, totally inclusive or completely exclusive possible answers merely encourage test-taking strategies that have nothing to do with the knowledge learned. In order to measure higher-order thinking skills properly, multiple-choice questions must require students to analyze material that is similar to the content they originally encountered in their course and to answer a question or several questions based on the new material. The material presented in the question can be in the form of paragraphs, charts, maps, pictures, graphs, or anything that is directly related to the course content. Teachers who want to use these detailed types of multiple-choice questions must keep in mind that such questions place a high demand on students' reading abilities and require more time to complete.

Summary

Each of these types of selected-response questions can be scored easily and quickly and can be used to assess student understandings across a broad array of factual course content. However, students may be able to guess the correct answer, with true/false having the highest probability, multiple-choice having moderate probability, and matching questions having the lowest probability (based on 7 to 10 perfect matches). Today, no curriculum is solely devoted to unambiguous facts and knowledge; therefore, it is inappropriate for teachers to use only selected-response questions to assess student learning. Selected-response questions are appropriate assessment tools when they examine unambiguous knowledge and skills and the type of understandings that were emphasized during instruction. For example, if a series of lessons taught only the names and functions of the individual parts of the human circulatory system, questions that examine the names and functions of the individual parts of the human circulatory system are perfectly appropriate. However, asking students questions that examine how all body parts work together within an integrated system would be completely inappropriate unless these explicit connections were taught and demonstrated by the teacher. Moreover, even if these explicit connections were taught and demonstrated, selected-response questions are not the best way to examine such intricate understandings and descriptions of integrated systems. For a proper examination of such detailed understandings, a constructed-response question is best. It is highly recommended, therefore, that selected-response questions be used as part of a broad array of teacher-generated assessment methods wherein the types of questions are appropriate for the respective content covered and how it was taught.

Constructed-Response Questions

The most commonly used constructed-response-type items are short-answer, restricted-essay, and essay questions. Like selected-response questions, all three types are generated from the learning objectives that guide teachers' lesson plans. However, unlike selected-response questions, all three types require students to provide an answer rather than merely select one. The requirement to generate an answer eliminates a student's ability to simply recognize a correct answer that may have been forgotten or is only vaguely understood. In other words, the probability of students guessing the correct answer to a constructed-response question is extremely low. Another unique feature of constructed-response questions is that teachers must gauge or judge the correctness of the answer. Where possible, it is highly recommended that students be given the benefit of the doubt for answers that are close to the intended answer but not necessarily perfect, even if only partial credit is awarded. Teachers can easily accomplish this by asking students something like, "Can you please tell me what you meant by this word/term/phrase?" and then judging the correctness of the written answers based on students' explanations. There are two reasons for taking this generous perspective. First, most teachers adhere to constructivist perspectives of education; they believe that students use and interpret language differently when constructing their own knowledge. Therefore, in testing situations, teachers have to expect that students will use varied or imprecise words/terms/phrases to convey the critical meaning of the required answer. Second, and perhaps most important, if teachers want their students to be consistently active learners instead of passive recipients of information, they must let their students know that their efforts to learn are valued. Nothing will dampen a student's enthusiasm for learning faster than the perceived unfairness of not getting credit for an answer that "means the same thing."

Short-answer questions

These questions typically come in two formats. In the first format, students have to answer direct questions by writing a word, phrase, or a few sentences to provide a correct answer. For example, "Who discovered insulin, and what country was that person from?" or "Name the national park that is located on the west coast of Newfoundland, and briefly describe the predominant elements of its geography." These types of questions contain one main point or one primary concept that may have several related parts. Depending on a teacher's overall emphasis for the course, students write their multiple-part answers either in point form or in complete sentences. The second format for short-answer questions, commonly called fill-in-the-blank questions, requires students to demonstrate their understandings by completing a sentence. The blank, which indicates where a critical piece of content knowledge is missing, can be at the beginning, in the middle, or at the end of the sentence. The rest of the sentence provides the student with the context for the answer. Fill-in-the-blank questions should contain only one main point and ask for only one response.

Both formats of short-answer questions are excellent examples of the purposeful connections that teachers can make between instruction and assessment, because these questions can mimic, exactly, the types of questions teachers constantly ask when teaching. When students then encounter similar questions on a test, they are familiar with the language used and the thinking required. Therefore, it is much easier for them to demonstrate what they have learned. It should be noted that while short-answer questions place less demand on reading skills than do multiple-choice questions, they place a higher demand on understanding, because they eliminate the simple recognition of correct answers. Like most of the selected-response items described above, short-answer questions typically involve Bloom's Knowledge and Comprehension levels and are best used for unambiguous fundamental facts. Therefore, they work very well as formative assessment tools if teachers plan to assess higher-order skills later in the unit. Like true/false questions, short-answer questions are excellent substitutes for multiple-choice items when it is difficult to generate a number of wrong answers.

Restricted-essay and essay questions
While short-answer questions typically place a low cognitive demand on students' knowledge and thinking, both restricted-essay and essay questions typically demand higher-order thinking. This is accomplished by requiring students to compose extended responses to statements, scenarios, or problems. These types of questions are best used when teachers want to get a comprehensive picture of student understandings. The basic difference between a restricted-essay and an essay question is the scope of the question asked and the length and depth of the response required. Restricted-essay questions are best used when time is a factor; in these cases, the unrestricted-essay response may become an unfair examination of the students' ability to write under pressure. Like all other test questions, essay questions must be designed with clarity in mind. The prompting statements, problems, or scenarios must be unambiguous, even though they deal with more complex topics. Essays can be used to examine all levels of Bloom's taxonomy once basic knowledge is consolidated. They are effective because they allow students to demonstrate what they know, particularly when they are asked to defend their position using important concepts taught in the course. While guessing is virtually eliminated, essay questions place a high demand on writing skills. It should also be noted that there is a curricular trade-off that teachers need to keep in mind when using restricted-essay and essay questions. While these types of questions allow teachers to examine an issue more deeply, they do so at the expense of limiting the content covered on a test. Therefore, teachers should make sure that these restricted-essay and essay questions delve primarily into the broader and more critical issues taught in a unit.

Essay questions are obviously inappropriate for early elementary students who are still learning complex language skills. Prior to Grade 4/5, it is readily apparent that most students are not able to accurately convey their knowledge and skills in a written format. However, once these skills are well consolidated in the later elementary grades, students should be able to respond to fairly simple essay questions. Restricted-essay questions are good assessment tools to use starting in Grade 4/5, but only if students have had experience with essays (e.g., homework and seatwork) and only if they have had experience writing drafts and revising and editing their work. Once students reach middle school and beyond, essays are more appropriate measures of knowledge and abilities. By this time in their cognitive development, students are able to handle more complex questions that require critical thinking.

> **think box**
>
> If you were an instructor preparing a test on this chapter of the textbook, what type of assessment questions would you include? What factors would you consider when designing the test and the test questions? How would you describe the test to students?

One of the best ways that teachers can help students prepare for essay questions is to specifically point out the conceptual differences between various parts of the curricular material. By purposefully demonstrating the difference between "knowing" factual information, such as the various names and functions of the different parts of the circulatory system, and "applying" knowledge, such as describing how the entire system is integrated or works together, teachers are making it clear to students that they either have to think about and study facts or think about and study the associations between various facts. By making these types of direct and explicit connections between how the content is taught and how the content will be assessed, teachers further enhance the validity of their tests. This explicitness also motivates students to study and learn, because they can predict what tests will require of them.

The critical element in using essay questions is to make sure that each essay is marked using the same evaluative criteria. The reliability of the marking scheme (its ability to grade all essays fairly and accurately) is critical to further improving the validity of the essay question. The assessment mechanism that outlines all the potential elements of a correct response to a restricted-essay or essay question is called a marking **rubric**. Just as designing assessment questions precedes deciding what to teach and how to teach it, designing all the critical response elements of a marking rubric precedes assigning the question on a test or assignment. When designing assessment questions, teachers ask themselves, "What do I want my students to know?" Similarly, when designing a marking rubric, teachers ask themselves, "What do I want my students to tell me to indicate that they have learned the material related to this question?" By knowing in advance exactly what the complete answer is, based on specific learning objectives from lesson plans, teachers are more likely to ask more precise and more comprehensive questions. Constructed in this manner, essay questions accurately reflect what was taught and are fair, reliable, and valid assessments of student learning.

One of the keys to designing a good marking rubric is to distinguish the important content criteria from the important writing elements. In other words, teachers must separately grade what was written and how it was written. For example, if there are 10 critical parts to the complete answer for a particular essay question, the teacher must decide whether or not a student's answer must contain all 10 parts in order to receive a perfect score. Or would it be more appropriate, based on how the material was taught, to award a perfect score for only 8 of the 10 parts? The teacher must also decide whether or not students who are very good writers will get better marks than those who do not write as well. Are spelling, grammar, and punctuation important enough to be graded? If conveying or eliciting emotion is not a critical aspect of an English essay, how are marks awarded if an answer does this exceptionally well/poorly/not at all? As you can see, determining, in advance, the various degrees of latitude that will be allowed when marking all types of essays is as important as making sure the specific answer criteria are met.

Some elements of an essay response can be easily marked by comparing them against a checklist of the concepts that must be included. Even so, teachers must be prepared to determine whether or not partial marks will be awarded if a key concept is implied but not precisely indicated. Other elements of essay answers will have to be graded via a rating scale whereby students get different marks for varying degrees of correct answers. Awarding more or fewer marks for these types of elements usually depends on the quality and precision of the explanations. Therefore, it is best if the rubric includes the bare minimum answer, the perfect answer, and several points in between. Then the teacher can consistently and confidently award different marks for each variation and justify such differences to students, parents, and administrators (if necessary). In all instances, regardless of the number of marks awarded for a particular question or test, the total score determined by the rubric should add up to 100%. Students readily identify with percentage scores rather than a grade of 120 marks, for example.

In summary, using a rubric that includes explicit criteria provides for more consistent and reliable marking and virtually eliminates teachers' judgments based on prior expectations of student performance. When employed in this manner, rubrics are concrete evidence on which constructive criticism of student learning performances can be based; thus, they are supportive of the precise instructional goals teachers are expected to fulfill. It should be noted that rubrics are also designed to evaluate other complex academic performances such as group assignments, comprehensive projects assigned as long-term homework, science-fair projects, in-class presentations, and portfolios of student work.

Annette places the material she has just read in an envelope for Mr. Hayes. She is sure that he will learn a great deal from this overview of assessment, but there is one more paper she wants to include, because it specifically addresses her personal approach to assessment. She wrote this paper back in July while attending Dr. Cameron's course. She picks up the binder marked "Ed Psych Summer Course" and flips to the assignment. Before placing it in the envelope, she quickly skims over it to be sure it matches the overall assessment plan she has for this school year.

Assignment—My Use of Assessment Tools

My approach to teaching is primarily based on direct instruction and problem-based learning. Therefore, throughout my units and lessons, I place a strong emphasis on encouraging my students to develop their overall knowledge base and to expand their thinking and problem-solving skills. In order to properly assess the wide range of curricular knowledge/skills covered in my courses and to allow all of my students an equal opportunity to demonstrate their learning, I use a variety of assessment tools. This does not mean, however, that I use the different types of assessment tools that are available indiscriminately; rather, it means that I carefully choose an array of assessment tools that match my instructional methods and goals. In this way, my assessment system is designed to provide consistent and uniform measures of performance.

Authentic Assessment

Within a well-constructed assessment system, grade weighting is determined by considering the teaching and curricular emphases. I utilize various types of selected- and constructed-response assessment tools based on their respective appropriate applications. These forms of assessment constitute about 40–45% of my students' overall grades. The other 55–60% of their grades comes from **authentic assessments**, because this is an accurate reflection of the percentage of time, effort, and emphasis that my students and I dedicate to meaningful learning. These tests or assignments ask students to use their knowledge and skills to carry out academic tasks that replicate, or are similar to, those found in real-world activities. By duplicating the problem-solving processes inherent in having to resolve meaningful and real-world problems, I find that students improve their problem-solving skills and learn to think beyond providing simple answers that require no justification. For example, based on a series of related science lessons, I had a group of students participate in a project that required them to gather and analyze data about a local ecosystem that was showing early signs of abuse and deterioration. The students had to devise a plan of action to help restore the viability of the ecosystem. Based on my constructive comments about the data and the comments of an expert, a local biologist whom I recruited to help with the project, the students finalized their own recommendations on how to enhance the area's biodiversity and water cleanliness. As an important evaluative feature of this process, one that typically distinguishes authentic assessment from other forms of assessment, the mentor and I provided feedback as part of the project activities. In other words, the students received feedback about their recommendations before finalizing them; the intent was to have them rethink or defend their recommendations as necessary. Then the biologist helped me guide the students as they actually implemented their ideas at the site.

It is important to point out that I learned the hard way that not all curricular topics lend themselves to precise real-world applications. In my previous attempts to use more real-world scenarios in my teaching and assessment formats, I found that many were so contrived that they appeared disingenuous. Not surprisingly, these applications did not go over well with my students. Therefore, globally, I use the term "authentic assessment" to indicate that my overall approach to assessment is an authentic reflection of my teaching and curricular emphasis; in my classrooms, student assessment includes as many real-world applications as possible.

By definition, the best forms of authentic assessment are open-ended student-selected projects/assignments (chosen from a teacher- or teacher–student-generated list) that are accomplished within an extended time frame, usually two to four weeks. If assigned as a group project, the marking rubric should provide criteria for both group and individual contributions and, where possible, allow for individual creativity and ingenuity. Clearly defined shorter problems can also be used in a test format; the only limitation is that authentic-assessment problems or questions, such as essay questions, restrict the scope of the curriculum that can be evaluated in one test. I try to make ample use of project- and test-based authentic assessments, because there is clear research evidence that these types of assessment tools are excellent for distinguishing between students' abilities to represent problems, explain concepts, present solutions logically, and self-monitor learning during both instruction and project completion. This approach also leads to far richer discussions with my students about the content of the assessment; there are far fewer conversations about whether an answer is merely right or wrong.

Portfolios

The final piece in my assembly of assessment tools is the **portfolio**: a collection of a student's work that demonstrates his or her abilities, achievements, and growth over time in a particular curricular area, as well as his or her range and diversity within and across specific curricular topics. Because portfolios are growth-oriented as well as product-oriented, they provide

Guiding Principles

Authentic Activities, Problems, and Questions

It is becoming increasingly evident that society's transition from a manufacturing-based to a knowledge-based economy necessitates a rethinking and reshaping of teaching and instruction. To better understand whether there is a need for alternative forms of both knowledge and instruction, Canadian scholars Carl Bereiter and Marlene Scardamalia (2012) examined the instructional objectives and methods tied to the rising importance of knowledge creation. They concluded that students, as part of their learning process, need to more actively participate in the knowledge creation process rather than only viewing, learning, and using knowledge as consumers. To accomplish this, the authors recommended that teachers engage students in more design work: the ability to work creatively with knowledge—distinct from working creatively on tasks that use knowledge. Working on ideas, as opposed to using ideas to do work, typically addresses the following practical concerns:

1. What is this idea (concept, design, plan, problem statement, theory, interpretation) good for?
2. What does it do and fail to do?
3. How could it be improved? (p. 701)

Bereiter and Scardamalia identified four constructivist instructional approaches that use authentic tasks to prepare students to work creatively with knowledge. While the term "authentic task" applies to each of the activities, problems, and questions used in the approaches, each approach has a slightly different but important meaning for the term. The identified approaches and their respective connotations of authenticity are

- learning by design (Holbrook & Kolodner, 2000)—the challenge for students is to design something that can be built and tested; authenticity means designing things that actually work and that appeal to students' interests in toys and games;
- sophisticated versions of project-based learning—student-designed inquiry is organized around investigations to answer important questions; authenticity means activities and issues drawn from real-life concerns and controversies;
- problem-based learning—students are engaged in solving important problems; authenticity means that these problems are modelled as closely as possible on problems currently encountered in the real world; and
- knowledge-building—students build models, conduct experiments, and write reports as a means of producing an innovation or advancing a knowledge frontier; authenticity means the problems and questions used are the ones that students actually wonder about (p. 705).

Applying sound assessment principles to evaluate the student learning provided by these four instructional approaches will, necessarily, result in authentic assessment.

systematic feedback about student development (Hebert, 2001) and are representative of real change. The two basic forms of portfolios are writing and artistic collections. The writing portfolio has the broadest range of applications in education, because schooling predominantly requires students to write in order to indicate their learning. Nearly all topics in all curricular subjects can be the focus of a student's portfolio—social studies, math, English, languages, physical education, technology, and vocational education, to name a few.

Under my guidance, all my students are individually responsible for developing their own portfolios and for selecting appropriate contributions. To make their portfolios truly effective, I make sure each one is directed or regulated by a specific learning outcome (or two) that the student and I agree upon. The student writes the learning outcome statement(s) on the outside flap of his or her portfolio folder. I also ask the student to indicate a growth time frame and the different categories for possible entries. Eventually, the portfolio contains student-, teacher-, and student–teacher-selected items, and from time to time the student is required to reflect on the contents of the portfolio and his or her own growth and progress. I always have my students include examples of their seatwork, homework, draft copies, final copies, and a series of reports. The main criterion for portfolio selection is that the item must be a clear indication of student growth relative to the learning outcome(s) and previous entries. Where practical, the portfolio should also contain copies of the stimulus material that were analyzed or reflected upon, such as newspaper or magazine articles, pictures, printed reports or other information from the Internet, and even excerpts from recommended curriculum resources. Ideally, the portfolio will contain a broad array of a student's work, and it will reflect all of his or her abilities and achievements. The portfolio should never become just a convenient place to store everything the student completed over a particular period of time.

An added feature and benefit of the portfolio is that my ongoing evaluation of these student productions results in formative as well as summative grades. Based on student growth and

performance indicators, formative evaluations help me determine the changes I need to make to my instructional plans; these evaluations help students better understand the direction and purpose of their portfolios. Perhaps the most important feature of portfolios is the fact that a student's accomplishments are all in one place rather than stored haphazardly or discarded or lost. In my classrooms, students have always taken great pride in their portfolios. They are quite enthusiastic about reflecting upon their learning and growth as they review the work they have collected. I always encourage students to specify, realistically, where they think growth and improvement have been demonstrated. This is efficiently accomplished, because students simply have to compare their work products to the learning outcome(s) that were identified when the portfolio was first conceptualized. These self-evaluations are particularly effective for students who do not experience a lot of scholastic success; they act as reminders of the student's ability to persevere and make progress toward his or her learning goals.

The marking and grading of portfolios is typically **criterion-based assessment** in that the teacher evaluates whether the portfolio (and each selection within it) has met the established standards (criterion) for good performance. These standards are mostly teacher-determined, but a reasonable proportion can also be student-and-teacher-generated. Depending on what the teacher wants to emphasize, each of the established standards can be scored in one of two ways:

1. present/correct = 1 or absent/wrong = 0; or
2. on a 5-point descriptive scale such as poor = 1, acceptable = 2, average = 3, above average = 4, and excellent = 5.

Because portfolios are mostly growth-oriented, all evaluative criteria should reflect desired changes within the student and should never be reflective of comparisons with other students. Figure 5.2 contains the six different evaluative criteria I used for a social studies portfolio, scored on a five-point scale. The portfolio focused on urban versus rural development, a unit of study that was presented over a four-week span in a high school classroom. During those four weeks, my students were required to write five reports. The primary learning outcome was for the students to improve their expository report-writing; therefore, there was no evaluation of their basic writing skills. These were not the writing attributes that required growth at that time.

> **Each of the following criteria will be scored on a scale of 1–5:**
> - demonstrates an understanding of the nature of the problem,
> - presents information in a logical fashion (opening, support/argument, conclusion),
> - makes appropriate use of urban/rural and city/farm statistics,
> - incorporates appropriate media reports (both positive and negative commentary),
> - integrates statistics and media reports, and
> - provides logical conclusions and recommendations (where possible).

FIGURE 5.2 Social Studies Writing Portfolio—Evaluative Criteria

Annette pauses to make a note to herself. She realizes she forgot to tell her students that she will also allow them to drop their lowest mark from each of their portfolios. This is consistent with what she told them about dropping their lowest test or assignment mark each term. However, she will also have to explain to them that because portfolios are growth-oriented, they will only be allowed to remove an item if they replace it with a piece of work that reflects improvement in their understanding or application of the original concept. This will reinforce the emphasis the portfolio places on growth rather than on simple replacement, and it will also encourage self-regulation, especially in terms of responsibility.

Annette puts down her pen and continues reading the assignment she completed for Dr. Cameron. She knows that Mr. Hayes will probably have questions for her after he reads it, so she wants to be prepared to discuss her assessment views with him. She is acutely aware that her views on assessment are quite different from those used in the school in the past few years.

Evaluating Effectiveness of Assessment Tools

Every teacher wants his or her students to do well and know all the correct answers to all test questions. This would indicate that the instruction was effective and students learned all that they were supposed to; everybody would be satisfied. In reality, this rarely happens. Instead of being disappointed at this regularly occurring phenomenon, I have developed an appreciation for how the disparity between what I teach and how well my students learn can actually be used to improve tests. Based on my teaching and on how my questions correspond with Bloom's taxonomy of cognitive skills, I build my tests based on the expectation that some questions will be answered correctly by all students. These are usually Knowledge and Comprehension questions and, depending on the emphasis of the unit of instruction, may include some questions from the Application category. While this sounds like simple and "easy" testing, I know that students will not be able to answer most of these questions if they did not take notes, ask questions, and study. I also expect that the majority of my students will get numerous other questions correct but, again, only if they have worked hard and paid attention in class. These slightly tougher questions address Application skills and perhaps Analysis skills and understandings. Finally, there are usually a few questions (about 10%) that I expect to be answered correctly by a smaller percentage of my students, those who truly understand the content and can make higher-order connections between concepts (usually 20–25% of my students). I certainly do not want most of my students to find these particular questions difficult, and there is no doubt that I would prefer that all students could answer all such questions correctly. Rather, the reality of teaching and learning is such that these types of questions will solicit answers that demonstrate complete understandings of complex concepts and the ability to transfer this thinking to other similarly complex concepts. Students acquire these types of knowledge and skills by attending all classes, paying attention and taking notes as needed, asking and answering questions in class, doing all seatwork and homework assignments to the best of their ability, seeking help to clarify misunderstandings, and diligently preparing and studying for tests and exams. In other words, if students work hard, these educational activities will help them develop skills that will allow them to answer Analysis, Synthesis, and Evaluation types of questions. Unfortunately, much as I encourage them, not all students do so.

It is also clear, however, that poor student responses to particular test questions or assignments cannot be solely attributed to a lack of work or studying. While the primary purpose of assessment is to determine whether students have learned and its secondary purpose is to assign grades, neither of these purposes are properly served if assessment tools do not ask questions that elicit proper student responses. Therefore, the final process in my assessment system is a procedure whereby I evaluate whether or not my assessment tools (all questions in all tests) have been effective. I complete this process by carefully reviewing all questions and respective responses that are graded, including those assigned as homework. I typically complete this task after I have finished grading an assignment or test, but of course I am also aware of it while I am doing my marking. I operate from the premise that, in theory, all my questions should be appropriate and should elicit suitable responses from my students, because both the questions and the answers were derived from the specific learning objectives I used in my daily lessons. However, I know from experience that it is not unusual for critical parts of some lessons to be overlooked, for the emphasis of a lesson to get a little off the mark, or for students to interpret the material differently from what I intended. Despite all of my careful planning and preparation, these things tend to happen occasionally. There is also the slight possibility that the overall emphasis of the test questions produced by my Table of Specifications did not exactly match what I did during my lessons. By reviewing all questions and answers and eliminating the questions that were ineffective, I find that I avoid the following pitfalls that research cites as common in teacher-based assessments: (a) questions that do not reflect the intended learning outcomes; (b) unfair grading due to poor questions; (c) students feeling that tests are intended to trick them and that therefore they are unable to truly demonstrate their learning; and (d) the loss of valuable feedback on how to improve both teaching and assessment practices, because no effort was made to determine why some questions did not produce the desired results.

As I examine each assessment question and the various answers that my students provided, I keep the following guidelines in mind and apply them differentially based on (a) the type and level of question asked, (b) the answer the question was intended to solicit, (c) how I taught/emphasized the material, and (d) my expectations for correct responses based on my knowledge of the students' abilities.

Guidelines for Determining the Effectiveness of Assessment Questions

1. A question that does not solicit proper responses from the majority of students is a poor question and must be eliminated from the grading scheme (e.g., answers are all over the map, many responses missed the intent of the question, many students indicated confusion about the question during the test). This is particularly true if the majority of students includes those whose knowledge/skills and work/study habits are exemplary.
2. If a constructed-response question solicits very few or no perfect answers, the mark allocation must be revised so as not to penalize anyone. For example, if a perfect response is worth 5 marks and only one or two students get 5 while the majority of students get 2s, 3s,

and 4s, either the value of the question should be revised to 4 or 3 or the entire question should be eliminated from the grading scheme.
3. When grading constructed-response answers, give students the benefit of the doubt by awarding partial marks for "near misses that mean the same thing" rather than no marks. This rewards effort and indicates that learning is valued, even if perfection was not achieved.

Once I have identified the poorly performing questions using these guidelines, I go back to my lessons and my Table of Specifications to decipher why the question did not do what I intended. I look for mismatches between the material I taught, how I taught it, how I tested for it, and how the students responded. In the rare instance where this in-depth process does not clear up the ambiguity, I review the question(s) with my students to determine whether the intent of the question was understood and why the question elicited a different-than-intended response. In all instances, I make appropriate changes to my lessons, teaching methods, or assessment tools to make sure that there is continuity between instruction, learning, and assessment. By doing a careful review and making necessary revisions, I improve the overall validity and reliability of my assessment system. In other words, my assessment questions become better reflections of the material I taught and how I taught it, and the answers they elicit become true indicators of student learning.

As Annette places this final material aside for Brian, she recalls the discussions she and her colleagues had in Dr. Cameron's class when they each presented their views on assessment. When these discussions became too focused on which forms and types of assessment were "better" than others, Dr. Cameron always reminded them to spend more time discussing and evaluating assessment tools in terms of appropriateness of application. He was adamant that the best application of assessment tools occurs when each is purposefully connected to specific learning objectives. Annette is eager to follow his advice this year. The variety of complementary assessment tools that she has planned to include in her assessment system will be closely tied to learning objectives. She feels confident that this approach will ensure that she always has a full understanding of student progress.

The Student Teacher's Role in the Classroom

It was not unusual for Annette to be the first to arrive at school in the morning, so she is surprised and impressed to see Aaron, her student teacher, waiting by the school door when she arrives the next morning. They chat and exchange pleasantries as she opens various parts of the school. Aaron explains that the reason he is so early is that he was not sure how long it would take to get to the school from his house. "Conscientiousness—hmmm, gets full marks from me," Annette says to herself while getting a pot of coffee going. After making sure her material is in order for the first class of the day, she has 30 uninterrupted minutes to talk with Aaron before the students begin to arrive.

"Well Aaron," Annette begins, "this morning I'd like to make you familiar with our class rules so that you get off on the right foot as soon as the students enter the classroom." Annette leads Aaron to the large posters on the wall. "I believe quite strongly that how the classroom is managed is vital to optimizing teaching. Believe me, nothing makes teaching more frustrating than an out-of-control environment. So the first thing I'd like to show you is our lists of classroom rules. Each of these rules was designed by either me or the students, and we all agreed on how each one would be implemented. As you can see, some are specific to the different age groups in the room. Together, they're the basic behavioural guidelines that we use to set the overall tone and atmosphere for the school. At this point, the students and I have lived by these rules fairly successfully, but like a lot of things in teaching, they've needed some adjustments along the way."

Annette explains a condensed version of the process she went through to implement DCM and describes how and why some of the rules had to be adjusted. "The reason I'm sharing this with you now," explains Annette, "is that I'm going to make sure that when I introduce you to the students, they immediately become aware that you're my co-leader in this group, not someone they can treat differently or expect different treatment from."

"Oh, okay," says Aaron tentatively.

"Don't worry," Annette replies reassuringly, "I've already done the same with Mr. Parker, our resource-room teacher, and Mrs. McCarthy and Mr. Hayes, our educational assistants, and it has worked out fine."

"But the kids are going to know that I'm a student teacher and I'm new here, so are they actually going to believe I'm your co-leader?"

"Well, I'm still the person who is ultimately responsible for everything that happens, but when it comes to everyone's behaviour and managing the classroom according to the rules, you will hold the same status as all the other adults. You see, unless the students understand that you and the rest of the adults in the school have the authority to make sure the rules are followed, good behaviour will probably only happen when I'm present or when the principal, Mrs. Nugent, is around. Not only would that send the wrong message about your status, but it would make the entire process we went through a waste of time."

"So, what do I do if someone steps out of line? Oh, and are you going to be around when I'm teaching?" asks Aaron, quickly putting the two events together.

"I'll be here when you first start teaching, but after a while I'll probably start spending some one-on-one time with some of the students outside the classroom. But don't worry, every one of our rules is based on common sense and has fairly straightforward consequences. I'll be here to help you with problem incidents if they happen. Besides, we all put so much time and effort into setting up the rules that the students will quickly let you know what to do, especially when they're entitled to a reward or if the right consequence isn't implemented."

"I think I can handle that," says Aaron a little more confidently.

"Yes, I'm sure you can," Annette replies encouragingly, "and remember, you also have to be able to recognize and support the good behaviours that we want to see in the classroom. For example, as you see on our chart we aren't merely striving for the absence of disrespect, which is a common baseline in many classrooms. We decided as a group that the whole tone of the room will be better if everyone takes the extra step of showing respect for one another . . . that's why we have rewards for good behaviours as well."

"I get it. You're rewarding preferred behaviours in order to replace bad behaviours. I bet they like the rewards a lot more than the punishments."

"For sure," Annette laughs, "but you'd be surprised at how often the students forget what they're supposed to do and revert to their old habits and of course get into trouble."

Aaron is surprised. "Really? Most of the rewards look pretty enticing, even to me, and I'd have thought they'd want them so much they'd stop breaking the rules."

"Yes, but let's take teasing for example," states Annette with more than a touch of exasperation. "The students are so used to doing it that it just happens naturally, especially when they get a little wound up. Mind you, it happens far less now than at the beginning of the year, but it's the one 'accident' that keeps cropping up. In fact, it's one of the consequences we had to reconsider. It didn't take long for everyone to realize that there's a difference between a slip-up and outright teasing. We needed to recognize that difference by establishing appropriate consequences for each of these actions. Obviously, the consequence for a slip-up is now less serious than the one for outright teasing. I only agreed to the change, however, after we had a meaningful discussion to drive home the understanding that teasing is hurtful no matter the intent."

"Did the students get it?"

"Right away," confirms Annette. "All I did was ask a few students to talk about how they felt when they were teased. It got a little emotional, but as the discussion went on, more and more students shared how teasing hurt even when they knew the other person wasn't trying to be mean to them. The real surprise to everyone was that almost every student in the classroom had experienced hurt feelings because of teasing."

Aware of the time, Annette moves on to the topic of instruction. "Let's formulate a tentative plan about what you'll teach. In my experience, it's better to start off slowly. I'll give you limited teaching duties at first so that you can do them well and enjoy the experience. Then you can gradually take on more responsibilities. How does that sound?"

"Sounds great to me," Aaron responds. "I can't wait to get started. And I should let you know that social studies was one of my majors, so I'd be happy to help you with that subject right away. I could mark all those assignments for you if you like." Aaron obviously saw the stack of social studies assignments sitting on the desk.

"You know Aaron, that's a very nice offer, but much as I could use a hand, I'd prefer to mark all the assignments myself, since I know precisely how the assignment fits into what I've taught. However, let's see how the week goes, and maybe we can work something out. Then you'll see what I mean."

Aaron is obviously a little disappointed that his offer has been turned down, but he has little time to dwell on it. The students have started arriving, and they are immediately curious about his presence in their classroom. Annette explains who he is and the role he will play in their school activities. Aaron also speaks to the students and easily gains their full attention when he starts to talk about his interest in sports. From the students' initial responses, Annette feels confident that Aaron will be a great asset to the classroom.

Annette's Journal

October 5, 2013

I'm enjoying this teaching placement more and more. What appeared to be a daunting challenge has turned into a completely positive experience. The students are friendly and eager to learn, and they are certainly buying into my approach to teaching and learning. I know that our discussions about assessment have been a little stressful for them, but now that they understand that I intend to be fair when assessing how well they're learning, they seem a little more relaxed. Even Anna, who has an obvious problem with test anxiety, told me that this was the first time a teacher ever explained assessment to her, and now she thinks she will be able to view tests a little differently. As she said to me, "Now I can see that tests are just as much for teachers as they are for students. If I do poorly on a test, then both the teacher and I have to find a better way for me to learn the material." Her comments reminded me of why I love teaching!

As a favour to Dr. Cameron, I now have a student teacher in my classroom. Aaron has a lot to learn about the profession, but he seems sincere, conscientious, and open to my suggestions and advice. The students love him. I think that has a lot to do with his open acceptance of each one of them, despite their varying ages and their obvious strengths and needs. He has a knack of being able to find ways to include them all in whatever activity he is overseeing. Of course, the students especially like him to accompany them to the gym. He's very athletic and has a great deal of knowledge about sports. All of these attributes will help him become an effective teacher. I must remember to tell him about my professional development experiences this past summer—even after teaching for several years, I learned so much from one in-depth course. I guess teachers are really only very experienced students . . . Aaron will do just fine if he remains willing to refine his skills throughout his career in education.

With most of my plans well in place, it's time to turn my attention to the needs of some students in particular. I don't have an extensive background in special education, so thankfully Mr. Parker is here to help me with this part of my teaching. He has already helped me better understand ADHD and the challenges that Zach faces on a daily basis, but I know there are a few other students in my classroom who have difficulties with learning, so I also want to find ways to help them. My goal for the coming week is to work closely with Mr. Parker to identify these students and determine a plan of action for each one of them.

Annette's Exploration of the Research

Ercikan, K. (2012). Developments in assessment of student learning. In P. A. Alexander & P. H. Winne (Eds.), *Handbook of educational psychology* (2nd ed., pp. 929–952). New York, NY: Routledge.

After Aaron has been in the classroom for a few weeks, Annette allows him to grade some papers under her supervision. She notices immediately that he wrote very few comments on most papers. His naïve justification for providing limited feedback is that most of the papers were well done and any errors he found were minor, usually involving grammar or writing style. It is also evident that most of the comments he did make focused on students' weaknesses; he rarely commented on what the students did well. When Annette probes further, it is clear that Aaron expected certain aspects of the papers to be well done, and if they were, he marked them correct and moved on. She also notes that he does not understand the intrinsic value of providing students with written feedback, because he appeared more caught up in assigning a correct numerical grade for each paper.

To find a way to gently but firmly change his perspective, Annette shares with Aaron how Anna's simple question "What does a mark really tell us?" continues to trouble her. She describes how Anna asked it in reaction to Annette's explanation of how she and her classmates could learn more and perform better if Annette provided them with shorter but more frequent tests and assignments. Annette explains to Aaron that not all tests and assignments warrant extensive feedback about learning performance, since that is impractical, but she emphasizes that students appreciate constructive comments on their assignments and they also find it helpful when parts of some tests are reviewed to clear up misunderstandings. To reinforce this message, Annette gives Aaron a copy of Ercikan's (2012) paper, which had been required reading in Dr. Cameron's class, and asks him to read it over so they can talk about it.

After school the next day, Annette has some errands to run, so she meets Aaron at the local coffee shop for an informal conversation about the paper. She wants to hear his views about Ercikan's work, and she also wants to reduce the formality of the exercise by speaking with him outside the school environment. Her intentions are realized when Aaron comments that he appreciates the more casual surroundings. Over coffee and muffins, their discussion focuses on how the article emphasizes the importance of teachers' providing students with feedback based on assessment results.

Ercikan's Views

Ercikan analyzed and distilled historical and evolving developments in student assessment and concluded that the true value of assessment lies in the provision of evaluative feedback to students, not simply in the assignment of a grade. Ercikan, in citing Black and Wiliam's (1998) extensive review of more than 250 books and articles on classroom assessment, stated clearly that "ongoing assessment by teachers, combined with appropriate feedback to students, can have high impact on learning" (p. 931). Except for summative assessments or grades for which student feedback is mostly irrelevant (final exams), feedback is essential in order for students to monitor and regulate their learning. Ercikan summarized four critical aspects of education that are positively affected by ongoing and constructive feedback based on student assessments:

Student self-esteem: To maintain and promote student self-esteem, feedback should focus on positive qualities of student responses/assignments and include advice on how responses can be improved.

Student self-assessment: Training in self-assessment teaches students the purpose of learning, makes clear connections between assessment tasks and learning outcomes, requires realistic views of personal performance, and allows students to govern their learning and studying accordingly.

Interaction in learning environments: Opportunities for students to express their understandings are necessary if assessment is to support the teaching and learning process. Question-and-answer sessions allow teachers to respond to and orient students' thinking, clarify misunderstandings, and demonstrate the thinking processes used to learn and manipulate information.

Teacher–student dialogue: This type of dialogue is more thoughtful and reflective and explores understandings more deeply than question-and-answer sessions. It is designed to engage students in thoughtful exploratory dialogue with ample time for thinking and reflecting upon understandings.

In summary, assessment is best immersed in an interactive teaching and learning environment; it should foster student self-esteem and self-assessment; and it should be the catalyst for thoughtful and meaningful curricular conversations between teachers and students.

Implications for Teaching

As their discussion comes to an end, Aaron tells Annette that he can see evidence of the critical elements of Ercikan's article in her overall approach to assessment. She takes the opportunity to point out that it had also shaped her overall approach to teaching. Aaron thanks Annette for opening his eyes to the value of open and honest teacher–student communication, whether it be dialogue regarding classroom behaviour or a discussion about a student's performance. He indicates that it is the most important teaching tool he has learned during his practicum.

Annette's Resource List

Academic Journals

Phi Delta Kappan
Practical Assessment, Research and Evaluation

Books

Borich, G. D., & Tombari, M. L. (2004). *Educational assessment for the elementary and middle school classroom* (2nd ed.). Upper Saddle River, NJ: Prentice Hall.

Hebert, E. A. (2001). *The power of portfolios: What children can teach us about learning and assessment.* San Francisco, CA: Jossey-Bass.

Popham, W. J. (2013). *Classroom assessment: What teachers need to know* (7th ed.). Upper Saddle River, NJ: Pearson Education.

Russell, M., & Airasian, P. (2011). *Classroom assessment: Concepts and applications* (7th ed.). New York, NY: McGraw-Hill Higher Education.

Websites

Bloom's Taxonomy—Rubrics for Teachers
www.rubrics4teachers.com

Growing Success: Assessment, Evaluation, and Reporting in Ontario Schools
www.edu.gov.on.ca/eng/policyfunding/growsuccess.pdf

Principles for Fair Student Assessment Practices for Education in Canada
www.bced.gov.bc.ca/classroom_assessment/fairstudent.pdf

Student Assessment in B.C.'s Public Schools
www.bccpac.bc.ca/sites/default/files/resources/studentassessmentbcparentguide_2007.pdf

From the Authors' Notebook

This chapter emphasized how teachers can build and implement their own unified approach to assessment and be confident that it will result in accurate indicators of student progress. Such an approach is a natural complement to the instructional principles described in Chapter 4, and more specifically, it allows teachers to use student assessment data to improve their teaching.

Reflecting on Practice

Consider the information you have read in this chapter as well as the knowledge you have acquired through instruction, classroom discussions, and classroom activities. Then take the time to write down your thoughts about these learning experiences. Consider how your perspective on educational psychology may have changed. In addition, respond to the following questions:

- How confident do you feel about your ability to design effective student assessment tools?
- What more do you need to know about student assessment, and where might you find this information?

Chapter Summary

In this chapter, the following concepts were highlighted:

- Just as the learning objective forms the basis of every daily lesson plan, it also has direct connections to student assessment.
- The critical factor in appropriate classroom assessment is question and test validity.
- The Table of Specifications is the blueprint for constructing precise and effective tests.
- Assessment is more than simply the act of designing a variety of selected-response or constructed-response questions to include on tests and assignments; assessment must also reflect the instructional methods used by the teacher.
- Authentic problems can play an important role in meaningful and appropriate assessment practices.
- Providing assessment feedback about performance motivates student learning.
- Analyzing student performance across all assessment tools improves both instruction and assessment.

New Terms

authentic assessment
constructed-response question
content validity
criterion-based assessment
portfolio

rubric
selected-response question
summative assessment
Table of Specifications

These terms are defined in the Glossary at the end of the text.

Review Questions

- How is the learning objective connected to assessment?
- What are the three types of classroom assessment, and how do they differ?
- What is test validity, and why is it important?
- What is the purpose of a Table of Specifications?
- What are the different types of assessment questions, and how are they best used?
- What are the benefits of using authentic problems in student assessment?
- What kind of assessment feedback should teachers provide to students?

EARLY DECEMBER
Individual Differences— Intellectual Abilities and Challenges

6

From the Authors' Notebook

This chapter provides the reader with insights into intellectual and learning-ability differences that teachers must take into account as they prepare and deliver instruction. The chapter also outlines the underlying premises governing the design and delivery of special education and describes how the philosophy of inclusion is resulting in more students with exceptionalities being educated in the regular classroom. In addition, it introduces the reader to the high-incidence categories of exceptionality and depicts how a detailed approach to psycho-educational assessment results in the data necessary to construct the types of individualized and differentiated instruction that have proved effective for students with special needs. Combined, the information in this chapter provides a wide-ranging perspective on individual differences that will serve teachers well as they contemplate how they can modify and adapt their instruction to suit the educational needs of all students.

Primary Learning Objectives

After reading this chapter, you should understand

1. the concept of intelligence;
2. the differences and similarities between Gardner's and Sternberg's models of intelligence and their respective importance when considering the design and implementation of classroom instruction;
3. what special education is, what it is not, and how intelligence plays a role in its conception and delivery;
4. controversial topics in special education such as labelling and education placements;
5. what the discerning ability and inability criteria are for the high-incidence exceptionalities;
6. what is meant by the term "inclusion";
7. the role of the Individualized Education Program (IEP); and
8. the differences and similarities between cognitive styles, learning styles, and temperament.

Parent Concern—Our Son Doesn't Seem as Smart as the Other Students

Annette has invited Jacob's parents to meet with her after school. She is eager to talk with them after a disturbing phone call she received from Jacob's mother the night before. While Annette had presumed all was well after the first reporting period and the first parent–teacher interview, it is now obvious that Jacob's parents have some real concerns about their child's abilities. Mrs. White sounded very distressed when she said, "Jacob just doesn't seem as smart as the other students . . . he isn't learning as quickly as we thought he would. We'd like to find out what his IQ is . . . maybe he needs some special help in order to learn." Rather than try to respond to Mrs. White over the phone, Annette invited both Mr. and Mrs. White to meet with her in person. She knows how important it is to address these fears and concerns right away.

Because Annette has a few hours to spare before they arrive, she pulls out the material she has on individual differences to see if there is any information that might help Jacob's parents better understand their son's abilities. She expects that Mr. and Mrs. White may ask for some reading material to take home with them, so she keeps this in mind as she begins to peruse the articles she has collected over the years.

Intelligence

While there is no universally agreed-upon definition of intelligence, most descriptions of this construct allude to two fundamental and interrelated cognitive functions—the ability to learn from experience and the ability to adapt to one's environment. Within the past decade or so, a third ability—knowing about and controlling one's own thinking—has been added to the majority of contemporary descriptions of intelligence. This is a logical addition, given the prevailing emphasis on information processing.

From an educational perspective, it is best to think of **intelligence** as groups of intellectual behaviours, both goal-directed and adaptive, that can have a significant impact on how, and how well, students learn. Goal-directed mental abilities satisfy the brain's constant desire to understand the world, and adaptive mental abilities satisfy the brain's need for timely changes in thinking that ensure survival in a constantly changing world. It is also apparent that intelligence operates in a hierarchical fashion with three distinct levels of abilities (Carroll, 1997). At the top of the hierarchy, there is an overarching general intellectual ability. This ability is facilitated by eight secondary abilities that carry out different classes of cognitive tasks. Both the overarching and secondary functions are supported by a bottom level that is made up of more than 70 specific information-processing actions (see Figure 6.1).

Of the eight secondary abilities, the trio of **fluid intelligence**, **crystallized intelligence**, and **visual-spatial (broad visual perception) reasoning** are considered the most important, and based on their definitions, it is easy to see why these three abilities are considered the workhorses of the brain. Fluid intelligence is the ability to understand abstract and/or new concepts by utilizing flexible and pattern-seeking thinking. It is also the ability to draw inferences and

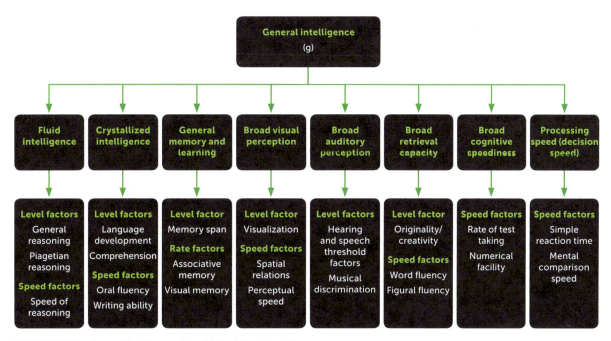

FIGURE 6.1 Carroll's Hierarchical Model of Intelligence

Source: Woolfolk, A. E., Winne, P. H., Perry, N. E., & Shapka, J. (2010). Educational psychology (4th ed., p. 107). Toronto, ON: Pearson.

understand relationships independent of acquired knowledge. The term "fluid" denotes that it can be applied to many types of cognitive tasks. It is viewed as a basic brain function that increases with age until the adolescence period, when it slowly begins to diminish. Because of its basic nature, it is not influenced by one's culture or environment. On the other hand, crystallized intelligence is the ability to apply culturally and environmentally influenced problem-solving skills. It involves the use of accumulated knowledge and skills; therefore, it draws substantially on information stored in long-term memory. In other words, crystallized intelligence is heavily influenced by experience. It can increase throughout the lifespan until about age 65–70. Fluid and crystallized intelligence are attributed to two separate brain systems, but they share an important interdependence that is critical for educators to understand. There is strong evidence that teachers' concerted and purposeful requirement for students to use basic fluid intelligence functions such as abstract reasoning, problem-solving, and quantitative reasoning can increase their crystallized abilities such as verbal skills, language development, reading comprehension, and sequential reasoning.

The last of the trio of important secondary intellectual abilities is visual-spatial reasoning, the ability to use and manipulate visual images and visual relationships when learning and problem-solving. This skill is sometimes referred to as thinking in pictures, but it is also the ability to visualize, for example, what the back of a house looks like when you are looking at it from the front. This is a particularly important mental function for educators to consider, because a substantial portion of curricular content is represented by images such as maps, charts, pictures, models, and videos. There is clear evidence that while this is an innate cognitive ability, it can be enhanced with instruction and practice.

Is Intelligence a Structure or a Process?

In addition to supporting the three-cognitive-functions model, many contemporary educational psychologists view intelligence from a systems perspective—theoretical viewpoints that describe broader conceptions of intelligence. These perspectives tend to be more descriptively inclusive in an attempt to demonstrate that individuals can be intelligent in many different ways.

Intelligence as Structures

Gardner's (1983) theory of multiple intelligences (MI) contends that there are eight (or more) separate intelligence structures: linguistic, logical–mathematical, spatial, bodily–kinesthetic, musical, interpersonal, intrapersonal, and naturalistic (see Table 6.1). At one point, existential intelligence was postulated as a ninth, but it has since been discarded. According to Gardner, each intelligence structure uses different and separate symbol systems, and each originates from a distinguishable part of the brain.

MI theory suggests that each person has varying levels of ability within each of the eight intelligences. Therefore, every student has a unique cognitive profile that does not necessarily match with the highly verbal–linguistic and logical–mathematical emphasis that dominates most schools. Gardner's original conceptualizations of the system decried, and even denied, any amount of coalescence among these eight separate structures. However, several researchers have demonstrated statistical connections among several of them. In fact, in the more than 30 years since Gardner's theory was proposed, there has been no verification of the separateness of the structures, and as a result the differences between the structures are viewed as semantic at best. Moreover, some researchers have recently suggested that the absence of separateness among the eight structures is further evidence of the existence of a global general intelligence, the very definition of intelligence that Gardner was trying to dispel in the first place. The contention that a global structure of general intelligence exists is well supported in the research literature, because, unlike MI theory, all other multiple-domain conceptions of intelligence indicate strong relationships among all listed areas.

TABLE 6.1 The Theory of Multiple Intelligences

Intelligence	Core Components of the Intelligence	Example of a Person Who Uses this Intelligence Heavily	School Activities to Develop the Intelligence
1. Linguistic	Sensitivity to the sounds, rhythms, and meaning of words; understanding of the different functions of language	Poet, journalist	Discussion of metaphor and onomatopoeia
2. Logical–Mathematical	Sensitivity to, and capacity to discern, logical or numerical patterns; ability to handle long chains of reasoning	Scientist, mathematician	Calculating the distance from one corner of a building diagonally to the other by knowing the formula for the area of a triangle
3. Spatial	Capacity to perceive the visual–spatial world accurately and to perform transformations on one's initial perceptions	Navigator, sculptor	Using perspective in drawing pictures
4. Musical	Ability to produce and appreciate rhythm, pitch, and timbre; appreciation of the forms of musical expressiveness	Composer, violinist	Determining the melody or tempo of a song
5. Bodily–kinesthetic	Ability to control one's body movements and to handle objects skillfully	Dancer, athlete	Playing pin-the-tail-on-the-donkey; square dancing
6. Interpersonal	Capacity to discern and respond appropriately to the moods, temperaments, motivation, and desires of other people	Therapist, salesperson	Listening to both sides of an argument between classmates
7. Intrapersonal	Access to one's own feelings and the ability to discriminate among them and draw on them to guide behaviour; knowledge of one's own strengths, weaknesses, desires, and intelligences	Actor, novelist	Role-playing a literary character to gain insight into one's own frustrations
8. Naturalistic	Ability to spot and understand patterns in nature	Geologist, explorer	Observation of patterns in the kinds of plant life in a forest setting

Source: Gardner, H., & Hatch, T. (1989). Multiple intelligences go to school: Educational implications of the theory of multiple intelligences. *Educational Researcher, 18*(8), 6. Reprinted by permission of SAGE Publications.

The most common critiques of MI theory state that (a) the model is based on theoretical rationale and educated intuitions rather than on pure research data and (b) the eight intelligences are merely other-word labels for talents or personality types. More pointed criticisms argue that the overall definition of the theory strongly suggests that all individuals are equally, but differently, intelligent. This position is considerably problematic, since no other theory has made this assertion, nor is the idea even remotely supported by more than 100 years of empirical research.

While MI theory has not gained widespread acceptance within the research community, the notion that there are multiple intelligences has been embraced within education, primarily because the basic premise of the theory appeals to two fundamental tenets of teaching and learning. We know that students think and learn differently, which in turn means that different ways of teaching are needed. Instruction should purposefully involve a variety of teaching methods, such as lectures, demonstrations, and teacher–student discourse, as well as a variety of information presentation modes, such as verbal, auditory, pictorial, and kinesthetic, instead of only one or two of each. The predominant message inherent within MI is that teachers need to break away from the constant and nearly exclusive use of methods that emphasize verbal–linguistic and logical–mathematical skills and intelligences at the expense of the other skills and intelligences. This message has parallel implications for methods of assessment and the types of questions used to determine student learning. It is almost a given within education that the use of multiple teaching methods and modes results in better learning for far more students and encourages teaching for depth of understanding rather than simply breadth of coverage. From the students' perspective, a teacher's adherence to MI theory can give them more learning opportunities specifically attuned to their particular way(s) of thinking and learning. In the final analysis, if MI theory causes teachers to teach differently so as to accommodate students who learn and process information differently, then educational practice is much better off for it. However, having said that, there is currently little empirical support for the value-added effectiveness of MI theory when it is adopted on a school-wide basis. Like many other concepts in educational psychology, teachers need to completely understand MI theory, then judiciously select and apply the aspects of it that may enhance their students' learning.

Intelligence as Processes

Whereas Gardner's theory emphasizes a series of independent intelligence structures, Sternberg's (1985; Sternberg & Williams, 2002) triarchic theory of human intelligence emphasizes a series of interdependent intelligence processes that people use to learn and solve problems. The theory is made up of three interrelated sub-theories—analytic/componential, creative/experiential, and practical/contextual. According to Sternberg, one's facility with each, and/or in combination, results in more or less intelligent behaviours. Figure 6.2 depicts the triarchic theory of intelligence.

Analytical/Componential intelligence
Analytical/componential intelligence involves the interrelated basic thinking processes that drive intellectual behaviour. Sternberg arranged these cognitive processes into a

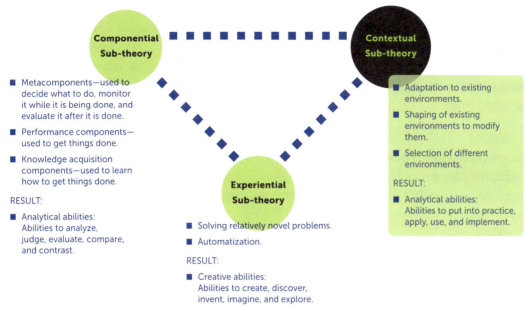

FIGURE 6.2 Sternberg's Triarchic Theory of Intelligence
Source: Sternberg, R. J., & Williams, W. M. (2002). *Educational psychology* (p. 130). Boston, MA: Allyn & Bacon.

three-component hierarchy: (1) meta-components are higher-order executive processes used to plan, monitor, and evaluate one's thinking as tasks are completed (such as writing a persuasive essay); (2) performance components are the processes used to implement the thinking governed by the meta-components (such as choosing a topic, gathering related information, and writing the essay); and (3) knowledge-acquisition components are the processes used in learning how to solve problems (such as learning how to decide the relevance of a topic, how to do related research, and how to write the essay to persuade the reader). Obviously, some components deal with very specific tasks while others deal with broader classes of tasks.

Creative/Experiential intelligence

Creative/experiential intelligence involves the various thinking mechanisms people use to cope with new experiences, either by using insight (finding a creative way to deal with a new problem) or by automaticity (the efficient/automatic use of thinking skills to problem-solve). It is marked by novel approaches to problem-solving and turning non-routine thinking processes into routine and effortless cognitive abilities.

Practical/Contextual intelligence

Practical/contextual intelligence involves understanding one's self well enough to choose to live and work in environments or contexts that provide the highest probability of success and then either

think box

How would you describe your own intelligence in terms of Gardner's and Sternberg's theories? How have your abilities and challenges influenced your school experiences and your career path? Have you, or any of your teachers, made any accommodations to address your specific learning needs? If accommodations have been made, what effect did they have?

adapting to or reshaping these contexts to ensure success. It is similar to creative/experiential intelligence in that it is influenced by one's surroundings and particularly by cultural effects. However, whereas analytical/componential and creative/experiential intelligences are mostly thinking process–oriented, practical/contextual intelligence is mostly action-oriented and applicable in everyday life. Some refer to this as tacit intelligence—knowing how as opposed to knowing what.

Summary
Sternberg's model of more intelligent behaviour involves the use of meta-cognitive thinking to regulate highly automaticized information-processing and problem-solving skills to maximize the success potential evident in one's chosen environment. In short, it is goal-oriented adaptive behaviour. The only criticism of Sternberg's theory to date is that it is perhaps too broad and too inclusive.

The Source of Intelligence

In the early discussions of what intelligence is, what it represents, and where it comes from, there were vociferous arguments supporting both the nature (an individual's genetic predisposition) and the nurture (an individual's environment) sides of the debate. The debate has subsided considerably since the cognitive revolution in psychology in the 1970s, and the agreed-upon conceptualization is that both nature and nurture make considerable, but different, contributions to various intelligent behaviours. In essence, it is agreed that genetic makeup sets the limits of one's intellectual potential and the environment determines how much of that potential is realized. It may be helpful to think of one's genetic contribution as a bookcase that has finite dimensions for length, width, and depth. The entire inner space of the bookcase is divided into a variety of different-sized compartments—small, large, narrow, wide, thick, thin, deep, and shallow. It is one's environmental contribution in the form of cognitive stimulation and experience that determines the degree to which each of the compartments is filled with knowledge and skills. This filling-up process determines a person's intelligence; keep in mind that a person's maximum intellectual ability will not exceed the overall capacity of the bookcase. While the shape and size of the various compartments are set by our genetic code, the structural composition of the compartments can change depending on the amount and type of environmental stimulation an individual encounters. For example, as described earlier, the compartments that form crystallized intelligence will increase over one's lifetime if the environment continually presents challenging and attainable learning tasks. Similarly, while the filling-up process mostly occurs because of environmental stimulation, small portions of some spaces in some compartments will automatically be filled by inherent cognitive skills that are not environmentally dependent, such as those associated with fluid intelligence. Finally, it is also helpful to envision that many of the shelves and partitions have small or large holes that act as connective pathways between compartments. These connections allow for the interactions between associated cognitive skills that are evident in many school-related tasks.

Why Is It Important for Teachers to Understand Intelligence?

The foremost and concomitant objectives of schooling are to impart domain-specific knowledge to students while helping them develop their cognitive abilities. To simultaneously achieve both objectives, teachers present content information in a variety of ways and ask students to both comprehend and manipulate it in order to accomplish various educational tasks. These learning processes expand students' knowledge bases, teach them how to learn, and, in combination, result in better problem-solving and critical-thinking skills. Therefore, it is important for teachers to understand intelligence because (a) intellectual ability is what drives learning processes and (b) the experiential/environmental aspects of intellectual ability, such as crystallized intelligence, can be improved through learning. Furthermore, knowing about intelligence is even more imperative given that not all students learn at the same rate or in the same manner, nor can all students successfully accomplish all educational tasks to the same degree. The broad range of student intellectual abilities that teachers encounter in classrooms obviously has a direct impact on how they will conduct their teaching. It is no surprise, then, that the hallmark contribution of educational psychology to teaching and learning is a clearer understanding of individual differences in cognitive functioning, or intelligence.

By knowing in advance that obvious or subtle differences in cognitive abilities will likely be evident in all classrooms, teachers can anticipate and predict these differences and plan for suitable instructional accommodations. Because all classrooms in Canada contain students with exceptionalities, their cognitive abilities and inabilities must be understood to appreciate the complete range of cognitive skills that teachers will encounter. Differences in general intellectual abilities among all students in any one classroom, however, are not as readily noticeable as differences in their abilities within specific domains such as math, writing, reading, analyzing, and problem-solving. This is why it is important to examine student differences by looking at the underlying cognitive processes that enable domain-specific performances rather than by focusing on how "smart" students are. For example, with such specific understandings, teachers can help students become better problem-solvers or readers, which can significantly improve their academic performance and progress. Teachers cannot, however, necessarily help students become more intelligent to the same degree.

An Example of an Intelligence Test

One of the most widely used individually administered intelligence tests is the Wechsler Intelligence Scale for Children, more commonly called the WISC–IV. It is designed for children from six years and 0 months to 16 years and 11 months and provides measures of global intellectual functioning and measures of four specific cognitive indexes. Brief descriptions of the cognitive demands of the tasks contained in the subtests that comprise the four index scores are presented in Table 6.2.

Based on a variety of literature regarding the WISC–IV, it appears that the global score and the four domain-specific index scores provide good information when determining a child's eligibility for special education services.

TABLE 6.2 Cognitive Indexes of the WISC–IV

Index	Cognitive Demand	Description
Verbal Comprehension	Similarities	Identify commonalities in unrelated stimuli
	Vocabulary	Name pictured objects and define read-aloud words
	Comprehension	Understand verbal directions, specific customs, and mores
	Information	Answer specific factual questions based on learning
	Word Reasoning	Deduce a common concept from described clues
Perceptual Reasoning	Block Design	Manipulate blocks to reproduce visually presented design
	Picture Concepts	Select pictures from various groups to form another group
	Matrix Reasoning	Select missing portion of matrix from five possible responses
	Picture Completion	Identify missing parts of a picture within a time frame
Working Memory	Digit Span	Recall orally presented digits (forward or backward)
	Sequencing	Recall or manipulate orally presented numbers and letters
	Arithmetic	Use arithmetic operations to orally solve math problems
Processing Speed	Coding	Associate symbols with shapes or numbers and copy onto paper within a time limit
	Symbol Search	Search, find, and indicate target symbols within a time limit; search group symbols within a time limit
	Cancellation	Mark target pictures within random or structured arrangements of pictures within a time limit

Source: Adapted from Salvia, J. S., Ysseldyke, J. E., & Bolt, S. (2010). Assessment in special and inclusive education (11th ed., pp. 258–259). Boston, MA: Wadsworth/Cengage Publications.

Annette stops reading to make some notes. It will be important to help Jacob's parents understand that determining how "smart" he is compared to his peers is not a productive exercise. As well, their desire to know his IQ must not be an exercise in determining a "number." Rather, it will be more beneficial to Jacob if his learning is portrayed and understood in terms of his cognitive strengths and challenges. While it is relevant to assess whether or not Jacob has acquired the knowledge and skills expected of a child his age, it is most important to view him as a unique and capable learner who may need some assistance in acquiring the specific skills he must have in order to be successful in school.

Annette is not sure that Jacob has any significant learning challenges, but she decides to read more about exceptionalities and **special education** in order to refresh her knowledge of this most important field. Since inclusive education is the accepted practice in Canada, she knows that at some time in her career she is likely to find herself teaching children from all the different categories of exceptionality. Undoubtedly, knowing more about these exceptionalities will also help with the identification of children with special needs, and perhaps more important, it will enable her to immediately recognize when a student's situation warrants extra attention. One thing Annette has learned over the years is that all students, not only those identified as having an exceptionality, can exhibit significant skill deficits. Early identification of these deficits is critical to students' future academic success.

think box

What questions might Annette ask Jacob's parents in order to better understand their concerns about his abilities and his school performance? What information from Jacob's early childhood may be relevant to the current discussion?

Special Education

The movement to provide an appropriate education for students with special needs evolved from the civil rights movement of the 1960s. Prior to that, specialized educational services throughout North America were minimally available and, if available, were mostly delivered in institutional settings. The vast majority of these institutional services lacked pedagogical frameworks, and while some programs focused on skill development, most did little to prepare students with disabilities to integrate into society as contributing adults. For example, even in the 1960s and early 1970s, it was common for high schools to focus on trying to teach students with exceptionalities how to read and write when what these students really needed was instruction and experience with job skills and life skills. In 1975, United States Public Law 94-142 changed this situation in the US by requiring a free, appropriate public education for all children between the ages of three and 21, regardless of their disabilities. Since then, PL 101-476 changed the name of PL 94-142 to the Individuals with Disabilities Education Improvement Act (IDEA) and required all schools to design programs that would specifically prepare high school students with disabilities for successful transition to post-secondary education or the workforce. While Canada does not have federal, provincial, or territorial laws governing special education, all Canadian educational jurisdictions adhere to the fundamental principles contained in IDEA. Therefore, except for specific legal issues, special education is so similarly practised in Canada and the United States that even experienced educators would be hard-pressed to determine which country students with exceptionalities were being educated in, based on their individualized programs.

Despite the many advances in special education, it is still sometimes erroneously portrayed as a mysterious process that happens separately from the mainstream of regular schooling. Nothing could be further from the truth. Special education is nothing more than good teaching that is prepared and conducted slightly differently in order to accommodate the special learning needs of students with exceptionalities. This basic premise is strongly supported by the foundational assumption that all students can be taught. There is consistent evidence that once teachers understand precisely the types of cognitive functions that students with exceptionalities can and cannot perform efficiently, they can adjust their teaching and classroom management techniques to properly accommodate these learners.

The key to successful special education, therefore, is specialized instruction based on the proper assessment of children's abilities. Without assessment information, suitable educational programs cannot be designed, and teachers can only guess as to what they can do to help children learn and grow academically. It is no coincidence that the assessment process that determines whether or not a child has an exceptionality involves determining his or her strengths and deficits in terms of cognitive abilities and obtaining a better understanding of his or her social behaviour. All defining criteria for all categories of exceptionality require indices of cognitive, academic, and behavioural abilities, because learning and socialization are precisely the two primary functions of education. Therefore, if we consider intelligence to be goal-directed adaptive behaviour, then both achieving academic goals and socially adapting to one's environment must be considered intelligent school behaviour. In fact, it was because of children with exceptionalities that the very first intelligence test was created. At the turn of the twentieth century, the French government noticed that some students did not learn as well as others. Alfred Binet (1857–1911) was commissioned to develop a test to determine which students would benefit from special classes and which students should continue to receive their education in ordinary schools. Not surprisingly, numerous other measures of intellectual ability/abilities have been developed since that time, and all have been precisely and indelibly associated with educational tasks. Why? Because the underlying cognitive skills that make up intellectual ability significantly affect student learning potential, and, more important, the ways that students learn significantly affect how teaching is designed and conducted.

Who Are the Students Who Receive Special Education?

No group of students better defines the broad range of possible human intellectual ability than students with exceptionalities. **High-incidence exceptionalities**—sometimes called mild disabilities—typically include learning disabilities, behavioural disorders, giftedness, and intellectual disabilities. It would be extremely rare for a teacher not to encounter students who fit into these categories, especially those with learning disabilities and behavioural disorders such as ADHD. In addition, many teachers will also encounter some students with **low-incidence exceptionalities**—sometimes called moderate and severe disabilities—which typically include autism, hearing and visual impairments, serious health impairment, and multiple disabilities. The intellectual abilities and capacities exhibited by these students cover the entire spectrum—from extremely high to extremely low and all variations in between.

Controversies Surrounding Special Education

Two predominant and related controversies have dogged special education throughout its nearly 60-year formal history. First, there is a perception that the definitional terms used to identify categories of exceptionality are somehow stigmatizing labels that do little to advance a child's education. This is a specious argument, since neither the use of different terms nor regulations regarding these terms could ever monitor or stop the harmful intent that could render any term negative or stigmatizing. Moreover, the current preferred practice within the discipline is to use person-first language, such as "students with learning disabilities" instead of "learning-disabled students," to emphasize that schooling focuses first on the individual and then on accommodating his or her disability.

The second controversy involves arguments about where and how special education should take place—in regular classes, specialized segregated classes, or pull-out programs. This controversy was most prevalent when separate schools or segregated classes within schools were the dominant delivery mechanisms for special education services. This argument has dissipated considerably within the past 10 to 15 years because of the widespread adoption of the educational philosophy of **inclusion**. This modern perspective on special education advocates that all students with exceptionalities should be educated within regular classrooms to the greatest extent possible. More specifically, it means that the regular classroom will be the first placement option for students with special needs rather than just one of several placement options.

Today, all Canadian provinces and territories have adopted the educational philosophy of inclusion, and the vast majority of students with high-incidence exceptionalities are taught in regular classrooms. However, some students are provided with appropriate educational programming in suitable classroom placements other than the regular classroom. While controversies over labelling and educational placements have abated, there is growing concern within inclusive classrooms that students with various behavioural disorders are having a significant negative effect on the quality of education provided to all other students, including other students with

Building an Inclusive Practice

In the past 20 years, there has been a considerable change in educators' perceptions of special education. Views of special education have evolved from a predominant deficit culture—with a behavioural emphasis on rote skill acquisition and a focus on labels and procedures that had to be followed—into a perspective that (a) is much more accepting of differences, (b) understands that learning and social differences exist along continua, and (c) focuses strategic teaching interventions on both a student's strengths and his or her needs. Most important has been the transformation from the separateness of special education into the acceptance denoted by inclusive education.

Banks et al. (2005) presented a broad-spectrum analysis of what teachers need to know and be able to do in order to construct and operate within an inclusive practice. A comprehensive synthesis of the most salient points of that analysis is presented below.

Teachers should know

- how to develop a supportive classroom community in which all students feel safe with the teacher and with each other;
- the principles of child development, learning, language development, classroom management, and how to assess how and what students are learning;
- the nature of various disabilities and the fact that certain disorders occur on a spectrum from very mild to very severe; and
- how to raise pertinent questions and communicate professionally about serious educational issues that require debate and may create conflict.

In addition, teachers should be able to

- develop and use a basic repertoire of strategies and adaptations to help students gain appropriate access to the material being taught and revise teaching strategies as necessary;
- observe, monitor, and assess students to gain accurate feedback about their learning and development;
- provide direct instruction on how children should interact with their peers; and
- communicate with parents and professionals about the findings of assessments and contribute to and implement Individualized Education Programs (IEPs).

According to Banks et al., "teachers who are prepared to teach students with exceptional needs become more skillful teachers of all students because they develop deeper diagnostic skills and a wider repertoire of strategies that are useful for many students who learn in different ways" (p. 255).

exceptionalities. Most educators agree that a child with a behavioural disorder, such as ADHD or autism, has the unequivocal legal right to an education in the regular classroom; however, this right cannot undermine the equal legal right afforded to all other students in the class.

Individualized Education Programs

What is not acknowledged often enough within special education is the fact that labelling and placement controversies have significantly abated over the years because of substantial advances in the appropriateness and specificity of a child's IEP, or **Individualized Education Program**. According to Edmunds and Edmunds (2014b), the IEP:

> . . . is a document that outlines a student's individualized educational goals, the services that a student with exceptionalities will receive, the methods and strategies that will be used to deliver these services to ensure that goals are met, and the placement in which all of these will be provided (p. 37).

It stands to reason, therefore, that the better this specialized and individualized program addresses a child's specific and appropriate educational needs, the less concern there will be about where the child is to be educated and the less likely it will be that vague or inaccurate terms will be used to describe the child. According to Edmunds and Edmunds, the following three questions are key to the assessment and IEP process:

1. How do we determine the strengths and needs of students with exceptionalities?
2. What specialized programming is needed to meet the needs of students with exceptionalities, and how does it get constructed?
3. What do teachers have to know and do differently to properly implement specialized programming? (p. 34)

It is the **psycho-educational assessment** that reveals how students with exceptionalities are different from their peers and what individual strengths and needs they have. This assessment is best described as the objective, valid, and reliable process of collecting data on current levels of intellectual, academic, and social functioning for the purpose of making educational decisions. A psychologist determines the focus of the assessment by reviewing the comprehensive descriptive information provided in the referral. These details form the starting point for the testing procedure and allow the psychologist to choose a series of appropriate tests, most of which are standardized tests and norm-referenced tests (e.g., intelligence tests, academic achievement tests, test of perception and perceptual-motor skills, and tests of social and emotional behaviour). The results, along with those provided by other professionals (e.g., speech language pathologists, physical therapists, occupational therapists, and social workers), are used to construct the specialized programming contained in students' IEPs.

Edmunds and Edmunds describe the overall assessment and IEP process in terms of the six phases that govern referral, assessment, and educational intervention (see Figure 6.3). This is the process used (with some variation) throughout the Western world. It is evident from the cyclical function of the process that ongoing review and evaluation are required and that the IEP is not a static document.

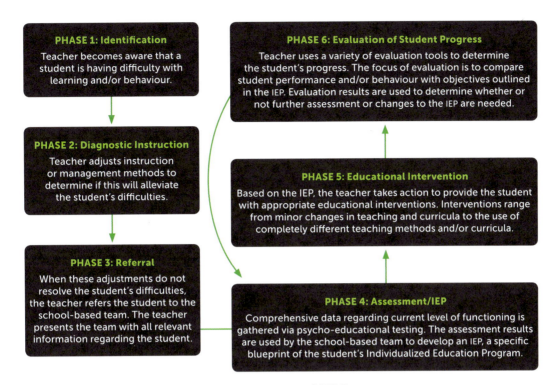

FIGURE 6.3 The Six Phases of the Assessment and IEP Process

Source: Edmunds, A.L., & Edmunds, G.A. (2014b). Special education in Canada 2e. © Oxford University Press Canada 2014. Reprinted by permission of the publisher.

Despite the vital role of the IEP, teachers often lack information about its development and use, and even when it is understood, the process of dealing with what can be a four- to eight-page document is viewed by many educators as onerous and excessive paperwork. The task of properly implementing the IEP is made especially challenging and time-consuming by the legal requirement in most Canadian jurisdictions that the IEP must be reviewed every 12 months. According to Edmunds and Edmunds:

> If the IEP is to be an accurate representation of a student's current state of functioning and act as the student's educational road map for the school year, this amount of change is logical, but probably too time-consuming given their length (p. 54).

Too often, probably because of its heightened legal stature, the IEP contains duplicates of general information, assessment results, or other material that is extraneous to the spirit and intent of the document. The IEP is intended to be an educational blueprint, not a catch-all repository. To eliminate educators' perceptions of the IEP being an onerous paper chase, Edmunds and Edmunds (2014b) sought to focus the content of the IEP into its functional elements. Based on an extensive review of numerous conceptualizations of the IEP, including those provided by the Council for Exceptional Children (CEC, 2000), the IDEA legislation (US Department of Education, 2000), and the Ontario Ministry of Education (2004), the authors designed 12 fundamental questions to be used when formulating an IEP (see Figure 6.4). These questions address the fundamental elements for effective IEP construction found in all IEP frameworks.

1. Who is the student and how old is he or she?
2. What grade is the student in, what school year is it, and who are the teachers who will implement this plan?
3. Why was the student referred in the first place? This alerts the student's teachers to the types of behaviours to watch for.
4. How is the student currently doing in his or her courses/subjects? Barely mastering something is different from struggling with it, which is different from failing it.
5. What does the student do well, struggle with, and/or not do at all?
6. What do we want the student to accomplish over the term/school year?
7. What have teachers done previously that has proven successful? This provides insights as to the continued use of particular interventions and how to make minor modifications to them if needed.
8. Based on the student's strengths and needs, what curricular learning outcomes have to be omitted, added (in the case of students who are gifted), or modified? These are often called short-term objectives, but we feel that it is better if they are more precisely expressed as learning expectations.
9. What accommodations, adaptations, or modifications are needed to allow the student to successfully attain his or her learning expectations?
10. Are there any unique circumstances that need to be considered, such as whether the student will participate in province-wide testing?
11. How and when will the student's progress be evaluated and reported?
12. Who has agreed that this document constitutes the student's plan for the year?

FIGURE 6.4 Twelve Fundamental Questions for IEP Formulation

Source: Edmunds, A. L., & Edmunds, G. A. (2014b). Special education in Canada (2nd. ed., pp. 48–50). © Oxford University Press Canada 2014. Reprinted by permission of the publisher.

Based on these questions, Edmunds and Edmunds constructed a one-page IEP that would suffice for all students with mild disabilities. Using an IEP of this length would be beneficial to teachers, because students in this group represent 89% of all Canadian students with exceptionalities. Figure 6.5 contains an example of a one-page IEP that was designed using the 12 fundamental questions. This one-page document replaced a student's original six-page IEP while retaining all the significant and required information.

The Cognitive Abilities of Students with Exceptionalities

The following sections provide brief cognitive profiles of the types of students with exceptionalities who are likely to be educated in regular classrooms—students with ADHD, students with autism spectrum disorder, students who are gifted and talented, students with mild intellectual

Individualized Edsucation Program

Student Name: Karl Hildebrandt **Date of Birth**: June 28, 2003 **Age**: 11

Date/Grade/Teacher(s): September 1, 2014/Grade 5/Jill McCarthy

Reason for Referral: dramatic reduction in academic performance; not reading at grade level.

Current Levels of Achievement by Relevant Subject:

Reading	—	Level 3 in Grade 4 expectations
Writing	—	Level 2 in Grade 4 expectations

Student Strengths and Needs Derived from Assessment: positive attitude towards learning; above-average cognitive abilities; hard worker; verbally expressive; good general knowledge; creative; difficulty with reading, spelling, and mathematics; can be hyperactive and impulsive; is not well organized.

Short-Term Learning Expectations:

Reading	—	Term 1	Level 4 in Grade 4 expectations
		Term 2	Level 1 in Grade 5 expectations
		Term 3	Level 2 in Grade 5 expectations
Writing	—	\multicolumn{2}{l}{make appropriate progress within each reporting period as Karl moves from Level 2 to Level 3 in Grade 4 expectations.}

Long-Term Learning Goals:

Reading	—	Level 2 in Grade 5 expectations
Writing	—	Level 3 in Grade 4 expectations

Successfully Implemented Teacher Interventions: reminders for following instructions and turn-taking; reading aloud improved with practice; written work improved with revision and editing; reminders to remember math symbols have improved achievement.

Learning Expectations Omitted/Added/Modified: Karl is expected to fulfill all the Grade 5 learning expectations except for those noted above for reading and writing.

Required Accommodations/Adaptations/Modifications: cueing from educational assistant or teacher; use of manipulatives in math; teacher provides written notes where appropriate; allowed a scribe and extra time for independent tasks and tests; use of quiet work area.

Special Considerations: candidate for use of assistive technology.

Description of Progress Indicators: evaluations according to Grade 4 and 5 expectations.

Schedule of Progress Indicators: reported according to Grade 5 assessment periods.

Principal's Signature: _____ Date: _____

Parent/Guardian Signature(s): _____ Date: _____

Student Signature: _____ Date: _____

* In the province of Ontario, four levels of achievement are identified for each learning expectation (Level 1—limited achievement, Level 2—some achievement, Level 3—considerable achievement, and Level 4—a high degree of achievement).

FIGURE 6.5 Example of a One-Page IEP

disability, and students with specific learning disorders. Their abilities are described in terms of the cognitive strengths and weaknesses that typically occur within these populations with the full understanding that each description may not necessarily apply to all students in any particular category. It is best to view cognitive abilities as a continuum of skills that range from highly efficient to highly inefficient. Except in very rare cases, the cognitive abilities of students attending school are not functions that either exist or do not exist. For example, students may be good critical thinkers or poor critical thinkers, or good at math or poor at math; it is not the case that some students have critical thinking abilities or math skills, while others have none of either or both. It is also important to acknowledge that the cognitive abilities and inabilities described here do not apply only to students with exceptionalities. The continuum of highly efficient to highly inefficient skills applies to students without exceptionalities as well. While most students not identified as having an exceptionality are able to learn fairly efficiently and perform nearly all of the educational tasks presented to them, some non-identified students have cognitive efficiencies and inefficiencies similar to those of identified students.

In a similar fashion, the instructional methods described for each of the categories of exceptionality are presented with the full understanding that these are general teaching guidelines that have proved beneficial for most students within each category. It should be noted that many of these methods will have to be specifically adapted or modified to suit a student's needs or to suit a teacher's unique way of teaching. Differentiated instruction, sometimes called **differentiated learning**, is a teaching and learning philosophy that emphasizes the purposeful use of a variety of instructional strategies to properly address students' diverse learning needs. In this approach, teachers adapt and tailor instruction and curriculum to suit students' needs rather than expecting students to adapt their learning to suit one-size-fits-all teaching methods. Furthermore, truly differentiated instruction is more than making sure that a wide variety of teaching methods is used; it is instruction designed to engage students in classroom activities that stimulate their particular learning needs, strengths, and preferences. Differentiated instruction is beneficial for all students, but it is particularly important when addressing the diverse academic potentials of students with exceptionalities.

Each child's IEP will contain details about the specific curricular and instructional modifications that need to be implemented. All of the suggested instructional approaches will be familiar to teachers, since these approaches emanate from research on excellent teaching practices. In order to accommodate students with exceptionalities, teachers will use some approaches much more often and others much less often, or not at all, depending on the needs of the student and the learning objectives of the curricula. Regardless of the teaching approaches used, however, *all* students function best when they are in supportive learning environments. They need classrooms that foster psychological security through proactive behavioural management; classrooms that offer predictability, structure, and routines as well as clearly established rules, rewards, and consequences; and classrooms that encourage and promote academic and personal growth.

Students with ADHD

Students with behavioural, mental, and emotional disorders are categorized as having an emotional disturbance. According to the Individuals with Disabilities Education Improvement Act (2004a), an emotional disturbance is defined as a condition exhibiting one or more of the following characteristics over a sustained period and to such a degree that educational performance is adversely affected:

- an inability to learn that cannot be explained by intellectual, sensory, or health factors;
- an inability to build or maintain satisfactory interpersonal relationships with peers and teachers;
- inappropriate types of behaviour or feelings under normal circumstances;
- a general pervasive mood of unhappiness or depression;
- a tendency to develop physical symptoms or fears associated with personal or school problems.

Attention deficit hyperactivity disorder (ADHD) is an emotional disturbance caused by a deficiency, imbalance, or inefficiency in brain chemicals that affects certain brain regions. It is diagnosed according to criteria found in the *Diagnostic and Statistical Manual of Mental Disorders* (DSM-V) of the American Psychiatric Association (2013) (see Figure 6.6).

In the vast majority of instances, individuals with ADHD do not carry out inappropriate behaviours deliberately, and if asked, they are typically remorseful and able to describe the appropriate behaviours that are expected of them. What they cannot do, however, is properly regulate their thinking and behaviour. Behavioural problems, which can appear as minor problems or irritations in the early years, will probably develop into more significant problems in the later school years when more self-control is expected and more independent learning is required. On the positive side, however, this also means that behavioural interventions can be implemented to help students with ADHD engage in preferred school behaviours.

ADHD is not simply a behavioural diagnosis. The research is clear that as many as one in four students with ADHD also demonstrate executive function, working memory, and learning deficits that place them at high risk for academic failure despite the fact that they are of average, or higher, intelligence. Because of their intellect and average-to-better language skills, these individuals often appear to others as articulate and capable, yet they behave badly and do not do well in school. The most frequent frustration expressed by teachers is that these students somehow do not perform what they know. This only fuels the common misperception that students with ADHD act out on purpose either to bother people or to avoid doing school work.

Cognitive Skill Profile of Individuals with ADHD

There is considerable consensus that while each individual with ADHD is unique, the following cognitive abilities and inabilities are common within this population. It should be noted that most of the cognitive strengths listed are enhanced by learning environments that purposefully establish opportunities for these skills to develop.

Abilities
1. While behavioural interference results in less efficient initial learning, students with ADHD are very capable of storing learned knowledge and skills in long-term memory and retrieving them when necessary.
2. They are creative and imaginative problem-solvers; they have excellent brainstorming skills and, with guidance, can provide insightful views that other students miss.

According to the DSM-V, the following criteria (A, B, C, D, and E) must be met for a diagnosis of ADHD:

A. A persistent pattern of inattention and/or hyperactivity-impulsivity that interferes with functioning or development, as characterized by (1) and/or (2):

1. Inattention: Six (or more) of the following symptoms have persisted for at least six months to a degree that is inconsistent with developmental level and that negatively impacts directly on social and academic/occupational activities:
    a. Often fails to give close attention to details or makes careless mistakes in schoolwork, at work, or during other activities (e.g., overlooks or misses details, work is inaccurate).
    b. Often has difficulty sustaining attention in tasks or play activities (e.g., has difficulty remaining focused during lectures, conversations, or lengthy reading).
    c. Often does not seem to listen when spoken to directly (e.g., mind seems elsewhere, even in the absence of any obvious distraction).
    d. Often does not follow through on instructions and fails to finish schoolwork, chores, or duties in the workplace (e.g., starts tasks but quickly loses focus and is easily sidetracked).
    e. Often has difficulty organizing tasks and activities (e.g., difficulty managing sequential tasks; difficulty keeping materials and belongings in order; messy, disorganized work; has poor time management; fails to meet deadlines).
    f. Often avoids, dislikes, or is reluctant to engage in tasks that require sustained mental effort (e.g., schoolwork or homework; for older adolescents and adults, preparing reports, completing forms, reviewing lengthy papers).
    g. Often loses things necessary for tasks or activities (e.g., school materials, pencils, books, tools, wallets, keys, paperwork, eyeglasses, mobile telephones).
    h. Is often easily distracted by extraneous stimuli (for older adolescents and adults, may include unrelated thoughts).
    i. Is often forgetful in daily activities (e.g., doing chores, running errands; for older adolescents and adults, returning calls, paying bills, keeping appointments).

2. Hyperactivity and Impulsivity: Six (or more) of the following symptoms have persisted for at least six months to a degree that is inconsistent with developmental level and that negatively impacts directly on social and academic/occupational activities:
    a. Often fidgets with or taps hands or feet or squirms in seat.
    b. Often leaves seat in situations when remaining seated is expected (e.g., leaves his or her place in the classroom, in the office or other workplace, or in other situations that require remaining in place).
    c. Often runs about or climbs in situations where it is inappropriate (in adolescents or adults, may be limited to feeling restless).
    d. Often unable to play or engage in leisure activities quietly.
    e. Is often "on the go," acting as if "driven by a motor" (e.g., is unable to be or uncomfortable being still for an extended time, as in restaurants, meetings; may be experienced by others as being restless and difficult to keep up with).
    f. Often talks excessively.
    g. Often blurts out an answer before a question has been completed (e.g., completes people's sentences; cannot wait for turn in conversation).
    h. Often has difficulty waiting his or her turn (e.g., while waiting in line).
    i. Often interrupts or intrudes on others (e.g., butts into conversations, games, or activities; may start using other people's things without asking or receiving permission; for adolescents or adults, may intrude into or take over what others are doing).

B. Several inattentive or hyperactive-impulsive symptoms were present prior to age twelve years.

C. Several inattentive or hyperactive-impulsive symptoms are present in two or more settings (e.g., at home, school, or work; with friends or relatives; in other activities).

D. There is clear evidence that the symptoms interfere with, or reduce the quality of, social, academic, or occupational functioning.

E. The symptoms do not occur exclusively during the course of schizophrenia or another psychotic disorder and are not better explained by another mental disorder (e.g., mood disorder, anxiety disorder, dissociative disorder, personality disorder, substance intoxication or withdrawal).

Based on these criteria, three presentations of ADHD are identified:
  (1) ADHD, combined presentation
  (2) ADHD, predominantly inattentive presentation
  (3) ADHD, predominantly hyperactive-impulsive presentation

FIGURE 6.6 Diagnosing ADHD

3. Because they consider multiple options simultaneously, these students are flexible and more open to different ideas.
4. When stimulated and directed, the motivational drive and perseverance of students with ADHD can help them overcome cognitive skill deficits.

Inabilities
1. The persistent inattentive, impulsive, and hyperactive behaviours of students with ADHD interfere with learning because learning processes require focused attention, good judgment, the ability to deal with frustration and wait for an outcome, attention to detail, and a good sense of time and timing.
2. These students have problems with working memory—the ability to hold selected pieces of information in memory while using parts of it to solve problems or while completing other cognitive functions.
3. They have difficulty recognizing interpersonal boundaries and correctly interpreting social cues contained in spoken language, body language, and facial expressions.
4. Students with ADHD have problems understanding and expressing language.
5. They have trouble finishing what they start.
6. They lack organizational skills.
7. They have executive-function problems with planning, prioritizing, organizing, persistence, multi-tasking, and monitoring.

When their behavioural and cognitive/academic inefficiencies are considered together, it must seem to these individuals that school was purposefully designed to demand the very skill sets that they do not have. It is not hard to imagine how frustrating academic tasks are for these students.

Instructional Approaches for Students with ADHD

While about 25% of students with ADHD have some cognitive deficits that negatively affect learning, the poor academic performance and progress exhibited by most students with ADHD primarily occurs because their problematic behaviours significantly interfere with the teaching and learning process. Therefore, the academic success of students with ADHD is wholly dependent upon educational interventions that address behavioural as well as learning concerns. The psychological and social issues pertaining to their behavioural problems must at least be in an acceptable and manageable state before any level of efficient learning can be expected. Specific behavioural interventions for teachers to follow/utilize will be found in each child's IEP as a result of the assessment process that identified the student's special needs. These interventions will typically encourage students to display behaviours that are conducive to learning, and they will likely be aimed at enhancing social acceptance. Nonetheless, these student-specific interventions will not work well unless they are implemented within a well-managed classroom, a classroom that prevents most discipline problems and models and requires acceptable behaviour.

In general, because of their average-to-better intellectual abilities, academic success for students with ADHD will depend on their ability to attend to their teachers, stay focused on academic tasks, and meet classroom behavioural expectations. These are the skills that will enable them to learn the required material, finish required assignments, and participate in classroom activities and discussions. Teachers can facilitate these important skills and processes by always using carefully structured lessons that introduce, explain, and summarize each topic. To significantly help students with ADHD, all academic interventions should strive to reduce the cognitive demand of the tasks that are processed in working memory. This can be done by helping students break tasks into smaller, workable units and by providing them with executive functioning cues and prompts that help organize and guide their thinking. While teachers generally do this for all students, they will have to do this specifically and constantly for students with ADHD. This slight adaptation is an excellent example of how good teaching methods can be implemented differently in order to benefit students with special needs.

Students with Autism Spectrum Disorder

As indicated by Edmunds and Edmunds (2014b), autism spectrum disorder (ASD) is classified as "a neurodevelopmental disorder that incorporates several previously separate diagnoses, including autistic disorder, childhood disintegrative disorder, Asperger's disorder, and pervasive developmental disorder not otherwise specified" (p. 250). This new definition distinguishes between three levels of severity as outlined by the DSM-V (American Psychiatric Association, 2013)—requiring support, requiring substantial support, and requiring very substantial support.

A diagnosis of ASD is based on the fact that the child demonstrates qualitative impairments in both social interaction and communication and has restricted, repetitive, and stereotyped patterns of behaviour, interests, and activities (see Figure 6.7). Individuals with ASD can display a wide spectrum of abilities (see Table 6.3).

Cognitive Skill Profile of Individuals with ASD – Level 1

The decision to include students with ASD in regular classrooms is mostly determined by their ability to effectively interact with teachers and peers rather than by any educational criteria. There is considerable consensus that while each individual with ASD is unique, the following cognitive abilities and inabilities are common among those who are high-functioning (Level 1) and best able to succeed in a classroom setting.

Abilities
1. Students who are high-functioning may have very good memory skills.
2. They may have the ability to focus intently.
3. They may have excellent auditory and visual perception when dealing with well-known information.
4. While they may have a sophisticated vocabulary at a young age, they are almost exclusively literal language users who have difficulty with the nuances of figurative language.
5. While behavioural interference may result in less efficient initial learning, these students may be quite capable of retrieving learned knowledge and skills from long-term memory.

According to the DSM-V, the following criteria (A, B, C, D, and E) must be met for a diagnosis of ASD:

A. Persistent deficits in social communication and social interaction across multiple contexts, as manifested by the following, currently or by history:
   1. Deficits in social-emotional reciprocity, ranging, for example, from abnormal social approach and failure of normal back-and-forth conversation; to reduced sharing of interests, emotions, or affect; to failure to initiate or respond to social interactions.
   2. Deficits in nonverbal communicative behaviours used for social interaction, ranging, for example, from poorly integrated verbal and nonverbal communication; to abnormalities in eye contact and body language or deficits in understanding and use of gestures; to a total lack of facial expressions and nonverbal communication.
   3. Deficits in developing, maintaining, and understanding relationships, ranging, for example, from difficulties adjusting behavior to suit various social contexts; to difficulties in sharing imaginative play or in making friends; to absence of interest in peers.

B. Restricted, repetitive patterns of behaviour, interests, or activities as manifested by at least two of the following, currently or by history:
   1. Stereotyped or repetitive motor movements, use of objects, or speech.
   2. Insistence on sameness, inflexible adherence to routines, or ritualized patterns of verbal or nonverbal behaviour.
   3. Highly restricted, fixated interests that are abnormal in intensity or focus.
   4. Hyper- or hypo-reactivity to sensory input or unusual interest in sensory aspects of environment.

C. Symptoms must be present in the early developmental period (but may not become fully manifest until social demands exceed limited capacities or may be masked by learned strategies in later life).

D. Symptoms cause clinically significant impairment in social, occupational, or other important areas of current functioning.

E. These disturbances are not better explained by intellectual disability or global developmental delay.

FIGURE 6.7 Diagnosing Autism Spectrum Disorder

TABLE 6.3 Levels of Severity in Autism Spectrum Disorder

Severity Level for ASD	Social Communication	Restricted, Repetitive Behaviours
Level 3 Requiring Very Substantial Support	Severe deficits in verbal and nonverbal social communication skills cause severe impairments in functioning; very limited initiation of social interactions and minimal response to social overtures from others.	Inflexibility of behaviour, extreme difficulty coping with change, or other restricted/repetitive behaviours markedly interfere with functioning in all spheres. Great distress/difficulty changing focus or action.
Level 2 Requiring Substantial Support	Marked deficits in verbal and nonverbal social communication skills; social impairments apparent even with supports in place; limited initiation of social interactions and reduced or abnormal response to social overtures from others.	Inflexibility of behaviour, difficulty coping with change, or other restricted/repetitive behaviours appear frequently enough to be obvious to the casual observer and interfere with functioning in a variety of contexts. Distress and/or difficulty changing focus or action.
Level 1 Requiring Support	Without supports in place, deficits in social communication cause noticeable impairments. Difficulty initiating social interactions and clear examples of atypical or unsuccessful responses to social overtures of others. May appear to have decreased interest in social interactions.	Inflexibility of behaviour causes significant interference with functioning in one or more contexts. Difficulty switching between activities. Problems of organization and planning hamper independence.

Source: Reprinted with permission from the *Diagnostic and Statistical Manual of Mental Disorders*, Fifth Edition, Copyright © 2013 American Psychiatric Association. All Rights Reserved.

Inabilities

1. Students may have problems staying on point and concluding lengthy discussions, even when the topics are of high interest.
2. Although proficiency with well-known information, they may have problems with new tasks involving visual-spatial perception, auditory perception, or visual memory.
3. They may have problems with proprioception (awareness of body in space), balance, and finger–thumb apposition.
4. These students may find it difficult to identify and describe personal emotions.
5. They may have a tendency toward anxiety and depression.

By definition, the cognitive skills of individuals with ASD–Level 1 are efficient enough to enable them to complete all school tasks. Schooling is enhanced when the abilities of those with ASD are encouraged to flourish within environments that facilitate the management of their highly distressing symptoms such as poor communication, obsessive/repetitive routines, and non-verbal vulnerability. At the same time, educators must take advantage of the linguistic and verbal strengths of these students in an effort to teach them age-appropriate social, communication, and vocational skills. Encouraging students to use their abilities to help compensate for their inabilities fosters independence and enhances self-esteem, both of which contribute to learning.

Instructional Approaches for Students with ASD

Perhaps more than any other category of students with exceptionalities, students with ASD benefit from well-structured classrooms that provide individualized or small-group instruction. The best instructional approaches for students with ASD reflect a teacher's systematic attention to the primary characteristics of the disorder; the goal is to reduce or eliminate the persistent behavioural interferences that typically compromise learning.

The explicit teaching of social skills and social interaction preferences has also proved beneficial with these students, especially those who are high-functioning. By seating a student with ASD next to an understanding "peer buddy," the teacher has another person who can serve as a social translator. It is often better to have a peer translate an event or occurrence into "what really happened" or "what that really meant," rather than to have the teacher doing it all the time. In terms of expressive communication, the translator can also be taught to reframe what can appear to be unintended, rude, and immature behaviours common within the ASD population. It would be beneficial to educate all classroom peers about how individuals with ASD are prone to highly literal interpretations of words and phrases and how they tend to blurt out what appear to be highly insensitive comments and questions.

Because many students with ASD are overwhelmed by noise, crowds, and/or perceived chaos, teachers should provide alternatives to attending loud and noisy school gatherings, such as assemblies, or have the students experiment with ear plugs or headphones to help block out troubling noise. Also, it is beneficial to introduce the student to one or two other trusted adults within the school who are available to help prevent or defuse crises.

While all students do well in structured environments, students with ASD absolutely thrive on routine and predictability. Teachers should use a variety of highly visible schedules and time frames to help their students reduce their lack-of-structure anxiety. If changes to routines are pending, teachers should explain them well in advance and provide frequent reminders leading up to the event. It is also beneficial to have students verbalize the ensuing changes to make sure that they have effectively processed them. In a similar fashion, teachers should use reminder notes for assignments and refer to previous conversations to clarify changes—this takes advantage of the students' excellent rote memory. Finally, teachers should make extensive use of visuals, graphics, models, and technology, because these modes are the highly preferred learning mechanisms of students with ASD.

Students Who Are Gifted and Talented

Students who are gifted and talented are usually easily identified by their outstanding performance on school-related tasks. These students represent 3–5% of the general population. The following definition from Marland's (1972) report to the US Congress continues to be the most widely used across Canada and the United States:

> Gifted and talented children are those identified by professionally qualified persons who by virtue of outstanding abilities are capable of high performance. These are children who require differentiated educational programs and/or services beyond those normally provided by the regular school program in order to realize their contribution to self and society. Children capable of high performance include those with demonstrated achievement and/or potential ability in any of the following areas, singly or in combination: general intellectual ability, specific academic aptitude, creative or productive thinking, leadership ability, and visual and performing arts (p. 10).

Cognitive Skill Profile of Individuals Who Are Gifted and Talented

The following cognitive abilities of students who are gifted and talented are described in relation to the five different categories identified by Marland.

Abilities

1. High general intellectual ability, as measured by an IQ test, typically refers to a wide knowledge base and high levels of performance on tasks that address vocabulary, memory, abstract knowledge, and abstract reasoning; it translates to an IQ score that is at least two standard deviations above the mean.
2. Specific academic aptitude is marked by outstanding performance (97% or higher) on domain-specific achievement tests (e.g., writing, math, science).
3. Creative or productive thinking is typically demonstrated by an uncanny ability to bring independent or seemingly unrelated elements together to result in new products or ideas that are meaningful.
4. Leadership ability is evident when an individual is able to successfully guide a group through the process of reaching a common goal; group dynamics are considered and negotiation skills are used when solving problems.
5. Visual and performing arts abilities are marked by special talents in visual arts, music, dance, or drama.

Teachers and parents often describe students with gifts and talents in terms of their superior ability to learn, retain, and manipulate vast amounts of detailed information very quickly. They exhibit heightened and rapid cognitive functioning in many areas, including the ability to (a) reason, (b) make part-to-whole and whole-to-part associations, (c) problem-solve, (d) develop deep specific interests, (e) use advanced vocabulary, and (f) sustain concentration/focus. With advances in our understandings about cognition and learning, these students are more often being described as having extremely efficient learning strategies, integrated and more broadly applicable metacognitive problem-solving abilities, and the motivation to learn and excel.

Inabilities

Students who are gifted and talented typically do not demonstrate cognitive inabilities per se, but it is not unusual that their average or above-average skills in some areas appear considerably weaker than their most superior abilities. It should be noted that there is a common misperception that these students do not have many friends or have significant social interaction problems. Research does not support this fallacy; in fact, there is considerable evidence that most students who are gifted and talented typically receive high ratings on social acceptance, social conduct, sensitivity, and social responsiveness. Lewis Terman's landmark research into the lives of 1528 students identified as being gifted in the 1920s revealed that these individuals were more emotionally stable and better adjusted than average and had lower rates of delinquency and emotional difficulty. Nonetheless, adjustment problems do appear to be more common in individuals with extremely high intellect, typically an IQ greater than 180. It is quite likely that the social adjustment problems that occur in this small faction have been erroneously applied to the entire gifted population.

As has been stated, students who are gifted demonstrate few cognitive inabilities; however, students who are identified as being gifted and as having a learning disability (commonly referred to as **twice-exceptional learners**) demonstrate a wide range of inabilities that can include difficulties with the processing skills involved in reading and writing, poor social skills, and some anti-social behaviours. These challenges explain the predominant school-performance problems typically associated with this population. According to Nielsen (as cited in Nielsen & Higgins, 2005), the other cognitive inabilities that can stem from an identified learning disability include

- deficient or extremely uneven academic skills that can lead to a lack of academic initiative and school-task avoidance;
- processing deficits that may cause students to respond slowly, work slowly, and appear to think slowly;
- difficulty with long-term and short-term memory;
- gross- or fine-motor difficulties exhibited by clumsiness, poor handwriting, or problems completing paper-and-pencil tasks;
- a lack of organizational and study skills;
- difficulty thinking linearly, resulting in an inability to understand cause and effect or to follow directions;
- extreme impulsivity; and
- high distractibility.

Instructional Approaches for Students Who Are Gifted and Talented

The primary goal of all good teaching is to constantly present students with learning tasks that are challenging but attainable. This is even more important for students who are gifted and talented because of their rapid learning rates, their highly capable and flexible cognitive skills, and their broad knowledge and interest bases. Teachers must be aware that classroom instruction will be less than challenging for these students if curricular topics and selected modes of presentation are not carefully and constantly monitored for appropriateness. Otherwise, boredom with school activities may lead to a lack of interest in learning, which unfortunately can result in problematic and disruptive behaviours and/or dropping out of school. In this regard, students who are gifted and talented are said to be one of the most underserved student populations.

The three most common forms of instructional approaches used in Canada for teaching students who are gifted and talented are (1) congregated classes or schools, (2) acceleration programs, and (3) enrichment programs. Congregated classes or schools put all identified students together in either specially designated classes or schools and provide them with a form of education that more precisely matches their knowledge and skills regardless of age or grade. For example, the curricular combination for a group of students in a Grade 5 class may include the Grade 5 social studies course, the Grade 6 English course, the Grade 7 math course, and the Grade 8 science course. The grade level of the various courses is not important. The critical point, especially given all we know about cognition and learning, is that the curricular topics are assembled to meet the specific educational needs of these students. Again, this is a clear demonstration of how regularly occurring instruction can be used, with little or no modifications, to educate students with special needs.

Acceleration and enrichment programs can be delivered in either congregated or regular classroom settings. Acceleration programs allow students to progress through the curriculum as quickly as they can, as long as they are demonstrating that their learning is full and comprehensive. Enrichment programs give students the opportunity to delve into curricular topics in broader and deeper ways than are typically provided in the regular curriculum. Unfortunately, very few of the arguments for and against both acceleration and enrichment are founded on learning principles; most arguments for using or not using either, or both, are based on edu- and socio-politically influenced issues such as perceived elitism, high costs, high teacher-to-student ratios, and the myth that students who begin school early and advance far more rapidly than their same-age peers are somehow susceptible to poor social adjustment. From the perspective of educational psychology, there is no question that both acceleration and enrichment should be implemented. This view is based on established learning principles and the fact that challenging learning has a strong positive influence on motivation.

Acceleration methods should be used to keep students from being exposed to topics they have already mastered, and enrichment activities should be used to encourage sophisticated and thought-provoking work about topics that warrant such detailed investigations. The benefits of curriculum acceleration are obvious to all, and such advances are often enriching on their own. True enrichment, on the other hand, is less obvious and, if not done carefully, is negatively viewed as "busy work" by many in the discipline. According to Renzulli and Reis (1997), there are prescribed criteria for ensuring that enrichment achieves its objectives and does not require students to simply do more of the same. Type I enrichment involves more advanced levels of involvement in a topic, Type II enrichment involves activities designed to develop higher-level thinking and research skills, and Type III enrichment involves individual and small-group investigations of complex real-life problems.

A common problem for teachers is finding time to do all the wonderful and interesting things that are possible when acceleration and enrichment are utilized. One way for teachers to gain time for design and implementation is to use curriculum compacting—a common educational process that allows teachers to eliminate curricular topics already mastered or not needed. Curriculum compacting is warranted when, in relation to specific topics, students consistently exhibit high mastery, accuracy, and an interest in advancing their knowledge and skills. Based on the required learning objectives for the course, teachers can decide what can be skipped or briefly touched on in order to allow more time for the advanced or enriched material. In the early grades, compacting should be mandated for the basic academic skills involved in reading, writing, math calculation, spelling, and other academic processes (such as doing research projects) in which further instruction will render no skill advancement. In the later grades, compacting should be used for objectives or topics that have been mastered or those that will be learned very rapidly. Regardless of which instructional approach is used, or what it is called, the underlying learning maxim that should always be adhered to is that all academic tasks need to be challenging but attainable.

Students who are gifted and talented typically prefer the company of older classmates whose verbal and cognitive skills and academic interests are comparable to their own. There is considerable evidence that where individually appropriate, students who progress rapidly and graduate early are better off in every regard, including socially and academically. Furthermore, students provided with instruction that is tailored to the specifics of their IEP do better in school than those placed in non-specific gifted classes or programs.

Students with Mild Intellectual Disability

According to the American Association on Intellectual and Developmental Disabilities (AAID; 2014), an intellectual disability originates before age 18 and is characterized by significant limitations in both intellectual functioning and adaptive behaviour. Adaptive behaviour refers to three skill types—conceptual (e.g., language and literacy), social (e.g., interpersonal interactions), and practical (e.g., activities of daily living). Deficits in these kinds of skills significantly limit a person's ability to meet expected age-level and cultural standards for maturation, learning, school performance, and personal independence/social responsibility.

Cognitive Skill Profile of Individuals with Mild Intellectual Disability

Intellectual disabilities are classified according to four levels of severity as indicated by an IQ score: mild (between 50/55 and 70), moderate (between 35/40 and 50/55), severe (between 20/25 and 35/40), and profound (below 20/25). Approximately 85% of all individuals with intellectual disability fall into the "mild" category. Because intellectual disability is not only defined by an IQ score, the AAIDD developed a diagnostic classification system. It focuses on an individual's capabilities and results in a classification based on a person's required support across nine key areas: (1) human development, (2) teaching and education, (3) home living, (4) community living, (5) employment, (6) health and safety, (7) behaviour, (8) social, and (9) protection and advocacy. The four possible support classifications are

1. intermittent support—occasional, as-needed support, mostly during times of stress or crisis—the predominant level or type of support typically required for individuals with mild intellectual disability;
2. limited support—usually marked by a consistent and/or time-limited need (but not an intermittent/occasional need) such as a school-to-work transition;
3. extensive support—usually requires daily support in one or more environments such as school (special education teacher), work (supervised workshop), home (long-term living support), and leisure (supervised/facilitated sports); and
4. pervasive support—life-long, high-intensity, daily supports for most adaptive areas.

Abilities

With early diagnosis and consistent and supportive schooling, individuals with mild intellectual disability can acquire functional academic skills to about the Grade 6 level, and as adults, some can become fairly self-sufficient and live independently with appropriate supports. Teachers are most likely to encounter students with mild intellectual disability in regular classrooms, because these students have the potential to achieve academic growth when provided with appropriate supports and modifications.

Inabilities

In general, students with mild intellectual disability are slower and less efficient at learning than other students. Their overall learning inefficiency is roughly consistent with their overall IQ. They commonly demonstrate specific cognitive deficits in memory, attention, language, and executive functioning. While students with mild intellectual disability find it hard to remember things, they are able to learn new skills, but they do so slowly and require much more practice. As well, they typically have great difficulty transferring newly learned skills to different environments or tasks. Despite numerous intervention studies over the past three decades, researchers have not yet found the key to enabling efficient and effective transfers.

Rates of emotional and behavioural problems are also much higher in children and adolescents with intellectual disability, and due to their poor social skills (both expressive and receptive/intuitive), these students are vulnerable to verbal abuse, rejection, victimization, and exclusion from social settings. These students also have considerable difficulty understanding social rules and predicting/realizing the results of their actions and typically cannot solve new social problems without help.

Instructional Approaches for Students with Mild Intellectual Disability

There are many specific instructional approaches that teachers can use with students who have mild intellectual disabilities, but all fall into the following three general and proven overarching strategies: (1) provide more time for learning and practice than usual; (2) where possible, contextualize all activities within daily life; and (3) include students in both social and academic activities rather than only one or the other.

Students with mild intellectual disabilities function best when engaged in concrete operational learning activities and, with help, can learn to read, do basic math calculations, and understand basic concepts in science and social studies. They will, however, typically struggle to understand what they read beyond the straightforward ideas expressed within simple sentence structures. These students will have difficulty learning new skills; thus, it is important for teachers to ensure students are focused when instruction is provided, particularly instruction that is broken down into several steps. Because of difficulties with long- and short-term memory, lots of practice—and even over-learning—is often required to ensure mastery. These students tend to have receptive and expressive language disorders that result in them speaking less frequently, using shorter sentences, having difficulty understanding questions, and lacking the ability to repair communication when it breaks down. At times, it will appear that they do not follow directions when, in fact, they simply do not understand the verbal directions and/or the task assigned and/or the connections between the two.

Students with mild intellectual disabilities typically have a high external locus of control; they often believe they are not responsible for their actions and are more likely to look to others to initiate and complete tasks. Teachers can address these behaviours by building a foundation of successful learning experiences upon which more challenging activities can be added. This approach, when combined with as much familiarity as possible, will encourage students to work more independently, and it will also help with generalizing learned skills to different situations.

Most students with mild intellectual disabilities will be involved in life-skills programs. These programs must be taught via direct instruction that makes extensive use of modelling, prompting, guided practice, and independent work, and the instruction must provide suitable reinforcement at each stage. Teachers who provide instruction using explicit language and present school work in a simple, step-by-step format are far more successful than teachers who use inferential language or expect students to transfer learning from one task to another.

Students with Specific Learning Disorders

Students with learning disabilities, or specific learning disorders as they were recently named in the DSM-V (American Psychiatric Association, 2013), represent 50–70% of all students with exceptionalities whom teachers will encounter in regular classrooms. Their cognitive abilities span a broad spectrum of strengths and weaknesses. In fact, the biggest instructional dilemma for teachers is that most students with a specific learning disorder (SLD) will simultaneously demonstrate considerable cognitive strengths alongside highly notable cognitive inefficiencies. It is not unusual, for example, for a student with a SLD to demonstrate high verbal proficiency (receptive and expressive) yet demonstrate very poor reading and writing skills. Teachers not familiar with this type and level of discrepancy are justifiably confused when they encounter an articulate and seemingly bright student who cannot read or write well enough to properly handle appropriate academic tasks.

The breadth and range of skills and weaknesses exhibited by students with SLDs is also reflected in the expansive criteria of the learning disability definition. According to the Council for Exceptional Children (CEC, 2006a, 2006b), in general, individuals with learning disabilities typically have average or above average IQ but do not achieve the same academic proficiency as their peers. In other words, they exhibit a discrepancy between their cognitive ability and their academic achievement. The pervasive educational conundrum regarding these students, therefore, is how and why students with average or better intelligence do so poorly in school. A careful examination of the definition of learning disabilities provided by the Learning Disabilities Association of Canada (LDAC, 2013) helps to illustrate why this occurs:

"Learning Disabilities" refer to a number of disorders which may affect the acquisition, organization, retention, understanding, or use of verbal or non-verbal information. These disorders affect learning in individuals who otherwise demonstrate at least average abilities essential for thinking and/or reasoning. As such, learning disabilities are distinct from global intellectual deficiency.

Learning disabilities result from impairments in one or more processes related to perceiving, thinking, remembering, or learning. These include—but are not limited to—language processing, phonological processing, visual-spatial processing, processing speed, memory and attention, and executive functions (e.g., monitoring, planning, and decision making).

Learning disabilities range in severity and may interfere with the acquisition and use of one or more of the following:

1. oral language (e.g., listening, speaking, and understanding),
2. reading (e.g., decoding, phonetic knowledge, word recognition, comprehension),
3. written language (e.g., spelling and written expression), and
4. mathematics (e.g., computation, problem solving).

Learning disabilities may also involve difficulties with organizational skills, social perception, social interaction, and perspective taking.

Unfortunately, there is no single definition of learning disabilities that is universally adhered to in Canada, and it is not unusual to find educators using conceptual definitions of the exceptionality that differ from the operational criteria used by the psychologists who render the diagnoses. Changes in the US identification process for learning disabilities have sought to change educators' reliance on definitional and discrepancy models to the use of a model that is more instruction-based. As of 2004, the Individuals with Disabilities Education Improvement Act (2004b) permitted the use of responsiveness-to-intervention (RTI) as a supplemental criterion for identifying students with learning disabilities. The objective of the change was twofold: (1) to decrease the number of students identified as having a learning disability when their poor achievement is actually due to poor instruction and (2) to intervene earlier when academic problems surface rather than wait for the two-year discrepancy criteria to be confirmed. At this point, there is no formal or mandated RTI definition. In general, RTI is an individualized assessment and intervention process that utilizes a problem-solving framework to identify students' academic problems. It then advocates the use of proven instructional research to design educational interventions. According to the National Center on Response to Intervention (2010):

Response to intervention integrates assessment and intervention within a multi-level prevention system to maximize student achievement and to reduce behavioural problems. With RTI, schools use data to identify students at risk for poor learning outcomes, monitor students' progress, provide evidence-based interventions and adjust the intensity and nature of those interventions depending on student's responsiveness, and identify students with learning disabilities or other disabilities (p. 2).

In the RTI model, students experiencing difficulties are provided with ever-increasing curricular interventions that are continuously monitored for instructional effectiveness that results in learning. Students who do not respond well to RTI are deemed to need specialized educational services. The current criticisms of RTI are that (a) on its own, it is not sufficient to identify a specific learning disorder, (b) students' inabilities may be masked by their strong compensatory abilities during interventions, and (c) its no-cost approach may replace the formal and costly assessment process.

Cognitive Skill Profile of Individuals with Specific Learning Disorders

Lerner and Kline (2006) provided a comprehensive outline of the range of cognitive and behavioural challenges that students with learning disabilities typically experience (see Table 6.4). The most common and predominant academic difficulty within this population is a struggle with written language. These students generally have great difficulty understanding what they read, and they find it equally difficult to properly express what they know through writing. Given the strong learning connections between reading and writing, and the extensive use of printed text in most academic tasks, difficulties with both create a significant obstacle for these students and their teachers. Even the subject of mathematics presents a challenge, since math curricula currently focus more on tasks that involve reading, deciphering relevant information, and making problem-solving decisions than on straightforward calculation tasks.

What can be inferred, but is not readily evident, from Table 6.4 is that the two most common and predominant cognitive skill deficits within this population are inefficient information processing in short-term memory and inefficient metacognitive skills. Metacognitive, or executive functioning, skills are the overarching cognitive tactics used to (a) plan a learning task, (b) choose an appropriate strategy to execute the plan, (c) properly employ the strategy, (d) monitor the efficiency of the strategy during its use, and (e) evaluate the final outcome relative to the initial objective. Relative to their peers, individuals with SLDs tend to have limited repertoires of learning strategies, and they do not readily or easily generate new strategies when they encounter new learning challenges. This is a major problem, because learning strategies are the specific cognitive tactics that individuals use to (a) understand and learn new information and skills, (b) efficiently integrate this new information into what is already known, and (c) recall it when needed. To make matters worse, students with SLDs are frequently unable to recognize when a strategy is not resulting in efficient learning. Moreover, these students are also inefficient at focusing on relevant material to which they need to apply all of the above skills. It is not difficult to imagine how these skill deficits can make independent learning, such as homework and seatwork, especially difficult. Unfortunately, many of these students become passive

TABLE 6.4 Common Learning and Behavioural Characteristics of Students with Learning Disabilities

Characteristic	Description
Disorders of attention	Does not focus when a lesson is presented; short attention span, easily distracted, poor concentration; may display hyperactivity
Poor motor abilities	Difficulty with gross-motor abilities and fine-motor co-ordination (exhibits general awkwardness and clumsiness)
Psychological processing deficits	Problems processing auditory and/or visual information (difficulty interpreting visual and auditory stimuli)
Lack of phonological awareness	Poor at recognizing sounds of language (cannot identify phoneme sounds in spoken language)
Poor cognitive strategies for learning	Does not know how to go about the task of learning and studying; lacks organizational skills; passive learning style (does not direct own learning)
Oral language difficulties	Underlying language disorders (problems in language development, listening, speaking, and vocabulary)
Reading difficulties	About 80% of students with learning disabilities have disabilities in reading (problems learning to decode words, basic word-recognition skills, or reading comprehension).
Writing difficulties	Difficulty with written expression, spelling, and handwriting
Mathematics	Difficulty with quantitative thinking, arithmetic, time, space, and calculation
Social skills	Does not know how to act and talk in social situations; difficulty establishing satisfying social relationships and friendships

learners, not because they do not want to take responsibility for their learning but because they simply do not know how to learn and cannot do so efficiently even when they try.

What is also not evident from Table 6.4 is that these cognitive and metacognitive skill deficits initially appear as minor difficulties in the early years and then develop into more significant hindrances in the later grades when schooling requires more sophisticated and complex learning, usually executed independently. The students' lack of both specific and overarching cognitive tactics presents a perplexing problem for teachers. While they realize that these students would obviously benefit from learning-strategy instruction, they also know that even if taught the strategies, the students might not use them expeditiously and might not recognize when a strategy is inefficient. Thus, despite a teacher's best efforts to provide these students with effective and independent learning processes, the teacher still has to provide ongoing monitoring and supervision.

While the above descriptions of students with SLDs may appear to imply homogeneity, this is not the case. Students with learning disorders have widely discrepant and often subtle variations in their abilities and inabilities. Because of this heterogeneity, each individual student must undergo a rigorous assessment process if their strengths and needs are to be precisely identified. Without proper assessment indicators, teachers will not be able to change or modify their instruction accordingly. However, with the completion of an excellent assessment, wherein specific strengths and weaknesses are identified, teachers will be able to make appropriate accommodations. This assessment–instruction approach has resulted in many more individuals with learning disabilities graduating from high school and going on to post-secondary education—a considerable improvement from the past.

Finally, it is worth noting that ADHD is a commonly co-occurring condition for children with learning disabilities. According to Lerner and Kline (2006), 25–40% of individuals with learning disabilities have co-occurring ADHD, and 30–60% of individuals with ADHD have a co-occurring learning disability. There is considerable evidence, however, that the two conditions are not causally related, since neurological research strongly suggests that different brain regions are involved in each of the two conditions. However, there may be more overlap between these regions than was previously thought; recent research has revealed that individuals with ADHD and individuals with LD have very similar cognitive and metacognitive deficits.

Instructional Approaches for Students with Specific Learning Disorders

As mentioned, although all students with learning disabilities have different cognitive strengths and challenges, problems common to the population include slow and inefficient reading, slow conceptualization (organization) and execution of essay-writing (writing mechanics), and frequent math calculation errors. Seriously affecting all of the above problems are noted deficits in learning-strategy generation and use and deficits in metacognitive functioning. Therefore, while specific instructional approaches for students with SLDs are typically derived from their IEPs, the two types of intervention that appear to produce the best results in terms of improved academic performance are (1) learning-strategy instruction and (2) assistance with metacognitive functions.

A cognitive strategy is a mental tactic that is purposefully used to learn or problem-solve when the steps for complex learning or problem-solving are not evident or provided, such as when students encounter new information or a new problem. For example, the steps in writing up a science lab using a template are precise, clear, and evident, whereas the steps and processes used in reading for meaning are not. Therefore, the mind has to develop and execute a strategy in order to gain understanding while carrying out the process of reading. Strategies to accomplish this usually involve the self-asking and the self-answering of questions. In fact, one of the best components of many strategies is the question "Does this make sense?"

For most students, devising and implementing cognitive strategies is immediate and highly efficient. However, for students with SLDs, their strategies and the various steps in their strategies have to be broken down and explicitly taught. Therefore, the focus of cognitive-strategy instruction should not be on the strategies used; rather, it needs to be on the way strategies are implemented. Based on Graham and Harris's (2003) self-regulated strategy development model, the emphasis on this type of implementation produces strategies that are habitual, flexible, and automatic. In order for this to happen, students must understand how a strategy works and why each step in the strategy is performed. To accomplish this, teachers follow six stages in strategy development, and while these stages are linear, they can be reordered or combined as the teacher sees fit. In fact, revisiting particular stages as needed will reinforce mastery and better develop students' metacognitive skills.

Stage 1   Develop and Activate Background Knowledge and Skills
Students with learning disabilities often lack essential background knowledge or skills to successfully use a strategy. Task analysis can be used to identify the basics. All skill deficits need to be addressed before introducing the strategy.

Stage 2   Discuss and Introduce the Strategy

Discussion of the strategy will actively involve students, provide ownership, and bring them to the point where they are self-regulated. The strategy is "sold" on the fact that it will result in improved academic performance. The benefits of getting more work done earlier can also be explained.

Stage 3   Model the Strategy

The purpose of modelling is to expose students to the thought processes of a skilled learner by discussing the "why" and "how" of various strategy steps, demonstrating that effort is essential, and showing how strategy use can result in better performance. This think-aloud process not only shows students what to do but also what to think.

Stage 4   Memorize the Strategy

Committing the strategy steps to memory allows students to focus on the task, not on remembering the steps. This reduces the load on working memory so it can become second nature to students.

Stage 5   Support the Strategy

Supporting the strategy occurs by scaffolding whereby teachers initially verbalize all or most of the strategy while the students execute it. Then, based on observations of strategy mastery, teachers increasingly shift responsibility for complete performance to the student. While independent strategy use is the objective, teachers should never eliminate their supervision of the process and leave students completely on their own. If errors or misapplications occur, previous stages in the process will have to be revisited.

Stage 6   Independent Performance

The ultimate objective is cognitive-strategy use that leads to improved academic performance. Students may adapt the strategy to meet their needs as long as it helps them successfully complete the intended academic task. Therefore, continued monitoring is required.

This instructional method is not a quick fix for students with SLDs. New strategies are always required as students progress through the curriculum. Reaching Stage 6 in one instance does not mean that the student can easily apply new strategies with the same independence. However, with continued instruction over time, students will become more proficient at transferring their skills.

Annette contemplates all that she has just read. Although she does not feel that Jacob has any problems similar to those described, she will certainly listen carefully to his parents' concerns, keep a close eye on his progress, and consult with Mr. Parker about Jacob's performance on the screening assessments conducted at the beginning of the year.

On the other hand, the reading material has piqued Annette's attention in regard to the academic performance of several other students. She is fairly sure that Anna is a gifted student, and perhaps Tara may fall into that category as well. She is also concerned about Katherine's learning difficulties, although she does not think that Katherine fits into any of the categories of exceptionality. Nonetheless, Annette will definitely speak with Mr.

Parker regarding these three students. After all, other than their parents, she is perhaps most aware of how these students learn. It is her responsibility to find effective instructional approaches that help them progress or, if necessary, refer these students for possible assessment by a qualified professional.

Annette's intuition has already led to more positive learning experiences for Brandon. His difficulty with written work has been confirmed by Mr. Parker, and with some simple accommodations (i.e., the use of a keyboard and oral rather than written testing), Brandon is performing much better in subjects that were previously quite challenging for him. Mr. Parker used a screening assessment tool (Beery-Buktenica Developmental Test of Visual-Motor Integration) to determine that Brandon does encounter significant difficulty when he is required to integrate his visual and motor abilities to produce written work. Mr. Parker was also able to confirm that Brandon has no other barriers to learning, as was previously suspected. Now that Brandon can demonstrate his knowledge and abilities without having to worry about the physicality of writing, he is quite successful in all academic areas. While Annette is extremely pleased that school has become less frustrating for him, she wishes these easily implemented accommodations could have been put into place much earlier in Brandon's schooling.

Just as Annette is about to close her file on "Individual Differences," she notices a paper prepared by Dr. Cameron. He said during the summer course that it was additional reading—something to consider when contemplating student differences. Annette is soon deeply immersed in the content.

Cognitive Styles, Learning Styles, and Temperament

Intelligence and the various cognitive abilities that make up intellectual activity can be considered our basic mental tools. The terms "cognitive style," "learning style," and "temperament" are used to describe our preferred ways of implementing these tools.

Cognitive style is a typical mode of perceiving, remembering, thinking, and problem-solving that is somewhat reflective of personality. Individuals who perceive patterns as wholes instead of independent elements are said to have a field-dependent cognitive style. These individuals tend to work well in groups and prefer global topics such as history and social studies, but they typically struggle at monitoring their own use of problem-solving strategies. Individuals who can perceive and analyze patterns in terms of elemental components are said to have a field-independent cognitive style. These persons are usually not as sensitive to social relationships, and they prefer science and math courses, where their tendency to monitor their own cognitive strategies provides success. Cognitive style is also described as being reflective or impulsive—reflective individuals are more patient and thoughtful when presented with academic tasks, while impulsive individuals are more spontaneous and reactive. As schooling progresses, a more reflective style is preferred because of the complexity of the material to be learned and the thoughtfulness required when writing about what has been learned. All students can be taught to be more reflective with specific instruction that emphasizes the importance of paying attention to metacognitive executive functions.

Learning style refers to the preferred mode of learning (i.e., auditory versus visual) and the preferred learning environment (e.g., working alone or in groups). When combined with cognitive style, learning style can have a significant influence on what gets done and where. For example, some students like to have the TV on when doing homework, while for others this is a major distraction. Still other students do not like working at home at all, preferring to do homework in the classroom or library.

There is little empirical evidence that matching instruction with either cognitive styles or learning styles has any significant effect on individual student achievement. Nonetheless, as in the case of multiple intelligences, teaching that considers and utilizes a variety of instructional options to allow for different styles will likely appeal to, and benefit, many more students than approaches that are one-dimensional. It should be noted, however, that teachers should not include these types of options simply for the sake of appealing to different cognitive or learning styles. This would be an inappropriate reason for making critical instructional decisions. Instead, teachers should make extensive use of these cognitive and learning preferences when they fit well within curricular demands and/or their overall approach to teaching.

The manner in which individuals typically behave in different environments and respond to various occurrences in their lives is referred to as their temperament. More specifically, temperament is described as a series of innate traits that account for the differences in the quality and intensity of individuals' emotional reactions. According to Thomas and Chess's (1977) original conceptual framework, there are nine key traits of temperament that are demonstrated on a continuum from low to high:

1. activity level (the amount of time spent in active movement);
2. adaptability (the ease with which one adapts to changes in the environment);
3. rythmicity (the regularity of bodily functions such as eating, sleeping, and eliminating);
4. distractibility (how easily environmental stimulation changes one's behaviour);
5. attention span and persistence (the length of time one is purposefully engaged in an activity);
6. approach/withdrawal (the way in which one responds to new objects or people in one's environment);
7. threshold of responsiveness (the degree of stimulation required to get a response);
8. intensity of reaction (the strength of one's reactions); and
9. quality of mood (the dominant attitude or feeling one demonstrates).

An analysis of these nine traits results in about 65% of all students being classified into one of three basic temperaments: (1) easy students (40%) are generally positive, highly adaptive without a lot of fuss, and they typically fall into systematic routines; (2) difficult students (10%)

are generally negative, reluctantly adaptive, and usually exhibit aggressive tendencies and poor self-control; and (3) slow-to-warm-up students (15%) are somewhat negative (certainly not positive), typically apathetic, and need lots of coaxing to make changes, especially changes that affect them significantly. These temperaments are stable through childhood into adulthood and are found in all cultures around the world.

For about 20 years, temperament was conspicuously absent from the factors that account for and describe intra- and inter-individual variations. This likely occurred because temperament is closely related to personality, and researchers were uncomfortable (or made to feel uncomfortable) investigating such a personal aspect of the human condition to potentially explain differences between individuals. However, temperament is re-emerging as all aspects of personality are being rigorously considered within socio-educational frameworks. As Edmunds and Edmunds (2014b) stated,

> ... temperament is an important factor to consider when dealing with students who have behavioural problems because it is a factor that is not explained or accounted for elsewhere. More importantly, we feel that the emotional intensity described by temperament is what makes behaviours less controllable by the individual and more problematic for others to deal with (pp. 71–72).

For teachers, understanding and considering that many students will demonstrate one of the three temperaments means that their teaching and their personal interactions with students will better respect and provide for individuality. Teachers may also consider that situational factors can cause a student's temperament to appear problematic. For example, a student with a low threshold of responsiveness will have great difficulty if constantly surrounded by and engaged in "busy" activities. Similarly, students with low activity levels may find repeated physical activities uninteresting. Both scenarios can lead to task avoidance strategies that are viewed negatively when, in actuality, all the student is trying to do is refrain from feeling highly uncomfortable.

Understanding students' temperaments can also help teachers reframe how student behaviours are interpreted. This provides teachers with an opportunity to anticipate and understand student reactions to particular comments and environmental stimuli. Positive teacher–student relationships are facilitated when teachers work with students rather than trying to change students. Helping students understand how their temperaments affect their lives, as well as the lives of others, helps to prevent or manage problems that may arise from differences among peers.

It also has to be stated, however, that recognizing temperament differences does not make the sometimes negative actions and consequences that result from them any more acceptable. It would be inappropriate to justify these behaviours (actions or verbal comments) with the rationalization that "this is just the way the person is." This type of explanation implies that because the behaviour is part of the individual's natural makeup, it cannot be judged or questioned.

Annette finds the information on temperament quite interesting. Since beginning her teaching career, she has always been quite aware of different cognitive styles and learning styles, but she has given little thought to the actual temperaments of her students. She immediately thinks of Amanda and Simon, who do not fall into the category of "easy students"—Amanda because of her negativity and intensity and Simon because of his reluctant adaptability and lack of responsiveness. In Amanda's case, her peers are already trying to avoid her because she tries to "boss" them around, and Annette has noted Amanda's resistance to direction, even at her young age. Simon, on the other hand, gets along fairly well with peers and adults but demonstrates a laissez-faire attitude to almost everything that occurs both inside and outside the classroom. While Annette has sometimes found it frustrating to deal with both of these students, she now realizes that it may not be simply a case of trying to change Amanda or motivate Simon. She decides to take a slightly different tack and follow the suggestions in Dr. Cameron's paper; she will try to anticipate and

The Aptitude x Treatment Interaction (ATI) Approach

Ask any experienced educator about the relationship between instruction and student academic performance, and they will eventually tell you that despite their best efforts in planning and delivering effective instructional programming, there are non-responders. These are students whose knowledge and/or skills do not improve even though they are exposed to well-developed curricula and excellent teaching. They are not students whose abilities and inabilities would typically cause them to be identified as students with exceptionalities. Nonetheless, they seem to fall between the cracks in education; they perform almost as poorly as many students with exceptionalities, but they do not receive any form of specialized instruction.

Fuchs (2012) argued that except in the case of students with exceptionalities, "there are very few attempts in schools to differentiate instruction by learner characteristics. Most everywhere, there is a one-size-fits-all approach, reflecting an assumption that all children will do well if only teachers select the right instruction and faithfully implement it" (p. 188). Building on the very early work of Cronbach (1957), Fuchs argued that more non-responders will have the potential for academic success if instructional practices are differentiated based on the meaningful interactions between student aptitudes and educational treatments (ATI). According to Cronbach, the ATI approach does not design educational treatments to fit the average student "but to fit groups of students with particular aptitude patterns" (p. 681).

Fuchs explained that early attempts to use ATI failed because (a) non-responders were exposed to poorly designed and executed instruction and (b) researchers could not envision how ATI could "fit productively between the regular classroom level and the special education level" (p. 203). His position was that while much is known about classroom instruction, instruction is not necessarily based on sound knowledge about non-responders. He concluded that by designing and selecting curricula, material, and instructional procedures based on the cognitive-linguistic profiles of groups of non-responders, the ATI approach would increase the likelihood that many would become responders. Finally, Fuchs made it clear that educators are not to confuse the ATI type of differentiated instruction for groups of non-responders with the individualized instruction afforded to students with exceptionalities. He preferred to conceptualize these two educational structures as supplementary approaches: "They are not synonymous, or in competition, with each other" (p. 203).

think box

Consider your own cognitive style, learning style, and temperament. How do you think they affect you as a teacher? What steps might you take to ensure that your cognitive inclinations do not restrict your use of teaching methods that are beneficial to students with other styles or temperaments?

understand Amanda's and Simon's reactions to comments and environmental stimuli and then make them more aware of how their responses affect those around them.

As Annette waits for Jacob's parents to arrive, she makes some notes in her students' files to reflect what she has learned from her readings. She is confident that not only can she address Mr. and Mrs. White's concerns about Jacob, but she can also help a number of other students in the classroom. Again, she is pleased to see how her increased knowledge of educational psychology is having a positive effect on her teaching and, more important, her students.

Annette's Journal

December 7, 2013

I'm currently facing my biggest challenge of all . . . helping to identify and address children's specific learning difficulties. Mr. Parker is encouraging me to trust my instincts, and while I generally do that when I teach, I'm a little more hesitant to apply the same approach to children who may have very special needs. Perhaps I'm feeling uneasy about this aspect of my job because in the past, students who required special services came to my class with detailed IEPs. I had no input into the identification process, and their special programs were already laid out for me.

Mr. Parker has been most helpful. And I'm so encouraged by the help we've been able to provide to Brandon. Just by removing the requirement to produce handwritten work, we've made school so much more enjoyable for him. He is a capable learner whose problems with visual-motor integration were masking his real abilities. It saddens me that he struggled for so many years. I'm also encouraged by my experiences with Mr. and Mrs. White, who came to me with concerns about Jacob's "not being as smart as the other students." While our meeting to discuss their concerns began with some very emotional conversation, by the end of the discussion I was able to somewhat allay their biggest fear—that Jacob was going to have lifelong difficulties with learning. We talked a lot about individual differences, especially about different rates of development, and the strengths and weaknesses that we all have in terms of our learning abilities. Perhaps most important was the list we generated of Jacob's strengths and weaknesses. It painted a clear picture of a very capable little boy who is definitely not advanced in his literacy and numeracy skills but certainly not significantly delayed either. After generating this list and examining it closely, Mr. and Mrs. White were no longer asking for an assessment to determine their son's IQ, but I did assure them that we would set up a meeting with Mr. Parker to discuss any assistance we might provide Jacob to ensure that his early skill development continues at an acceptable pace.

I have also spoken to Mr. Parker about the other students who came to mind when I was going through the special education reading material. He was quite open to discussing my concerns; we plan to take some preliminary actions in the coming weeks. Within this school district it takes some time to get an appointment with an educational psychologist, so in the meantime Mr. Parker and I are going to try some specific instructional interventions to further assess what I've observed in the classroom. We hope to be able to make learning more enjoyable for these students as well.

Annette's Exploration of the Research

Fuchs, L. S., Fuchs, D., Schumacher, R. F., & Seethaler, P. M. (2013). Instructional intervention for students with mathematics learning disabilities. In H. L. Swanson, K. R. Harris, & S. Graham (Eds.), *Handbook of learning disabilities* (2nd ed., pp. 388–404). New York, NY: Guilford Press.

Recently, during math class, Amanda commented to Annette that she finds learning language arts easier than learning math. "Why is math so hard?" she asked. "What am I doing wrong?" Annette knew Amanda was a bright and diligent student, so she decided to explore the research to see whether she, the teacher, was doing all that she could to help students with the learning and understanding of math concepts. She already knew that mathematics competence is critical to both student success in school and success after graduation. In fact, according to an article she read some time ago (Rivera-Batiz, 1992), math competence accounts for people's differences in employment, income, and work productivity, even after intelligence and reading ability are controlled.

Annette found a research article on the teaching of mathematics written by Fuchs, Fuchs, Schumacher, and Seethaler (2013). First, the authors provided background information on basic math facts and math word problems as well as details on how these aspects of math are typically taught. They then summarized the findings of a number of studies designed to investigate remedial efforts by teachers to improve students' abilities in these areas. Annette makes some important notes.

Salient Points

Based on their analyses, Fuchs et al. proposed a set of six principles that should be followed to ensure that interventions that address functional parts of the math curricula are effective:

1. Instructional explicitness: Teachers should directly share information and support student mastery. Instructional explicitness ensures the understanding of the structure, meaning, and operational requirements of mathematics. In other words, teachers should not rely on students' gaining knowledge and mastery from inductive approaches, because these approaches usually present a multitude of examples in the hope that students will eventually "notice" how the concept works.

2. Instructional design to minimize learning challenge: Teachers should focus on anticipating and eliminating student misunderstandings by using precise explanations and carefully sequenced instruction.

3. Strong conceptual basis for procedures: Teachers should make sure that students fully grasp why they are doing particular math functions.

4. Drill and practice: Teachers should combine a strong conceptual basis for procedures and engagement in directed drill activities with independent practice to increase students' capabilities across more math procedures and processes. The goal is an increased overall mastery of functional mathematics.

5. Cumulative review: Teachers should provide students with many opportunities for explicit reviews of what they have just learned. Teachers do this by successive and cumulative reviews of concepts so that each review also includes the content contained in the last review. Cumulative review is important because mathematics concepts are purposefully taught and learned in a cumulative fashion; what students are learning today builds on what they learned yesterday.

6. Motivators to help students regulate their attention and behaviour and work hard: Teachers should recognize that students with a learning disorder in mathematics often display attention, motivation, and self-regulatory difficulties that will negatively affect their learning. These students also typically experience many failures and therefore are afraid to try for fear that they will fail again.

The authors noted that while the vast majority of the student research participants benefited from the above principles, not all students with learning disorders in mathematics responded to the interventions. Some required more intensive and individualized instruction.

Implications for My Teaching

While I recognize that this research focuses on students with a learning disorder in mathematics, I believe that if these fundamental principles worked for students who struggled when learning math, they should work for all students. This stance is consistent with my belief that teaching students with exceptionalities is not something special; it is simply excellent teaching done slightly differently. At a minimum, these principles should complement my basic approach to teaching math, and I can add more complex instructional strategies if I feel they are needed. I also know that a few of my students struggle with math and stand to gain directly from this new research.

After considering the six principles, I realize that my instructional practice needs to be tweaked in two places. In the past, I have not been as diligent as I could be in anticipating and eliminating student misunderstandings, and I definitely can employ more successive and cumulative reviews. I will speak with Amanda about these changes and how they may help her over the next series of lessons. I will also tell her that if after these lessons she is still worried about her math skills, I will look into getting some one-on-one help for her. I will tell all my students that these two aspects of my teaching will be slightly different, and I will provide them with examples during the lessons. This discussion will give me the opportunity to share with the older students how educators rely on valid and reliable research to guide their teaching.

Annette's Resource List

Academic Journals

Behavioral Disorders
Exceptional Children
Gifted Child Quarterly
Journal of Autism and Developmental Disorders
Journal of Communication Disorders
Journal of Developmental and Physical Disabilities
Journal of Emotional and Behavioral Disorders
Journal of Intellectual Disabilities
Journal of Learning Disabilities
Journal of Special Education
Journal of Speech, Language, and Hearing Research
Journal of Visual Impairment and Blindness
Journal on Developmental Disabilities
Roeper Review

Books

Bender, W. N. (2007). *Learning disabilities: Characteristics, identification, and teaching strategies* (6th ed.). Boston, MA: Allyn & Bacon.

Demchak, M., & Greenfield, R. (2002). *Transition portfolios for students with disabilities*. Thousand Oaks, CA: Corwin Press.

Edmunds, A. L., & Edmunds, G. A. (2014). *Special education in Canada* (2nd ed.). Don Mills, ON: Oxford University Press.

Karnes, F. A., & Bean, S. M. (Eds.). (2009). *Methods and materials for teaching the gifted* (3rd ed.). Waco, TX: Prufrock Press.

Kennedy, D., Banks, R., & Grandin, T. (2011) *Bright not broken: Gifted kids, ADHD, and autism*. San Francisco, CA: Jossey-Bass.

Lerner, J. W., & Johns, B. (2008). *Learning disabilities and related mild disabilities* (11th ed.). Belmont, CA: Wadsworth.

Rief, S. (2005). *How to reach and teach children with ADD/ADHD: Practical techniques, strategies, and interventions* (2nd ed.). San Francisco, CA: Jossey-Bass.

Snell, M., & Brown, F. (2010). *Instruction of students with severe disabilities* (7th ed.). Upper Saddle River, NJ: Pearson.

Swanson, H. L., Harris, K. R., & Graham, S. (2013). *Handbook of learning disabilities* (2nd ed.). New York, NY: The Guilford Press.

Websites

ADD & ADHD in Children
www.helpguide.org/mental/adhd_add_signs_symptoms.htm

Canadian Association of the Deaf
www.cad.ca

Canadian Down Syndrome Society
www.cdss.ca/en//main.htm#

Canadian National Institute for the Blind
www.cnib.ca

Canadian ADHD Resource Alliance
www.caddra.ca

Children and Adults with Attention Deficit/Hyperactivity Disorder
www.chadd.org

Council for Exceptional Children
www.cec.sped.org

LD Online
www.ldonline.org

Learning Disabilities Association of Canada
www.ldac-taac.ca/index-e.asp

National Center for Learning Disabilities (US)
www.ncld.org

Students with Intellectual Disabilities: A Resource Guide for Teachers
www.bced.gov.bc.ca/specialed/sid

Teaching LD
www.teachingld.org

From the Authors' Notebook

This chapter addressed the importance of understanding the concept of intelligence in relation to individual differences. It is clear that intelligence affects student learning; this was exemplified through detailed descriptions of the high-incidence exceptionalities. In conjunction with the specific and practical instructional suggestions provided, it is clear that understanding the philosophical nature of inclusion is crucial for teachers, because the vast majority of students with exceptionalities are now educated in the regular classroom. The chapter also emphasized the vital role that the psycho-educational assessment and IEP processes play in the education of students with special needs.

Reflecting on Practice

Consider the information you have read in this chapter as well as the knowledge you have acquired through instruction, classroom discussions, and classroom activities. Then take the time to write down your thoughts about these learning experiences. Consider how your perspective on educational psychology may have changed. In addition, respond to the following questions:

- How confident do you feel about your ability to teach in an inclusive classroom?
- What more do you need to know about students with exceptionalities, and where might you find this information?

Chapter Summary

In this chapter, the following concepts were highlighted:

- Intelligence is the ability to learn and adapt.
- Gardner's multiple intelligences is a systems approach to intelligence, while Sternberg's triarchic model is a processing approach.
- Special education is nothing more than exemplary teaching that is designed and delivered slightly differently to accommodate the learning and behavioural needs of students with exceptionalities.
- Labelling and education placements are two of the most contentious issues in special education.
- The high-incidence exceptionalities represent 80% of all students with special needs; students who fall within a particular category of exceptionality exhibit similar yet unique combinations of abilities and inabilities.

- Inclusion is the philosophical position adopted across Canada that contends that the regular classroom should be the first-option placement for students with exceptionalities.
- The IEP is the legal document that guides the curricula and instruction provided to students with exceptionalities.
- Cognitive style and learning style are learning-mode preferences, while temperament is an individual's natural way of reacting to his or her environment.

New Terms

analytical/componential intelligence
creative/experiential intelligence
crystallized intelligence
differentiated learning
fluid intelligence
high-incidence exceptionalities
inclusion
Individualized Education Program

intelligence
low-incidence exceptionalities
practical/contextual intelligence
psycho-educational assessment
special education
twice-exceptional learner
visual-spatial reasoning

These terms are defined in the Glossary at the end of the text.

Review Questions

- What is intelligence, and how does it relate to education?
- How might a teacher use Gardner's and Sternberg's models of intelligence in the classroom?
- What knowledge do teachers need to acquire in order to construct an effective inclusive practice?
- What are the six phases in the assessment and IEP process?
- What cognitive profile is typical of students with the following diagnoses: ADHD, autism spectrum disorder, gifted, mild intellectual disability, and specific learning disorder?
- Why is it important to understand a student's cognitive style, learning style, and temperament?

EARLY FEBRUARY
Socio-Cultural Considerations

7

From the Authors' Notebook

As part of a democratic society, student diversity must be acknowledged and celebrated, not merely accommodated. This chapter explores the social and cultural differences that can affect student learning and academic achievement. It outlines how teachers must be prepared to understand these differences and purposefully attempt to mitigate them. The chapter also describes how, through the development of a critical consciousness and an enhanced understanding of multiculturalism, a teacher can minimize the potentially negative effects of numerous socio-cultural factors.

Primary Learning Objectives

After reading this chapter, you should understand

1. how and why all students are influenced by individualism and community;
2. why race, class, gender, culture, language, and educational achievement are issues of individuality, not of group membership;
3. why a knowledge of cultural frames is necessary;
4. how social and cultural differences lead to disparate educational opportunities;
5. what stereotype threat is and how it can contribute to educational inequities;
6. how socio-economic status can contribute to educational inequities;
7. the scope of multicultural education;
8. why developing a teacher's critical consciousness is crucial to effective multicultural education;
9. what teachers need to know and do in order to construct a culturally responsive practice;
10. what risk and protective factors influence the education of Aboriginal students;
11. that factors including stereotype threat, socio-economic status, and student culture, race, ethnicity, religion, and gender do not have to negatively affect achievement; and
12. the positive effect that an instrumental value of education has on student engagement.

Cultural Differences in *The Little Red Schoolhouse*

Unbeknownst to Annette, Liam and Jacqueline did not go out for morning recess; instead, they are working on their social studies projects. As Annette walks by the lunchroom on her way to the photocopier, she overhears them talking about which students do the best social studies projects and who usually gets the highest mark—typical topics of conversation in all students' lives. Annette does not want to eavesdrop, but the discussion turns to Caleb and what she hears is disconcerting.

"He does okay in math, but he never does good projects," says Jacqueline. "He doesn't really seem to try. He's more interested in being outside or playing sports."

"Yeah, maybe it's because he's Cree," states Liam. "I have to work on my projects at home, but Caleb always gets to go on fishing and camping trips with his family. Maybe that's why he knows so much about animals and stuff. Anyway, I don't think he likes school very much . . . when we had to do that science project together last month, I ended up writing our whole report. You're right about sports though—he's good at everything we do in gym class. He always gets picked first for dodge ball, even by the older kids."

"Well, even though he doesn't seem to like school, I like him," says Jacqueline with certainty. "He makes me laugh, and he always shares the snacks he brings for recess."

"I like it when he tells the stories he learned from his father," Liam responds, "like the one about the eagle that he told us on the playground yesterday. I think he's doing his social studies project on something about the Cree people. That'll be pretty easy for him because he can use all the stories he knows. He probably won't even use any books from the library."

"Nope," Jacqueline smiles, "and he'll probably be late handing in the project to Ms. Elkins. And he probably won't get a good mark either, because he never seems to do what Ms. Elkins asks us to do. Too bad he can't just get a mark for telling stories . . . then he'd get the best mark in the whole class."

Liam nods his head. "Yeah, but he doesn't care what mark he gets anyway. He's happy as long as he can spend time in the gym."

The students' conversation seamlessly shifts to their own projects and the looming deadline. As Annette continues toward the photocopier, she thinks it is remarkable that all of what Liam and Jacqueline have just said was stated quite matter-of-factly, with no overtones of prejudice or negativity. While it was not the most glowing endorsement of their classmate, all of it was true. It is apparent that they accept Caleb for who he is and do not judge him based on his academic performance. They also seem to recognize that Caleb is far more capable than his grades indicate.

Annette realizes that even though several months of school have passed, she knows very little about this likeable boy who often gives up on his school work and sometimes becomes disruptive in class. While her classroom management plan has reduced Caleb's problematic behaviours, she has not seen any significant gains in his academic progress. Her second review of Caleb's file does not reveal much more than what Annette already knows about him, but it does make clear that his "acting out" behaviours and poor academic performance started when he was in Grade 3. Prior to that, he was well-behaved and received fairly acceptable grades, although he still did not perform up to his academic potential according to comments by previous teachers. One very interesting note in the file was written by his mother. She expressed concern about the report that Caleb was acting out in school, because she did not observe the same type of behaviours at home. She said she would do what she could to help him understand that his behaviours at school were inappropriate. Annette had met with Caleb's mother at the end of the first reporting period, and they had discussed Caleb's apparent lack of interest in school at that time. Mrs. Johnston seemed sadly resigned to the fact that her son "is just a boy who doesn't like school very much."

> **think box**
>
> Do you think it is important for Annette to understand the intricacies of the Cree culture in order to help Caleb? Would knowing these intricacies lead to instruction that is likely to have a significant positive impact on Caleb's scholastic attainment? Is knowing about the Cree culture more or less important than knowing about Caleb and his family?

Later in the day, Annette speaks to Mrs. Nugent. The principal confirms that while Caleb's behaviours have not been terribly problematic, he is showing more and more disinterest in school. "Annette, what concerns me is that I've seen all this before. We have a student here who seems quite capable in many ways, but his grades continue to drop and his behaviours are telling us that he isn't happy with school. If this continues over the next few years, he'll probably become more of a problem in the classroom and eventually get so far behind his peers that he'll begin skipping school, or he may even choose to drop out. It's so important that we try to address Caleb's situation as quickly as we can." After more discussion with Mrs. Nugent, Annette has a tentative plan. While she will familiarize herself with Caleb's First Nations background, she will put most of her efforts into finding out more about Caleb the individual.

Over the next several days, Annette makes a point of talking to Caleb more often. While he is quiet and reserved for the most part, he provides a veritable wealth of information about a variety of topics when prompted, and he seems to undergo a personality transformation when he is in storytelling mode. It is also clear that what Caleb knows and understands is not reflected in his grades. Annette suspects that the assessment and grading tools used in past years did not allow Caleb to properly demonstrate what he knows.

As they talk and he grows more comfortable with her, Annette discovers that most of Caleb's acting out behaviours are caused by his struggles and frustrations with organizing and processing written information, both when reading and when writing. "It makes perfect sense," Annette realizes. "Caleb's behaviour problems surfaced in Grade 3, exactly when his schooling went from learning to read to reading to learn. For an aural/oral learner like Caleb, the switch from listening to the teacher to learning from printed material, and then having to print or write to demonstrate his knowledge, must have posed significant problems. He probably didn't naturally or automatically make the adjustment like other students, and because his parents are predominantly aural/oral learners as well, they thought everything was fine. That's why Caleb's track record for homework completion was so poor—while education is highly valued in his home, the written word is simply not a priority."

Annette also discovers that Caleb is not overly concerned about the grades he gets. While he says he would like higher marks, he seems to be content with the report cards he takes home. After some thought, Annette decides that if she works carefully, she can probably accomplish four things at the same time: she can teach Caleb how to organize and make better sense of print materials; she can get him to finish his work on time; she can show him that he can get grades that better reflect his knowledge and abilities; and she can reduce his frustrations and resulting problematic behaviours. "It also won't hurt for his classmates to see him as a capable, productive, and well-behaved student," Annette muses.

Several days later, during seatwork in social studies class, Annette uses Caleb's pending project as the focal point of their conversation. She asks him to make a brief written outline of the information he wants to include. When he balks, as she had anticipated, Annette says, "Let's do it just like you would if you were going to tell me a story about your project from start to finish. You can tell me that story, can't you?"

"Um, yes . . .," Caleb answers warily.

Annette senses his discomfort. "Well, putting it down on paper is pretty much the same thing. All I want you to do is write down the title of your project at the top of the page and then underneath the title, write one or two key words that you will use to start your story." She waits as he cautiously puts pen to paper.

"See, that wasn't so hard," encourages Annette. "Now, write down a few more key words or phrases that will help you tell your story in the right order."

Caleb sets to work, but it is obvious from his limited notes that he is sticking to his minimalist approach. "Why do I have to do this? I don't like to write and do projects. I keep all the stuff I know in my head," he laments.

"Yes, I know you do, and I'm sure that you don't need all these notes."

"So, why do I have to do it?" he logically asks.

"Think of it this way," Annette says reassuringly, "what do you think your father would say is the most important thing about telling a story?"

Caleb's eyes brighten. "That's easy, he wants people to understand the story and learn from it. Then they can tell it to other people. You have to pay attention and listen carefully though, 'cause he doesn't like to repeat things."

"Exactly," states Annette, "so I want you to think of your outline as the information that will help me understand the story of your project, and then I can tell others about it."

"Can't you do it in your head like I do?"

"Yes, I could if I only had to understand your story but not if I have to understand the stories of all the students. Besides, learning to write about what you know is an important part of school. Your outline will help you to clarify and organize all the points you want to include in your project." She looks back at Caleb. He has his head down and has already started to make some notes.

It seems that now that Caleb understands the purpose of making notes, he is intent on crafting a far more meaningful outline. To help him further, Annette demonstrates how to use a few library books and some items from the Internet to gather additional information, but it is obvious that Caleb already "knows" most of what will go into his project. She later shows him how to expand the outline into a written report, and while this task is a bit of a struggle, Annette finds that he gets the job done and stays on track because of her reminders to simply focus on telling "a really good story."

A week later, it is time for the culminating social studies activity—each student must make a formal presentation of his or her project to the rest of the class. "Me and My Culture," Caleb begins nervously but proudly, "by Caleb Johnston . . . can you all sit in a circle so that I can tell you my story?" From that point on, the class is transfixed as Caleb tells his story from memory, referring only occasionally to his notes and, all the while, modestly but consciously assuming the persona of a storyteller.

"I'm from the Cree Nation, but you already know that. Many years ago, my people lived a very different life from the life your ancestors lived. They spoke a different language, lived in wigwams, travelled by canoe, wore different clothing, used bows and arrows, and ate foods like moose and elk. Ms. Elkins helped me find some pictures to show you what it was like for the Cree people way back then, and I drew some myself." Caleb passes the pictures and drawings to his classmates and continues to tell them more about his Cree ancestors. Once he has covered the past, he brings his audience back to the present. "You may think I'm different because I'm Cree, but I'm only a little bit different and mostly the same as you. I live in a house, not a wigwam. My family has a truck, not a canoe. We speak English, not Cree. And we eat pizza and hamburgers, just like you. But when it comes to school, I'm a little bit different. I like listening to stories more than reading books. My mother says it's because I'm from an oral culture. That means that really, really old Cree stories are passed down through our people. We learn what we need to know from listening to these stories. My father tells me and my sisters all the stories that his father told him."

Caleb pauses, stepping out of his storyteller persona momentarily, and looks directly at Annette. "You know . . . I could tell you some of the Cree stories. Maybe everybody, not just the younger kids, can have story time on the carpet sometimes." Without waiting for answer, he immediately reassumes his character and continues.

"My Auntie says our storytelling and our own language and our land are part of who we are because they are part of our spirit. I learn most of the things I know from older people who know about our spirit, like my Uncle Jim. He can't read books, but he knows the answers to all of my questions. That's how I'm different from you. I like to learn most things from my elders, while you like to learn from books and from school."

"One way we are all the same is we don't like to get into trouble at school. But one way we are different is that you look at the teacher when she talks to you about doing bad things. I got into trouble last year when I didn't look at Mrs. Nugent when she was mad at me. I guess she didn't understand that in my culture it is more respectful if you don't look at your elders, but you still have to listen to what they say so you don't do it again."

"I'm the same as you because I like gym, playing games at recess, and going on field trips like the one we took to the fish hatchery, but I'm different because sometimes I just don't like doing homework and writing and stuff, and I'm never good at getting things done on time. My father says that I'm just like him. I like to do things when I'm ready, and that's important. But he says that school is different and it's something I need to work on. He says he knows I can do it because I'm never late for road hockey with my friends or for visits with my Uncle Jim." Laughter erupts in the classroom. When things settle down, Caleb continues. "My parents tell me that I should try my best in school but that the most important thing is to be a good person and get along with everyone and respect my elders."

"I guess another way I'm sort of different from you is how I feel about animals and nature. The Cree Nation respects nature because of our beliefs and traditions that come from our ancestors. Remember the other day when Liam caught that frog and put him in a container with water in it? I asked Liam to let him go, but Liam said that he wanted to keep him. He left the container by the swings and said he would feed him insects every day. That made me sad because I wanted the frog to be free and to be able to go back to the pond behind the school. That's why I left the school grounds when I wasn't supposed to. I took the frog back to the pond. Liam was kind of mad when I told him what I did, but we worked it out later."

"I mostly like school but not when we do boring stuff or when I get in trouble. Ms. Elkins says I'm getting better, like when I was doing this project. I like everyone in school, but Liam is my best friend, and he comes over to my house a lot. Sometimes I go to his house but not on Sundays, 'cause that's when we go to my Auntie's for supper. I really love hockey, but that has nothing to do with my culture, that's just about me. That's it. I'm finished. If you want to know any more about Cree people, you can just ask me." Immediately, several students put up their hands, eager to ask Caleb some questions.

Guiding Principles

Diverse Learners

It has been obvious for some time that teachers have to be prepared to teach a broad and diverse spectrum of student populations. This does not mean simply allowing for diverse populations within all classrooms. Rather, it means purposefully encouraging diversity and making the academic achievement of these populations, and all other populations, a primary educational goal. A comprehensive analysis of what teachers need to know and be able to do in order to accomplish these specific socio-cultural objectives was conducted by Banks et al. (2005). According to these authors, openly encouraging and supporting student diversity is in keeping with the democratic roots that underpin all of the fundamental tenets of public education. To support these democratic ideals, teachers must seek to eliminate disparities in students' educational opportunities, and students must experience democratic classrooms and culturally responsive curricula. Banks and his colleagues advocate that teachers adhere to the following precepts:

1. When teachers use knowledge about the social, cultural, and language backgrounds of their students when planning and implementing instruction, the academic achievement of students can increase.
2. Most teachers are of European descent from middle-class backgrounds and speak mainly English, while many of their students are from racial and ethnic minorities, live in poverty, and speak a first language other than English; thus, most teachers do not have the same cultural frames or points of reference as their students.
3. Teachers need to be aware of the embedded structural conditions that determine the disparate allocation of educational opportunities within schools—the types of courses, curricula, and teaching offered to different students.
4. Teachers must take action to alter the disparate educational opportunities afforded to groups of students who differ from one another racially, culturally, and socio-economically.
5. Teachers need to be aware of family and community values, norms, and experiences so they can help students across the boundaries that sometimes exist between home and school (pp. 233, 236–237).

In reviewing the research on teacher competencies required for the diverse educational landscape that all teachers encounter on a daily basis, the authors note that while technical competence in teaching and classroom management is essential, it is not sufficient for effective teaching. "Teachers' attitudes and expectations, as well as their knowledge of how to incorporate the cultures, experiences, and needs of their students into their teaching, significantly influence what students learn and the quality of their learning opportunities" (p. 243).

Later that day, Annette is still smiling when she thinks of the progress she has made with Caleb. Her inquisitive nature leads her to think more about the effects that socio-cultural issues have on students and their school experiences. While her summer course in educational psychology included some emphasis on this topic, she is sure that Dr. Cameron can point her in the direction of some specific reading material. She decides to send him an e-mail.

Socio-cultural Issues

Annette Elkins <annette_elkins@schoolmail.com>

Date: Monday, February 10, 2014 3:22 PM

To: Andrew Cameron <acameron@university.ca>

Hello Andrew,

Sorry it's been a while since I've written. As you can imagine, school has kept me extremely busy, and I have to say that I'm enjoying every minute of it.

Today was one of the highlights of my year so far. I made significant progress with a student who was showing no interest in academic tasks despite his obvious intellectual abilities. It took some comments by his peers to open my eyes to the socio-cultural factors that were influencing his behaviour. Once I took these factors into account, I was better able to reach this student. Today he submitted his completed social studies project (on time, I might add) and gave a class presentation within a storytelling circle that had all of us mesmerized. Needless to say, I'd like to learn more about socio-cultural issues. Can you recommend some reading material on this topic?

As always, I appreciate your help!

Annette

Not long after sending the e-mail, Annette receives a response from Dr. Cameron.

Re: Socio-cultural Issues

Andrew Cameron <acameron@university.ca>

Date: Monday, February 10, 2014 4:10 PM

To: Annette Elkins <annette_elkins@schoolmail.com>

Attachments: Socio-Cultural Considerations.doc

Hello Annette,

It was great to hear from you. I was wondering how things were going in your Little Red Schoolhouse. Your practicum student, Aaron, came back to class with lots of great stories about your students and the good things you're doing with them. Thanks again for making time for him.

Your comment on the storytelling circle reminded me of something I read recently on the "language of circles" (www.edu.gov.on.ca/eng/aboriginal/Guide_Toolkit2009.pdf):

> *Circles represent important principles in the Aboriginal worldview and belief systems—namely, interconnectedness, equality, and continuity. According to traditional teaching, the seasonal pattern of life and renewal and the movement of animals and people were continuous, like a circle, which has no beginning and no end. Circles suggest inclusiveness and the lack of a hierarchy. They are found throughout nature—for instance, in the movement of the seasons and the sun's movement*

from east to west during the day. Circles are also used in the construction of teepees and sweat lodges; and the circular willow hoop, medicine wheel, and dream catcher are powerful symbols.

Talking circles symbolize completeness and equality. All circle participants must be respected and listened to. All comments directly address the question or the issue, not the comments another person has made.

In the circle, the object that symbolizes the connectedness to the land—for example, a stick, a stone, or a feather—can be used to facilitate the circle. Only the person holding the "talking stick" has the right to speak. Participants can indicate their desire to speak by raising their hands. Going around the circle systematically gives everyone the opportunity to participate. Silence is also acceptable—any participant can choose not to speak.

I've also attached some reading material on socio-cultural issues that are relevant to teaching. As you know, these issues are most pertinent in Canada where teachers are facing much diversity in their classrooms. Just take Ontario for example . . . here are some statistics from StatsCan and the Census of Canada (www.edu.gov.on.ca/eng/policyfunding/equity.pdf) that speak volumes:

Language: Ontarians reported more than 200 languages, as "mother tongue." The proportion of Ontarians reporting English or French as a mother tongue is declining. In 2006, 69.1% of Ontarians reported English as their mother tongue, and 4.2% of the population reported French as their mother tongue.

Aboriginal peoples: Between 2001 and 2006, Ontario's Aboriginal population grew nearly five times faster than the non-Aboriginal population. The Aboriginal population is also younger than the non-Aboriginal population. More than a third (35.7%) of the Aboriginal population consists of children and teenagers aged 19 and under.

Families: Between 2001 and 2006, the number of lone-parent families increased by 11.2%.

Same-sex couples: Between 2001 and 2006, the number of self-identified same-sex couples increased by 40%.

Newcomers: Ontario continued to be the province of choice for more than half (52.3%) of the 1.1 million newcomers who arrived in Canada during the 2001–6 period. More than half of these newcomers will settle in areas outside of Toronto.

Visible minorities: The 2006 census enumerated an estimated 2.7 million Ontarians who identified themselves as members of the visible-minority population, representing more than half of Canada's total visible minorities. Between 2001 and 2006, Ontario's visible-minority population increased more than four times faster than the population as a whole (not counting those who self-identified as Aboriginal).

Religion: By 2017, about one-fifth of our population will be members of diverse faith communities, including Islam, Hinduism, Buddhism, and Judaism, in addition to a growing number of individuals without a religious affiliation.

This picture of what is happening in Ontario is true of the whole country. Schools are much more diverse than they ever were. In order for all students to thrive, teachers must fully understand socio-cultural issues.

Let me know if you have any questions.

Keep in touch,
Andrew

Annette quickly scans the e-mail, nods when she reads about the significance of circles, prints out the attachment, and begins to read.

Socio-cultural Perspectives

The raison d'être of educational psychology is to understand the cognitive, behavioural, affective, and motivational abilities and capacities of students so that teachers can best meet their learning needs. Within this contemporary view, students are seen as independent participants struggling to come to grips with two harmonizing yet contrasting personal dilemmas: to be apart from their world and act within a unique identity and exclusive purpose (individualism) and to be a part of their world and act within a shared identity and common purpose (collectivism). The balancing act for an individual is basically "How much do I want/need to be me?" and "How much do I want/need to be like everyone else?" This strategic dance involves the emergence and development of pre-eminent innate biophysical endowments as they are affected by socio-cultural surroundings. Individuals have an essential genetic predisposition that gives rise to fundamental cognitive, social, and linguistic functions that enable this intricate dance. While these basic functions are shaped by social contexts, they are not caused or replaced by them.

However, some social-cultural theorists do not view students as independently and willfully operating within their world to improve their own knowledge, understandings, and resultant behaviours. In fact, the more radical views contend that

> All social-cultural perspectives understand persons as actually constituted by socio-cultural practices, not just influenced or affected by them. . . . Social-cultural perspectives in educational psychology do *not* understand historical, cultural, contextual, and interpersonal practices of schooling and teaching as factors that affect the cognitive and motivational strategies of learners and the instructional goals and methods of teachers (Martin, 2012, pp. 596, 611).

This contention is reminiscent of the age-old nature-versus-nurture debate, the debate now shifting from its previous focus on intelligence, which is less socially constructed, to an emphasis on teaching and learning, which is more socially constructed. Like the nurture-begets-intelligence supporters of old, the culture-begets-learning line of thinking in the current debate has failed to reconcile how and why its overarching and deeply rooted philosophical arguments are out of step with its still-yet-to-be-proven scientific claims. Moreover, this entrenched socio-cultural perspective has ardently deflected all and frequent suggestions by modernists to, at minimum, create a recognizable taxonomy of socio-cultural views. Social-cultural theorists claim that such an endeavour "is fraught with difficulties of oversimplification, unduly restrictive categorization, and highly debatable placements of programs of inquiry . . . given that cultures and societies are constantly changing in inexplicable ways that cannot be predicted with anything like certainty" (Martin, 2012, pp. 599, 610). In essence, a taxonomy of any sort would be the antithesis of this stringent theoretical perspective. This is problematic for contemporary educational psychologists, because without a taxonomy, or model, or a set of theoretical givens, let alone practical and replicable applications, the contention that knowledge and knowers are constructed and constituted because of socio-cultural influences is far too susceptible to interpretation. If socio-cultural manifestations are always changing in inexplicable and unpredictable ways, they can never be responsibly explained, pinned down, or held accountable; they are merely descriptions of what is. A further problem for educational psychology theorists is that if demonstrable permutations of a theory's hierarchy, complete with attributes and flaws, cannot be conceived or portrayed, then an entity or an observation is only what it is at the moment.

Given that educational psychology is mostly about reasonably predictable relationships between various and numerous entities, it is difficult to discern the benefits of a perspective that overtly eschews predictability. More specifically, in terms of educational practice, if teachers are to effectively plan, conduct, monitor, reflect upon, and adapt their teaching to suit ever-changing classroom conditions, they must do so from an instructional position of reasonable consistency. Otherwise, teaching becomes a theoretically baseless function from which no purposeful activities, remedies for mishaps, or accommodations for behavioural or learning problems can be effectively designed. This does not mean, however, that the factors put forward by various theoretical perspectives and grounded research do not provide valuable insights into how and which social and cultural influences need to be seriously considered within the larger education sphere; rather, it means that these influences are not nearly as preponderant as claimed.

Differences within Identified Groups

When it comes to teaching and learning, the unifying belief among educational psychologists is that all students can be taught. Commensurately, in order to reach all students, teachers must understand the various social and cultural values, beliefs, norms, and expectations that accompany each child to school every day. These social-identity factors can emanate from a student's race, culture, gender, and/or socio-economic status and are thought to influence how students learn, how much they learn, and how well they learn. Having said this, the prevailing research does not support the often advocated position that significant learning influences, both positive and negative, can be derived from an individual's cultural background or ethnicity. While there do appear to be some trends in learning and achievement that may characterize a member of a particular group, the variability within all such identified groups (i.e., race, gender, culture, ethnicity, religion, nationality, geography) is far too great to draw inferences about any particular individual. In other words, there are as many differences, and degrees of differences, between individuals from within any of these groups as there are between group members and non-group members. For example, some research indicates that most students of Asian descent attain high achievement outcomes, but there are so many Asian students who do not attain high achievement that it would be incorrect and misleading to say that a student is likely to have high achievement *because* he or she is Asian. It is possible, however, that the research on this aspect of education is limited, because most of such data is based on broad racial and ethnic categories rather than on subgroups within such categories. Nonetheless, even the results that emanate from studies that identify specific subgroups within various ethnic groups have to be interpreted with such broad strokes that they have little relevance to any one student in any particular teacher's classroom.

Positioning Cultural Identity within the Individual

All other things being equal, a teacher's understanding of the intricacies of a particular culture or ethnicity is unlikely to have a significant positive impact on the scholastic attainment of any one student from that culture or ethnicity. This is also important from both a theoretical and practical perspective, because it would be inconceivable to ask all teachers to fully understand all the nuances of each and every culture or ethnicity in order to effectively teach all students. The consensus within educational psychology is that conceptualizing culture or ethnicity as sets of characteristics embodied by all individuals within a group does nothing more than promote stereotypical thinking and misperceptions. There is no question, however, that having intimate understandings of the diversity of students is both important and useful for the harmony of any teacher's classroom. After all, these classrooms are home to students from widely different backgrounds. It is also important, therefore, that all teachers and students be exposed to and educated about social and cultural diversity. Contemporary views on culture and ethnicity within educational psychology advocate that cultural identity should not be positioned within the group; rather, it needs to be properly and personally contextualized within the individual. In this way, culture is neither perceived as nor indicative of group membership; it is constructed and understood as a set of shifting continua that are shared among individuals but held differently by each individual. In this light, individuals' cultural or ethnic identity comes from how they balance their own personal and cultural influences against those exerted by competing social environments. It is from within this established and individualized perspective that teachers can certainly be expected to attune their cultural and ethnic understandings to a student's contextualized individuality. The teacher should know the child's family and community and understand how particular influences from these contexts may, or may not, need to be considered.

The Critical Consciousness of Teachers

There is a growing acknowledgment that teachers cannot meet the educational needs of students from diverse populations solely with exemplary content knowledge and impressive pedagogical skills. Howard and Aleman (2008) further this notion by suggesting that simply adding teacher understandings of race, class, gender, culture, language, and educational equity is also not enough for teachers to be responsible and effective. They argue that teachers need to acquire a **critical consciousness** disposition. Deriving support from several other researchers, they describe this disposition as

- political values and beliefs . . . teachers' critical consciousness about the social and political context of society and education (Howard & Aleman, 2008);

- an ideological clarity . . . teaching is always a political endeavour . . . teachers should have an awareness of the cultural capital that students bring to the classroom and know how to take advantage of the rich array of cultural, social, and community resources at their disposal (Moll & Arnot-Hopffer, 2004); and
- a socio-cultural consciousness . . . recognizing that people's ways of thinking are significantly influenced by race, class, gender, and language, and the hierarchical social systems in which they are located (Villegas & Lucas, 2002).

Howard and Aleman's steadfast position is that a critical consciousness is required to combat and alter the established ways of schooling that appear to legitimize inequitable social hierarchies and social practices through non-critical constructions of curriculum, policy, pedagogy, daily interactions, and discipline. They posit that this critical consciousness takes teachers' hegemonic thinking to task and requires them to reflect on the effects their practices have on their students. This way of thinking allows teachers to design and implement all sorts of learning activities "without requiring students to relinquish their cultural integrity in pursuit of academic success" (p. 166).

Building a Culturally Responsive Practice

In addition to having or developing a critical consciousness to guide their practice, teachers need to know how to incorporate the cultures, experiences, and needs of culturally and ethnically diverse students into their teaching. Banks et al. (2005) conducted a comprehensive analysis of what teachers need to know and be able to do in order to accomplish this specific socio-cultural objective.

The authors' foundational position is that teachers must develop a reciprocal and interactive orientation toward their practice whereby they and their students work together to construct cultural meanings out of the content. They caution, however, that while teachers must apprise themselves of various cultures and differences, they must be careful not to fall victim to acquiring the damaging cultural stereotypes that can result from superficial understandings. In keeping with the contemporary views on cultural influences expressed in the educational psychology literature, the authors clearly state that "it can be dangerous to attempt to transmit shorthand knowledge about a list of different cultures to prospective teachers" (p. 247).

To avoid this problem, Banks et al. portray a teacher's culturally responsive practice as one that builds a broad cultural knowledge and instructional base that grows and changes as students, contexts, and school-subject matters shift. All of the knowledge and actions listed below, therefore, are specifically related to individual students and their cultural community, because "cultural connections between the school and children's communities have often led to increased achievement" (p. 244). Teachers must, therefore, know the following:

- how to examine their own cultural assumptions to understand how these concepts shape starting points for practice;
- how to inquire into the backgrounds of their students so they can use what they learn to inform instructional decisions;
- how to develop a broad range of teaching strategies and approaches that meet the needs of culturally diverse learners and to know when and how to use them under a range of different circumstances;
- how to interpret cultural symbols from one frame reference to another, how to mediate cultural incompatibilities, and how to establish links across cultures that facilitate the instructional process; and

continued

- how to develop a curriculum that takes into account the understandings and perspectives of different groups, includes multiple representations of content, and is responsive to the particular cultural context within which they teach (pp. 243–252).

Based on the cultural understandings derived from the above, teachers must then do the following:

- celebrate their students as individuals and as members of their specific cultures;
- form and maintain connections with their students within their social/cultural contexts;
- incorporate cultural knowledge into instruction via community-based research;
- link classroom content to students' cultural experiences;
- modify interaction and participation structures;
- implement culturally relevant instructional methods;
- allow the use of multiple languages while teaching the target language;
- emphasize cooperation rather than competition and feature cooperative learning strategies and student-initiated discourse and participation; and
- where appropriate, develop and modify assessment strategies that are sensitive to cultural differences (pp. 243–252).

The authors conclude that teachers definitely face a considerable challenge in developing a culturally responsive practice, because the diversity they are trying to understand and incorporate, as reflected in individual students, is constantly in flux. This is not only because the students change, but also because the community that influences them changes as well. Having said this, Banks et al. emphasize that this challenge is a worthy educational endeavour; it is evident that mitigating the differences that can exist among students is crucial to producing more equitable student outcomes.

Stereotype Threat and Socio-economic Status

There are two very important socio-cultural considerations that warrant careful examination by teachers, because they can, and do, influence student learning and achievement. The effects of both stereotype threat and socio-economic status have been shown to have significant implications in the classroom.

Stereotype Threat

Stereotype threat (ST) is the fear, existing either in your own eyes or in the eyes of others, that your behaviour will confirm an existing negative stereotype about your identity group. This fear results in an impairment of performance because it generates a compounded cognitive and emotional burden that reduces working memory capacity and undermines actual ability. Based on the original work of Steele and Aronson (1995), research has repeatedly shown that when permanent characteristics such as race, ethnicity, or gender are highlighted before testing situations (e.g., telling black and white college students that a test will determine their intellectual ability—thus potentially eliciting the stereotype that blacks are less intelligent than whites), test performances are negatively affected (Steele & Aronson, 1995; Steele, Spencer, & Aronson, 2002). Unfortunately, it is not necessary that the individual believe the stereotype; he or she only needs to be aware that it exists. It is also unfortunate that this negative influence can both extend beyond poor academic performance to other life functions and apply to all groups who have a stereotypical identifying trait, not just minority groups. There is evidence that consistent exposure to stereotypes, such as women performing poorly in engineering or men being ill-suited for nursing, can negatively affect the way an individual values their chosen domain of study or work. A more insidious effect of ST is that affected students will disidentify with their domain of choice and disengage from striving for success within it despite a demonstrated ability to achieve. This results in self-defeating rationalizations such as "math is not for girls" and "only smart people know computers," and it lowers expectations such that performance and attraction to the domain are further affected. Similarly, there is also evidence of a reverse ST effect whereby the performance of one group is positively affected when they perceive that their comparison group is negatively stereotyped as poor performers on the task at hand.

What is vital for teachers to understand about this research is that ST can be brought on by seemingly innocuous comments, not only by overt, direct, and obviously negative statements. Additionally, the students most vulnerable to ST are those who have strong ties to their identity group. This has significant implications for how teachers and students conduct themselves in classrooms. Statements that are typically perceived as lighthearted or teasing jabs about an identity group must be considered as having serious ramifications. And while the obvious reaction to such a comment would be to tell someone, "it was just a joke," this body of research indicates that the underlying psychological unease remains with the individual and continues to play an undermining role in his or her achievement. Vulnerability to ST is greater in students who strongly identify with academic achievement and are members of groups that are perceived to perform poorly in school. Conversely, and of vital importance to teachers, is the fact that ST vulnerability is decreased by the degree to which an individual believes that a target skill is important. This means that teachers need to emphasize, perhaps even overemphasize, that students' abilities for success in school are malleable and can be positively affected by constantly attempting and re-attempting to master new content and skills. This positive and self-regulating perspective changes students' social cognitions as they pertain to academic achievement and changes their perceptions about how they will approach learning in school. Thus, while the research indicates that there may be broad trends toward group differences in achievement for a wide variety of groups, these differences may be better explained by the effects of ST than by the effects of race, ethnicity, culture, or gender. Therefore, both ST and group achievement are best addressed at the individual student level.

A further problem with stereotyping is that because stereotypes are often oversimplified conceptualizations of a group, based on assumed common attributes and sometimes very loosely related variables, they often pave the way for **prejudice**—an unjustified and usually negative perception about an individual based on membership

think box

How does Annette's implementation of Dynamic Classroom Management relate to the possible reduction of stereotypes, prejudice, bias, and discrimination in her classroom? What additional classroom activities might Annette implement to ensure that both the younger and the older students understand and respect the attitudes and behaviours of their peers?

or association with a particular group (wherein a group can be just about any collection of individuals that have a set of common attributes). Stereotypes and prejudice, and by extension discrimination and bias, are human interactive attitudes and actions that typically occur when negative attributions are attached to individuals who are relatively unknown to us. Because these attitudes and actions are learned behaviours, there is much that teachers can do to diminish or eliminate their proliferation.

Socio-economic Status

The second significant socio-cultural consideration for teachers is **socio-economic status** (SES), which indicates an individual's social class based on education, occupation, and income. While SES indicators can also include relative comparisons of power and influence, background, and prestige, these descriptors pertain more to one's perceived status than to one's actual economic leverage. In Canada, there are five levels of SES: lowest, lower-middle, middle, upper-middle, and highest. Numerous studies over several decades have consistently revealed that more than any other social or cultural attribute, SES has by far the greatest impact on scholastic achievement. Even though there is achievement variability within all SES levels, the variability is not enough to dismiss the fact that the higher one's SES, the greater the likelihood that average or higher levels of academic achievement will be attained, and vice versa. In fact, the SES–achievement relationship is so prevalent that it holds true regardless of other socio-cultural factors such as race, gender, and ethnicity. In terms of education, individuals from different ethnic groups have been shown to have more in common as a result of their SES levels and perceived values of education than they have in common because of their cultural or ethnic connections. Moreover, while some achievement-level differences can be found for variously defined groups, these differences are mitigated once SES is removed as a contributing factor. Within any identified group, however, there will be students who outperform or do not measure up to the achievement patterns of their SES level. In the larger picture, because SES is the strongest contributing factor to meaningful differences in student achievement, teachers must be aware of these differences and do what they can to moderate them.

Children's SES is determined by their parents' occupations and income levels. Low SES parents tend to have less education, lower-status jobs, and lower incomes and tend to have negative perceptions of the value and importance of education as well as a mistrust of public institutions such as schools. Of all the factors considered when determining SES, poverty is the most negative influential factor when it comes to effects on achievement. Poverty, therefore, puts children at significant risk for poor development of their physical, emotional, and intellectual capacities and abilities. When compared to students from higher SES levels, students from poor homes do not have as much exposure to the types of resources (e.g., books, tutoring, computers, and out-of-school programs) that enhance learning and achievement. They are at high risk for reading and writing difficulties, and they experience far greater instances of receiving special education services, having to repeat grades, exhibiting detrimental

think box

Consider Simon, one of Annette's students. How might knowing that he is from a lower SES family help Annette address his absences from school, his lack of effort on academic tasks, and his general lack of motivation? What types of interventions might Annette implement to help Simon become more interested and engaged in school activities?

attitudes toward school, and failing to complete high school. Furthermore, their home environments tend to expose them to more personal and social stressors. Overall, there is a clear indication that the vast majority of the observed differences in academic performance across SES levels are due to economic hardships and a scarcity of related resources, particularly during the summer months when school does not play a role in children's lives.

Effect of parenting style

Students from lower SES groups are also far more likely to experience a style of parenting different from that of students from other SES groups. Research examining how parental attitudes and practices systematically affect student scholastic success reveals that parenting style plays a significant role. As a result, there are noteworthy implications for teachers. Baumrind's (1991) model of parenting style classifies parent behaviour into three patterns. The **authoritarian parenting** approach attempts to shape, control, and measure children's behaviours against fairly rigid standards; conveys a strong emphasis on respect for authority, obedience, and traditional values; and mostly discourages open discussion of such topics and children's objections. Conversely, the **permissive parenting** approach is openly tolerant and accepting of nearly all children's actions, rarely making behavioural demands or invoking restrictions, and does not purposefully distinguish between acceptable and unacceptable actions. Finally, **authoritative parenting** is a parental style that involves a constant series of balancing acts: between expectation demands and encouragement to achieve, between establishing rules and meting out discipline, between fostering student independence and providing parental influence, and between open communication and direct advice. Under an authoritative structure, children come to understand that they are valued members of their families. They also know, however, that they have to respectfully adhere to established family parameters for the betterment of the cohesive unit. This attitude is fostered by a collective understanding of all the parameters, not solely by the enforcement of such parameters.

Both the authoritarian and the permissive approach are related to lower grades, with the authoritarian parenting type having the strongest negative effect on achievement. The authoritative parenting approach, on the other hand, is associated with higher grades, better overall school engagement, and higher levels of parental involvement in schools—especially for adolescent children. Furthermore, children who grow up in homes that adopt an authoritative style tend to have higher levels of cognitive competence. It has been suggested that this is likely due to the ongoing reasoned and logical discussions initiated and required in order to function in these environments. Relative to SES, students from lower SES groups are far more likely to experience authoritarian approaches than the other two types of parenting. Students from higher SES groups are more likely to experience authoritative approaches. In addition, while positive attitudes about the values and benefits of education are evident across all SES levels, this attitude is more prevalent among middle to high SES families.

Effect of teaching style

Teachers are not in any position to make significant changes to a student's SES, but they are in an excellent position to ameliorate and offset the negative influences that SES can have on achievement. Through exemplary teaching practices conducted within classrooms that are free of stereotypes and other behavioural stressors, students from all SES levels can attain high levels of achievement, including success at the post-secondary level. Adopting an authoritative approach to teaching can also offset some of the negative factors associated with SES and achievement. Amid all the factors that can negatively affect student learning and achievement, and later levels of employment and income, education can be the great equalizer. In and of itself and across all other mitigating influences, educational success fosters better jobs and higher incomes as well as providing greater access to higher education. For this reason, education has been shown to break generational cycles of poverty and low educational attainment. In the United States, for example, there is evidence of substantial and sustainable changes in achievement performances on the part of several minority groups. The pervasive benefits of education follow a logical pattern and progression. Children who do well in school grow into better than average educated parents whose SES moves upwards, whose attitudes toward education are more positive, and whose approach to parenting will likely be more authoritative and constructive. Subsequently, their own children may benefit indirectly from many positive attitudinal and societal effects, but most important, they will benefit directly from the academic achievement that is typically associated with higher SES.

In addition to providing good teaching and a psychologically secure learning environment, teachers can support students who come from poor or dysfunctional homes by making a point of providing extra help rather than waiting for these students to ask for assistance. Teachers can also counteract the negative effects of authoritarian or permissive approaches to parenting by explicitly negotiating more independent and self-directed student activities (both social and academic). It is also vital that teachers share how education was, and is, important in their own lives and demonstrate how it has been beneficial to a wide variety of individuals from various SES levels. Moreover, for students from traditionally disadvantaged groups, it would be beneficial for teachers to discuss at length the rewards and values they gained from finishing school and going on to post-secondary education. All these activities should be accompanied by teacher suggestions and comments that make it clear that these rewards are mostly a product of hard work and positive attitudes toward school. In conjunction with discussions about how students can positively adapt their malleable cognitive skills to produce higher achievement, students who hear success stories are more likely to think, "I can do it" rather than "I can't do it." Student perceptions and motivations about schooling can also be enhanced by discussions about how a good education can affect their future lifestyles.

Multicultural Education

The primary focus of teachers is to understand each individual student's personal identity and how it is formed relative to their associations with various groups. These social and cultural influences affect how innate traits and characteristics are manifested so that each individual can succeed within their social and cultural surroundings. Canada is rich in cultural diversity and, as a society, has embraced the influences brought to this country by many different ethnic groups. The dilemma for educators is no longer whether or not multicultural education should be taught; it is more about how the topic should be emphasized when it is taught. In Canada, multicultural education strives to promote cultural identity and intergroup tolerances while at the same time attempting to reduce prejudice toward ethnic minorities. Overall, the aim of multicultural education is to develop cultural understandings of—and mutual respect for—different beliefs, values, and social practices. This perspective values diversity as a pervasive educational element that contributes to the fabric of Canadian society in positive ways. From this perspective, school is seen as the predominant vehicle by which students from diverse ethnic groups are assimilated into the Canadian mainstream. This approach is different from the melting-pot concept, which advocates exchanging one's cultural identity for that of the majority in order to become a valued member of the group. The Canadian mosaic is an acknowledged heterogeneous multicultural society within which schools play a significant role in preparing students for complete participation and interaction.

Different Views

There are three slightly different views of multicultural education. First, some educators and researchers feel strongly that diversity should be valued above all and that no culture should be portrayed as superior or dominant. This approach to multicultural education attempts to avoid marginalizing minority groups by critically examining the assumptions held by the dominant culture. It also seeks to prevent unwarranted pressure for students from these groups to assimilate and potentially lose their cultural identity. The second view of multicultural education stresses the values of the dominant culture in an effort to provide students with better opportunities to understand and function within it. Advocates of this perspective contend that understanding diversity is not as important as learning how to survive in the real world. Proponents of this view feel that students must be alerted to the preferred and non-preferred behaviours that will affect their success within the dominant culture. This approach emphasizes the similarities that bind groups and individuals rather than differences that draw or force them apart. The third and probably most contemporary view of multicultural education is a synthesis approach—the focus is on both the values of the dominant culture and the values of diversity. This blended perspective exposes students to the complete range of possibilities available but also purposefully stresses the importance of acquiring knowledge, skills, and behaviours that will allow them to function successfully in the larger community. It encourages lifestyles that recognize individuals' own cultures, but not to the extent that it excludes or ignores the real world that surrounds them. This is particularly important when it comes to social rules and judicial laws. Within this synthesis approach, individuality and societal membership are equal-opportunity experiences that students must strike a balance between in order to establish their social identity.

Banks's Model

There is no consensus about the preferred approach to teaching multicultural education, but there is agreement that the five dimensions suggested by Banks (2001) need to be considered. Banks's model (see Figure 7.1) for multicultural education goes beyond the integration of content, because simple changes to the curriculum about what to teach are not enough. Attempts to do so are bound to include ethno-specific information that is irrelevant to some students while leaving out other information that is highly pertinent. The dimensions provided by Banks

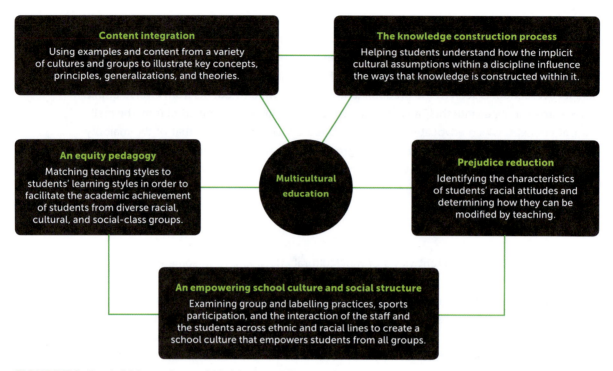

FIGURE 7.1 Banks' Dimensions of Multicultural Education

Source: Reprinted with permission of James A. Banks from James A. Banks, CULTURAL DIVERSITY AND EDUCATION: FOUNDATIONS, CURICULUM AND TEACHING (6th Edition). Boston: Pearson Allyn and Bacon, page 5.

are an attempt to construct a universal model of multicultural education that is relevant to all students. The model, therefore, includes (a) helping students understand how beliefs influence knowledge, (b) reducing prejudice, (c) teaching to benefit all students, and (d) creating social structures that support the development and learning of all students.

Aboriginal Education

In Canada, Aboriginal education is receiving considerable attention. Unfortunately, much of this attention revolves around poor rates of achievement. The Congress of Aboriginal Peoples (2010) noted that the rates of Aboriginal students completing high school in Canada lag far behind those of non-Aboriginal students. In response to this situation, the congress identified both risk and protective factors that may affect the Aboriginal student's engagement in school.

Risk factors:
- early school failures;
- moving from school to school (e.g., reserve school to public school);
- difficulty transitioning from elementary to secondary school (e.g., no local high school);
- lack of parental support;
- poor home–school communication;
- lack of qualified teachers with a strong degree of proficiency in Aboriginal languages and Aboriginal studies;

- lack of resources for educators who have to teach Aboriginal content;
- negative teacher attitudes toward Aboriginal students;
- having to perform adult roles (e.g., some Aboriginal students work and/or have children of their own);
- living in remote communities;
- poor access to technology; and
- having special needs.

> **think box**
>
> How did the schools that you attended promote cultural identity and intergroup tolerances? To what extent did you have the opportunity to develop cultural understandings of different beliefs, values, and social practices? How did these opportunities, or lack of opportunities, affect your school experiences?

Protective factors:

1. **Early intervention**—students who feel connected to school and have positive school experiences are more engaged.
2. **Resiliency**—learning leadership skills and being empowered to contribute in the classroom helps students to face adversity.
3. **Positive self-image**—students who are provided opportunities to explore their identities in a positive manner are more motivated to achieve.
4. **Engagement by families**—when parental confidence about formal education is high, positive relationships develop between families and teachers.
5. **Community involvement**—students who are involved in their communities are more successful at school.
6. **Relevant programming**—students are more engaged when the curriculum reflects Aboriginal language and culture.
7. **Connections to Aboriginal role models and supports**—students feel more comfortable in school when they have contact with people like themselves (e.g., Aboriginal counsellors and elders).

It is clear, then, that the issues within Aboriginal education are similar to those of multicultural education. Simply changing the curriculum is not enough. As Banks (2001) highlighted in his model of multicultural education, student success is best achieved through content integration, an equity pedagogy, an empowering school culture and social structure, a knowledge construction process, and prejudice reduction.

Conclusion

In summary, culture and society are pervasive elements of all learning environments. They influence social interactions and establish overarching frameworks that dictate what is good and bad, true and false, and acceptable and unacceptable, among numerous other intrinsic values. However, except for ST and SES, cultural and societal influences do not significantly affect student achievement, because within-group achievement variability for all identified groups is greater than between-group variability. This means that once ST and SES influences have been considered and mitigated, student achievement is primarily a function of good teaching, regardless of a student's culture, race, ethnicity, religion, or gender.

When Annette finishes reading, she goes back and re-reads the last sentence. The phrase "student achievement is primarily a function of good teaching" resonates strongly with her, and she reflects on what she has accomplished in her classroom to date. She knows that the tone and atmosphere of her classroom resounds with a strong and focused desire for academic and behavioural success. She feels that her constructivist bent allows her students to formulate and construct their own knowledge and their own knowledge-producing structures. Additionally, she knows that her use of universal instructional design conceptualizes teaching as an inclusive and equitable process, which, because it is designed to meet the needs of the least able students, makes it more effective for the diverse needs of all students in her classroom. Moreover, she has purposefully chosen meaningful tasks inherent in problem-, project-, and inquiry-based learning that will positively influence student achievement and student self-regulated learning because of the options provided. Because learning involves skill acquisition, cognitive understanding, and the formation of cognitive processes, all of which are generated by thinking, she has formulated her instruction to invoke active student thinking rather than passive remembering. And finally, all this has taken place in an environment that has as its ultimate goal the psychological well-being of all students. It is an environment that is collectively and democratically constructed around the tenets of mutual respect and responsibility. Together, this collection of instructional principles encourages and values diverse approaches to learning and, perhaps more important, promotes opportunities for all students to express their learning in diverse and individualized ways. Annette confidently concludes that her teaching is made up of several elements that promote student diversity and individuality while adhering to the fundamental requirements of schooling. "It wasn't easy creating this type of balance," she murmurs to herself, "but it's something we all benefit from. I know I'll have to continue to stay on top of things, though, or else the balance might be easily upset. Monitoring what happens in the classroom, and making modifications where needed, is key."

Annette's Journal

February 14, 2014

Just when teaching and learning begins to seem so complicated, along comes a solution to a problem that is rather obvious and simple to implement. I'm referring of course to Caleb. His apparent lack of interest in anything academic left me perplexed for some time. I always knew he was quite capable, so I spent my energies trying to motivate him to behave in class and be more positive about school tasks. Motivating him to take part in physical or outdoor activities was never a problem. His lack of interest seemed to be centred around any type of seatwork, and that extended to homework assignments as well. It wasn't until I overheard Liam and Jacqueline talking about Caleb that I more seriously considered his cultural background as being a major factor in his school behaviours. This set me on the path to learning more about who Caleb is, both as a person and as a learner.

I totally enjoyed working with Caleb over the past few weeks. I probably learned more than he did. However, I'm most satisfied knowing that Caleb finally had a very positive school experience. He received one of the highest marks in the class for his social studies project, and more important, he earned respect and admiration from his classmates. I also think he realized how capable he is, and this should go a long way toward his achievement in other areas, even those tasks that do not have a storytelling component.

I've followed Caleb's advice and have given all students in the class an opportunity to take part in storytelling circles. We had our first get-together on the carpet yesterday. I invited Caleb to lead us off with a story, and he did a fine job. He had everyone, including me, transfixed by his every word. I was surprised when Troy put his hand up immediately after Caleb finished. He said he wanted to tell us a story too. He obviously identified in some way with Caleb, because his story was related to his Asian background. Troy doesn't have the storytelling skills that Caleb has, but his story was sweet and sincere. Everyone clapped for him when he was done. There is no doubt that we will continue to have these storytelling sessions on a regular basis. They're not only opportunities for students to learn more about each other, but they also give students the chance to shine and feel respected by their peers.

Annette's Exploration of the Research

Okagaki, L. (2012). Ethnicity and learning. In P. A. Alexander & P. H. Winne (Eds.), *Handbook of educational psychology* (2nd ed., pp. 615–634). New York, NY: Routledge.

Annette's success with Caleb led to a discussion with her educational assistants about how one's ethnicity affects learning. She found an interesting study in the *Handbook of educational psychology* that she shared with Mr. Hayes and Mrs. McCarthy. Her conversation with them included the following information:

> In a comprehensive review of ethnicity and learning, Okagaki (2012) presented several reasons why students, especially those from ethnic minorities, disengage from schooling and typically attain low achievement levels. A universal strategy, employed by adolescents across all ethnic groups, for disengaging from school is to publicly distance oneself from the appearance of working hard because working hard and having an academic orientation brings feelings of alienation from one's peers. In many cases, students go to great lengths to keep their peers from knowing about their academic successes.
>
> According to Okagaki's (2012) review of the literature, another predominant reason for disengagement among ethnic minorities is the perception held by many that working hard in school will not pay off. These individuals seek other venues in which to achieve and will disengage from trying to achieve in domains where they perceive that discrimination may keep them from succeeding. This causes a disidentification with particular domains that are traditionally viewed as beyond the purview of many minorities.
>
> There is also evidence that underachieving ethnic-minority students have different goals and values about education, ones that significantly contribute to their lack of motivation to achieve and are a major part of the process by which minorities disengage from school. Their perceptions of admirable and respectable individuals lean more toward low-achieving than high-achieving peers. This causes a crucial disconnect between their aspirations and the aspirations typically held by educators for these students.
>
> Okagaki concluded that a general belief in the value of education is not as important for ethnic-minority students as is a fundamental belief in the instrumental value of education. Instrumental value is the degree to which individual students believe that doing well in school will produce direct benefits for their lives. This belief, in concert with a teacher's avoidance of tacit or overt forms of ST, can contribute significantly to student engagement and achievement and can help overcome the belief that there are discriminatory barriers to one's education-related successes. This position is also consistent with the philosophy espoused by many educators that hard work can make a difference. From this perspective, teachers are appealing to the social identities of individual students, not utilizing blanket perceptions about groups. "We too often assume that others are acting out of the same world view that we hold and explain their behaviours in ways that are consistent with our existing theories. . . . Working with people who have different cultural perspectives provides opportunities for making familiar phenomena new and different" (p. 630).

Annette's Resource List

Academic Journals

American Educational Research Journal
Educational Psychologist
Educational Researcher
International Journal of Multicultural Education
Journal of Educational Psychology
Journal of School Psychology
Sociology of Education

Books

Alberta Teachers' Association. (2010). *Here comes everyone: Teaching in the intercultural classroom.* Edmonton, AB: Alberta Teachers' Association.

Clauss-Ehlers, C. S. (2006). *Diversity training for classroom teaching: A manual for students and educators.* New York, NY: Springer.

Websites

Aboriginal Perspectives: A Guide to the Teacher's Toolkit
www.edu.gov.on.ca/eng/aboriginal/Guide_Toolkit2009.pdf

Anti-Racism and Multicultural Education: Some Current Activities in Canada
www.safehealthyschools.org/whatsnew/racism.htm

Culturally Responsive Educational Practices
http://education.alberta.ca/admin/fnmi/collaborativeframework/themes/culturally-responsive.aspx

Four Directions Teaching
www.fourdirectionsteachings.com/

Manitoba First Nations Education Resources
www.mfnerc.org/index.php?option=com_content&task=category&sectionid=14&id=92&Itemid=116

Promising Practices in Aboriginal Education
www.maei-ppw.com/

What Is Stereotype Threat?
www.reducingstereotypethreat.org/definition.html

From the Authors' Notebook

This chapter emphasized the importance of understanding student diversity and how addressing this diversity can have a significant impact on teacher instruction and learning. It outlined how teachers must be prepared to understand student differences and act to mitigate their potentially negative effects on achievement. It also addressed how teachers can accommodate socio-cultural differences by acquiring both a critical consciousness and multicultural understandings; together, these contribute to the construction of a teacher's culturally responsive practice.

Reflecting on Practice

Consider the information you have read in this chapter as well as the knowledge you have acquired through instruction, classroom discussions, and classroom activities. Then take the time to write down your thoughts about these learning experiences. Consider how your perspective on educational psychology may have changed. In addition, respond to the following questions:

- How confident do you feel about your ability to create a culturally responsive practice?
- What more do you need to know about addressing diversity in the classroom, and where might you find this information?

Chapter Summary

In this chapter, the following concepts were highlighted:

- Individuals struggle to be a part of the world and apart from the world.
- Race, class, gender, culture, language, and educational achievement are issues of individuality, not group membership.
- Some theorists contend that socio-cultural factors constitute the individual, not merely influence that constitution.
- Cultural frames are socially constructed points of reference.
- While social and cultural differences can lead to disparate educational opportunities, education can be the great equalizer if properly framed and implemented.
- Effective multicultural education goes beyond the integration of content.
- A culturally responsive practice incorporates the cultures, experiences, and needs of culturally and ethnically diverse students on an individual basis.
- An instrumental value of education is the degree to which students believe that doing well in school will produce direct benefits.

New Terms

authoritative parenting
authoritarian parenting
critical consciousness
permissive parenting

prejudice
socio-economic status
stereotype threat

These terms are defined in the Glossary at the end of the text.

Review Questions

- Why should cultural identity be positioned within the individual?
- How do social and cultural differences lead to disparate educational opportunities?
- What is stereotype threat, and how can it contribute to educational inequities?
- How does socio-economic status contribute to educational inequities?
- How is parenting style related to lower socio-economic status?
- What is the contemporary view of multicultural education?
- What is a critical consciousness disposition, and why is it important for educators to acquire such a disposition?
- How can a teacher construct a culturally responsive practice?
- What are the risk factors for low achievement by Aboriginal students?
- What effect does an instrumental value of education have on student engagement?

END OF SCHOOL YEAR
Standardized Achievement Tests

8

From the Authors' Notebook

Standardized tests are used for a wide variety of purposes in education. This chapter outlines these purposes, addresses the controversy surrounding the tests, and differentiates between standardized achievement tests and both aptitude and teacher-made tests. The reader is also introduced to design issues that are now considered critical to the development of valid large-scale standardized tests, such as the connections that are needed between test content and classroom curricula.

Primary Learning Objectives

After reading this chapter, you should understand

1. how standardized tests are used by Canadian provincial and territorial governments;
2. what a standardized test is and is not;
3. the difference between standardized achievement tests and teacher-made tests;
4. the difference between standardized achievement tests and aptitude tests;
5. stakeholders' views of standardized achievement testing;
6. the essential elements that must be addressed when making improvements to standardized tests;
7. the importance of connections between classroom curricula and standardized tests;
8. how teachers can help students prepare for standardized tests;
9. how standardized test results should be used in educational decision-making; and the importance of constructed responses and performance results reporting.

Determining Student Achievement

Like many Canadian teachers, Annette was involved in the administration and supervision of several **standardized tests** during the school year. Because she had students from many grades in her classroom, she administered at least one of these tests every month from January onwards. As she updates her students' files, she thinks about her next meeting with Mr. Hayes and Mrs. McCarthy. Earlier in the year, she asked them to make a list of questions that they would like her to address in their weekly get-togethers. Some of their questions were about standardized testing, and there had never been enough time to really discuss the topic fully. Now that the school year is almost over and there are no pressing issues, she has decided to make this the focal topic of their next meeting. While considering what she should talk about, she recalls a brief but important conversation she had with Aaron, the student teacher who spent time in her classroom during the fall term. They were discussing the unique teaching situation she found herself in and the equally unique student-teaching placement he was experiencing. As was often the case, their talk turned to assessment.

"I noticed from the student files that you tested all the students when school started," Aaron said. "Why did you do that? Wasn't it awfully early to test the students? And weren't you busy just trying to get everything organized at that point?"

"Yes, of course I was busy," replied Annette, "but I wanted to be sure that when I started teaching I was making the correct assumptions about the students' current levels of knowledge and skill development. I also wanted to see who potentially might need extra attention."

"You mean you tested all the students across all subjects?"

Annette smiled. "No, not all subjects. I just prepared diagnostic tests for language arts and math for the younger group and English and math for the older group. The results were quite revealing."

Aaron was taken aback. "Wasn't that a lot of work? After all, you were new to the school and the community, and you didn't know anything about the students who would be in your class. On top of that, I know how much work it must have been to make two tests from scratch for every grade—one in English and the other in math."

"Oh no," laughed Annette, amused at the bewildered look on Aaron's face. "I used the end-of-year tests the students wrote last June as the basis for my tests. I put that information together with the information in this year's curriculum guides to develop the questions, and you have to remember that the tests were quite short."

"I know, but that seems like an awful lot of work, even though it's a good idea. Why didn't you just use a few standardized tests? From what I've learned, they provide information that is especially useful at the start of a school year, they're easily administered, you can get them for almost every subject and grade level, and they have scoring keys for easy marking. I've even seen them advertised for sale on the Internet by commercial test developers, and they're not that expensive."

"You're right on all accounts except that I've learned that the results from those types of tests are not really the best measures to use when you want to develop learning expectations or goals for specific courses. They're very good for differentiating between groups of students for instructional reasons, I'll grant that much, but I only have one or two students in each grade, so the test results wouldn't have served me very well at all. And you have to realize that these types of tests are even less informative when you want to set learning expectations for individual students. They may indicate global areas of curricular strength or need, but they're really only a general starting point for further assessment. I wanted to be very precise when developing my expectations and goals. And, of course, I knew the students would be more comfortable and less stressed if they were familiar with the assessment material."

After thinking about Aaron's comments on standardized tests and the questions posed by Mr. Hayes and Mrs. McCarthy, Annette decides that she needs to do some research before the meeting with her educational assistants. She turns to Dr. Cameron once again for advice.

Testing Issues

Annette Elkins <annette_elkins@schoolmail.com>

Date: Thursday, June 12, 2014 7:02 PM

To: Andrew Cameron <acameron@university.ca>

Hello Andrew,

Well, here we are, almost at the end of the school year. I'm not sure where the time went, but I do know that both the students and I are ready for a break. After our year-end party on the 20th, I'm leaving for a three-week trip to Europe. I'm quite excited because I'm finally going to visit Venice, a place I've always wanted to experience.

Before I sign off for this school year, I hope you don't mind responding to one more request. The whole issue of standardized achievement tests versus teacher-made tests has been on my mind. In the fall, I had a conversation with Aaron about this topic, and now I'm about to discuss standardized testing with the educational assistants. As you know, I like to make my own tests to evaluate student achievement. I'm not sure I can fully explain the role that standardized tests play in student learning, even though I administer them every year. Do you have any reading material on this topic?

Thanks again for all of your help. You're a terrific mentor! I've learned so much more about teaching just by having you as my sounding board.

Annette

The next afternoon, Annette receives a response from Dr. Cameron.

> **Re: Testing Issues**
>
> **Andrew Cameron <acameron@university.ca>**
> **Date:** Friday, June 13, 2014 2:22 PM
> **To:** Annette Elkins <annette_elkins@schoolmail.com>
> Attachments: Testing Issues.doc; G&M Testing.doc
>
> Hi Annette,
>
> I'm so glad to hear that you'll soon be off to Europe for a holiday. You certainly deserve the break after the effort you've put into your teaching this year—remember, it's extremely important to take the time to recharge your mind and body. Try to leave school behind as you focus on yourself for a few weeks.
>
> Your comments about testing are reflective of how and why, in the past decade or more, educational psychologists have argued for a major shift in the way that educational assessment is conceptualized, designed, and practised. One of my colleagues wrote a paper on large-scale standardized testing issues (see attached). I've also sent a copy of a newspaper article that will give you a real flavour of what is happening in Canada. I hope these help you and your colleagues to better understand the current issues.
>
> Enjoy your travels,
>
> Andrew

She reads the e-mail and prints the two documents, hoping they will contain some interesting information that she can share with Mr. Hayes and Mrs. McCarthy. She also wants to be prepared for any questions that her students or their parents might have in the future.

Testing Issues

Since the 1990s, government institutions and educators have used various standardized tests to evaluate teacher competencies, conduct large-scale analyses of student abilities, and set performance standards to improve score interpretations. In Canada, some standardized tests are required for all students across the country. For example, for many years, all 13- and 16-year-old Canadian students completed **achievement tests** that examined concepts in mathematics, reading, writing, science, inquiry, and problem-solving. Since 2007, this approach has changed; now, only the math, reading, and science performances of 13-year-olds are examined.

In terms of provincially mandated standardized achievement testing, nearly all Canadian provinces and territories use this type of testing. However, there are considerable differences in how and why testing programs are conducted. For example, in Ontario, under the auspices of the Education Quality and Accountability Office (EQAO), all Grade 9 students in any given year complete a standardized mathematics test; all Grade 10 students complete a standardized literacy test; and all Grade 3 and Grade 6 students complete reading, writing, and mathematics tests. While Ontario does not yet have standardized exit exams for all Grade 12 subjects/courses, many provinces have successfully used provincial subject/course graduation exams for several decades. The two primary purposes of these exams are to determine whether students can (1) graduate from high school and (2) enter a post-secondary institution. In British Columbia, Grade 12 students write provincial examinations with the test worth 40 per cent of their Grade 12 mark. In Alberta, provincial exams in mathematics, science, and English comprise 50 per cent of a Grade 12 student's final mark. Saskatchewan students write provincial math, science, reading, and writing standardized tests in various two-year cycles, but these results do not factor in final grades. In Manitoba, provincial exams in English and math count for 30 per cent of a Grade 12 student's final mark. Quebec Grade 11 students write standardized tests in history, science, English, and French that comprise 50 per cent of their final grades. Students in New Brunswick must pass the Grade 9 reading and writing assessment in order to graduate. All Nova Scotia Grade 12 students write standardized tests in English and math worth 30 per cent of their final grades. Newfoundland and Labrador Grade 12 students write standardized tests in English, French, biology, chemistry, math, physics, geography, and history that count for 50 per cent of final grades.

> **think box**
>
> Think back to your time in school. Do you remember completing any standardized achievement tests? What do you remember about these testing experiences (e.g., the types of tests, teachers' explanations of why you had to complete the tests, how your peers responded to the testing sessions, your own feelings about taking these tests, and what you were told about the test results)?

What Is a Standardized Test?

A standardized test, which is administered to large groups of individuals, is simply a test that (a) contains the same questions for all test-takers; (b) is administered to all individuals in the same fashion, under the same conditions, and within a specified time; and (c) is always scored in a systematic and uniform manner. While teacher-made tests are based on the learning objectives emphasized in one classroom, standardized achievement tests are based on the learning objectives that should be common in all classrooms. Based on these elements of uniformity, standardized achievement tests are typically used in Canada by provincial governments to determine whether or not students have acquired the knowledge, skills, and attitudes required or provided by their schooling. From a broader perspective, these wide-scale assessments are also used to help determine the effectiveness of education systems.

Achievement versus Aptitude Tests

The standardized achievement tests used in the large-scale assessments described above are not to be confused with the standardized **aptitude tests** used by psychologists, psychometrists, and educators when conducting psycho-educational assessments (see Chapter 6). While both achievement and aptitude tests are constructed, administered, and interpreted based on the same psychometric principles of standardization, they are designed and used for very different purposes. An aptitude test is a specific ability test that assesses a student's specific cognitive, social, and behavioural skills. It answers the question "What is the student able to do?" versus the question answered by achievement tests, "What knowledge/skill level has the student achieved?" A psycho-educational assessment also usually includes topic- or skill-specific achievement tests (e.g., reading, spelling, math, writing), but these tests are quite different from the more generalized achievement tests administered province- or territory-wide and nationwide in Canada. The achievement tests used in large-scale assessments are designed to provide broad overviews of academic performance for large groups of students. They are typically **criterion-referenced tests**—a student's score is reflective of how well he or she performed relative to established standards or criteria. By contrast, the aptitude tests used in psycho-educational assessments are designed to provide specific insights into a student's abilities and inabilities. They are typically **norm-referenced tests**—a student's score is reflective of how well he or she did in comparison to all other students who completed the same test. In other words, the student is compared against the norm. Another principal difference between these two types of tests is that large-scale achievement tests primarily serve a summative and evaluative function, while psycho-educational aptitude tests primarily serve a diagnostic function.

Stakeholders' Views of Standardized Testing

It is interesting to note that the original purpose of broadly applied standardized testing programs was to assess the overall effectiveness of instruction as an indication of teacher effectiveness, not to examine the academic progress of students. It is ironic then, and considerably disappointing,

that when large-scale assessment results are typically reported in the media, the consistent and predominant discussion involves detailed comparisons of schools or groups of students, with little attention being paid to the overall quality of education or the effectiveness of instruction. Nonetheless, supporters of standardized tests are convinced that such tests are the best way for society to hold educators accountable for student learning and the best way to make sure school systems and teachers are dutifully executing their educative responsibilities. For example, the Fraser Institute's *Report Card on British Columbia Elementary Schools* (Cowley & Easton, 2008) indicated that an overwhelming majority of BC parents (83%) supported the province-wide testing of reading, writing, and mathematics. It stated that "the best way to gather real and relevant data is through standardized testing" (*Vancouver Sun*, 2008, June 19). The authors of a more recent Fraser Institute report (Cowley, Easton, & Thomas, 2012) reported that in 2011, 604,000 individual school reports and school comparisons of BC elementary schools were downloaded by parents and others. Obviously, parents are very interested in this type of information.

However, not all stakeholders support standardized testing. Teachers in particular have presented many legitimate arguments against the use of standardized testing. Some argue that the tests are biased in that they only examine certain types of knowledge or skills and/or that they produce different types of results for different groups (e.g., those who differ in race, ethnicity, class, and/or gender). This is of particular concern when test results alone are used to determine successful graduation and/or college and university entrance. The inherent problem in placing such value on admissions tests is that even though the tests are reliable and may appear valid, the decision-making process about who gets in, and who does not, can still be biased in terms of test content and/or group differences.

Other teachers argue that the high-stakes nature of standardized achievement tests is extremely stressful for students and teachers, infringes on teachers' ability and freedom to teach, consumes inordinate amounts of time, and coerces teachers into teaching to the test. In teaching to the test, teachers—because of enormous public, school board, or within-school pressure for their students to perform well—place more time and emphasis on the standardized test content at the expense of other more valuable curricular content.

Educators also argue that provincial standardized testing does not increase student learning, nor does it improve their motivation to learn. For example, the Fraser Institute's first report (Cowley & Easton, 2008) noted that the B.C. Teachers' Federation did not approve of the British Columbia Foundation Skills Assessment of elementary reading, writing, and mathematics and was attempting to persuade parents to withdraw their children from participating. The teachers felt that the fault lay not with the testing methods but with the government's focus on benchmarking student learning (*Vancouver Sun*, 2008, June 19). In a similar vein, there is a feeling among numerous teachers that standardized tests affect how, and which, learning expectations are developed and that these expectations are vastly different from what is taught in classrooms. Their principal argument here is that the content examined in the government's tests is not reflective of the content teachers are mandated to teach by government curriculum guides.

Another common concern expressed by educators focuses on the security of standardized tests. Most of these tests rely heavily on tight test security in order to validate both the scores assigned and the evaluative interpretations that follow. Once a test becomes available to the public, test security is breached, the test loses its validity, and it must be replaced.

It is obvious, then, that many teachers feel that standardized tests do little to improve the teaching and learning process. Two primary factors support this argument: (1) these tests are not derived from the same curricular objectives as the subjects/courses that teachers teach, and (2) the results from wide-scale assessments are reported to educators far too late to be of any instructional benefit. While it could be argued that a potential benefit of late test results is that teachers can make instructional changes for the subsequent year, these changes do nothing for the students who just completed the test. Furthermore, having to make instructional changes indicates that something was wrong with the test or with the instruction provided or with both. This is another compelling reason that the concepts examined in standardized tests should be more precisely aligned with curriculum content. If they are not, test results may help determine the progress and effectiveness of educational systems, but they do not provide any benefit for individual students; hence, their contribution toward improving instruction is notably suspect on several fronts. When examined from a more philosophical position, Graham and Neu (2004) contend that standardized testing is a "big brother" technique of government that operates indirectly at a distance yet seeks to directly manage populations. They suggest that by subjecting all participants in education systems to considerable public scrutiny, standardized testing contributes to the construction of governable persons.

Misconceptions

Finally, it is important to note that there are several misconceptions (mostly negative) about standardized achievement tests designed and implemented by Canadian provincial and territorial governments. In many cases, these misconceptions have developed because the term "standardized test"—with its emphasis on standardization—also correctly refers to intelligence tests, personality tests, commercially available achievement tests administered in numerous US schools, and a wide assortment of tests used for employment entry and progression. Each of these tests has appropriate and inappropriate uses, and over time numerous concerns have been expressed about their design, implementation, and interpretation practices. For example, many media and academic reports have accurately reported the inappropriate use of intelligence test results to classify students or deny students entry into particular academic programs. Additionally, there are bona fide reports of similar widespread misuses of large-scale standardized achievement tests provided by commercial developers. It should be noted that the heightened attention given to high-stakes assessment and standardized testing, especially in the US, is due to the significant emphasis placed on standards-based assessment within the No Child Left Behind Act of 2001.

Without understanding that these standardized tests are vastly different from those used by Canadian provincial and territorial governments, some government representatives—as well as the media, the public, and even various stakeholder groups within education—erroneously assume that their negative qualities are also present in provincial and territorial achievement testing. A simple Google search of the term "standardized testing" turns up an unwieldy plethora of pointed examples. This is not to imply, however, that provincially mandated achievement testing is without fault. Rather, it is important to acknowledge and understand that some of the criticisms and rhetoric directed at provincial and territorial governments regarding standardized achievement testing is considerably off the mark.

Guiding Principles

The Purpose, Outcomes, and Future of Standardized Testing

Since the standards-based reform movement of the 1980s, the enduring mantra used to justify large-scale standardized assessment has been accountability. Given that education in Canada is, for the most part, a publicly funded enterprise, governments need to be able to show their constituents that they are getting excellent value for the significant dollars spent. In their review of the research on external, large-scale assessments, Shepard, Hammerness, Darling-Hammond, and Rust (2005) determined that the intended purposes of these types of tests are to

- determine student performance in the essential elements of schooling;
- monitor achievement trends over time;
- identify and/or modify the instructional methods that best produce student progress;
- evaluate educational programs; and/or
- hold districts, schools, and teachers accountable (pp. 306–307).

Large-scale assessments may be used, for example, to identify schools that do or do not do well in raising the scholastic achievement of particular groups of students (e.g., female or male students or students who live in a certain region of the country). Based on the data, instructional changes may need to be incorporated or educational policies may have to be altered or both.

The authors also determined that the accountability assessment improvement movement has led to more testing programs that include more open-ended problem-solving questions to better reflect the challenging learning goals found in most classrooms. They reported that "a number of studies have shown that these kinds of large-scale assessments can influence instruction in demonstrably positive ways . . . [but] are also accompanied by negative effects . . . [and] there is limited evidence that standards based reforms . . . have contributed to improvements in student achievement" (pp. 309–310).

Citing Pellegrino, Chudowsky, and Glaser's (2001) landmark report, the authors concluded that educational policy-makers, especially those responsible for developing large-scale tests, need to pay closer attention to curriculum-embedded testing systems instead of purposefully separating large-scale test concepts from classroom instructional concepts. This change in approach would provide for both the complexity of classroom learning and still ensure the comparability of test data. For classroom and large-scale assessments to work properly together, they will need to

- be designed from the same basic curriculum frameworks;
- address the same and full range of cognitive demands;
- incorporate similar tasks and meaning for eliciting student proficiency;
- use common standards for judging the quality of student work; and
- use the same underlying continua or benchmarks representing how student proficiencies are expected to develop over time (Shepard, Hammerness, Darling-Hammond, & Rust, 2005, p. 308).

The legitimacy of accountability is dependent on closing the divide between what is taught and assessed by teachers in classrooms and what is assessed by large-scale standardized achievement testing.

Constructing Better Standardized Tests

Regardless of their good qualities and benefits, their poor qualities and drawbacks, and their potential to be seen as infusing more government into the lives of educators and students, there is considerable room for improvement in standardized tests. First, it is best that educators think of all tests as useful but imperfect instruments. Second, it is also worthwhile to keep in mind that even tests of the highest quality can be problematic if they are used for invalid applications. In fact, while most test scores are accurate numerically, all test scores are inevitably subject to someone's interpretation, and because these interpretations are often used for significant educational decisions, the definition of test validity has evolved in the past 15 years to explicitly include an indication as to whether test scores are being used properly. The discipline of educational psychology, in particular, has made considerable strides in realizing better understandings about (a) test construction and design, (b) the intricacies of the cognitive processing being assessed, and (c) the beneficial instruction and assessment interactions that can enhance teaching and learning. As Ercikan (2012) stated, when evaluating any form of test—either classroom-based or provincially mandated—it is critical to focus, above all else, on determining whether or not the assessment serves student learning.

There is no question that educators need to strike a delicate balance between the public's rightful need for accountability and their students' rightful need for proven and effective assessment methods. The first part of that balancing act has to be the judicious and appropriate weighting of standardized test scores against other indices of student achievement when making educational decisions. In Canada, it is fair to say that most governments involved in the design, development, administration, and interpretation of provincially mandated tests realize that good educational assessment is made up of much more than the results of such tests. In 2013, the Alberta government took this a step further when they announced that their Provincial Achievement Tests would be replaced by a new series of computer-based tests called Student Learning Assessments. According to the education minister (Global News, 2013, May 9), these new tests would be "centered around the student, and centered around assessment for learning, as opposed to assessment of learning."

The second part of the balancing act between the need for accountability and the need for effective assessment methods, and certainly the most important one from the perspective of educational psychologists, is the issue of generating a more concerted effort toward matching what tests test with what teachers teach. Attention to this curricular and conceptual match would go a long way toward satisfying the desire of provinces and territories to have more centralized curricula and better indices of achievement (Earl, 2003). It would also satisfy teachers' widespread concerns that standardized tests cannot be supported from a pedagogical standpoint (Froese-Germain, 1999) because of the obvious "chasms" between test content and classroom content.

Five Essential Elements

Educational psychologists like to think of education as a three-legged stool that is equally supported by curriculum (what to teach), instruction (how to teach it), and assessment (how to determine whether students have learned). These three fundamental facets of the educational process are not only important, they are critically interdependent; if one fails, they all fail, and worse yet, the entire educational enterprise collapses. If large-scale assessment is not a complementary procedure that both enhances teaching and learning *and* improves curricular design, then, because of its guaranteed accountability-driven presence, it undermines education. Popham (2003) argued that in order for large-scale assessments to improve teaching and learning, they need to meet the following five essential requirements:

1. The test must assess important curricular goals.
2. The curricular goals must be teachable.
3. The assessed knowledge and skills must be clearly described and accurately reflect effective learning.
4. The test must be specific enough to directly guide instruction.
5. The assessment process must be minimally intrusive on classrooms.

Popham's five essential elements are necessary because, according to the complaints voiced by numerous educators and parents, large-scale assessments (a) do not assess curricularly relevant goals; (b) assess goals that are not teachable, are not clearly described, and do not reflect effective learning; (c) do little to guide instruction; and (d) are considerably intrusive. Therefore, we are seeing a growing awareness that assessments used solely for accountability purposes need to be replaced by assessments that provide specific information about student cognitive processes and the learning mechanisms that contribute to academic progress. This is not to say that large-scale assessments are not needed; rather, it is a clear indication that reported performance results need to clearly indicate what students are able to do. Chudowsky and Pellegrino (2003) took Popham's assertion that assessment needs to support learning a step further. They argued that while research on learning, knowledge development, and competency has made great strides and can be applied in practical ways, these results are rarely incorporated into large-scale assessments. According to Chudowsky and Pellegrino, therefore, the foremost requirement for assessments that are truly supportive of student learning is the inclusion of clear and precise articulations about the underlying concepts being assessed. This means, in no uncertain terms, that the questions used in standardized tests must be derived from the same learning objectives used for instruction.

Ideally, then, a standardized achievement test in which students' scores are compared to established criterion-based standards is developed through rigorous processes of design and pilot testing. For example, consider the following scenario: A provincial ministry of education wants to know how well sixth-grade students in school board XYZ are doing in math compared to the rest of the Grade 6 students in the province. They ask Grade 6 math curricular experts (including practising teachers) to design a test that is reflective of the entire curriculum. When doing so, these experts pay strict attention to the curricular goals and learning objectives contained in the provincially mandated Grade 6 curriculum guide. They create a series of multiple-format questions for each and every topic and objective covered in the guide. (While standardized tests have historically included mostly multiple-choice questions, recent advances in assessment practices have resulted in a more widespread use of constructed-response questions, because they better assess students' reasoning, thinking, and problem-solving skills.) They then present all the questions to a wide variety of Grade 6 teachers across the province (who are not involved in the design process) to make sure the questions accurately represent the curriculum taught. Based on teacher feedback, additions and deletions are made, and the resulting questions are equally divided into three different tests so that each test contains questions that measure performance across all curricular topics.

In a pilot session, the different tests are then administered to different sets of Grade 6 students using a standardized administration procedure (i.e., same amount of test-taking time, same conditions, same time of year). Each specific set of students writes an identical test. Educators involved in the pilot testing, along with the test developers, are present to observe the process and make notes about issues that may be relevant to the results and about test revisions or administration adjustments that still need to be made. The results from the three different tests are then carefully examined. In order to report performance results that clearly reflect what students are able to do, classification systems that indicate performance categories by levels of abilities are developed. Finally, the very best questions are selected, and a final draft of the test is compiled.

The test is then administered to another, larger set of Grade 6 students that is as representative as possible of all the Grade 6 students in the province (e.g., urban students, rural students, from private and public schools). Based on student results, and once scores are adjusted for any testing anomalies, scoring criteria are finalized, and a test manual is prepared. The completed test is then administered according to its standardized procedure to all the Grade 6 students in school board XYZ. The scores of the students in school board XYZ are then compared to the established criteria. For example, if the average score on the test for the representative sample is 38 out of 50, the province can report that students who scored above or below 38 are either above or below the provincial standard for Grade 6 math. This is an accurate and fair interpretation of their math performance compared to the rest of the Grade 6 students in the province. It should be noted that subsequent versions of this test will include exemplary questions from the existing test as well as new questions that accurately reflect any curricular changes or pedagogical innovations. Changes such as these will necessitate pilot testing, and if changes are extensive, the establishment of new criterion standards will be required.

Connections between Classroom Curricula and Standardized Tests

According to Popham (2003) and Chudowsky and Pellegrino (2003), the key to excellent standardized assessment is making sure that the learning objectives tested match the learning objectives taught. Canadian provinces and territories are in an enviable position when it comes to constructing high-quality standardized achievement tests for their students. This is because provincial and territorial governments (a) develop and publish the curriculum guides that teachers use as the basis for instruction and (b) governments that design the standardized tests can construct them based on the learning objectives contained in their own curriculum guides. For example, in 2008, EQAO, the independent arm's-length agency of the Ontario government responsible for achievement testing, announced that 84% of first-time eligible Grade 10 students successfully met the literacy standard for reading and writing examined by the 2007–8 Ontario Secondary School Literacy Test (OSSLT). The OSSLT is based on the expectations contained in the Ontario Curriculum, and EQAO test developers visit a number of schools every year to observe the approaches educators are using to improve student achievement (Education Quality and Accountability Office, 2008).

Preparing Students for Test-Writing

Standardized achievement tests will continue to be a common and predominant feature on the educational landscape in Canada. Teachers, therefore, have an important preparatory role to play if all students are to have an opportunity to perform well. A teacher's first obligation is to teach well. Nothing contributes more to student achievement than excellent teaching conducted with passion and rigour. It is also important for teachers to convey positive attitudes about standardized tests and to present them as educational challenges rather than as time-consuming burdens or interruptions. This can be accomplished by educating students about test formats and procedures. Using their own tests, teachers can simulate the use of time limits and the types of questions that students will find on standardized tests and involve students in marking a few questions of each type to familiarize them with scoring formats. It is also helpful for teachers to teach students to be test-wise by demonstrating how to do the following: (a) read test instructions carefully; (b) complete the easy questions first; (c) make sure they allot enough time for each section of the test; and (d) check that the correct answers are filled in on the answer sheet. Facilitating the development of test-taking skills such as these benefits students by reducing test anxiety and enabling optimal performance.

Interpreting Test Results

The best way for teachers to interpret results from standardized achievement tests is to think of a student's reported score as an additional piece of information that can serve two main purposes. The first purpose is that it can help teachers develop a better overall picture of a student's academic progress. Considering the student's score as just one part of the picture is critical, because teachers only ever see the scores and rankings of provincial tests; they do not typically see any of the affective elements that may have contributed to, or could have detracted from, a student's final score. Therefore, five important questions need to be asked when evaluating a standardized test score:

1. Does the score or data make sense? Is it an accurate reflection of the child that I have come to know?
2. How does this score match with other achievement indicators he or she has displayed in my classroom?
3. Does the score reveal considerable growth in learning, a plateau of learning, or a regression in performance?
4. Is it possible that the student had a bad day?
5. Does the score reflect the learning that took place over the whole year/course, or does it merely reflect some of the topics covered?

The second purpose of a student's standardized test score, when considered as part of the whole group's performance, is to highlight curricular content areas and learning processes that are either well consolidated or need further attention. By extrapolation, this may also mean considering modifications to instructional practices. However, teachers have to keep in mind that this will require considerable professional judgment. While standardized achievement test scores, like all other test scores, are direct indicators of how well something has been learned, they are only indirect indicators of how well something has been taught.

As previously mentioned, most standardized provincial test results are provided to educators far too late to be of benefit to the students who completed the test in any given year. This exemplifies how these tests are disconnected from the primary purpose of education—student learning. Nonetheless, the results of these tests can be of considerable benefit to teachers if they view them as information that provides professional opportunities for instructional improvement. Based on this interpretive perspective of test results, it becomes even clearer why the content of the questions used in standardized tests has to match the learning objectives contained in the content taught to students. This focus on the term "learning objectives" as opposed to "content" is very purposeful. Teachers and students can make creative use of a variety of content or subject matter to achieve the same learning objective. It is not uncommon, particularly in project-based learning environments, that students derive the same basic learning from material that varies considerably. The use of similar-but-different content to achieve common learning objectives gives teachers the flexibility and freedom to teach according to their professional insights and experiences without compromising provincial standards.

Summary

Developments in student assessment will continue to emerge as more and more researchers strive to align tests for accountability with tests for improved teaching and learning. As the focus on assessment turns more toward the cognitive processes examined by test items and moves beyond standardized results, researchers in educational psychology will lead these advances because of their inherent connections to teaching, learning, and assessment.

Canadian Standards for Standardized Achievement Testing

The *Principles for Fair Student Assessment Practices for Education in Canada* (1993) contains the principles and guidelines that are generally accepted as indicative of fair assessment practices within Canada. It is safe to say that these principles are also adhered to in most other parts of the world involved in educational testing. Because assessments ultimately depend on professional judgment, particularly in terms of how test results are interpreted and applied, this document lays out the issues to be considered in exercising such judgment. The ultimate goal is fair and equitable assessment of all students. Part B of the document describes

. . . the development and use of standardized assessment methods used in student admissions, placement, certification, and educational diagnosis, and in curriculum and program evaluation . . . [with] guidelines particularly pertinent for mandated educational assessment and testing programs developed and conducted at the national, provincial, and local levels (p. 14).

The principles and guidelines are organized into four interrelated domains. In the fourth domain, Implementing Mandated Assessment Programs, the authors of the document are very careful to point out that the joint committee that created the guidelines "has not taken a position on the value of mandated assessment and testing programs. Rather, given the presence of these programs, the intent of the guidelines . . . is to help ensure fairness and equity for the students being assessed" (p. 20). As a result, the guidelines advise that where the administration of an assessment method is required, test developers and test users should do the following:

- inform all persons with a stake in the assessment (administrators, teachers, students, parents/guardians) of the purpose(s) of the assessment, the uses to be made of the results, and who has access to the results;
- design and describe procedures for developing or choosing the methods of assessment, selecting students where sampling is used, administering the assessment materials, and scoring and summarizing student responses;
- interpret results in light of factors that might influence them (important factors to consider include characteristics of the students, opportunity to learn, and comprehensiveness and representativeness of the assessment method in terms of the learning outcomes to be reported on);
- specify procedures for reporting, storing, controlling access to, and destroying results;
- ensure reports and explanations of results are consistent with the purpose(s) of the assessment, the intended uses of the results, and the planned access to the results; and
- provide reports and explanations of results that can be readily understood by the intended audience(s), and if necessary, employ multiple reports designed for different audiences (p. 20).

Annette is encouraged by the information that describes how educational psychologists are working hard to improve assessment practices in schools. Prior to her summer course and her subsequent readings, she was not aware that the discipline of educational psychology played such an integral role in this aspect of education. However, now she knows differently because, just as the research indicated, the assessment system she used during the current school year proved effective—her students responded positively to the assessment components, and they were obviously motivated by assessment feedback. Annette now turns to the newspaper article that Dr. Cameron recommended. She is interested in learning more about the current viewpoints of Canadian stakeholders.

Canadian Debate over Standardized Testing

The Globe and Mail, May 31, 2013

The Debate over Standardized Testing in Schools Is as Divisive as Ever

Rachel Giese and Caroline Alphonso

"It's getting closer," teacher Erin Hamilton tells her Grade 6 class at Lougheed Middle School in Brampton, Ont. "It's becoming a reality."

"It" is the annual series of tests administered by the Education Quality and Accountability Office, or EQAO, which to the kids stands for Evil Questions Attacking Ontario. By the end of next week, they and every other student in Grades 3 and 6 across the province will have spent six hours (over three days) writing provincially mandated assessments of reading, writing, and math skills.

Just thinking about what lies ahead makes Ms. Hamilton's crew tense.

"It's scary," says Maneesha Johal, 12. "I'm feeling nervous. It's what the government sees; they look at how we've done."

And the government is increasingly proud of what it sees, trumpeting a steady rise in the number of children able to meet its standards—and thus adding lustre to Ontario's reputation in the global race to produce the best and the brightest.

But the nature of standardized testing—a constant concern to teachers and parents across the country, as well the youngsters put under the microscope—is in dispute to such a degree that at least one province is having second thoughts.

Last month, Alberta announced that next year it will begin to phase out its renowned Provincial Achievement Tests (PATs), one of the older and more comprehensive of the exams conducted in Canada.

The move by the nation's top performer in international rankings has reignited the national debate over standardized testing, which critics accuse of encouraging rote learning and forcing teachers to tailor their efforts "to the test." In response, supporters argue that there is no better way to ensure that schools perform properly and the education system remains accountable.

Parents are caught in the middle, trying to weigh their children's angst (and often that of teachers) against a natural curiosity to know just how well schools stack up against each other—an exercise that has caused problems in the United States and Britain, even as it provides real-estate agents with a valuable sales tool.

Stress notwithstanding, testing appears to be popular with the public at large. One survey conducted by the EQAO (which also tests math skills in Grade 9 and literacy in Grade 10) found that 64 per cent of respondents felt it helps to keep the system accountable to taxpayers as well as parents; in a second one, 69 per cent of elementary-school parents said it's important to know how a child is faring in relation to a provincial standard.

Those who conduct the tests insist that they aren't intended to pit schools against each other, but the Fraser Institute has no such qualms. Every year, the conservative think tank issues report cards that use results from BC, Alberta, Ontario, and Quebec to rank schools from best to worst.

Peter Cowley, director of the institute's school performance studies, has co-written all of the report cards and insists that not only are the rankings of public interest, "it is a dereliction of duty" if ministries of education and school boards ignore them.

He has heard all the criticisms—that the rankings are elitist and biased, that they are simply tools used by real-estate agents to market neighbourhoods with "good" schools, that they provide only a narrow measure of student ability, that they stress out students and teachers, that some schools will go to extreme lengths to prep students.

In response, he says, "there should be no pressure and no stress, and no teaching to the test. If teachers are doing their job, then kids should already have the required knowledge." The tests, he adds, are based on provincial curricula and written, administered, and graded by teachers.

Yet teachers are particularly opposed to testing, which they argue does not promote learning even as it undermines their professionalism. Rather than South Korea, which has fostered a culture of testing and rocketed to the top of the international education charts, they point to Finland, which vies for the lead without putting kids through six hours of grilling.

So some observers predict that, without standardized exams to keep its system in check, Alberta will soon find itself "in a race to the bottom," as Michael Zwaagstra, a research fellow at Frontier Centre, a Winnipeg-based think tank, wrote recently in the *Calgary Herald*.

But Carol Henderson, president of the Alberta Teachers' Association, dismisses the PATs as "30-year-old tests for 20th-century learners."

She has taught Grade 3, had her classes tested, and says the results provided no information that teachers do not already have simply by observing students and assessing their regular tests, assignments, and discussions.

The new Student Learning Assessment (SLA) that Alberta is developing—after years of discussion—will be computer-based and, rather than make students wait until spring, take place at the beginning of the school year. As well, the emphasis will be on such skills as problem-solving, critical thinking, and creativity rather than knowledge of specific subjects. Pilot testing of the SLA for Grade 3 will begin next year, followed by Grades 6 and 9 in 2015 and 2016.

Will the new approach overcome the fact that, given the expanding demands placed on education by revolutions in technology, transformations in the work force, and the rising economic power of developing nations, the appeal of standardized tests is difficult to ignore? After all, they offer an ostensibly objective assessment to parents concerned about their children's future.

Charles Pascal, former chair of the EQAO and a professor at the Ontario Institute for Studies in Education at the University of Toronto, says that using tests to compare schools is misguided. It creates "a lot of anxious white noise" that "comes from the fear of not being as good as the school next door."

He concedes that as a result, "there are people at school boards who put pressure on schools to up their test scores."

South of the border, this kind of pressure led to a recent scandal in Atlanta that left 35 educators facing criminal charges after standardized test results were falsified. Similar incidents have taken place across the United States, spurred by the use of student scores in teachers' performance reviews and merit-pay decisions.

According to a joint statement by the presidents of the state and national teachers' federations, the scale of the Atlanta incident "crystallizes the unintended consequences of our test-crazed policies."

According to Prof. Pascal, the EQAO—founded in 1996—is a means to an end. He cites a number of successful schools, including those with socio-economically disadvantaged student populations, that have used their results to galvanize the leadership to secure more resources and to develop new programs.

"The importance for me is not in ranking or comparing schools," he explains, "but rather in finding out how children are faring and then putting information into action."

Marguerite Jackson, the EQAO's chief executive officer, agrees. "Data is stimulus for action," she says. The province supports schools that want to improve their math and literacy performance by providing grants for such resources as technology, peer mentors for teachers and principals, and enhanced curriculum.

As well, EQAO results indicate that student performance is improving: For instance, 73 per cent of Grade 6 students met the standard in writing in 2010—almost a 40-per-cent rise from 2000, when the figure was just 53 per cent.

Others remain unconvinced. Large-scale tests "are asked to assess too many things," argues Daniel Laitsch, an associate professor of education at Simon Fraser University. He feels that, no matter what the stated purpose, they are meant to measure, along with student achievement, that of teachers, schools, curriculum, and entire jurisdictions as well, which stretches their validity in appraising any of them.

In fact, Prof. Laitsch calls testing students "an atrocious way to evaluate teacher effectiveness, without any research to support the theory."

Toronto resident Maxeen Paabo agrees and has decided that her son will not participate in this year's Grade 3 tests. She researched the issue and reached her conclusion even before the school year began.

"I think the way it is now and the way it's being used politically is wrong and it's a misuse of resources," she says.

"What the ministry [of education] said is that it is used on a student level, on a class level, and on a school level to make improvements. But my understanding on the ground is that that isn't really happening, that teachers' regular classroom assessments are doing all that work."

But the sixth graders at Lougheed (coincidentally named for the Brampton-born grandfather of Alberta's late premier Peter Lougheed) are not staying home on test day.

To help them take the "evil questions" in stride, Ms. Hamilton leaves candy on their desks, lets them play outside and, by far the biggest treat, gives no homework for three days.

She feels one of the testing's shortcomings is the fact that it is standardized and so treats everyone the same even though children learn at different rates and on different levels. "In the classroom, we're modifying and accommodating where needed," she says. "EQAO doesn't give them that same nicety."

And does it really keep the system on track? In fact, the correlation between standardized testing and achievement appears to be fuzzy. With myriad factors affecting the education system—among them demographic and economic changes, fluctuation in education budgets, shifts in curriculum—it's impossible to say unequivocally that where scores have gone up, it's in any way because of standardized tests.

For example, others assess Canada's schoolchildren. The Council of Ministers of Education, Canada administers cyclical tests across the country to determine levels of performance in math, reading, and science. And international bodies, such as the Organisation for Economic Co-operation and Development (OECD), compare millions of secondary-school students in about 70 countries.

In both cases, the assessments are based on random samples of students, rather than putting everyone to the test. Despite the EQAO's positive signs, the most recent OECD results released in 2009 showed Canada to be slipping both in reading and math.

The debate about standardized tests may soon become moot.

Alberta's new SLAs aim to address many of the concerns of critics, by broadening the definitions of skills and capability. They are also less stress-inducing and will no longer alienate the teachers who have to administer them. It's not even clear yet that the results will be made public.

This new model may prove to be a bellwether, but there are no plans in Canada to do without testing, like Finland. Darlings of the global education community, the Finns regularly score near the top of the OECD survey even though they emphasize autonomy in teaching, rely very little on marks in the primary years, and limit homework as well as tests. Their system is nimble, independent and decentralized—the antithesis of the rote-learning, test-obsessed education model.

Paul Taillefer, president of the Canadian Teachers' Federation, says Canada could learn from Finland, where education is a collective responsibility, not a competition. What's more, he says, while testing for literacy and numeracy has its place, the current model of large-scale assessments is missing "a whole gamut of 21st-century skills."

"We're handcuffing our teachers with the narrow focus of these assessments," he says. "More time should be spent on individual strengths and weaknesses. We are training our students to be responsible citizens, just and caring human beings. We want to give them a bank of knowledge they can use to take on the world. (© The Globe and Mail Inc. All Rights Reserved.)

Annette takes a moment to digest what she has read. The article highlights some very important points about testing. She realizes that standardized testing in Canada has some very contentious issues that she would like to mull over with her colleagues. She looks forward to hearing their opinions.

After reading all of this information on testing, Annette feels reassured about her own assessment practices. While she has always taken her students' performance on standardized achievement tests into consideration when determining their learning progress, she has never allowed these test results to be the sole, or even the major, factor in evaluating student learning. The message she will continue to give to parents, students, and her teaching team will be that student progress is determined by a wide range of fair and valid assessment practices. Never will a student's learning be determined or judged on the basis of one test. As she finalizes the end-of-year student progress reports, she feels confident that the results she is documenting for each student are an accurate reflection of their learning.

Annette's Journal

June 19, 2014

It's hard to believe that in a few days, the doors of The Little Red Schoolhouse will close for the summer. I have never worked so hard in my whole teaching career, and never has it been so rewarding. And I owe most of my success to Dr. Cameron's educational psychology course that I took nearly a year ago. While I always understood "what" to teach and "how" to teach, this is really the first year I felt like I understood the "why" behind what I was doing. From doing all my prep work last August, to the implementation of DCM, to the development of a fair assessment system, to tackling special learning needs . . . my teaching had a very specific purpose every step of the way. Most important, I had a clear vision of what needed to be accomplished and how to do it.

I have seen such growth in my students. They all embraced my honest and fair approach, and while we had a few bumps along the road with some minor behaviour management issues and a less than full commitment to a few academic tasks, we were able to work through these problems in a manner that didn't detract from our efforts to create a positive learning environment. I'm proud of all my students, but especially proud of Zach—for working so hard to manage his ADHD behaviours, Caleb—for teaching us all about cultural differences, and Brandon—for accepting the accommodations he initially resisted but obviously needs in order to excel academically.

Despite all of our successes, I'm still concerned about Jackson and Simon; both boys come from families who do not place a high value on education. While I did my best to encourage and motivate them at school, I still couldn't completely negate the effects their home life have on their academic achievement. I'll continue to work with them next year, because I want them both to see that learning can not only be fun but it can also lead to a better life down the road. I think they may need to see and hear that from someone else besides me, so I plan to arrange for mentors to work with them during the next school year.

I think I have learned as much as, or more, than my students this year. I know now that

- a knowledge of educational psychology is critical to teachers;
- teachers can benefit immensely from having a mentor like Dr. Cameron;
- creating a positive learning environment is not that difficult if you select a proven approach to behaviour management and implement it consistently;
- creating an effective teaching team (i.e., educational assistants, resource personnel, student teachers) is time-consuming at first but well worth it in the end;
- finding ways to help a student often just requires getting to know the student and listening carefully to what he or she has to say about learning tasks;
- teacher intuitions can help identify students who require special services; and
- teachers have to be as open to learning as their students.

Time to sign off for this school year . . . I wonder what next year has in store for me and my students—I can't wait to find out!

Annette's Exploration of the Research

Ercikan, K. (2012). Developments in assessment of student learning. In P. A. Alexander & P. H. Winne (Eds.), *Handbook of educational psychology* (2nd ed., pp. 929–952). New York, NY: Routledge.

When reading the material on testing sent to her by Dr. Cameron, Annette was drawn to the statements made by Kadriye Ercikan. She decided to learn more about Ercikan's views, so she found the article "Developments in assessment of student learning." In this article, Ercikan reported on his extensive review of all the contributions that allow large-scale assessments to better serve student learning, as opposed to primarily serving accountability agendas. He revealed that performance-level scoring is one of the most positive recent developments. Performance-level scores are ordered classifications of student performance that accurately describe and clarify assessment results. They allow for better and more justifiable interpretations of student progress.

According to Ercikan's findings, the critical element in determining accurate performance levels is adhering to an established standard-setting procedure that translates student scores into expected levels of competency, skills, and knowledge. By accurately establishing critical and consistent cut-off points for various levels of performance, educators significantly enhance the validity of interpretations of such scores. This validity is needed because the interpretations of scores from large-scale assessments are coming under more intense scrutiny. More important, performance-level descriptors are much better understood by students, parents, and teachers.

What is of utmost importance to educators is that since the mid-1990s, several new and exemplary methods for setting standards for performance assessments have been developed that provide inestimable benefits. There is now a detailed and systematic process that requires educators to make critical judgments about a student's overall test performance rather than merely considering responses to multiple-choice questions. Because performance assessments are polytomously scored (option weighting that assigns differential values to each response option)—and because performance tests are usually designed to assess multiple attributes, skills, or knowledge—the focal point for test designers has turned to panelists' judgments. And because performance assessments typically use fewer test items/tasks, panelists must carefully consider (a) each of the items used, (b) the classifications of examinees based on other school-related performances, and (c) the classifications of all potential responses (Hambleton, Jaeger, Plake, & Mills, 2000). This process allows test designers to bring large-scale assessments more in line with the typical assessment processes used by teachers in classrooms.

According to Ercikan, "Although considerable effort is being made to develop assessments for accountability purposes . . . reducing [curricular] constructs into more easily assessed but less educationally desirable outcomes . . . [is] not necessarily moving assessment in a positive direction" (p. 947). On the other hand, the author optimistically indicated that performance assessments "are expected to move assessment practice in classrooms as well as at large-scale levels closer to learning and instruction" (p. 947). This is primarily because performance assessments are designed to assess processes that are directly related to both learning and product outcomes and they can be used in a variety of different learning environments.

Annette concludes from Ercikan's review that educational psychologists are actively searching for methods and procedures that can produce more reliable and valid performance-level scores. She expects that as these researchers continue their quest, more attention will be paid to cognitive processes, rather than simply curricular content, and that a higher premium will be placed on classroom processes than on student performances on standardized achievement tests.

Annette's Resource List

Academic Journals

Applied Measurement in Education
Applied Psychological Measurement
Educational Assessment
Educational Measurement: Issues and Practice
International Journal of Testing
Journal of Educational Measurement

Books

Airasian, P. S. W., Engemann, J. F., & Gallagher, T. L. (2007). *Classroom assessment: Concepts and applications.* Toronto, ON: McGraw-Hill Ryerson.

Kubiszyn, T., & Borich, G. (2007). *Educational testing and measurement: Classroom application and practice.* New York, NY: John Wiley & Sons.

Web Links

Canadian Test Centre
www.canadiantestcentre.com

Teaching to the Test: What Every Educator and Policy-Maker Should Know
www.umanitoba.ca/publications/cjeap/articles/volante.html

Real Accountability or an Illusion of Success?
http://testingillusion.ca/wp-content/uploads/2013/01/illusion_of_success_EN.pdf

The New Face of Standardized Testing in Schools
www.canadianfamily.ca/kids/the-new-face-of-standardized-testing-in-schools

What Is My Child Learning?
www.edu.gov.on.ca/eng/parents/curriculum.html

From the Authors' Notebook

This chapter outlined the purposes of standardized tests, the criticisms and controversy surrounding them, and the differences between standardized achievement, aptitude, and teacher-made tests. It also detailed the outcomes that have resulted from nation- and province-wide systemic testing and presented changes that educational psychologists believe will improve future test development.

Reflecting on Practice

Consider the information you have read in this chapter as well as the knowledge you have acquired through instruction, classroom discussions, and classroom activities. Then take the time to write down your thoughts about these learning experiences. Consider how your perspective on educational psychology may have changed. In addition, respond to the following questions:

- How well do you understand standardized achievement tests?
- What more do you need to know about standardized testing, and where might you find this information?

Since this is your last reflection on the knowledge you acquired in this course, take time to consider your entire learning experience.

- What is the most important concept you have learned?
- How has this course better prepared you to be an effective teacher?

Chapter Summary

In this chapter, the following concepts were highlighted:

- Standardized curriculum-based assessments are used by provincial and territorial governments to make wide-scope educational decisions and/or individual student decisions.
- When the media and public criticize standardized tests, aptitude tests are not the tests in question.
- Province- and territory-wide achievement tests are carefully designed and tested for appropriateness.
- Common learning objectives between classroom curricula and standardized tests will produce better tests.
- The Canadian standards for testing were established to guide fair student assessment.
- Test-performance levels translate numerical scores into meaningful interpretations of student performance.

New Terms

achievement test

aptitude test

criterion-referenced test

norm-referenced tests

standardized test

These terms are defined in the Glossary at the end of the text.

Review Questions

- What is a standardized test?
- How are standardized achievement tests used in Canada?
- What is the difference between standardized achievement tests and teacher-made tests?
- What is the difference between standardized achievement tests and aptitude tests?
- How do different stakeholders view standardized achievement testing?
- How can standardized tests be improved?
- How can teachers help students prepare for standardized tests?
- How should standardized test results be used in educational decision-making?
- What are the benefits of performance results reporting?

Glossary

achievement tests Tests that provide broad overviews of academic performance for large groups of students

adaptation An innate drive to adjust to one's surrounding environment

analytical/componential intelligence The ability to think abstractly and process information effectively

aptitude test A specific ability test that assesses an individual's specific cognitive, social, and behavioural skills

authentic assessment Designed to measure the application of knowledge and skills

authoritarian parenting Attempts to shape, control, and measure children's behaviour against fairly rigid standards

authoritative parenting Provides clear guidelines for children and balances that with responsiveness, respect, and encouragement

backward design Developing instruction and assessment based on learning goals

behaviourism Learning theory that focuses on observable behaviours that are believed to be acquired through conditioning

Bloom's taxonomy The classification of learning objectives based on six categories: knowledge, comprehension, application, analysis, synthesis, and evaluation

classroom discourse research Investigates the role of open classroom discussion in student learning

classroom management Actions taken to create a psychologically secure classroom

cognitive strategy A cognitive procedure used to learn/understand new material

constructed-response question Type of test item that requires the student to generate an answer (e.g., completion, short answer, essay)

constructivism Actively and meaningfully constructing one's own knowledge and understanding

content validity Degree to which a test represents the domain it is intended to measure

creative/experiential intelligence The ability to form new ideas by combining what may at first appear to be unrelated facts or information

criterion-based assessment The measurement of student learning using specific curricular criteria

criterion-referenced test Scores are reflective of how students performed relative to established criteria

critical consciousness Perceiving social, political, and economic oppression and taking action against it

crystallized intelligence The ability to apply culturally/environmentally influenced problem-solving skills

descriptive research Research that describes populations or situations but does not draw conclusions

diagnostic assessment Determination of a student's current level of knowledge prior to instruction

differentiated learning Teaching that emphasizes meeting the needs of all learners by adjusting content, process, product, and/or learning environment where appropriate

direct instruction Teaching that emphasizes explicit instruction executed within well-planned lessons

ecological theory A framework of environmental systems within which an individual interacts

ethnographic research The in-depth examination of cultural occurrences

executive cognitive function A set of higher-order mental processes that control and regulate thought and action

experimental research The examination of relationships between variables that can provide indicators of causal effects

extrinsic motivation Behaviour that occurs as a result of external factors such as rewards

fluid intelligence Ability to understand abstract or new concepts by utilizing flexible and pattern-seeking thinking

formative assessment Determination of a student's level of understanding on an ongoing basis during the instructional period

high-incidence exceptionalities Mild disabilities that include learning disabilities, behavioural disorders, giftedness, and intellectual disabilities

idiographic research The in-depth examination of individual cases or events

inclusion When appropriate, students with exceptionalities are educated in the regular classroom with their same-age peers

Individualized Education Program The document that outlines a student's education goals, services required, implementation methods and strategies, and location of delivery

intelligence Ability to learn from experience, adapt to one's environment, and understand and control one's own thinking

intrinsic motivation Behaviour that occurs as a result of internal factors such as a desire to learn

language-acquisition device Chomsky's concept of a universal innate ability that humans have to acquire their native language at a very young age

low-incidence exceptionalities Moderate to severe disabilities that include autism spectrum disorder, sensory impairments, serious health impairments, and multiple disabilities

metacognition Understanding and monitoring one's own cognitive systems—thinking about thinking

norm-referenced test Scores reflect how students performed relative to all other students who completed the same test

permissive parenting Expresses tolerance and acceptance of nearly all children's actions

portfolio Collection of student work that can be used for assessment purposes

positive behaviour support A decision-making framework that guides selection, integration, and implementation of best evidence-based academic and behavioural practices

practical/contextual intelligence Ability to adapt to changes in the environment in order to maximize one's strengths

prejudice An unjustified and usually negative perception of an individual based on his or her association with a particular group

process-outcome research Measuring process variables and determining whether they affect the outcome of an intervention

psycho-educational assessment The comprehensive process of collecting psychological, social, and achievement data for the purpose of making educational decisions about individual students

qualitative research In-depth examination of behaviour and the motivations that drive it through studies of small groups of individuals; data are descriptive rather than predictive

quantitative research Examination of associations between variables using statistical methods; data are numerical and can often be generalized to larger populations

reciprocal determinism An individual's behaviour constantly influences and is influenced by personal factors and the social environment

reliability Producing the same results across repeated trials

resiliency The dynamic process whereby an individual exhibits positive behavioural adaptations when encountering significant adversity

rubric A scoring tool that explicitly states the performance expectations for a test or assignment

scaffolding Providing just enough support to prompt learning

schema A mental representation of an item or happening

selected-response question Type of test item that requires the student to choose an answer (e.g., multiple choice, matching, true/false)

self-concept How someone thinks about or perceives himself or herself

self-efficacy Belief about one's capability to produce certain levels of performance in order to influence events that affect one's life

self-esteem A person's subconscious beliefs about how worthy, lovable, valuable, and capable he or she is

socio-economic status Indicator of social class based on education, occupation, and income

special education Schooling that is constructed and delivered to suit the needs of students with exceptionalities

standardized test A test that (a) contains the same questions for all test-takers; (b) is administered to all individuals in the same fashion, under the same conditions, and within a specified time; and (c) is always scored in a systematic and uniform manner

stereotype threat Fear that one's behaviour will confirm a negative stereotype about one's identity group

summative assessment Determination of a student's level of knowledge and skills after all instruction has been provided

Table of Specifications An assessment procedure that lists the instructional topics to be covered by a test and the number and type of test questions associated with each topic

temperament Traits that account for differences in individuals' emotional reactions

theory A well-substantiated set of ideas intended to explain facts or phenomena

theory of mind The ability to attribute mental states to self and others in order to understand and predict behaviour

twice-exceptional learner Students who are both gifted and learning-disabled

universal instructional design An educational framework that focuses on providing students with diverse learning needs equal access to classroom teaching and learning

validity Measuring what is intended to be measured

visual-spatial reasoning The ability to understand, manipulate, and draw relationships among visual images when learning and problem-solving

zone of proximal development Tasks that a student cannot complete independently but can complete when given assistance

References

Ackerman, P. L., & Lohman, D. F. (2012). Individual differences in cognitive function. In P. A. Alexander & P. H. Winne (Eds.), *Handbook of educational psychology* (2nd ed., pp. 139–162). New York, NY: Routledge.

Alberta Education. (2014). *Culturally responsive educational practices*. Retrieved from http://education.alberta.ca/admin/fnmi/collaborativeframework/themes/culturally-responsive.aspx.

American Association on Intellectual and Developmental Disabilities. (2014). *Definition of intellectual disability*. Retrieved from http://aaidd.org/intellectual-disability/definition#.Ux3iGuddXxo.

American Psychiatric Association (APA). (2013). *Diagnostic and statistical manual of mental disorders* (5th ed.). Washington, DC: APA.

Anderson, P. (2002). Assessment and development of executive function (EF) during childhood. *Child Neuropsychology, 8*(2), 77–82.

Bandura, A. (1977). *Social learning theory*. Englewood Cliffs, NJ: Prentice Hall.

Bandura, A. (1986). *Social foundations of thought and action*. Englewood Cliffs, NJ: Prentice Hall.

Banks, J. A. (2001). *Cultural diversity and education: Foundations, curriculum, and teaching* (4th ed.). Boston, MA: Allyn & Bacon.

Banks, J., Cochran-Smith, M., Moll, L., Richert, A., Zeichner, K., LePage, P., . . . (with McDonald, M.). (2005). Teaching diverse learners. In L. Darling-Hammond & J. Bransford (Eds.), *Preparing teachers for a changing world: What teachers should learn and be able to do* (pp. 232–276). San Francisco, CA: Jossey-Bass. Reprinted with permission from John Wiley & Sons.

Baumrind, D. (1991). Effective parenting during the early adolescent transition. In P. A. Cowan & E. M. Hetherington (Eds.), *Family transitions (Advances in family research series)*. Mahwah, NJ: Lawrence Erlbaum.

Bereiter, C., & Scardamalia, M. (2012). Education for the knowledge age: Design-centered models of teaching and instruction. In P. A. Alexander & P. H. Winne (Eds.), *Handbook of educational psychology* (2nd ed., pp. 695–713). New York, NY: Routledge.

Berk, L. E. (1996). *Infants and children: Prenatal through middle childhood*. Boston, MA: Allyn & Bacon.

Berliner, D. C. (2012). Educational psychology: Searching for essence throughout a century of influence. In P. A. Alexander & P. H. Winne (Eds.), *Handbook of educational psychology* (2nd ed., pp. 3–25). New York, NY: Routledge.

Berliner, D. C., & Calfee, R. C. (Eds.). (1996). *Handbook of educational psychology*. New York, NY: Macmillan.

Black, P., & Wiliam, D. (1998). Inside the black box: Raising standards through classroom assessment. *Phi Delta Kappan, 80*, 139–148.

Bloom, B. S., Englehart, M. B., Furst, E. J., Hill, W. H., & Krathwohl, O. R. (1956). *Taxonomy of educational objectives: The classification of educational goals. Handbook 1: The cognitive domain*. New York, NY: Longman.

Bransford, J., Derry, S., Berliner, D., & Hammerness, K. (with Beckett, K. L.). (2005). Theories of learning and their roles in teaching. In L. Darling-Hammond & J. Bransford (Eds.), *Preparing teachers for a changing world: What teachers should learn and be able to do* (pp. 40–87). San Francisco, CA: Jossey-Bass.

Bredo, E. (2006). Conceptual confusion and educational psychology. In P. A. Alexander & P. H. Winne (Eds.), *Handbook of educational psychology* (2nd ed., pp. 43–57). Mahwah, NJ: Lawrence Erlbaum.

Bronfenbrenner, U. (1979). *The ecology of human development*. Boston, MA: Harvard University Press.

Bronfenbrenner, U., & Morris, P. A. (1998). The ecology of developmental processes. In W. Damon & R. M. Lerner (Eds.), *Handbook of child psychology* (5th ed., Vol. 1, pp. 993–1028). New York, NY: Wiley.

Brooks, R. B., & Goldstein, S. (2007). Developing the mindset of effective students. In S. Goldstein & R. B. Brooks (Eds.), *Understanding and managing children's classroom behavior: Creating sustainable, resilient classrooms* (2nd ed., pp. 208–225). Hoboken, NJ: John Wiley & Sons.

Brophy, J. (2012). Observational research on generic aspects of classroom teaching. In P. A. Alexander & P. H. Winne (Eds.), *Handbook of educational psychology* (2nd ed., pp. 755–780). New York, NY: Routledge.

Calfee, R. C. (2012) Educational psychology in the 21st century. In P. A. Alexander & P. H. Winne (Eds.), *Handbook of educational psychology* (2nd ed., pp. 29–42). New York, NY: Routledge.

Carroll, J. B. (1997). The three-stratum theory of cognitive abilities. In D. P. Flanagan, J. L. Genshaft, & P. L. Harrison (Eds.), *Contemporary intellectual assessment: Theories, tests, and issues* (pp. 122–130). New York, NY: Guilford Press.

Case, R. (1992). *The mind's staircase: Exploring the conceptual underpinnings of children's thought and knowledge*. Hillsdale, NJ: Lawrence Erlbaum.

Case, R. (1998). The development of conceptual structures. In W. Damon (Ed.), *Handbook of child psychology* (5th ed., Vol. 2). New York, NY: Wiley.

CEC (Council for Exceptional Children). (2000). *Creating useful individualized education programs (IEPs)*. Retrieved from www.cec.sped.org/AM/Template.cfm?Section=Home&TEMPLATE=/CM/ContentDisplay.cfm&CONTENTID=1568.

CEC (Council for Exceptional Children). (2006a). *Learning disabilities*. Retrieved from www.cec.sped.org/AM/Template .cfm?Section=Learning_Disabilities&Template=/TaggedPage/TaggedPageDisplay.cfm&TPLID=37&ContentID=5629.

CEC (Council for Exceptional Children). (2006b). *New flexibility in testing students with disabilities a positive step*. CEC Position Document. Retrieved from www.cec.sped.org/AM/Template.cfm?Section=Search&template=/CM/HTMLDisplay.cfm&ContentID=6247.

Chan, J. C. K., McDermott, K. B., & Roediger, H. L. (2006). Retrieval-induced facilitation: Initially non-tested material can benefit from prior testing of related material. *Journal of Experimental Psychology: General, 135*(4), 553–571.

Charles, C. M. (2002). *Essential elements of effective discipline*. Boston, MA: Allyn & Bacon.

Chase, C. I. (1999). *Contemporary assessment for educators*. New York, NY: Longman.

Chomsky, N. (1957). *Syntactic structures*. The Hague, Netherlands: Mouton.

Chomsky, N. (1965). *Aspects of the theory of syntax*. Cambridge, MA: MIT Press.

Chudowsky, N., & Pellegrino, J. W. (2003). Large-scale assessments that support learning: What will it take? *Theory into Practice, 42*, 75–84.

Congress of Aboriginal Peoples. (2010). *Staying in school: Engaging Aboriginal students*. Retrieved from www.abo-peoples.org/wp-content/uploads/2012/10/Stay-In-School-LR.pdf.

Cooper, H. M. (1989). Synthesis of research on homework. *Educational Leadership, 47*(3), 85–91.

Cooper, H. M., & Valentine, J. C. (2001). Using research to answer practical questions about homework. *Educational Psychologist, 36*, 143–153.

Cowley, P., & Easton, S. (2008). *Report card on British Columbia's elementary schools*. Vancouver, BC: Fraser Institute. Retrieved from www.fraserinstitute.org/researchandpublications/publications/5527.aspx.

Cowley, P., Easton, S., & Thomas, M. (2012). Report card on British Columbia's elementary schools, 2012. Retrieved from www.fraserinstitute.org/research-news/display.aspx?id=2147484266.

Cronbach, L. J. (1957). The two disciplines of scientific psychology. *The American Psychologist, 12*, 671–684.

Cyrenne, P., & Chan, A. (2012). High school grades and university performance: A case study. *Economics of Education Review, 31*(5), 524–542.

Darling-Hammond, L., Banks, J., Zumwalt, K., Gomez, L., Gamoran Sherin, M., Griesdorn, J., & Finn, L. (2005). Educational goals and purposes: Developing a curricular vision for teaching. In L. Darling-Hammond & J. Bransford (Eds.), *Preparing teachers for a changing world: What teachers should learn and be able to do* (pp. 169–200). San Francisco, CA: Jossey-Bass.

Deci, E. L., & Chandler, C. (1986). The importance of motivation for the future of the LD field. *Journal of Learning Disabilities, 19*, 58–59.

Deci, E. L., & Flaste, R. (1995). *Why we do what we do: Understanding self-motivation*. New York, NY: Guilford Press.

Deci, E. L., Hodges, R., Pierson, L., & Tomassone, J. (1992). Autonomy and competence as motivational factors in students with learning disabilities and emotional handicaps. *Journal of Learning Disabilities, 25*, 457–471.

Dewey, J. (1934). The need for a philosophy of education. In J. A. Boydston (Ed.), *John Dewey, The later works, 1925–1953, Volume 9: 1933–1934* (pp. 194–204). Carbondale, IL: Southern Illinois University Press.

Dreikurs, R., & Cassel, P. (1992). *Discipline without tears* (2nd ed.). New York, NY: Plume.

Duncan, G. J., Dowsett, C. J., Claessens, A., Magnuson, K., Huston, A. C., Klebanov, P., . . . Japel, C. (2007). School readiness and later achievement. *Developmental Psychology, 43*(6), 1428–1446.

Earl, L. (2003). *Assessment as learning: Using classroom assessment to maximize learning*. Thousand Oaks, CA: Corwin Press.

Edmunds, A. L. (1999). Cognitive credit cards: Acquiring learning strategies. *Teaching Exceptional Children, 31*(4), 68–73.

Edmunds, A. L., & Blair, K. (1999). Nova Scotia teachers' use of the cognitive credit card. *ATEC Journal, 5*(1), 7–13.

Edmunds, A. L., & Edmunds, G. A. (2005). Sensitivity: A double-edged sword for the pre-adolescent and adolescent child. *Roeper Review, 26*(1), 69–77.

Edmunds, A. L., & Edmunds, G. A. (2014a). Behaviour management network. Retrieved from www.edu.uwo.ca/dynamic-classroom-management/index.asp.

Edmunds, A. L., & Edmunds, G. A. (2014b). *Special education in Canada* (2nd ed.). Don Mills, ON: Oxford University Press.

Edmunds, A. L., & Edmunds, G. A. (2014c). The sensitivity of precocious child writers: More evidence of the double-edged sword. *Roeper Review, 36*(3), 178–189.

Edmunds, A. L., & Noel, K. A. (2003). Literary precocity: An exceptional case among exceptional cases. *Roeper Review, 25*(4), 185–194.

Education Quality and Accountability Office (EQAO). (2008). *Ontario student achievement: EQAO's provincial report on the results of the 2007–2008 Ontario Secondary School Literacy Test*. Toronto, ON: EQAO.

Elawar, M. C., & Corno, L. (1985). A factorial experiment in teachers' written feedback on student homework: Changing teacher behavior a little rather than a lot. *Journal of Educational Psychology, 77*(2), 162–173.

Ercikan, K. (2012). Developments in assessment of student learning. In P. A. Alexander & P. H. Winne (Eds.), *Handbook of educational psychology* (2nd ed., pp. 929–952). New York, NY: Routledge.

Erikson, E. H. (1963). *Childhood and society* (2nd ed.). New York, NY: Norton.

Erikson, E. H. (1968). *Identity, youth, and crisis*. New York, NY: Norton.

Erikson, E. H. (1980). *Identity and the life cycle* (2nd ed.). New York, NY: Norton.

Evertson, C. M., & Weinstein, C. S. (Eds.). (2006a). *Handbook of classroom management: Research, practice, and contemporary issues*. Mahwah, NJ: Lawrence Erlbaum.

Evertson, C. M., & Weinstein, C. S. (2006b). Classroom management as a field of inquiry. In C. M. Evertson & C. S. Weinstein (Eds.), *Handbook of classroom management: Research, practice, and contemporary issues* (pp. 3–15). Mahwah, NJ: Lawrence Erlbaum.

Fallona, C., & Richardson, V. (2006). Classroom management as a moral activity. In C. M. Evertson & C. S. Weinstein (Eds.), *Handbook of classroom management: Research, practice, and contemporary issues* (pp. 1041–1062). Mahwah, NJ: Lawrence Erlbaum.

Froese-Germain, B. (1999). *Standardized testing: Undermining equity in education*. Ottawa, ON: Canadian Teachers' Federation.

Fuchs, D. (2012). Cognitive profiling of children with genetic disorders and the search for a scientific basis of differentiated education. In P. A. Alexander & P. H. Winne (Eds.), *Handbook of educational psychology* (2nd ed., pp. 187–208). New York, NY: Routledge.

Fuchs, L. S., Fuchs, D., Schumacher, R. F., & Seethaler, P. M. (2013). Instructional intervention for students with mathematics learning disabilities. In H. L. Swanson, K. R. Harris & S. Graham (Eds.), *Handbook of learning disabilities* (2nd ed., pp. 388–404). New York, NY: Guilford Press.

Gardner, H. (1983). *Multiple intelligences*. New York, NY: Basic Books.

Gardner, H., & Hatch, T. (1989). Multiple intelligences go to school: Educational implications of the theory of multiple intelligences. *Educational Researcher*, 18(8), 6.

Geiser, S. (with Studley, R.). (2003). UC and the SAT: Predictive validity and differential impact of the SAT I and the SAT II at the University of California. *Educational Assessment*, 8(1), 1–26.

Geiser, S., & Santelices, M. (2007, June 13). Validity of high-school grades in predicting student success beyond the freshman year: High-school record vs. standardized tests as indicators of four-year college outcomes. *CSHE.9.07*. Retrieved from http://cshe.berkeley.edu/publications/publications.php?id=265.

Gettinger, M., & Kohler, K. M. (2006). Process-outcome approaches to classroom management and effective teaching. In C. M. Evertson & C. S. Weinstein (Eds.), *Handbook of classroom management: Research, practice, and contemporary issues* (pp. 73–96). Mahwah, NJ: Lawrence Erlbaum.

Global News (2013, May 9). *Alberta gets rid of Provincial Achievement Tests*. Retrieved from http://globalnews.ca/news/548713/alberta-gets-rid-of-provincial-achievement-tests.

Goldstein, S., & Brooks, R. B. (2007a). Introduction. In S. Goldstein & R. B. Brooks (Eds.), *Understanding and managing children's classroom behavior: Creating sustainable, resilient classrooms* (2nd ed., pp. 3–21). Hoboken, NJ: John Wiley & Sons.

Goldstein, S., & Brooks, R. B. (2007b). Creating sustainable classroom environments: The mindset of effective teachers, successful students, and productive consultants. In S. Goldstein & R. B. Brooks (Eds.), *Understanding and managing children's classroom behavior: Creating sustainable, resilient classrooms* (2nd ed., pp. 22–42). Hoboken, NJ: John Wiley & Sons. Excerpted content on p. 29. Reprinted with permission from John Wiley & Sons.

Graham, C., & Neu, D. (2004). Standardized testing and the construction of governable persons. *Journal of Curriculum Studies*, 36(3), 295–319.

Graham, S., & Harris, K. R. (2003). Students with learning disabilities and the process of writing: A meta-analysis of SRSD studies. In H. L. Swanson, K. R. Harris, & S. Graham (Eds.), *Handbook of learning disabilities* (pp. 323–344). New York, NY: Guilford Press.

Gresham, F. M. (2002). Social skills assessment and instruction for students with emotional and behavioral disorders. In K. L. Lane, F. M. Gresham, and T. E. O'Shaughnessy (Eds.), *Interventions for children with or at risk for emotional and behavioral disorders* (pp. 242–258). Boston, MA: Allyn & Bacon.

Guskey, T. (2005). Mapping the road to proficiency. *Educational Leadership*, 63(3), 32–38.

Hambleton, R. K., Jaeger, R. M., Plake, B. S., & Mills, C. N. (2000). *Handbook for setting standards on performance assessments*. Washington, DC: Council of Chief State School Officers.

Hebert, E. A. (2001). *The power of portfolios: What children can teach us about learning and assessment*. San Francisco, CA: Jossey-Bass.

Hoffman, J. L., & Lowitzki, K. E. (2005). Predicting college success with high school grades and test scores: Limitations for minority students. *Review of Higher Education*, 28(4), 455–474.

Holbrook, J., & Kolodner, J. L. (2000). Scaffolding the development of an inquiry-based (science) classroom. In B. Fishman & S. O'Connor-Devilbiss (Eds.), *Fourth International Conference of the Learning Sciences* (pp. 221–227). Mahwah, NJ: Lawrence Erlbaum.

Howard, T. C., & Aleman, G. R. (2008). Teacher capacity for diverse learners: What do teachers need to know? In M. Cochran-Smith, S. Feiman-Nemser, D. J. McIntyre, & K. E. Demers (Eds.), *Handbook of research on teacher education: Enduring questions in changing contexts* (3rd ed.). New York, NY: Routledge, Taylor, & Francis/The Association of Teacher Educators.

Individuals with Disabilities Education Improvement Act (2004a), 34 CFR Pt. 300.8(c)(4)(i) (1997).

Individuals with Disabilities Education Improvement Act (2004b), Pub. L. No. 108-446, 118 Stat. 2647–2799 (2004).

James, W. (1899/1983). Talks to teachers on psychology. In G. E. Myers (Ed.), *William James: Writings 1878–1899*. New York, NY: Library of America.

Johnson, F. L., & Edmunds, A. L. (2006). *From chaos to control: Understanding and responding to the behaviours of students with exceptionalities*. London, ON: Althouse Press.

Kohlberg, L. (1969). Stage and sequence: The cognitive-developmental approach to socialization. In D. A. Goslin

(Ed.), *Handbook of socialization theory and research* (pp. 347–380). Chicago, IL: Rand McNally.

LaConte, R. T. (1981). *Homework as a learning experience. What research says to the teacher.* Washington, DC: National Education Association.

Lane, K., Falk, K., & Wehby, J. (2006). Classroom management in special education classrooms and resource rooms. In C. M. Evertson & C. S. Weinstein (Eds.), *Handbook of classroom management: Research, practice, and contemporary issues* (pp. 439–460). Mahwah, NJ: Lawrence Erlbaum.

LDAC (Learning Disabilities Association of Canada). (2013). *LD defined*. Retrieved from www.ldac-acta.ca/en/learn-more/ld-defined.html.

Lerner, J. W., & Kline, F. (2006). *Learning disabilities and related disorders.* Boston, MA: Houghton Mifflin.

Lewis, T. J., & Sugai, G. (1999). Effective behavior support: A systems approach to proactive schoolwide management. *Focus on Exceptional Children, 31*(6), 1–24.

Maag, J. W. (2004). *Behavior management: From theoretical implications to practical applications* (2nd ed., pp. 151–197). Belmont, CA: Thompson Wadsworth.

Marland, S.P., Jr. (1972). *Education of the gifted and talented: Report to the Congress of the United States by the U.S. Commissioner of Education and background papers submitted to the U.S. Office of Education* (2 vols.). Washington, DC: US Government Printing Office (Government Documents Y4.L 11/2:G36).

Martin, J. (2012). Social cultural perspectives in educational psychology. In P. A. Alexander & P. H. Winne (Eds.), *Handbook of educational psychology* (2nd ed., pp. 595–614). New York, NY: Routledge.

Masten, A. S., & Coatsworth, J. D. (1998). The development of competence in favorable and unfavorable environments: Lessons from research on successful children. *American Psychologist, 53*, 205–220.

Mayer, R. E. (2001). Changing conceptions of learning: A century of progress in the scientific study of education. In L. Corno (Ed.), *Education across a century: The centennial volume, one hundredth year book of the National Society for the Study of Education* (pp. 34–75). Chicago, IL: University of Chicago Press.

Mayer, R. E. (2003). *Learning and instruction.* Upper Saddle River, NJ: Merrill/Prentice Hall.

Mayer, R. E., & Wittrock, M. C. (2012). Problem solving. In P. A. Alexander & P. H. Winne (Eds.), *Handbook of educational psychology* (2nd ed., pp. 287–303). New York, NY: Routledge.

McCaslin, M., Bozack, A. R., Napoleon, L., Thomas, A., Vasquez, V., Wayman, V., & Zhang, J. (2006). Self-regulated learning and classroom management: Theory, research, and considerations for classroom practice. In C. M. Evertson & C. S. Weinstein (Eds.), *Handbook of classroom management: Research, practice, and contemporary issues* (pp. 223–252). Mahwah, NJ: Lawrence Erlbaum.

Moll, L. C. & Arnot-Hopffer, E. (2004). Sociocultural competence in teacher education. *Journal of Teacher Education, 56*(3), 242–247.

Morine-Dershimer, G. (2006). Classroom management and classroom discourse. In C. M. Evertson & C. S. Weinstein (Eds.), *Handbook of classroom management: Research, practice, and contemporary issues* (pp. 127–156). Mahwah, NJ: Lawrence Erlbaum.

National Center on Response to Intervention. (2010). *Essential components of RTI: A closer look at response to intervention.* Washington, DC: US Department of Education, Office of Special Education Programs, National Center on Response to Intervention.

National Research Council. (2000). *How people learn: Brain, mind, experience and school* (Rev. ed.). Washington, DC: National Academies Press.

Newmann, F. M. (1991). Promoting higher order thinking in social studies. Overview of a study of 16 high-school departments. *Theory and Research in Social Education, 19*(4), 324–340.

Nielsen, M. E., & Higgins, L. D. (2005). The eye of the storm: Services and programs for twice-exceptional learners. *Teaching Exceptional Children, 38*(1), 8–15.

No Child Left Behind Act of 2001, Pub. L. No. 107-110, 20 U.S.C. § 6301 *et seq.* (2001).

Noel, K., & Edmunds, A. L. (2007). Constructing a synthetic-analytic framework for precocious writing. *Roeper Review, 29*(2), 125–131.

Nucci, L. (2006). Classroom management for moral and social development. In C. M. Evertson & C. S. Weinstein (Eds.), *Handbook of classroom management: Research, practice, and contemporary issues* (pp. 711–734). Mahwah, NJ: Lawrence Erlbaum.

O'Donnell, A. M., D'Amico, M., Schmid, R. F., Reeve, J., & Smith, J. K. (2008). *Educational psychology: Reflection for action.* Mississauga, ON: John Wiley & Sons.

Okagaki, L. (2012). Ethnicity and learning. In P. A. Alexander & P. H. Winne (Eds.), *Handbook of educational psychology* (2nd ed., pp. 615–634). New York, NY: Routledge.

Ontario Ministry of Education (2004). *The individualized education plan (IEP): A resource guide.* Toronto, ON: Queen's Printer for Ontario.

Paris, S. G., Morrison, F. J., & Miller, K. F. (2012). Academic pathways from preschool through elementary school. In P. A. Alexander & P. H. Winne (Eds.), *Handbook of educational psychology* (2nd ed., pp. 61–86). New York, NY: Routledge.

Paris, S. G., & Winograd, P. (2003). The role of self-regulated learning in contextual teaching: Principles and practices for teacher preparation. A Commissioned Paper for the US Department of Education Project, *Preparing teachers to use contextual teaching and learning strategies to improve student success in and beyond school.* ERIC (ED479905).

Pellegrino, J. W., Chudowsky, N., & Glaser, R. (2001). *Knowing what students know. The science and design of educational assessment.* Washington, DC: National Academy Press.

Perry, N. E., Turner, J. C., & Meyer, D. K. (2012). Classrooms as contexts for motivating learning. In P. A. Alexander & P. H. Winne (Eds.), *Handbook of educational psychology* (2nd ed., pp. 327–348). New York, NY: Routledge.

Piaget, J. (1964). *The moral judgement of the child.* New York, NY: Free Press.

Piaget, J. (1970). Piaget's theory. In P. H. Mussen (Ed.), *Carmichael's manual of psychology.* New York, NY: Wiley.

Popham, W. J. (2003). The seductive allure of data. *Educational Leadership, 60,* 48–52.

Pressley, M., Borkowski, J. G., & Schneider, W. (1987). Cognitive strategies: Good strategy users coordinate meta-cognition and knowledge. In R. Vasta & G. Whitehurst (Eds.), *Annals of child development* (Vol. 4, pp. 89–129). Greenwich, CT: JAI Press.

Pressley, M., & Harris, K. R. (2012). Cognitive strategies instruction: From basic research to classroom instruction. In P. A. Alexander & P. H. Winne (Eds.), *Handbook of educational psychology* (2nd ed., pp. 265–286). New York, NY: Routledge.

Principles for fair student assessment practices for education in Canada. (1993). Edmonton, AB: Joint Advisory Committee.

Renzulli, J. S., & Reis, S. M. (1997). The schoolwide enrichment model: New directions for developing high-end learning. In N. Colangelo & G. A. Davis (Eds.), *Handbook of gifted education* (pp. 136–154). Boston, MA: Allyn & Bacon.

Rivera-Batiz, F. L. (1992). Quantitative literacy and the likelihood of employment among young adults in the United States. *Journal of Human Resources, 27,* 313–328.

Rose, D. H., & Meyer, A. (2006). *A practical reader in universal design for learning.* Cambridge, MA: Harvard Education Press.

Schunk, D. H., & Zimmerman, B. J. (2012). Competence and control beliefs: Distinguishing the means and ends. In P. A. Alexander & P. H. Winne (Eds.), *Handbook of educational psychology* (2nd ed., pp. 349–368). New York, NY: Routledge.

Schwab, J. J. (1973). The practical 3: Translation into curriculum. *School Review, 81,* 501–522.

Shanker, S. (2010). Self-regulation: Calm, alert, and learning. *Education Canada, 50* (3). Retrieved from www.cea-ace.ca/education-canada/article/self-regulation-calm-alert-and-learning.

Shepard, L., Hammerness, K., Darling-Hammond, L., & Rust, F. (with Snowden, J. B., Gordon, E., Gutierrez, C., & Pacheo, A.). (2005). Assessment. In L. Darling-Hammond & J. Bransford (Eds.), *Preparing teachers for a changing world: What teachers should learn and be able to do* (pp. 275–322). San Francisco, CA: Jossey-Bass.

Sockett, H. (2008). The moral and epistemic purposes of teacher education. In M. Cochran-Smith, S. Feiman-Nemser, D. McIntyre, & K. Demers (Eds.), *Handbook of research on teacher education: Enduring questions in changing contexts* (3rd ed., pp. 45–66). New York, NY: Routledge, Taylor, & Francis.

Spear, L. P. (2000). The adolescent brain and age-related behavioral manifestations. *Neuroscience and Biobehavior Review, 24*(4), 417–463.

Steele, C. M., & Aronson, J. (1995). Stereotype threat and the intellectual test performance of African-Americans. *Journal of Personality and Social Psychology, 69*(5), 797–811.

Steele, C. M., Spencer, S. J., & Aronson, J. (2002). Contending with group image: The psychology of stereotype and social identity threat. In M. P. Zanna (Ed.), *Advances in experimental social psychology, Vol. 34* (pp. 379–440). San Diego, CA: Academic Press.

Steinberg, L. (2005). Cognitive and affective development in adolescence. *Trends in Cognitive Science, 9*(2), 69–74.

Sternberg, R. (1985). *Beyond IQ: A triarchic theory of intelligence.* Cambridge, UK: Cambridge University Press.

Sternberg, R. (2008). Applying psychological theories to educational practice. *American Educational Research Journal, 45*(1), 150–165.

Sternberg, R. J., & Williams, W. M. (2002). *Educational psychology.* Boston, MA: Allyn & Bacon.

Stiggins, R. J. (1997). *Student-centered classroom assessment.* Upper Saddle River, NJ: Prentice Hall.

Stiggins, R. J. (2001). *Student-centered classroom assessment* (3rd ed.). Upper Saddle River, NJ: Merrill/Prentice Hall.

Sugai, G., Horner, R. H., Dunlap, G., Hieneman, M., Lewis, T. J., Nelson, C. M., . . . Wilcox, B. (2000). *Applying positive behavioral support and functional behavioral assessment in schools.* Washington, DC: OSEP Center of Positive Behavioral Interventions and Support.

The Globe and Mail (2013, May 31). *The debate over standardized testing in schools is as divisive as ever.* Retrieved from www.theglobeandmail.com/news/national/education/the-debate-over-standardized-testing-in-schools-is-as-divisive-as-ever/article12299369/?page=all.

Thomas, A., & Chess, S. (1977). *Temperament and development.* New York, NY: Bruner/Mazel.

UBC Centre for Teaching, Learning and Technology (2013). *Notes on reflective journals.* Retrieved from http://blogs.ubc.ca/coursedesign/2013/01/18/notes-on-reflective-journals-jan-24th-meaningful-course-goals.

US Department of Education (2000). *A guide to the individualized education program.* Washington, DC: Office of Special Education and Rehabilitative Services.

Vancouver Sun (2008, June 19). Editorial: *Standardized test results valuable if reported correctly,* p. A16.

Vercillo, K. (2012). *Why it is important for teachers to understand child development stages.* Retrieved from http://hubpages.com/hub/WhyTeachersMustUnderstandChildDevelopment.

Villegas, A. M., & Lucas, T. (2002). Preparing culturally responsive teachers: Rethinking the curriculum. *Journal of Teacher Education, 53*(1), 20–32.

Vygotsky, L. S. (1962). *Thought and language.* Cambridge, MA: MIT Press.

Vygotsky, L. S. (1978). *Mind in society.* Cambridge, MA: Harvard University Press.

Weinberger, N. M. (2001). Memory codes: A new concept for an old problem. In P. E. Gold & W. Greenough (Eds.), *Four decades of memory: A Festschrift honoring James L. McGaugh.* Washington, DC: APA.

Wentzel, K. R. (2006). A social motivation perspective for classroom management. In C. M. Evertson & C. S. Weinstein (Eds.), *Handbook of classroom management: Research, practice, and contemporary issues* (pp. 619–644). Mahwah, NJ: Lawrence Erlbaum.

Wigfield, A., & Eccles, J. S. (2002). Children's motivation during the middle school years. In J. Aronson (Ed.), *Improving academic achievement: Contributions of social psychology.* San Diego, CA: Academic Press.

Wigfield, A., Eccles, J. S., & Pintrich, P. (1996). Development between the ages of 11 and 25. In D. Berliner & R. Calfee (Eds.), *Handbook of educational psychology.* New York, NY: Macmillan.

Wiggins, G. P., & McTighe, J. (1998). *Understanding by design.* Upper Saddle River, NJ: Prentice Hall.

Wiggins, G. P., & McTighe, J. (2001). *Understanding by design* (2nd ed.). Upper Saddle River, NJ: Prentice Hall.

Woolfolk, A. E., Winne, P. H., Perry, N. E., & Shapka, J. (2010). *Educational psychology* (4th ed.). Toronto, ON: Pearson.

Index

abilities: adaptive, 193; goal-directed, 193; intellectual, 191–237; *see also* cognitive abilities
Aboriginal peoples: education and, 258–9; as students, 61; talking circles and, 266–7
acceleration programs, 217–18
accommodation, 50, 51
accountability: standardized achievement tests and, 275, 276, 277, 288
achievement: parenting style and, 255; SES and, 254
achievement targets, 125
achievement tests, standardized, 267–91
Ackerman, P. L., and Lohman, D. F., 140–1
acronyms, 47
adaptation (Piaget's term), 49–50
adaptive behaviour, 193, 218
adolescents: development of, 44; executive cognitive functioning and, 46–7
affect, 59–60
Alberta: standardized achievement tests in, 271, 276, 282, 285
Alberta Education, 61
American Association on Intellectual and Developmental Disabilities, 218
analysis (Bloom's taxonomy), 123–4; assessment and, 163
analytical/componential intelligence, 196–7, 198
Anderson, P., 44
application (Bloom's taxonomy), 123–4, 168
aptitude tests: standardized achievement tests and, 271–2
Aptitude Treatment Interaction (ATI), 229
assessment, 147–88; approaches to, 148–9; appropriateness of, 164; authentic, 173–4, 175; class discussion on, 154–9; communication on, 148–59; criterion-based, 177; design process of, 161–4; diagnostic, 21–2, 114–17, 159, 268–9; formative, 6, 159–60, 176–7; frequency of, 164, 165–6; instruction and, 113–25; issues in, 164–74; multiple intelligences and, 196; pre-instructional, 6, 22; psycho-educational, 204, 271–2;

purposes of, 159–61; SLDs and, 223; special education and, 201; standardized achievement tests as, 267–91; summative, 6, 161, 176–7; *see also* tests
assessment questions, 118, 159, 161–2; effectiveness of, 179–80; types of, 166–8; *see also* specific types
assessment tools, 158–9; evaluation of, 178–80; use of, 173–8
assessment-centredness, 131–2
assimilation, 50, 51
attention deficit hyperactivity disorder (ADHD), 102–5, 208–12; cognitive skill profile and, 209–11; diagnosis of, 209, 210; instruction and, 211–12; learning disabilities and, 224
attitudes and dispositions, 125
authentic assessment, 173–4, 175
autism spectrum disorder (ASD), 62, 212–15; cognitive skill profile and, 212–13; instruction and, 214–15; levels of, 213
autonomous morality, 62

backward design, 118–22; assessment and, 161, 162; elements of, 119
Bandura, A., 77
Banks, J., et al., 203, 245, 251–2, 257–8, 259
Banks's model, 257–8
Baumrind, D., 255
BEDMAS, 47
behaviour: adaptive, 193, 218; classroom, 76–9; motivation and, 76–7; positive, 78; self-regulated, 79, 104–5; teachers and, 90
behaviourism, 13
Bereiter, Carl, and Marlene Scardamalia, 175
Berliner, D. C., 10–11
best practices, 26
Big Five rules, 87–97
Binet, Alfred, 201
Black, P., and D. Wiliam, 184–5
Bloom, Benjamin, 122
Bloom's taxonomy, 122–5; assessment and, 163, 164, 171, 178; assessment questions and, 166–7, 168
brain: development of, 43–4
Bransford, J., et al., 132
Bredo, E., xvi

British Columbia: standardized achievement tests in, 271, 273
Bronfenbrenner, Uri, 65–6, 70
Brooks, R. B., and S. Goldstein, 88
Brophy, J., 26–7

Calfee, R. C., xvi
Canada: Aboriginal education in, 258–9; multiculturalism in, 256–7; special education in, 201, 202–3; standardized achievement tests in, 270–1, 273, 280–1; standardized achievement tests debate in, 282–5
Case, Robbie, 54
central conceptual structures, 54
central executive function, 140–1
challenges, intellectual, 191–237
challenging-but-attainable tasks, 55–6
Charles, C. M., 76
choices: needs and, 59; self and, 61–2, 66
Chomsky, Noam, 57, 70
chronosystem, 65
Chudowsky, N., and J. W. Pellegrino, 277, 278
classroom management, 6, 73–111; approaches to, 74–83; definition of, 77; principles of, 78; *see also* Dynamic Classroom Management
classroom tasks, 130
cognitive abilities: ADHD and, 209–11; ASD and, 212–13; assessment and, 163; as continuum, 208; exceptionalities and, 206, 208; gifted students and, 215–16; SLDs and, 222–4
cognitive credit card (CCC) model, 137–9
cognitive development, 45–6, 51–3
cognitive objectives, 122–5
cognitive readiness cue, 121
cognitive strategies, 128–9, 133–6
cognitive styles, 226–30; field-dependent, 226–7
cognitive verbs, 123–4
collectivism, 248
community–centredness, 131–2
competence, social, 107–8
competence beliefs, 29–30
components: intelligence and, 197
comprehension (Bloom's taxonomy), 123; assessment and, 163, 168, 171
concrete operations stage, 52
congregated classes/schools, 217

Index

Congress of Aboriginal Peoples, 258
consequences, 84, 86
constructivist approach, 24, 26, 127–8, 132, 133, 134; assessment and, 170, 175; PPIL and, 135
content validity: assessment and, 162–4
control beliefs, 29–30
conventional stage, 64
Council for Exceptional Children, 205, 220–1
Council of Ministers of Education, 285
Cowley, Peter, 283
creative/experimental intelligence, 197, 198
credibility: research and, 14
criterion-based assessment, 177
criterion-referenced tests, 272
critical consciousness, 250–2
Cronback, L. J., 229
crystallized intelligence, 193–4
culturally responsive practice, 251–2
curiosity, innate, 47–8, 54
curricular planning, 20–3; definition of, 22
curriculum: standardized achievement tests and, 277–9
curriculum compacting, 218
curriculum guides, 20–1, 114, 122; assessment and, 158

Darling-Hammond, L., et al., 22
Deci, E. L., 88
development: child and adolescent, 35–71; cognitive, 45–6, 51–3; definition of, 37; influences on, 37–9; language, 56–8; moral, 62–4; personal and social, 58–62; physical/biological, 43–4; principles of, 37–43; psychosocial, 60–1; rate of, 38–49; societal influences on, 64–6; "zone of proximal," 55
Dewey, John, 7, 13
Diagnostic and Statistical Manual of Mental Disorders (*DSM-V*), 209, 210, 212, 213, 220
diagnostic assessment, 21–2, 114–17, 159, 268–9
differences: individual, 191–237; socio-cultural, 239–65
differentiated instruction/learning, 208
direct instruction (DI), 128, 132–3
disabilities: learning (LD), 137, 216; mild intellectual, 218–20
disengagement: ethnic minorities and, 262

disequilibrium, 49; equilibrium and, 50, 51–4
disorders: *see* specific learning disorders (SLDs)
disruptiveness, 101–2
distractibility, 103–4
diversity, 239–65; encouraging, 245; self and, 61
Dreikurs, R., and P. Cassel, 76–7
Dynamic Classroom Management (DCM), 73, 75–83, 107; implementation of, 81–2

ecological theory, 65–6
Edmunds, A. L., 75; and K. Blair, 137; and K. Edmunds, 204–6, 228
education: Aboriginal, 258–9; "commonplaces" of, 8–9; inclusive, 200, 202–4; multicultural, 256–8; special, 199, 200, 201–26
educational psychology, 8–17; application of, 10; definition of, 8; history of, 12–13; planning and, 4–17; purposes of, 7–8; research in, 12–17
Education Quality and Accountability Office (EQAO), 270–1, 278, 282, 284
emotional disturbance, 208–9
emotionality, 59–60
enrichment programs, 217–18
environment: development and, 39; intelligence and, 198
equilibrium: disequilibrium and, 50, 51–4
Ercikan, K., 184–5, 276, 287–8
Erikson, E. H., 60–1, 64, 70
ethnicity: learning and, 262
evaluation (Bloom's taxonomy), 123–4
Evertson, C. M., and C. S. Weinstein, 76, 78
exams: design of, 162–4; *see also* assessment; tests
exceptionalities, 200; cognitive abilities and, 206, 208; high-incidence, 202–3; low-incidence, 202
executive cognitive functions, 44, 46–7
exosystem, 65

fairness: rules and, 84, 86
feedback: assessment and, 159–60, 185
First Nations students, 61
fluid intelligence, 193–4
formal operations stage, 52
formative assessment, 6, 159–60; portfolios and, 176–7

Fraser Institute, 273, 282–3
Fuchs, D., 229
Fuchs, L. S., et al., 231–3
function: central executive, 140–1; executive cognitive, 44, 46–7; language and, 58; slave, 140–1

Gardner, H., 194–6
gender: moral reasoning and, 63–4
general intelligence, 193
genetics: development and, 39; intelligence and, 198
Giese, Rachel, and Caroline Alphonso, 282–5
gifted and talented students, 215–18; definition of, 215; instruction and, 217–18
Globe and Mail, 282–5
Goldstein, S., and R. B. Brooks, 75, 90, 95, 107
"good information processing" model, 128
government: standardized achievement tests and, 270–1, 274
grade weighting, 173
Graham, C., and D. Neu, 274
Graham, S., and K. R. Harris, 224
groups: differences within, 249
guidelines, generic, 26–7

Hall, G. Stanley, 12
Henderson, Carol, 283
Herbart, Johann Friedrich, 12
heteronomous morality, 62
higher-order thinking skills: assessment and, 166, 169, 171
high-incidence exceptionalities, 202–3
homework, 150–2
"horizontal decalage," 54
Howard, T. C., and G. R. Aleman, 250–1
How People Learn (HPL) framework, 131–2
"How to Be a Successful Learner," 150

identity: crises in, 60–1; cultural, 250–1
inclusion: philosophy of, 202–3
inclusive education, 200, 202–4
individual differences, 191–237
individualism, 248
Individualized Education Programs (IEPs), 204–6; one-page, 206, 207
individuals: cultural identity and, 250–2
Individuals with Disabilities Education Improvement Act (IDEA), 201, 208, 221

infinite generativity, 58
information processing models, 128–30, 135–6
instincts, learning, 48–51
instruction, 113–44; ADHD and, 211–12; ASD and, 214–15; assessment and, 113–25, 147; cognitive/learning styles and, 227; differentiated, 208; direct (DI), 128, 132–3; gifted students and, 217–18; guiding principles of, 127–8; inclusive, 200, 202–4; learning-strategy, 224–5; meaningful, 129–30, 136; mechanisms of, 126–36; mild intellectual disability and, 219–20; multiple intelligences and, 196; SLDs and, 224–5; special education and, 201; starting point for, 114–17; theory and, 128–30
instructional goal, 118; see also learning objective
instructional practices, 130–1
intelligence, 193–200; analytical/componential, 196–7, 198; creative/experimental, 197, 198; crystallized, 193–4; definition of, 193; fluid, 193–4; general, 193; global, 199–200; as hierarchical, 193–4; multiple, 194–6; practical/contextual, 197–8; as processes, 196–8; source of, 198; as structures, 194–6; tacit, 198; tests of, 199–200, 201–2; triarchic theory of, 196–8; visual-spatial, 193–4
Inuit students, 61
IQ: learning disabilities and, 221; mild intellectual disability and, 218–19

Jackson, Marguerite, 284
James, William, xvi, 12, 13

knowledge (Bloom's taxonomy), 123; assessment and, 163, 168, 171
knowledge (Stiggins's achievement target), 125
knowledge-centredness, 131–2
Kohlberg, L., 63–4, 70

labelling: special education and, 202–4
Laitsch, Daniel, 284
language: development and, 56–8, 68; person-first, 202
language-acquisition device (LAD), 57–8
"language of circles," 246–7
learner-centredness, 131–2

learning: assessment of, 158–80; domain-specific, 54; early, 46; enhanced, 55–6; innate mechanisms for, 48–51; motivation and, 130–2; preschool preparation for, 46; psychological structures of, 48–51
learning disabilities (LD), 137; gifted students and, 216
Learning Disabilities Association of Canada, 221
learning disorders: see specific learning disorders (SLDs)
learning objectives, 117–25; assessment and, 161–2, 167
learning outcome statements, 176
learning-strategy instruction, 224–5
learning styles, 227
legitimacy: research and, 14
Lerner, J. W., and F. Kline, 222, 224
lesson plans, 22–3, 117–25; global, 139; template for, 120
life-skills programs, 220
low-incidence exceptionalities, 202

macrosystem, 65
Manitoba: standardized achievement tests in, 271
marking scheme, 172–3
Marland, S. P., Jr, 215
Martin, J., 248
Masten, A. S., and J. D. Coatsworth, 64
mathematics: instruction and, 136–8, 231–3
Mayer, R. E., and M. C. Wittrock, 130
mechanisms: innate learning, 48–51; instructional, 126–36
memory: long-term, 135; short-term, 135, 137; working, 128, 129–30, 140–1
mesosystem, 65
metacognition, 128; SLDs and, 224–5
Métis students, 61
microsystem, 65
mild intellectual disability, 218–20; support classification and, 219
milestones, development, 38–9, 42–3
misbehaviour, 76–7
morality: development of, 62–4; heteronomous/autonomous, 62
moral reasoning, 63–4
motivation: behaviour and, 76–7; extrinsic, 131; intrinsic, 131; learning and, 50–1, 130–2; needs and, 59; performance and, 55–6; resiliency and, 88; self-worth and, 66; social, 107

multicultural education, 256–8
multiple intelligences (MI), 194–6

National Academy of Sciences Committee, 131
National Center on Response to Intervention, 221–2
needs: fundamental psychological, 58–9; fundamental student, 88; psychosocial, 60–1
neo-Piagetian theories, 54
New Brunswick: standardized achievement tests in, 271
Newfoundland and Labrador: standardized achievement tests in, 271
No Child Left Behind Act, 274
non-responders, 229
norm-referenced tests, 272
Nova Scotia: standardized achievement tests in, 271

Okagaki, L., 262
Ontario: standardized achievement tests in, 270–1, 278–9, 282, 284
Ontario Ministry of Education, 205
Ontario Secondary School Literacy Test, 278–9
Organisation for Economic Co-operation and Development (OECD), 285
organization: innate drive for, 48–9

parenting: authoritarian, 255, 256; authoritative, 255; permissive, 255, 256; SES and, 255
Paris, S. G.: et al., 46; and P. Winograd, 25
Pascal, Charles, 283, 284
"peer buddy," 214
Pellegrino, J. W., et al., 275
performance: motivation and, 55–6
Perry, N. E., et al., xvii, 130
personality: temperament and, 228
phonological loop, 141
physical/biological development, 43–4
Piaget, Jean, 13, 49, 54, 68, 70; equilibrium and, 51; language and, 57; moral development and, 62; Vygotsky and, 55
placement: special education and, 202–4
planning: concepts of, 5–6; curricular, 20–3; in early August, 3–33; instructional, 23–7; teacher, 19–28
Popham, W. J., 277, 278

portfolios, 174–8; marking of, 177; types of, 175–6
positive behaviour support, 78
postconventional stage, 64
poverty, 254–5, 256
practical/contextual intelligence, 197–8
practice: "best," 26; culturally responsive, 251–2; inclusive, 203; instructional, 130–1; reflective, 7, 32
pre-instructional assessment indicators, 6, 22
preconventional stage, 64
prejudice, 253–4
preoperational stage, 52
Pressley, M.: et al., 128; and K. R. Harris, 134
principal: rules and, 97
Principles for Fair Student Assessment Practices for Education in Canada, 280–1
principles of development, 37–43
problem-, project-, and inquiry-based learning (PPIL), 135–6
problem-solving: assessment of, 173–4, 175; student, 133–6
products (Stiggins's achievement target), 125
prompt, 121
psycho-educational assessment, 204, 271–2
psychology: cognitive, 13; functional, 13; *see also* educational psychology
psychosocial development, 60–1
punishment, 86

Quebec: standardized achievement tests in, 271
questions: application, 166; assessment, 118, 159, 161–2, 166–8, 179–80; authentic, 175; constructed-response, 166, 167, 170–3, 179–80; effectiveness of, 179–80; essay, 171–3; fill-in-the-blank, 168, 170; linkage, 133; matching, 168; multiple-choice, 168–9; objective, 166, 167, 168–9; recall, 166; recognition, 166; restricted-essay, 171–3; selected-response, 166, 167, 168–9; short-answer, 170–1; transfer, 166; true/false, 168

real-world applications, 173–4
reasoning: moral, 63–4; Stiggins's achievement target, 125
reciprocal determinism, 77

reflective practice, 7, 32
rehearsal: as learning strategy, 46–7
relatedness, 58–9
relationships, classroom, 131
reliability: assessment and, 162; research and, 14
Renzulli, J. S., and S. M. Reis, 217
research: approaches to, 16–17; classroom discourse, 78–9; educational psychology and, 12–17; ethnographic, 16–17; experimental, 12, 16; idiographic, 16–17; methods of, 14–15; process of, 15; process-outcome, 75; qualitative, 16–17; quantitative, 12, 16
resiliency: motivation and, 88; student, 75
responsiveness-to-intervention (RTI), 221–2
rewards, 84, 91
"routine thinking expertise," 133
rubric, marking, 172–3
rules, 78–9, 83–100, 106; basic, 87–97; Big Five, 87–97; classroom, 6; collective, 62; mandatory, 86–7; principal and, 97

Saskatchewan: standardized achievement tests in, 271
scaffolding, 55
schemas/schemes, 49, 51
Schunk D. H., and B. J. Zimmerman, 29–30
Schwab, J. J., 8–9
select–organize–integrate (SOI), 129–30
self, 60–1
self-assessment, 185
self-concept, 61–2
self-determination, 58–9
self-efficacy, *xviii*, 59
self-esteem, 61–2, 185
self-evaluations: portfolios and, 176–7
Self-Monitoring Checklist, 104–5
self-regulated behaviour management, 79, 104–5
self-regulated learning (SRL), 24–5
self-worth, 58–9, 66
sensorimotor stage, 52
Shanker, Stuart, 24–5
Shepard, L., et al., 275
skills (Stiggins's achievement target), 125
slave functions, 140–1
social competence, 107–8
social skills, 64–5
societal influences: development and, 64–6

socio-cultural considerations, 239–65
socio-economic status (SES), 252, 254–6, 259
Sockett, H., 7
special education, 200, 201–26; controversy and, 202–4; intelligence test and, 199
specific learning disorders (SLDs), 220–5; cognitive abilities and, 222–4; definition of, 221; instruction and, 224–5
standardized achievement tests, 267–91; aptitude tests and, 271–2; curriculum and, 277–9; definition of, 271; essential elements of, 276–8; future of, 275; improving, 276; interpretation of, 279–80; issues in, 270–81; misconceptions about, 274; misuses of, 274; preparation for, 279; purposes of, 271–2, 275; stakeholders' views of, 272–4; standards for, 280–1
Steele, C. M., and J. Aronson, 252
stereotype threat (ST), 252–4, 259
Sternberg, R., 10, 196
Stiggins's achievement targets, 125
stimulus–response (SR) theory, 13
strategies: cognitive credit card, 137–9; cognitive, 128–9, 133–6; learning, 46–7
stress–performance connection, 56
structures: language and, 58; "of learning," 48–51
student-centred approach, 23–7
students, successful, 95
student teacher: role of, 180–4
Sugai, G., and T. J. Lewis, 78
summative assessment, 161; portfolios and, 176–7
synthesis (Bloom's taxonomy), 123–4

Table of Specifications, 163–4, 167, 179, 180
tacit intelligence, 198
Taillefer, Paul, 285
teacher-centred approach, 23–7, 127–8
teachers: as clinician–professional, 7; critical consciousness and, 250–2; intelligence and, 199; student, 180–4; student behaviour and, 90
teaching style: authoritative, 256; SES and, 255–6
teaching: approach to, 23–7; explicit, 132–3; *see also* instruction

temperament, 60, 227–9; three basic, 227–8
Terman, Lewis, 216
tests: achievement, 267–91; aptitude, 271–2; criterion-referenced, 272; design of, 162–4; intelligence, 199–200, 201–2; norm-referenced, 272; teacher-made, 271; *see also* assessment; standardized achievement tests
themes, 6
theories: application of, 10; definition of, 14; instructional, 128–30; *see also* specific theories
theory of mind, 62
thinking, higher-order, 166, 169, 171; *see also* cognitive abilities
thinking strategies, 128–9, 133–6

Thomas, A., and S. Chess, 227
Thorndike, Edward Lee, 12–13
triarchic theory, 196–7
twice-exceptional learners, 216

United States: poverty and education in, 256; special education in, 201; standardized achievement tests in, 283–4
universal instructional design (UID), 127

validity: assessment and, 162–4, 287–8; research and, 14
verbal protocol analysis, 134–5
verbs, cognitive, 123–4
Vercillo, K., 61
visual-spatial reasoning, 193–4

visuo-spatial sketch pad, 141
Vygotsky, Lev, 13, 55, 68, 70; language and, 57

Wechsler Intelligence Scale for Children (WISC-IV), 199–200
well-being: emotional, 75; psychological, 58–62
Wentzel, K. R., 107–8
Wiggins, G. P., and J. McTighe, 119
working memory, 128, 129–30, 140–1
writing skills: marking rubric and, 172

Yerkes–Dodson law, 55–6, 74

"zone of proximal development," 55
Zwaagstra, Michael, 283